EUROPE
AND THE
GERMAN QUESTION

AMS PRESS
NEW YORK

EUROPE
AND THE
GERMAN QUESTION

By

F. W. FOERSTER

NEW YORK
SHEED & WARD
1940

Library of Congress Cataloging in Publication Data

Foerster, Friedrich Wilhelm, 1869-1966.
    Europe and the German question.

    Translation of Europa und die deutsche Frage.
    Reprint of the 1940 ed. published by Sheed & Ward,
New York.
    Includes index.
    1. Germany—History. 2. European War, 1914-1918—
Germany. 3. Germany—Politics and government—20th
century. 4. Europe—Politics—20th century. I. Title.
DD94.F613   1975   943.08   70-180399
ISBN 0-404-56123-3

Reprinted by arrangement with Sheed & Ward Inc., New York, N. Y.

From the edition of 1940, New York
First AMS edition published in 1975
Manufactured in the United States of America

AMS PRESS INC.
NEW YORK, N. Y. 10003

CONTENTS

v

CONTENTS

PART II

INTRODUCTORY

DURING an historical crisis when the destiny of the world is being decided, personal reminiscences may seem an untimely impertinence. But the brief account of my life I propose to give is justified by the fact that my experiences and observations throw light on the development which is the subject of my book.

I must begin by insisting that although I am deprived of my nationality and live far from my native land my soul has never lost its fatherland. I address my fellow-countrymen not only as a patriotic German—whose patriotism however is given to a country still invisible—but also as a German who knows Europe and therefore believes it his vocation to explain to his people the reaction of the rest of the world to German aggression and thus help to pave the way for an eventual reconciliation between Germany and Europe.

It is no merit of mine but the gift of a fortunate inheritance and peculiarly favorable circumstances that I have remained immune from the intellectual and spiritual movements which have carried captive the vast majority of my countrymen since the foundation of the Second Reich. My father, director of the Berlin observatory, had been a pupil of Humboldt's and had remained faithful all his life to his master's profession of faith that the whole of past history teaches us that "in the life of nations under the protection of a Higher Providence a desire long cherished and directed to a noble ideal is finally satisfied." He was therefore the consistent opponent of everything for which Bismarck stood, for he was firmly convinced that the deep-rooted German desire to realize the ideal of international cooperation must finally triumph over all aberrations. He loved France; and his dearest friends were French, friends whom I inherited from him. During the first World War some of them visited me at Zurich where I had a house for the holidays. We could hear the thunder of the guns from the distant blue of the Vosges. Of Treitschke's bluster and his wildly applauding audience my father always spoke with the deepest sorrow. An indefinable compassion and sadness came into his voice when he spoke of a man who had sacrificed delicacy of feeling and calm, accurate and consistent thought to the diseased egoism or unchecked ambition which held him captive. It was in such tones that he spoke of the new Germany and all its heroes and bards. The noisy intolerant worship of success, which had not only taken possession of the rising generation but even seduced grey heads, he regarded as a serious and pitiable disease. That disease, he held, had alienated the people from the noble traditions of their past and imbued them instead with a hollow self-display.

I grew up in an atmosphere of loathing for Bismarck's work. I had inherited that loathing from my father. Many of the friends who had grown up with him were Bismarck's devoted collaborators. He was thus in a position to follow closely the important events and their psychological effects, and his entire political outlook was dominated by dread of the judgment which with an impressive certainty he foretold must be the result of his contemporaries' cynical worship of success and their unconcealed pact with lower powers. From my youth, my entire life and my whole thought were overshadowed by the doom which threatened my country. My presentiment of it made me a solitary figure even as a schoolboy.

Many who have known me only by my educational writings have been surprised by what seemed my sudden incursion into the political field. In fact my educational work had always been merely one particular expression of the general orientation of my thought and activity. I have always aimed at a renewal of the spiritual foundations of our culture, perverted, as it is, by an exclusive preoccupation with technique. In 1899 I inaugurated my work at the university of Zurich by a lecture on "Machiavelli and Political Morality" and I lectured on Comte's philosophy of humanity. Comte's noble subordination of politics to ethics had powerfully influenced my own thought in this domain. His *Réconstruction sans Dieu* appealed to the freethought in which I had been educated.

My entire work at that period could be regarded as an attempt to champion the humane and international Germany in the midst of the new Germany of science and technical industry by arguments adapted to modern conditions; and, by giving it a realist basis, to defend the old idealism against the disintegrating forces at work in the contemporary world.

On these lines I edited during the nineties the weekly review *Ethische Kultur*, and my radical criticism of Prussian militarism, Bismarck's Germany and the Pan-German mania was so outspoken that in 1895, for an article censuring a speech by the Emperor in celebration of Sedan, I was sentenced to three months' imprisonment and an academic career in the German Universities was made impossible. My educational work, intended to assist the emancipation of schools and education in general from the illusions of an age in which the intellect had become mechanized, had reference to and was determined by my wider task.

For that reason, in the introduction to my *Jugendlehre* I set out from the general position that the moral crisis of our technical age was due to the fact that mastery of the psychological forces of human nature had not kept pace with the technical mastery of the forces of external nature and that this might well lead to the collapse of our entire civilization, since the latter is based on centuries of religious and moral education.

It required many more years of study and experience

of life before I came to realize that all modern attempts to find a substitute for the work of Christianity as the foundation of culture and the trainer of souls rest on illusions out of touch with real life and are powerless to defend human society against the might of unrestrained greed and passion.

During the first World War I became acquainted with the writings of Constantine Frantz, Bismarck's great opponent. Scales fell from my eyes; I saw the abiding mission of my people, deep-rooted in the entire history of Europe, the mission to organize a confederation of Europe. It became clear to me that not only was there no contradiction, but on the contrary the most perfect harmony, between the universal tradition of the old Germany linking the nations together and the political requirements of Europe's greatest exporter. From the moment when, as a teacher in the Hoch Schule in Munich during the War, I proclaimed this conviction without reserve and declared— drawing all the consequences involved—that Germany's international mission defines her place in Europe and indicates the lines on which peace treaties should be concluded and is the fundamental principle for the solution of all the tasks confronting her, I began to be isolated.

Gradually I was cast out by a public long made captive to elements which, by dint of incredible exertions, had completely eliminated the old German tradition in favor of the new Prussian tradition of the power-state. I was officially condemned by the teaching bodies of all the German and Austrian Universities. For many I was a traitor pure and simple. But a large number of the students even in the school of history were on my side. After the War almost all my supporters left me. The young men who returned from the army, many of them officers, had been transformed—and the propaganda against the Allies completed the work.

At this point I must speak of my encounter and friendship with a man who came from a world entirely different from my own and whose agreement with my estimate of the political position, its causes and prospects, brought me no little encouragement at a time when I was completely isolated. He was the Bavarian Colonel Falkner von Sonnenburg, a friend of the Bavarian Minister for War, and during the closing years of the War the chief censor, wielding in this sphere a despotic authority. He was a man of high intelligence and thoroughly acquainted with the world outside. He had been himself a member of the General Staff and knew everything that went on behind the scenes. He is no longer living. To him I owe much information of the highest importance. He told me facts known to no other civilian. After the War he opened my eyes to the systematic restoration of the old military Reich organized by those who were assumed to have crept away to remote hiding-places.

Towards the end of 1917 I had been informed that he secretly shared my views. Late one evening I visited him, taking every precaution not to compromise him. After a few words we were discussing the subject of my visit. He pointed to a copy of a book I had written on *Politics and Conscience* which had been submitted to him as a censor. "I agree with every word you say. The German people is a noble steed ridden to its doom by a bad horseman. A training collar must be pressed tightly around the Prussian neck. Otherwise there will be no peace in Europe."

I thought, if that is your opinion I will unburden myself freely. And I did. From time to time he said, bringing down his fist on the table, "true, true!" About two o'clock in the morning we separated, friends. During the War he protected me and allowed no harm to come to me. After the War he visited me at Berne. As it happened, I was about to invite two German diplomats to dine with me. So I asked them to meet him. They were delighted to be dining with an officer of high rank, and thinking they were now three against one they launched into a violent attack on the Entente and the peace terms that had been imposed. I noticed how the Colonel grew more and more restive. At last he struck his glass and said, "A word, if you please." Then he spoke these unforgettable words, emphasizing every syllable with the anger of the true gentleman who could not endure the complaints of those who, having bullied others, refused to abide by the consequences of their behavior. "The German nation is behaving at present like an urchin who has broken every window and when he is put over his father's knee to receive a well-deserved whipping screams the house down. I am ashamed, ashamed. That is all I have to say."

I have often heard him say, "I am ashamed". It was his patriotic duty and mine to be ashamed of what no one else was ashamed of. This is vicarious shame which Heaven will surely accept. He told me that when as a young officer he was returning from China on a French steamer, German officers on board celebrated Sedan by drinking champagne in front of the crew, "I was ashamed—I was ashamed."

In his opinion the Treaty dealt far too mildly with those responsible for the War or guilty of outrages in its conduct; he held that it had neglected to provide for any efficient control. He blamed the post-War policy of France for its excessive leniency towards those who organized the propaganda against the Entente, and also for the tameness with which it tolerated German rearmament and the sabotage of reparations. We were, he said, living in an age of iron and unless Western civilization made up its mind to enforce respect from the incorrigible foes of peace, it would deserve its fate. As for those pacifists who urged the French to make concessions to the *soi-disant* German democrats who were wax in their masters' hands, concessions which would be abused by those who were organizing the war of revenge, he wished them to the devil—for the salvation of the German people.

He knew the Prussian Junkers thoroughly and used to say, "Believe me, I know those gentlemen; there is nothing, absolutely nothing, of which they are not capable. Prenez garde". In this he agreed with Freiherr von Stein who also knew them and who said of them, "They are a hybrid genus, in which something of a long extinct antediluvian animal still survives."

The conclusions and prognostications in this book were destined from the outset for my fellow-countrymen. They were put before them without intermission from 1916 until Easter 1933 when the victorious Nazis stopped the publication of my paper *Die Zeit*. It was all useless, as useless as my last attempt to save Austria had been. In Munich I became increasingly isolated. One old friend after another broke with me. A few convinced Christians were ashamed of the treatment I received. In the spring of 1918 the Catholic *Augsburger Postzeitung* published an article on my activities from which I quote the following:

"Let us confess the truth. One man, abandoned by all his friends, is devoting himself to what is in fact the cause of Christian morality, and we who call ourselves Christians find his words so unpalatable that we hardly perceive their harmony with our profession of faith. The purifying and atoning effect of confessing our own guilt; the moral victory won by judging our enemy justly; in short, the desire for peace shown by a heart warm with love of men—all these things which should be well-known and self-evident truths we look upon as eccentric."

In the same year my campaign against those who were seducing Germany was discussed at length in the Bavarian Landtag. One deputy after another repudiated me. The representative of Labor alone supported me. The Minister of Religion denounced me as a public danger. Ludendorff demanded my imprisonment. He was disappointed. For my friend, Colonel von Sonnenburg declared, "He is our man. We will not surrender him to you". The record of this debate can be found in the National Library at Munich.

After the revolution I visited Munich and invited the entire body of students to a lecture on the responsibility of the intelligentsia for the War. At this lecture I said what I knew to be the truth. I was howled down with cries of shame, shame. A little schoolmistress from Berlin made the unforgettable remark: "Because we have lost the War, are we therefore guilty?" In 1923, I spent several months in Germany, seeking to discover by lecturing up and down the country whether the time was ripe for a more thoroughgoing attempt to convert the élite. I achieved absolutely nothing. Everywhere I saw the old Germany arming behind the façade. From the Berlin Union of German Students I received a characteristic postcard. "YOU are to blame for our misfortunes—but vengeance does not sleep." Rathenau was murdered, Harden beaten within an inch of his life for daring to say, after the War, what every decent German should have said. At the end of July, I received the following warning from Colonel Sonnenburg:

"Dear Foerster: They are on your track. They intend to stop your mouth by imprisonment. Take the first train for Basle. Don't throw yourself in front of the German motor bus which is heading for the abyss. There is no sense in sacrificing your life now. Go abroad. Enlighten foreign countries about Germany, and from abroad enlighten so far as is possible the Germans".

His advice tallied with all my own impressions and conclusions. I returned to Switzerland and in 1926 went to Paris where I embarked on my task. Everywhere illusions prevailed which were fostered by the pacifists and socialists gathered in Paris. I warned the French and the Poles "Don't disarm, re-arm." I backed up my warning by evidence of the danger they had to expect and its psychological explanation. Then even the German pacifists with a very few exceptions turned against me and denounced me as a militarist. I was never more isolated than when Stresemann at Geneva made a violent onslaught upon me and said that I had been too long absent from Germany to be able to give a correct account of what was happening there. Only too soon it was plain that the reality would be far worse than my forecast. Then radical pacifists in France exclaimed: "Poincaré is to blame. Important concessions should have been made!"

It was a grotesque misconception of the facts. Even now there was complete ignorance of the character of those who possessed the real power in Germany, complete blindness to their inflexible determination to restore the old order and revive the entire programme of 1914. To them concessions were simply a proof of their opponents' weakness. To all this the French Left replied to me, "Yes, but we could have won the other Germany". A tiny minority perhaps. The rest were made captive immediately after the War by a gigantic propaganda which instilled into them an attitude of expectation which made any reconciliation impossible. A French laborer said to a German pacifist, "Who are you and your friends—a mere handful—nothing." And an old French lady said to me, "We two understand. I lost my father in the war of 1870, my husband was killed in the last war, and my son will be killed in the next. I feel what the German mentality is. It is incorrigible. God alone will put an end to it". You were right, unfortunately, only too right.

In London the British Overseas Bank invited me to a luncheon at which I had an opportunity to discuss the problem of Germany with a number of City financiers. I did not spare their illusions. They answered, "Yes, but we wanted to give Germany a chance all the same." "Yes," I retorted, "you have indeed given the worst element in my country a splendid chance." And I told them the language that should be used to the rulers of Germany, who regard every generous gesture as a sign of weakness. I told them, too, that every concession should be safeguarded by rigid conditions and cast-iron guarantees, indeed that no concessions should be granted until . . . at this point a Swedish financier who had been looking at me with an inscrutable expression from the opposite side of the table broke in, "That's true, I never heard anything truer. Yes, you Germans are like that. I've known them for the last thirty years. But it will take you two years to convince these Englishmen."

The first impression I made in England was unfavorable. The Englishman does not like a man who attacks his own country. By degrees my English listeners came to understand that I am a patriot, far more German than those who denounce me as a traitor, and that the conditions in Germany today cannot be compared with those of foreign countries.

Many a time as, from foreign soil, I looked at the blue mountains of my native land I was tempted to indulge the dream that yonder lay my true fatherland, not the fortress of nationalist barbarism. In 1916 during the War I was living in Switzerland. I found myself one day in March on the shore of Lake Constance. A thin mist lay over the surface, calm as a mirror. The German shore was indistinct and seemed completely cut off from the Swiss. Some gulls wheeled above the grey water. Over there, remote in the mist, lay Germany which was waging alone a gigantic war against an entire world. She was beyond the reach of any appeal, of any enlightenment. Every plea was rejected by the fearful combination of the noble and the base elements in Germany. With deep despondency I saw clearly that a peace of reconciliation between Germany and the rest of the world was a utopian dream and that only a crushing defeat of Germany's military power could give entrance to truth and prepare the way for a lasting reconciliation.

On another occasion I stood on the terrace before Basle Cathedral across the Rhine and saw the blue mountains of the Black Forest lying bathed in sunlight and the brown villages nestling among the soft folds of its valleys and among its vineyards. A deep homesickness came over me. For what? Had I not been exiled? Was not that world over there a completely alien world where I could not have borne to listen every day to the follies and frenzied utterances of Jingoism?

Many Germans wanted me to employ more moderate language. After the War, the editor of the *Koelnische Volkszeitung* wrote to me: "Before the War you had the nation's ear. By a host of political blunders you have lost it."

To which I replied, "There are men whose vocation it is to show political cleverness. There are other men whose vocation it is to make political blunders, that is, to utter truths which arouse passionate indignation and which may even lead to the speaker's banishment; but notwithstanding they do their work in the secret depths of the people's soul. The man who is not cast out by his contemporaries is no genuine educator. He who, when it is required of him, does not flatly contradict his people is not a guide but a traitor."

This book, the French and English translations of which will, I hope, enlighten foreign nations as to the underlying nature of the German problem and the meaning and limits of Germany's responsibility for the dissolution of Europe, is above all intended to acquaint Germans living outside the Third Reich with Germany's authentic tradition and with its European mission. But it also looks forward to a not too remote day when the Germans of the Third Reich, cut off from the truth by an unprecedented propaganda, may learn from it the chain of sin and doom in German history since Bismarck. *The German people cannot be reconciled with Europe till they have been reconciled with truth.* Moreover, for the honor of Germany this painful truth must at last be frankly declared by a German. "When I would keep silence it devoured my bones."

F. W. FOERSTER.

EUROPE
AND THE
GERMAN QUESTION

CHAPTER I

GERMANY'S RESPONSIBILITY IN EUROPE

SINCE the first World War most pacifists have been fond of talking about militarism on both sides and of a universal war-guilt, thus fostering the impression that all parties were more or less equally responsible for the catastrophe and that to blame Germany's policy as particularly responsible serves neither reconciliation nor truth. Such pacifism is, in reality, cheap. It can neither clear the general atmosphere nor produce in the German people the self-knowledge and the radical conversion from an aberration centuries old without which Germany must involve herself and Europe in a succession of disasters. Not until the German nation grasps the particular causes of the War of 1914, its own peculiar mentality since its "great success", its departure from its own best tradition, a tradition extending over a millennium, and its complete surrender to Prussianism, not till then can it truly understand itself and its recent destiny and apply this knowledge to its profit.

Certainly the other nations are not better than the Germans. But their defects and vices are of another order. Nor do all nations reach their moral nadir contemporaneously. The vice of modern Germany is militarism, a deification of war and its supposed blessings, unqualified belief in force, and contempt for international law. And for this very reason Germany was guilty of the World War. That guilt can be questioned by no one who sincerely seeks the truth, has genuine knowledge of pre-war Germany, and has studied the relevant documents. Germany's guilt strikes us in the face. The proofs of it are clear and convincing. Indeed they are so plain that to cover them up has required the determination to lie at all costs and a crusade of lies financed by millions of marks. Other nations besides Germany have sinned. But Germany has made of her sin a new biology, a new religion, or as an American writer has expressed it, "a philosophy of the earth spirit " which cynically rejects all the achievements of the past two thousand years.

I shall prove that in July 1914 Germany's policy was solely responsible for the outbreak of war. The German rulers were terrified at the possibility that peace might be preserved. On the opposite side the governments were terrified of war and what at the close of July Count Pourtalès, the German Ambassador at St. Petersburg, reported of Sasonow—"He clutches at every straw to preserve peace"— was equally true of all concerned *except* the Prussian general staff in Berlin and the Pan-German publicists, officials and representatives of heavy industry.

Prusso-German responsibility for the present state of Europe began about 1866. Before that date the German disease was indistinguishable from the general disease afflicting Europe. From the European disintegration which began with the Italian Renaissance and with Machiavellianism—which was certainly no German invention— Germany has but drawn the final and most fearful conclusions. This was pointed out by Graf Keyserling in an article published in the *Hibbert Journal* for October 1914. Germany's conduct, he argued, was not essentially different from that of other nations. But on the historical stage she had carried out a false morality (of which they were all alike guilty) with such a shocking logic, such astounding success, and such unabashed effrontery that the hatred of the entire world, which was in fact guilty of acting on the same immoral principle, was now directed against Germany alone. But precisely because the German people had carried out the false principle with such an appalling consistency and such whole-hearted devotion, it could be more radically cured of the disease than those nations which had but toyed with it.

Here we reach the heart of the problem: German and European responsibility for the present state of the world. Germany has always been the laboratory in which hypotheses put forward throughout the world have been consist-ently tested, lived, thought and carried out to the bitter end. German seriousness and German passion for logic are a force which can be employed in the service of error and evil. Reforming tendencies were at work throughout Europe. It was the German Luther who carried them to their logical conclusion: "Here I stand, I cannot do other-wise, God help me. Amen." There was freethought out-side Germany. Indeed France went far along that path of destruction, as Goethe observed in Strasbourg. But it was Germany that produced Nietzsche, the consistent denier and transvaluer of all Christian values who felt and thought out to its complete nihilism, which incidentally destroyed himself, the modern delusion that man is obliged, if he will be intellectually honest, to reject everything which cannot be justified by an abstract intelligence severed from its spiritual roots. "A rigid intellectual conscience fostered and rendered supreme by Christianity itself turns in me against Christianity. In me Christianity pronounces its own doom and defeats itself."

The same is true of the principle of isolated national sovereignty based on power, and the competition in strength which follows from it, the false principle which has replaced the *civitas humana* of medieval Christendom. It was not made in Germany but imported from the West, from Richelieu, Louis XIV, the French Revolution and Napoleon III. No doubt the principle represents *one* indis-pensable foundation of international order, namely the unique value of the individual nation. But since by itself it leads to a war of all against all, it must be supplemented by a principle of combination which controls its operation. Germany, however, under Prussian influence has lived and worked out the principle until it has become sheer mania, has exploded all the dynamite it contained and has applied it on a terrain where its realization must involve the most savage conflict and mutual destruction because nationalities are so mixed in Germany that it is impossible to demarcate any frontiers between them. A single alternative is then possible, either the enslavement of one nationality by another or supernational federation. A straight line runs from Fichte to Hitler. Everything follows in a strictly logical sequence, even the program of Pan-Germanism.

Germany has reduced to absurdity the principle of nationality as the sole determinant of Europe's political structure. She has carried it through to the utmost and now proclaims to the world, "This is your principle of nationality. This is the form it must assume if it is taken seriously and applied regardless of consequences." Germany is even logical when today she insists in isolating the German element in Eastern Europe—though in fact this is impracticable, since Eastern Europe and the mutual economic dependence of its peoples has been built historically upon the solidarity of mixed nationalities. Before and during the first World War the German—even the Austrian—attached value only to *his own* nationality and refused to recognize the equal rights of others. It was this attitude which produced the World War. The historical significance of the Treaty of Versailles lay in the fact that its provisions attempted to apply even to Eastern Europe the strict logic of nationalism. We see today that this solution was one-sided and must prove economically ruinous and morally indefensible *so long as it is not supplemented by a new and complete confederation*. Such a confederation however could have been set up only by Germany. And Germany could have accomplished the task only if she had frankly recognized the new order and the reparation it made for historic wrongs, an attitude which would have made it possible to ignore the new frontiers between peoples collaborating in mutual confidence. . . .

To sum up: Everything depended indeed upon Germany, the employment she made of her power, her recognition of facts, her fulfillment of the moral conditions on which alone frontiers could be thrown open, her admission of past mistakes. To expound this thesis in greater detail will be the task of the next chapter.

CHAPTER II

THE MEDIEVAL EMPIRE AND BISMARCK'S EMPIRE

THE CHRISTIAN AND GERMAN CONTINUATION OF THE ROMAN EMPIRE

WHEN did the conflict between Germany and Europe begin?

It is tempting to reply: during the barbarian invasions, which were a mass movement of the German tribes that in every direction broke into the Roman Empire. But we must not forget that from one point of view the German race has never been so intimately united with Europe or so completely identified with Europe as in the epoch immediately following this invasion. In that epoch it created and administered the new machinery of European unity, so that in spite of its original violence the invasion finally effected the first incorporation of the new racial elements into the traditional culture of the Mediterranean world. None of the great Teutonic leaders of that period— Theodoric, Alaric, Odoacer and finally Charlemagne— could escape the potent attraction of Greco-Roman culture. Those leaders did everything in their power to forge a firm bond with that culture and to continue its supernational tradition on a wider basis.

The starting-point of the divorce which occurred later and of all the conflicts it involved was undoubtedly the Treaty of Werden in 843 A.D. Charlemagne's empire was there divided; the Roman world was sundered from the German; and the latter, abandoned to itself and its anarchic passions until the day dawned when a new organizing power arose in the North-East, took possession of the shape-less German masses, substituted itself for the Latin culture, which had hitherto been the sole principle of order, and pushed Germany into an increasing opposition and finally into an open conflict with Western Europe.

That the fatal significance of the original separation did not escape the notice of far-seeing contemporaries is shown by a sonnet written in the year 843 by the deacon Florus of Lyons entitled "A Lamentation over the Division of the Empire," in which he foretold the dissolution of Europe which would arise from it. He says: "The interest of the whole has been forgotten, everyone is concerned only to defend his own right. The Empire is like a wall plainly threatened with destruction. It has lost its equilibrium, the cement has fallen out, all its parts are shaky." In truth, the thunder of the German artillery before Verdun, the hecatombs of French and German soldiers offered on its battlefield were the result of this original division.

Certainly the growing differentiation between the nations of Europe, as their individual characters became more marked, was an inevitable result of the historical process and in harmony with a general law of biology. Moreover, Christianity has promoted the development of individuality. But just because this was the course of development and because the European family of nations contains national differences so exceptionally marked, all the great minds of that epoch of ferment when Europe was taking shape, perceived that if this individualizing process was not to lead to the dissolution of Europe and to perpetual war, it must be counterbalanced by such a principle of unity as was supplied by the tradition of the Roman Empire renewed in a Christian spirit.

Kant, in his treatise on "Perpetual Peace," pointed out that international peace and the subordination of politics to morality were impossible, so long as isolated states were fighting for power; and could be secured only by a European federation. He quoted the fundamental biology of Europe: Europe can survive only as an organized and organic whole. This truth of international biology Rome had learned from her experience of the barbarian invasions. That is why she placed the Roman-Teutonic synthesis under the protection of the Catholic Church and the Catholic Church in turn under the protection of the Roman-Teutonic synthesis. Even when, as we should have expected, the separation effected in 843 A.D. laid the foundation of all the later divisions and disintegrations, *The Holy Roman Empire of the German People* after the separation of France continued for centuries to fulfill its functions as the center of a European confederacy and the secular basis of the united European Christendom. The tradition it embodied did not perish until the year 1866 in the break-up of the German confederation, whose statutes expressly declared that it was designed to promote the peace of Europe and the European balance of power.

THE DESTINY AND TASK OF GERMANY IN EUROPE

Very few foreigners, but also very few Germans, understand in the least the peculiar destiny of Germany, the true cause of the profound cleavage in the soul of the modern German, the appalling tragedy of German history, and the German conflict with Europe. But only when these things are understood is it possible to explain correctly the fathomless intellectual and moral disorder of the modern Germans and thus to be in a position to grapple with it. Even the Christian guides of the German people, whose vocation it is to throw light upon the disorder and apply a cure and to make its causes plain to foreign Catholics and to the Head of the Church, have remained to the present day helpless and ignorant in face of the mental attitude which inspires the entire policy of modern Germany and keeps the whole world in blind turmoil.

A solitary German writer has seen clearly into the abyss

of his country's destiny and has perceived the seemingly mortal cleavage it reveals, namely Bismarck's great counterpart, Constantine Frantz. Though of less genius than the Iron Chancellor, Frantz possessed a deeper understanding of the spirit of German history, the facts of the international situation, and the German character. His conclusions may be summarized as follows:

The entire development of modern Germany under the aegis of Prussian power and statecraft is an aberration incapable of survival, a departure from the entire spirit of German history, from Germany's true function in the life of Europe, from her character and her soul. It was a fundamental mistake to shape the development of modern Germany on lines dictated by the militarism of the North-Eastern frontier region, to copy the growth and example of the Western states, and like Hegel, Stahl and others, to be influenced by abstract theories of national sovereignty. As a result of her geographical position in the center of Europe, her distinctive history, the function she performed in the organization of medieval Europe and the supernational trend of her character produced by the cooperation of these factors, Germany had become something unique and incomparable with anything outside. She was not a state but an Empire, occupying a position intermediate between the domain of national and international law, a center of European federation, a bridge between East and West, between North and South, a mediator between opposites, a supernational reality entrusted with the heritage of Roman universalism purified, baptized and enlarged by Christianity with all the responsibilities attached to it.

The German Emperor, therefore, was not a German overlord of Europe, but, as it were, the holder of an international office, the president of a league of nations, whose function it was to harmonize their equal rights. It was

Germany's vocation to administer from her territory the tradition of Roman and Christian unity—nothing more and nothing less. The non-German peoples were conscious of a bond with the Empire, precisely because the latter had no intention of interfering with their national distinctions, still less of suppressing them. Those peoples were dependent not upon the Germans but upon the Christian ideal which the Germans represented and championed. The Empire was well-termed the Roman Empire of the German people, a title which far from offending the Germans was felt as an honor. It was a German genius, Charlemagne, who, captivated and enriched by both these inheritances, not only founded a united Germany but created the political union between Germany and Rome and at the same time paved the way in the East for the future incorporation into Europe of the Western Slavs. And it was the Roman Church that inspired his entire creation and thus became in the strictest sense the mother of the new Empire.

Rome provided the first answer to the German problem. Only Rome could create Germany. For the extremely diverse and often mortally hostile German tribes, who occupied the center of Europe, lacked every possibility of creating such a union, indeed, even the conception of it. The Church set before the German spirit a sublime goal at which to aim and provided a wide field for its activity. The mission she entrusted to it was nothing less than to maintain the equilibrium of Europe and in the process to discover its own. The medieval German Empire was a bulwark against the dissolution of Europe and reaped all the benefits which must accrue to the European center from such a function and such a protective task. Since this function has been abandoned and the bulwark of European unity removed, the whole of Europe has gone astray and Germany has become the center of anarchy and is engaged today in devoting all her national endowments, her economic organization and her science to the service of a total war.

It may be objected: the past is closed; medieval Europe has been dissolved by the era of national states; Germany could not have stood aside from this historical process.

The objection shows complete blindness to all the lessons of the last decades of European history. It has been drastically shown that the relations obtaining at present between the European powers must end in disaster unless the principle of unrestricted individualism is balanced by a principle of reconciliation and international organization which can harmonize the conflicting forces by subordinating them to a higher unity. It is astounding that not one of the great national organizers in Europe, from Richelieu to Bismarck, could foresee that a one-sided preoccupation with securing the rights of a single nation would be the surest way to destroy those rights and that, if the existence of the nation were to be preserved, a system of mutual guarantees must be organized, and a supernational framework elaborated, all this moreover as the weightiest task of any realistic policy which could look ahead and was worthy of the name. This plain truth passed unperceived. The entire sphere of international relations was abandoned to sheer anarchy, any concern with their regulation being denounced as utopian and unpatriotic.

THE GERMAN PROBLEM IS INSOLUBLE ON THE LINES OF NATIONAL SOVEREIGNTY

The German problem could, and still can, be solved only on European lines. Why is this? Because the European environment penetrates far into the German mass, the witness of a former federal bond with the non-German world, a bond which has been falsely interpreted under the influence of national blindness as a right to Germanize the foreigner—the claim which produced the War. On the contrary, the correct understanding and treatment of these relics of a former symbiosis of German and Slav might well have enabled Germany to unite Europe.

The bigots of nationalism must inevitably regard the presence of Slavonic populations in the Reich or, as in the old Austrian Empire, the coexistence of foreign nationalities in the same state, as a factor of disorder, as the incomprehensible survival of a chaotic era to be liquidated as speedily as possible, like the pillars of an ancient temple standing in the midst of a modern city. It was not understood that *these survivals reveal the true and natural law of the Teutonic world, the only form of government adapted politically and biologically to the central land of Europe.* German unity can be achieved only as part of the unity of Europe, not in opposition to it.

Hitler, carrying the principle of nationality to its logical conclusion, has demanded the inclusion of all Germans in a single state. But it is surely as clear as daylight by now— a fact which he sees himself—that in the actual situation, in which the nationalities of Eastern Europe are inextricably mixed, such a concentration of all Germans cannot be carried out without a war of annihilation against the states of mixed German and Slav population which are economically dependent upon the territories inhabited by Germans and cannot break up a symbiosis centuries old without bleeding to death from the operation. In short, it is an irrefutable truth that the German problem is absolutely insoluble on lines of national sovereignty. The erection of national sovereign states and the destruction of the former supernational political body will not only produce inevitable conflicts on a vast scale but is in glaring opposition to all Germany's economic needs, which require the most intimate and friendly relations with the countries of South-Eastern Europe.

Well might Frantz ask: "Can it ever be the true vocation

of the German people to form a great centralized state when her entire history vociferates the contrary? Can it be her vocation to break with her long historical past, to set up in its place an order dictated solely by utilitarian considerations, whereas it is her mission more than that of other peoples to hold fast the foundation of her historical development and, if need be, to defend it? And this is not only for her own sake, but for the sake of Europe that it may not founder in chaos."

GERMANY'S TREASON TO HERSELF!

From a supernational mission to a barrack state! This unparalleled treason to herself and her millennial history, effected under the influence of Prussian leadership, is the substance of German fate and explains completely her present mentality. We are told that the German character has undergone a revolutionary change. That is untrue. Certain elements within the German people, adherents of "Colonial Teutonism," as Lamprecht entitled the mental attitude of the Prussian border, have succeeded in dominating the entire nation. Otherwise the German character has not essentially changed. It has merely felt and thought itself into the adoption of ambitions which profoundly contradict its nature; and even in the attempt to achieve them it is not difficult to detect below the surface unalterable traits of the German character. The modern German, as Hermann Bahr observed, "is a commercial traveler mimicking the gestures of Wotan." The ancient, but at present perverted, impulse of the German soul towards totality, has surrendered itself to the cult of the totalitarian state and total war. Schubert, Beethoven, Hoelderlin, Schiller are today pressed into the service of this mania of national power to which the Germans, completely blinded, now dedicate the old German seriousness, kindness of heart and spirit of sacrifice.

The combination is not harmonious. But since the

Germans have believed all the lies served up to them for the past sixty years, they have reached an appalling state of disbelief in their neighbors' goodwill and are prepared to follow their national seducers with an unquestioning enthusiasm into any reckless undertaking in order to win for Germany the equality of rights of which she is still said to be deprived. They cannot perceive that this demand for equal rights—a demand whose precise meaning has never yet been defined—is justified only in so far as it is a protest against any exclusion of Germans motivated by envy or fear, but that beyond this point it distorts their entire view of Europe and of Germany herself. For, as we have already shown, Germany neither can nor should demand without special qualifications the same treatment as other nations, because in fact she is altogether different from them, with completely different responsibilities and possibilities, so that 'equality' turns out to be the most unjustifiable *inequality* and threatens the freedom of other nations. Europe is, therefore, justified in requiring the fulfilment of obvious moral conditions before making any concessions, whether of territory, rights or spheres of influence.

Hardly a single German today understands this fact, though it is the essential problem of the relations between Germany and Europe. But even while the medieval community of nations still persisted, was there not a moment when Europe suddenly began to suspect that Germany's imperial role was no longer functioning in the service of an ideal which was more than Teutonic but was already being exploited by German power-politics? It was surely this suspicion which later on produced that tragic chapter of history—Richelieu and Gustavus Adolphus.

To sum up: Germany is not a nation like the rest, but something unique and as such subject to unique conditions and endowed with unique possibilities. Her supreme mistake, which plunged her into ruin and made her a curse to the rest of Europe, has been precisely this demand to act exactly as other nations have acted, a demand which misconceives her position and is a treasonable refusal to fulfill the conditions under which alone she can exist in the center of Europe, as Europe is actually constituted, and under which alone she can reap all the advantages accruing from this central position.

The day may well be nearer than we imagine when the Germans, aroused from a hideous delusion and appalled by its results, will open their ears and their consciences to an appeal from the depths of the German tradition and turn with abhorrence from everything which for many decades has been presented to the world as 'German policy'. There is at present a 'British policy' which expresses the British character and history and which corresponds with the actual exigencies of Britain's situation in the world. There has been and is a 'French policy' which expresses the French spirit and tradition. But there is as yet no 'German policy' which expresses the German soul, is inspired by the spirit of German history, and is based upon the recognition of Germany's actual dependence upon the rest of the world. What is called the German policy has been simply a policy of Prussian aggrandizement. It has been imposed upon the German people, alienated from its genuine tradition by the militarist North-East, which was completely ignorant of everything truly German and had no conception of the fundamental presuppositions under which alone Germany can play a leading part in the world, nor even indeed of the conditions of any lasting power, so that every success was thrown away by this fatal blindness.

BISMARCK'S ACHIEVEMENT AND GERMAN FEDERALISM

The new German empire of Prussian extraction constituted no link between Germany and the world outside but, on the contrary, pushed her by degrees into an in-

creasing conflict with that world. The supernational
Empire of the Middle Ages, which was a genuine protector of law and peace in Europe, made Germany an
international power and by so doing conferred distinctive
endowments and powers upon her. Therefore it was that
even an Italian like Dante could, as a Christian world-
politician, pay enthusiastic homage to the German Emperor. Germany was able to perform this function of promoting international union, not only because she was
supported by the prestige and comprehensiveness of the
Roman-Christian tradition but, above all, because she
brought to the service of that tradition a talent for confederation. *For she knew how to combine with federal
association a high valuation of the unique character of each
nationality or tribe;* a combination which enabled her to
harmonize diversities and even contrasts. Germany was a
miniature Europe where Asia and Europe met, where any
undue centralization must be defeated by the variety and
strength of the living individual components and where,
accordingly, order could be produced only by free confederation which, when it functioned well, made it easier
to incorporate into a united European system numerous
foreign elements which were not prepared to surrender
their native traditions but which sought union with a center of civilization.

The European significance of the German medieval
organization was recognized abroad earlier than in Germany herself. The French Abbé St. Pierre, in his *Projet
pour rendre la paix perpetuelle en Europe,* appealed to
the example of the federal union of German peoples. The
new Empire founded by Prussia is, as Frantz observes,
related to the old as a barracks to a Gothic cathedral.

The religious division produced· by the Reformation
struck at the very roots of the Empire. Notwithstanding,
it continued to exist, though the union had become extremely loose. And in the nineteenth century once more a

federal bond began to be reconstituted between groups which had fallen apart into individualist isolation. The first attempts in this direction, to be sure, were not promising. The powerful effort and thought inspired by a realistic idealism, if sublime ideals were to rescue the nation from a deeply rooted particularism, were lacking. Modern German history has been particularist through and through, a struggle of each local group to sever itself from the rest and at the same time to retain as large a share as possible of the whole. Prussia and Austria were deeply involved in this particularism.

In such a situation the most important political task should have been to overcome particularism from within by opening up new and sweeping perspectives and by the progressive practice and understanding of cooperative organization; and thus to reconstruct Germany in the old federal spirit though with completely new political machinery. Instead, the centralization effected by Prussia was fundamentally nothing more than the victory of a more strongly organized individual group over the remaining groups, not the inner defeat of the particularist attitude or a genuine union of opposites. What was artificial and enforced stifled the native growth. And this principle of domestic policy was applied in the field of foreign policy. Frantz has shown how in the eighteen-sixties Prussia had a most valuable opportunity of entering into a federal union with Poland, in company with Austria. It would have erected a bulwark against Russian influence in Europe and by degrees have united all the Western Slavs with the Teutonic world in a new and free bond.

The opportunity was thrown away and all traditions pointing in that direction buried out of sight. The Prussian Junker in Bismarck had no comprehension of the rich inheritance of German history and culture. He saw nothing but a welter of individual states which had not been set in order and united by abstract ideas; nor could be, since the representatives of these ideas had no roots in the reality of German life and therefore did not perceive that a living German unity must be something totally different from a union of homogeneous nations. But instead of allying himself against abstractions with the primordial forces of German history and thereby reviving them for a new work of construction, Bismarck became as it were "The Buonaparte of the German Revolution" and its abstract and academic ideas. Though he was so contemptuous of the idealistic element in the revolutions, he was close to the revolutionaries. His link with them was the Prussian faith in force and the indifference to historical fact and to the continuity of the German Imperial tradition.

He had, therefore, nothing more at heart than to solve the German question by the simple expedient of *extending to the whole of Germany the Prussian conception of the State*, though it had no place for any of those old sublime ideas which had once made the German federation the exemplar of a united Europe. *Autocracy* superseded federation as the principle of unity. Force replaced the determination and establishment of law and legal rights. He thus founded the Empire, which Nietzsche denounced as the extirpation of the German spirit.

Frantz never tired of attacking Bismarck's policy from every angle. He charged him with pursuing at a momentous crisis in the history of his people a hasty and shortsighted policy completely devoid of intellectual greatness or real knowledge of the law governing German history. Bismarck possessed more will (Thumos) than understanding (Nous). He took for granted a political theory, which though dominant at the time was extremely superficial— that of the great national power—without stopping to enquire how far it represented a vital truth of international life, or whether it was applicable to the peculiar relations of Germany or was not simply a passing phase of political thought, an aberration which could arise only in the interregnum, when the medieval conception of the *civitas humana* had passed away and no great principle of international organization had as yet taken its place. This interregnum of mere national and territorial selfishness was accompanied by a truly lamentable state of political thought. Men had eyes only for the single state and completely overlooked international life with its realities, needs and conditions. From regarding intercourse between the nations as a matter which concerns even the domestic life of states and treating it accordingly, political thinkers had formed a thoroughly exaggerated conception of the sovereignty, self-assertion and self-sufficiency of the individual state, a conception completely incompatible with the actual growth of mutual dependence between the nations and with the increase in the tasks which could be accomplished only by their collaboration.

All modern German historians have been deeply enmeshed in this cult of the great nation hermetically sealed from the outside world and living in an international anarchy. Ranke, for example, described with the utmost interest barren changes in the preponderance of power as between one competitive great power and another. That the supremacy of France had yielded to the supremacy of a Prussian Germany he regarded as a fact of the first importance. He never asked what the world had gained by the change or "Whether by this competition with the Western powers and by this imitation of their development Germany might not have risked her genuine supremacy". It never occurred to him that in the future any policy worthy of the name must grapple with very different and more important tasks than striving for political preeminence. Those who wrote history from this point of view were inevitably blind to the sublime supernational mission of the ancient German Empire. Their readers received the impression that that Empire also had been simply a great German power which had now been re-awakened from centuries of torpor. *The enormous differ-ence between the old universal and supernational empire which for that very reason led Europe and the new nar-rowly Prussian national state was thus completely oblit-erated.*

BISMARCK AND HIS SUCCESSORS

It is often said that the blame for this disastrous policy lies not with Bismarck but with his successors. From the psychological standpoint this is a superficial view. Bis-marck was the first to base Germany's entire domestic and foreign policy unreservedly upon the Prussian army. Nor was the latter simply an instrument employed in the service of totally different aims. On the contrary, the su-premacy of the Prussian army, both inside and outside Germany, became itself the significance and the goal, both deliberate and unconscious, of a nation in uniform. Such a policy knew nothing of "You and I", but only "You or I", and was accordingly compelled to refer all disputes great and small to the final test of military strength. The demon that inspires the Prussian tradition willed it so. No doubt the Iron Chancellor was also a political chess player of genius, so that he was able for a long period to prevent his policy from producing the fruits which of its nature it must produce. When at length they ripened, his successors were blamed for them: men who every year were involved more deeply in the hideous tangle of difficulties which were but the final and inevitable product of the epoch of blood and iron and of the forces it had unleashed.

Bismarck had stood over these unleashed forces like a trainer over his wild beasts. With skilled hand he tamed them or set one against another, kept them occupied or terrorized them. But this policy could not in fact cope with the vast national problems of the new age. The suc-cessors of this great nation-tamer could not continue to

play his game with the consummate skill that had been
his. Moreover, even in his own time there were forces
which refused to obey any longer his beck and call. The
balance of power had shifted. Opponents had made up
for their former inferiority. It was time to inaugurate an
entirely new policy, a policy of international organization. But every previous tradition was against such a
policy. Blunder followed blunder. Every opportunity of
effecting a permanent settlement of differences was thrown
away. By degrees there became evident the implications
of a policy which had attempted to settle by an appeal to
brute force all the far-reaching conflicts of interest which
had arisen between the nations of the modern world. It
dawned on many minds, as they pondered in silence on the
state of mankind, that Bismarck's iron policy of national
defense by threats and terrorism could be effective only
so long as Central Europe possessed a considerable military supremacy; and as soon as the neighboring states had
caught up with the armaments of the Central Powers,
these methods must become not merely fruitless but positively harmful. Henceforward a country in this central
position must experience the historical truth of the text,
"He that taketh the sword by the sword shall perish."

What does it signify that under Bismarck the army was
still subordinate to the leading statesman? For it was precisely Bismarck's reliance on military force which raised
the army to the first place not only in the state but in the
German soul. Everything else followed from this. No
doubt a policy based on pure force, so long as it is carried
out by consummate statecraft, may avoid many collisions
and for a time present the semblance of genuine statesmanship. But it is radically limited, provokes more indignation and hostility among foreign powers than it can
control, and reckons with only one aspect of human nature, as on his part the pure idealist takes only man's
highest qualities into account. Both methods are insuffi-

cient. The abstract idealist is defeated by the lower forces he has left out of his reckoning; the statesman whose policy reckons only with the baser instincts in other peoples incurs the hostility of the nobler elements in humanity. Not only is he unable to employ in his service the moral forces active in the outside world, he discourages and corrupts them even in his own nation. And this one-sided realism is avenged more tragically and more lastingly than one-sided idealism.

It is all very well to argue that Bismarck would have avoided many of the mistakes his successors committed. This does not alter the fact that the appalling logic of his principle "Might before right", his blind refusal to take account of immaterial forces, and the intoxicating success of actions inspired by this spirit have not only alienated the contemporary German from his better self, but have also brought him into conflict with the profoundest realities of the political government of mankind. The background of all the fatal decisions which brought the German nation to disaster is precisely Bismarck's refusal to take account of justice. We have only to read the collection of documents published by W. Hopf bearing on the German crisis of 1866 to realize the utter contempt for justice with which Bismarck carried his plans through and the horror which his policy aroused at the time in many Germans who could look below the surface.

But unfortunately it must be admitted that even then there were a large number who retracted their protest when injustice had proved successful. When war was declared with Austria the celebrated jurist R. V. Jhering wrote as follows: "Never probably has a war been engineered with such revolting shamelessness and alarming recklessness . . . One's inmost soul rises against such an outrage against all the principles of law and morality . . . What a fearful future awaits us." The supreme tragedy of modern Germany lies in the fact not that such words were written but that only two months later the same man could justify the entire action because of Bismarck's splendid success. "I bow to the genius of a Bismarck. I have not only forgiven him for all he has done hitherto but have become convinced that what to us outsiders appeared arrogance was necessary . . . For such a man of action I would give a hundred men of impotent honor".

These two letters written by a man who had struggled all his life for the ideal of justice and indeed had insisted upon the personal responsibility of every individual to fight for its victory (in his pamphlet *Der Kampf ums Rechts*) are an important historical testimony to the mental attitude of German scholars in the nineteenth century: a completely impotent and abstract idealism, which the moment it was faced by stern realities withdrew from the struggle and left the field uncontested to a most brutal and shortsighted gangster policy.

BISMARCK DID NOT UNDERSTAND THE PROBLEM OF GERMAN UNITY

But one achievement at least must surely be put to Bismarck's credit, namely the foundation of a united Germany. To this the Austrian historian R. von Kralik has replied: "Bismarck was not the creator but the destroyer of German unity". For he excluded from his Little German solution of the problem the Austrian and Sudeten Germans. His reasons for this exclusion are further evidence of the fundamental mistake which vitiated this attempt to realize the ideal of German unity on Little German lines. Austria was excluded because it was organically united with non-German races.

That union, however, revealed the millennial trend and the significance of German history and should have reminded German statesmen that the entire racial result of that history made it possible to unite the German populations only within the framework of a new federal organization of Europe as a whole. Neither the Little German nor the Pan-German solution was compatible with the fact that in the South-East, German and non-German populations were united and inextricably mixed. The first World War was simply the inevitable consequence of ignoring this fact. If a second should break out it is more than probable that it will arise from the same conflict between the unhistorical Nationalist ideology of modern Germany and the unalterable mixture of races who have lived together for centuries.[1] Moreover from the economic standpoint this participation by many nationalities in a common life is a providential, indeed an indispensable, condition of survival for the states which have grown up in this region. The entire policy pursued by modern Germany in Eastern and South-Eastern Europe has been the very opposite of a realist policy. It has been dictated by purely ideological considerations which have attempted to solve the problem of Eastern Europe on Western lines.

When the Middle Ages opened, the Pope and the Emperor understood the supernational character of the German problem and provided the only possible solution. Certainly the German desire for unity expressed a fundamental need, was justified and progressive in tendency. But the right leaders were lacking, men who would take equal account of national and supernational needs. The idealists of nationality cared nothing for the real roots and conditions of Germany's existence and growth as a European power. Neither did the realists. They remained on the surface and showed no understanding either of the German or the European problem or of the intimate connection between both. Consequently a domestic policy was pursued which ran counter to the requirements of foreign policy, and a foreign policy which ran counter to the inmost nature of Germany—a desperate muddle which has perverted the German soul and completely disorien-

[1] Written in 1937.

tated German political thought in regard to foreign nations.

THE CHARACTER AND WORLD-PERSPECTIVE OF FEDERALISM

Federalism alone genuinely combats particularism and is alone capable of doing so. For it harmonizes the individual member with the whole, respecting the distinctive values of each, thus not making unity a mere uniformity. So far from weakening the central government, it places it on broader foundations and thus prevents a victory of that central government which would be the victory of a particular member over the whole body, such a victory in fact as was achieved when Prussia became the central authority. As Frantz observed, federation is a "double-edged principle." It regards every situation from two points of view and treats it accordingly: as possessing a distinctive value in itself and yet at the same time as serving a larger whole. And he points out very appositely that the solution of every social problem, both in the wider and the narrower sense, must thus be two-sided, whereas in Germany one-sided attitudes combat each other.

The revival, therefore, of federalism as the organizing principle of international relations, far from being a romantic attempt to resuscitate the past, is a matter of real and urgent importance in view of the problems of the present day. To reconcile the growing demand for self-determination with the equally urgent and pressing need for combination and for a central authority is, indeed, the problem which confronts our age. Can the Polish, Yugo-Slav, and Czecho-Slovak problems be solved otherwise than on federal lines? Is it not plain that the British Empire owes its central position and its cohesion solely to its logical embodiment of the federal principle in which it is the heir of the old Germany? The words spoken by General Smuts when Dutch South Africa entered the British Empire are true:

"In its fundamental principle", he said, "this Empire differs from any other that has ever existed, even the United States. We must always bear in mind that the British Empire is a society of nations, and as such does not seek to render uniform, amalgamate or denationalize its members, but on the contrary to promote a richer, fuller and freer life for each. In this Empire even peoples who, like my own, have in the past fought England on the battlefield, feel that they and their interests, language, religion and culture are as free and secure under the British flag as are those of British descent and blood".

At the Imperial Conference at Ottawa the proposal was brought forward that the conditions under which other countries could join the British Empire should be laid down. This proposal shows how the logical development of the British League of Nations has prepared the ground for a new world-federation and that beyond doubt federalism is the principle of future international organization: the only possible synthesis of autonomy and international law. It may yet happen that the Scandinavian countries will join the British Empire.

If Germany, instead of shrinking into an isolated national power in Hegel's sense, had extended the German federation, it is extremely probable that a league of the Central European nations would have come into existence. That league might have included Holland and Scandinavia, possibly also Poland. From its composition it would have been not a German bloc but the nucleus of a United States of Europe. It is not waste of time to consider such unfulfilled possibilities. Though a lost opportunity cannot be retrieved or the past undone, if the true causes of Europe's present state of hopeless anarchy and the desperate position of Germany, which cannot live in isolation and has forfeited the trust of the outside world, are clearly perceived, we shall have understood and learnt much and shall know what is the only direction in which salvation lies.

The curse of contemporary Germany is not her past aberration and the guilt she has incurred but the appalling fact that they are not recognized for what they are and not confessed, and that this knowledge has been made impossible because lies and self-deception have cloaked in the darkness of night the responsibility for past crimes and have obscured the chain of cause and effect.

THE LEAGUE OF NATIONS AND EUROPEAN CONFEDERATION

All the difficulties and weaknesses which have crippled the existing League of Nations are due to the fact that up to the present there is no link between the isolated national State with its rigid conception of sovereignty and this world-embracing League. Rabindranath Tagore called the League of Nations a "league of kettles on the boil". He saw no possibility of uniting in a fruitful collaboration the overheated and jealous egoisms of the member states who meet at Geneva. Once however there existed a European and German League of Nations based on Christianity. It broke down the isolation of the sovereign states and created a number of international bonds of a juridical and a federal nature which made possible common undertakings on a large scale, such as the Crusades, and such institutions as the truce of God and similar arrangements for securing peace.

The League of Nations as an ideal has not failed. It is the sovereign states which compose it, whose policy has been purely selfish, that have failed. They will continue to fail because there does not exist in their midst a supernational body to balance the rigidity of their nationalism and to form a bridge to supernational organization. Such, however, could be created by the power of the Christian ideal if it were applied once more to international relations and if it burnt into the conscience of all nations

"Sacredness of union" under the aegis of a higher good than the interest of the individual nation.

Nationalism cannot possibly be the last word of man's political arrangements. That is impossible, as it would be impossible to leave the coordination of private interests within a nation to an enlightened and liberal individualism. It cannot be the last word in international relations, since the unique political genius which enables the Englishman to be at the same time nationalist and enlightened and liberal is not possessed by other nations. They require an international organization, if they are to remain conscious of the reality of supernational interests and if the indispensable subordination of the particular to the whole is to be embodied and realized by a concrete institution. Beyond doubt the fundamental condition which must be fulfilled if national patriotism is to be reconciled with such an international institution is the development of a federal organization in Europe and elsewhere. Even British nationalism is liberal and enlightened only because it has been educated by a federal system. Coudenhove was right in maintaining that a European confederation is the indispensable preliminary to a world federation.

Such a federation, however, cannot be erected by a bureaucratic machine on the basis of an abstract conception of Europe. It must grow slowly and organically from a specific nucleus, a growth for which a mere Pan-European ideal is not a sufficient inspiration. The first condition which must be fulfilled is a radical change of mental attitude in the center of Europe, a political and moral conversion such as was envisaged by Frantz and Adam Mueller who 125 years ago taught that "Christ died also for states" and that a selfish and isolated national heathenism was untenable because it denied the moral and religious foundations of genuine statesmanship and of a God-given fact—the mutual independence of nations.

LITTLE GERMANISM AND PAN-GERMANISM SINCE 1848

Even before 1848—and immediately after the revolution, in the great assembly convened at Frankfurt—the question of the form which should be given to the political life of Germany was widely and vigorously debated. The conflict of views on the point was so great, the incompatibility of interests and traditions so glaring, that everyone who did not realize that important historical developments require time and patience shared the impatience and scorn which Bismarck felt for the general muddle, and which he expressed later in his *Gedanken und Erinnerungen*: "The Gordian knot of the German situation cannot be unloosed by the friendly consent of the parties but must be cut by the sword." In fact, the problem of Franco-German relations was treated in this fashion.

At that period three different solutions of the German problem were put forward. One of these was the Prussian, Northern and Little German solution, which would renounce Austria because it was united with non-German peoples. Another was the Pan-German narrower program, which invited the Germans in the Austrian Empire to separate from those foreign elements so that a state might be formed which would include all the Germans and none but Germans. The third was Pan-Germanism, a great German solution. It would preserve Germany's supernational character and organize and build up the German federation on central European lines, therefore including the entire community of races which constituted the Austro-Hungarian Empire. Evidently a living memory of the true nature of the German Empire was still operative. But no one looked beyond this central European horizon and viewed the German problem as a problem to be solved in the setting of Europe as a whole, as Frantz proposed it should be settled a decade later, when the Little German solution had already conquered public opinion.

Naturally, the chief supporters of the great Pan-German solution were to be found in Austria whose German population was not prepared to give up the historic union of Germans and non-Germans in one Empire, being well aware of its significance; but who also foresaw that their position would be very difficult if they had to confront these non-German populations as a mere fragment severed from the vast mass of Germans. How great the divergences of opinion were which clashed in this debate can be seen most clearly from the following utterance of Bismarck,[2] which sketches the future construction of a greater Prussian State in revealing language, and from which we see how the entire federal order of the Danubian Empire with its populations extending far into Eastern Europe was opposed to everything he was seeking to create: "There is no German people. Our policy is the absorption of Germany into Prussia and thereby the transformation of Prussia into Germany."

Possessed by this greater Prussian ideal, Bismarck, by exerting his entire strength of will and threatening to retire, compelled his king to hold aloof from the Diet of Frankfurt. "So thoroughly did Bismarck throw his personality into the struggle that he left the king's chamber in a rage he could hardly restrain. On his departure he burst his way through the doors and when back in his room broke a vase as an outlet for the mighty passion which devoured him."

O. Schuchardt has very aptly characterized this determination to create the greater Prussia which fatally debarred Germany from Eastern and South-Eastern Europe and led to a hopeless competition with the British Empire. "The arena of world politics," he wrote, "was entered with

[2] In the *Publizist*, 1865. Quoted by Rusch, *Bismarck und seine nachfolger bis zum Weltkrieg*. Olten. 1924.

a complete neglect of the most stubborn facts, and in this period of anxiety and national confinement the castle in the air of a greater Germany was built up on the far horizon out of gas and mist. The greater Germany which had formerly existed was recklessly demolished and our modern patriots acclaimed its destruction as the 'restoration of Germany'. But it was thought possible to erect a new German world-power on the shifting sands of the African deserts or in the swamps which skirt the shore of the Pacific."

It is significant that in the period of Bülow the necessity, which could not be evaded, to link Germany up with South-Eastern Europe, a necessity thrust upon her notice by her economic needs, revived the greater German ideal disguised in a Pan-German garb. But its advocates completely overlooked the fact that the peoples of South-Eastern Europe, now in process of acquiring nationality, were less disposed than ever to submit to a German domination. But error is always obliged at some point or other to testify to the truth. Here too this Pan-German dream reveals the fatal incompatibility between the Little German solution and the essential conditions of Germany's existence.

The Emperor Francis Joseph sponsored all the attempts made at the Frankfurt Diet to unite the entire Habsburg Empire with the rest of Germany. The supernational tradition was still so strong in Austria that on this point the Emperor felt himself supported by public opinion. But King William's seat at the Diet remained empty. It was the end of the Great German dream. Moreover, even the Great Germans did not show the same consistency in advocating their views as their opponents showed in working out their own. Schwarzenberg, for example, put too much faith in force and was too great a centralizer to be capable of thinking on genuinely federal lines. We cannot forget that his attitude towards Hungary shewed a profound inability to understand the respect for an historical growth entertained by genuine federalism. Certainly his project of a federal union of nationalities in South-Eastern Europe was sound. But his Viennese centralism could not solve the problem of Hungary. It was from him that the Emperor Francis Joseph learned the absolutist ideas of his first decade, indeed of his entire life.

My intention, in this necessarily brief treatment of the Frankfurt Diet, has been simply to show that in the middle of the last century the memory of the supernational foundations of the first Reich was still very much alive. It was clearly perceived that the greatest achievement of this German form of political life had been precisely the intimate bond it had effected between Germany and South-Eastern Europe; and the incalculable damage produced by breaking the bond could not be compensated by any successful employment of force by 'little Germany'. Indeed, the fact that the Germans were henceforward a minority in the Austrian Empire, but refused to abandon their claim to hegemony or to understand once more their peculiar federal mission, was a fundamental cause of the war of 1914. An untamable ambition to rule is, indeed, an attitude of mind from which even the most enlightened exponents of the revived Great German ideal cannot free themselves. The German, it would seem, is no longer capable of thinking about foreign politics otherwise than in terms of *Germans to the front*. Germany must lead and dominate. Germany must at all costs be of larger size and more powerful than other nations.

I must take this opportunity to reject most emphatically all such claims and to express my opinion that before the German will again be fit to assume the imperial role, he must serve for several centuries in the hallowed realm of humble service. Even before Hitler's advent, the world had had more than enough of German leadership. After this latest outbreak of German megalomania an extremely long period must pass before the disease of inflated egoism from which the German people are suffering can be cured. But Providence, working in accordance with that law by which It governs the world, will not delay very long before commencing the cure.

Though I have subscribed to Frantz's federal view of Germany's historical mission, I am careful to add; "It was so once." This interpretation of German history will one day assist the German people to recognize how far they have departed from what is deepest in their own nature and in the meaning of their history. Moreover, we cannot emphasize sufficiently the universal and abiding function of federalism and its special mission to solve modern international problems, and in particular to enable Germany to perform her future service to Europe.

Nothing seems to me more improbable than that, within any calculable future, Germany will again be called to be the *center* and the *leading power* of the European federation. There must be a *translatio imperii*. The day of the Slavs is dawning. Other peoples must take over what Germany, the scarecrow of armed power, has refused. Germany must no longer rule. She must serve. This reversal of position will prove her cure and her regeneration.

CHAPTER III

RICHELIEU AND THE FRENCH POLICY OF SECURITY

THE CREATION OF THE NATIONAL STATE

THE dissolution of the medieval community of nations is too frequently explained as due solely to the Reformation which, it is said, split Germany into two halves and broke up the Latin-Teutonic synthesis established by Charlemagne. In reality, the Reformation was itself but one effect among others of the profound disintegration which began with the Italian Renaissance and embraced all departments of human life. But disintegration is not always decomposition or a phenomenon of decay. A form of unity dependent on the conditions of a particular historical epoch may break up and release new forces which, by their own vitality and working in harmony with the altered external and internal conditions, create in due course a new form of unity. Augustine's phrase, *felix culpa*, will be applicable to the great historical experiment of national sovereignty if it produces a clearer vision of the limits of all autonomy and organizes the cooperation of government and liberty in a more mature fashion than was accomplished by their first combination after the tempest of barbarian invasion.

The new power of "the particular" was indeed itself the product of Christian centuries. During those centuries the blood of the Redeemer, of the martyrs, of the saints had poured its vitalizing stream into the veins of Europeans, had produced new individual capacities and novel powers of organization, and had developed new qualities of mind and spirit. In the cathedrals all these new energies rose proud and self-conscious heavenward. All these forces now sought to develop in blissful freedom and were tempted to regard themselves as self-sufficient. In every sphere they attempted to break down existing forms of central government, and they chafed against the traditional international order as a barrier to their individual action. This radical emancipation of man's intellectual and spiritual powers, which was based on self-deception —that is, on the failure to perceive the super-personal bases of the new individuality—was then abused by the lower powers as a vent for themselves, just as the creative emergence of the national groups from the old political union was exposed to abuse by purely selfish aims and isolated interests. But if we are to do justice to the era of dissolution we must never lose sight of the fact that the original cause of this violent assertion of particularism was the unprecedented fertilization of all the endowments and energies of the individual which Christianity had effected and the enormous increase of self-confidence to which it had led.

Moreover, the division began with the Church herself as a growing revolt of the national churches against the omnipotence of the Pope and the interference of the Curia. And this development was itself inevitable. For the higher clergy everywhere constituted the first-rank estate of the national nobility; and, as such, became increasingly committed to the particular interests of their respective nations. Had the Bishops wished to remain purely ecclesiastical functionaries, they should not have become feudal lords. When the Church everywhere entered the feudal system, she accepted the consequences.

To this was added the dissension between the spiritual and the temporal power. The medieval ideal demanded perfect harmony between the Papacy and the Empire. But their almost uninterrupted disputes and wars are notorious. And when the Church finally succeeded in defeating the Empire the medieval unity was in even greater peril. For the Empire had never contested that unity, though the Emperor had sought to be its supreme representative. The situation was worse now when, after the defeat of the Empire, the monarchs of the individual states asserted their power against the Church, particularly Philip the Fair of France in his quarrel with Pope Boniface. For the king did not put forward his claim as the representative of an institution common to the whole of Christendom but expressly as the ruler of a particular country, the representative of French national interests which for him were more important than the entire ecclesiastical system. This was a fundamental attack upon the basis of medieval unity and the beginning of the process which destroyed the political power of the Papacy. And to that date we must trace back the origin of everything characteristic of the modern political system—competition for power between all the individual states, and with it Machiavellianism, and the rejection of every higher ideal and responsibility.

But human history demands patience. When Jacob Burckhardt in his writings upon the civilization of the Italian Renaissance describes what he terms "the discovery of man", of nature and reality as a whole, he calls attention to the great secularist experiment made by modern man. In the long run this experiment must assist the restoration and deeper understanding of Christian truth and its lawful sovereignty over the entire edifice of human association. But when man sought to find norms for all his conduct, and especially in the political sphere, by interrogating the laws of nature and in particular the facts of human nature and human society, he believed that their witness would differ from that borne by the hallowed traditions of the Christian past. He forgot that the Founder of Christianity and His Apostles, as also the founders of the Christian churches and of the supernatural order of

Europe, had based their work on facts, facts however which were not merely apparent, temporary or superficial. Today we have reached the end of this vast experiment in "real" politics. The hour has come to draw from it all the conclusions to which it leads and once more to learn the lessons of history.

Richelieu will have successors who on the one hand will destroy by degrees the excessive centralization which was necessary only as a temporary expedient to meet a special danger, and on the other hand will devote a political genius equal to the great Cardinal's to reuniting the nations of Europe. In his study of Richelieu, Burckhardt aptly describes his work for France, when he speaks of "the principle of concentrated masculine rule carried to its utmost power," which, he says, "in the person of Richelieu successfully asserted itself against the dying medieval world and against the maternal government of compromise and flexibility which, as represented by Maria dei Medici, had become corrupt and selfish." If in the spirit of "masculine" rule and concentration of power the Habsburgs had forcibly broken the resistance of the German princes, and then in their relations with the outside world been inspired not by the will-to-power but by "the *maternal* principle of compromise and flexibility," Germany and Europe would have been spared incalculable suffering.

THE HABSBURGS, RICHELIEU AND CATHOLICISM

It is most comprehensible that the entire Catholic world is hostile to Richelieu and champions the supernational cause of the Habsburgs who were defending the Empire and with it the unity of Europe. While they were battling against the Protestant secession, a Catholic Cardinal, so runs this reading of history, attacked the defenders of German Catholicism from the rear.

It is not easy to refute the charge, which has lately been

repeated by Hilaire Belloc in his book on Richelieu. The problem however is far too complex to justify such one-sided charges. To place the position as far as possible in a true and fair light, I must go back to my statement of the enormous historical consequences which followed from the division of Charlemagne's Empire in the year 843. One of these inevitable consequences was Richelieu's achievement. Ever since that division there were two rival political systems in Europe which must one day struggle for supremacy. At first the significance of the split was concealed by centuries of cooperation between the members of European Christendom; that is to say, by the psychological after-effects of the Latin Christian ideal of unity. But when individualism and Machiavellianism spread from Italy to the rest of Europe, clouded the intelligence of rulers and diplomats, and gradually banished the policy of Christian supernationalism from international life, to pave the way for what is called real politics, the policy of the Holy Roman Empire itself was gradually, and often unconsciously, transformed into an unholy Machiavellianism.

Was it, for example, the policy of a Catholic and holy Empire, conscious of its responsibility for the unity of Europe, which led Austria to join with Frederick the Great in the crime of partitioning Catholic Poland? But the materialization and secularization of Habsburg policy had begun long before this. From an international policy it had slowly degenerated into a policy of German imperialism whose aim was the aggrandizement of the Habsburg family. Hence the position of France between Germany and Spain, whose world-renowned infantry had won the Emperor victory after victory, became more and more plainly one of encirclement by the great Habsburg powers. To break through and defeat their encirclement was, most intelligibly, the chief aim of the man who had resolved to rescue France from her domestic anarchy and her insecurity from foreign attack—Cardinal Richelieu, the Prime Minister of Louis XIII.

Since Richelieu desired no annexations but merely to secure the French frontiers it would have been easy for Ferdinand II at the price of very moderate territorial concessions to reach a solid agreement with the Cardinal. That the Emperor never made this attempt does not speak well for his intentions towards France. Ferdinand was infected already by the modern spirit of ambitious power and could not therefore pursue the genuinely German policy which at that juncture above all was so urgently required to counteract the purely individualist national policies. Consequently the French policy of defensive security thought it necessary to exploit the German civil war for its own ends. The moment Germany neglects to base her policy on a higher principle and indulges in power-politics, she is lost. The history of the Thirty Years War would have demonstrated this, had not its historians successfully concealed and distorted its causes.

When we contemplate the policy of the Habsburgs as a whole, we are compelled to admit that, although this imperial house rendered great service to Catholicism and to Austria, their *foreign policy* made no serious attempt to realize Christian principles. The *policy* of Catholic Austria was not inspired by a Catholic spirit; and for that reason was impotent to resist the disintegration of Europe. Certainly, in this, Ferdinand II was a child of his age. But it is unfair to censure Richelieu because in the struggle he too behaved as a child of his age and saw in the Emperor no longer the protector of Catholic Europe but the representative of the imperialist power-politics pursued by the German-Spanish bloc, and accordingly gathered allies from whatever quarter he could find them.

In view of these facts, Richelieu's alliance with the King of Sweden and with the Protestant German Princes will appear in a different light and can no longer be con-

demned as a mere betrayal of Catholic interests. The
Cardinal was convinced that the most venerable and deep-
rooted Catholic traditions were to be found in France, not
in the more modern Germany, and, therefore, that to save
France from being stifled by the German colossus was also
a vital necessity for the Catholic cause. Moreover, Richelieu set definite limits to his support of his Protestant
allies. His object was to prevent a dangerous increase
of the imperial power, not to make it possible for Protestantism to triumph in Germany. When, therefore, after
his first important victories, Gustavus Adolphus made him
the tempting offer to give to France the entire left bank of
the Rhine if he would grant him further subsidies, he
spent a whole night weighing the proposal from every
point of view and finally decided that as a Cardinal of the
Catholic Church and as Minister of Catholic France he
must reject the offer and pay no further subsidies.

FRANCE DIVORCED FROM EUROPE

On the other hand, in view of the tragic development
of the European problem and all the modern and contemporary results of the enmity between France and Germany whose deepest roots must be sought in Richelieu's
policy, the Cardinal's achievement is not in every aspect
so defensible as many of his champions have made out.
Richelieu came from a district in which the landowners
surrounded their estates with high stone walls. It is symbolic of the one-sidedly defensive character of the policy
he pursued in regard to Germany and Europe. But this
one-sidedness is common to the entire French nation, and
has been the source of everything that is tragic in the
history of modern France. France has filled the whole of
Europe with the scent of her garden, but the perfumes
of a high civilization cannot bind demons. France has
said, "Laissez-nous tranquilles," and left Europe to itself.
But, even in a state of chaos, Europe is still a whole, and

drags into its conflagrations even those who would remain outside.

Jacques Rivière has observed, "France is the guardian of the treasures of the individual life." Well and good. But has not France occupied herself too exclusively with her individual treasures? Alliances to defend her from the final consequences of the European anarchy are not enough. Before God and man a cold and unconcerned isolation from everything that is not "France" cannot be compensated by the great virtues of the French people nor yet by the handful of too enthusiastic French Europeans and friends of Germany who could not see that it was already too late and that the powers of darkness are not to be banished by conversations: though neither by stone walls. In this connection we should read what the acute and cold-blooded Bainville wrote in praise of Richelieu's policy. His language is terrifying in its unconcern for the nations beyond the French frontiers which are abandoned to their dissolution as though the living could sleep quietly with corpses and never succumb to the poisonous reek of their corruption. Bainville wrote: "France developed and perfected herself while Germany decayed and decomposed. To promote and to insure German anarchy was the masterstroke of French policy in the seventeenth century which crowned the toil and achievements of many generations and meant the triumph of France; France could henceforth live without fear side by side with her dangerous neighbor which was placed in a state of unarmed impotence."

Can we in truth call the French policy towards Germany great and successful when the threat, of which Bainville wrote that it oppressed France like a nightmare, is now thrice as great and has since 1866 never ceased to keep the French people in perpetual fear? Was it not precisely because Germany had been abandoned to its anarchy that Prussia was able to assume the function of organizing

German unity, with the result that France was bled white by wars and the whole of Europe has been transformed into an armed camp? Is Bismarck conceivable without Richelieu?

No doubt Richelieu died too soon. Confronted with a desperate situation which demanded a hasty decision, he had performed only the first act of a policy in which he displayed such genius that we may conjecture that he would have been able with his wide vision, his sense of measure and balance, his feeling for European realities, to do for Europe what he had accomplished with so sure a touch for France. In any case his work is a pledge that in the future his people will produce an organizer to complete the task of which he achieved but a fragment, a new representative of the Christian synthesis to unite France once more with Europe and Europe with France.

But it cannot be denied that the creation of a great French national and centralized state, while Germany was left in a condition of anarchy in the midst of an anarchic Europe, inevitably provoked the advent of a German Richelieu, wearing, to suit the German mentality, the boots of a huzzar instead of a Cardinal's robe, who setting out from the North-East, destroyed the inadequate defense erected by seventeenth-century France. Hitler has simply brought this counter-attack to its conclusion.

That the solution of a unified sovereign state, which indeed suited France but not Germany nor the situation in Eastern and South-Eastern Europe, must produce a crisis threatening to uproot Germany and Europe is another question. But that in the framework of a disintegrated Europe the anarchic condition of Germany, fostered, indeed deliberately created, by Richelieu and his successors, must one day tempt a German statesman to follow Richelieu's example, and that the creation of anarchy in the neighborhood of a well-ordered country could not permanently give security to France, is surely quite incontestable. That in view of the European disorder the question of German security must one day arise could have been foreseen. The least therefore that should have been done was to attempt to reorganize Europe, in some such reorganization as Napoleon envisaged later. Only thus could Germany have been saved from Pan-Germanism and from the hegemony of Prussia.

To sum up: In the traditional French policy of security there is a great weakness, due to the French retirement from Europe and to a fatal ignorance of the nature of the German problem and its special difficulties in regard to Eastern Europe. This weakness found expression once more in all the projects put forward after the year 1918 by followers of the Richelieu tradition for breaking up German unity once more. Their advocates indeed saw truly that the survival of the union created by Prussia must inevitably lead to the preparation of a second World War. It was undoubtedly the worst mistake of the Treaty of Versailles not to have foreseen this and not to have taken adequate measures to prevent it. But the problem of permanently preventing, after the German union has been forcibly dissolved, the reunion of the separated groups by propaganda, deceit and rearmament was a thousand times more difficult than they have ever recognized, so difficult that it could be solved only by organizing Europe. There is not in fact a single European problem soluble in isolation and by mere force. Europeans have no alternative but to reconstruct their ancient community in entirely new forms. But so long as this community does not exist, even in the treatment of nations that break the peace of Europe, how are European peace and security to be organized?

CHAPTER IV

THE ENTRANCE OF PRUSSIA INTO GERMAN HISTORY

THE ECCLESIASTICAL ORIGIN OF THE PRUSSIAN STATE

WHAT was the root-stock from which grew that historical power we call Prussia? How did Prussia rise to power? What enabled it to dominate completely the German soul? How did its conflict with Europe develop? How will that conflict end?

Amidst the dense primeval forest which covered the plain around the Weichsel, a picked body of knights from every part of Germany——with the special blessing of Rome and extensive privileges, employing administrative and economic methods, brought from the East and supported by the Hanseatic towns and settlers from the whole of Germany after a war of extermination that lasted for sixty years——founded a model state which gradually extended its territory to the Rhine and imbued Germany as a whole with its military spirit and love of order until the conflict with the entire world matured. This surely is one of the most dramatic chapters in the history of mankind. It will repay us to study the psychological and sociological factors which determined this development.

When the Crusaders were besieging the stronghold of Acco, some wealthy merchants from Luebeck and Bremen had pity on the wounded and took them into their tents. There they were nursed by German knights; as crusaders of other nations had long been nursed by the Templars and the Hospitallers. After the capitulation of Acco a hospital was erected with the assistance of those merchants and

the brotherhood of knights became a permanent institution (A.D. 1190). This was the origin of the Teutonic
Knights. It was also the origin of the foundation of Prussia.
It was symbolic of the future work of the Order in North-
eastern Germany that German burghers watched over its
cradle. For the later success of the Order depended entirely
on the cooperation between the Hanseatic towns and the
Knights. And so long as its greatness endured, the Order
continued to pray for its devout cofounders from Luebeck
and Bremen.

A generation later the Order had settled between
Western and Eastern Europe, tended the sick, drilled the
new crusading infantry and increased its settlement by
the sword. Its undertakings assumed a political importance
when Herman Von Salza became Master-General. Herman, who had been brought up at the court of Wartburg,
had been imbued with the secular culture of the age at
Frederick the Second's Court at Palermo, and had been
initiated there into the world-embracing ambitions of
imperial statecraft. The Hohenstaufen Emperor had himself learned this absolutism in the East where it was the
venerable Byzantine tradition. His highly developed financial system and his skill in ruling men were due to the
fact that he governed Sicily with the aid of a highly trained
bureaucracy, and practiced the utmost refinements of fiscal
administration and codified legislation. Those who later
have remarked upon the Byzantine character of Prussian
bureaucracy have not guessed that in the most literal sense
Prussia can, from one point of view, be called a Byzantine
creation and that the Prussian gift for administration was,
in the last resort, of oriental origin.

The peculiar mixture of administrative skill and technique and the lawless savagery displayed in the war waged
with the barbarians who poured into Asia Minor, had
been from the outset the distinctive feature of the entire
institution and its innate curse. To reward their services

in his war against the pagans, Cumans, king of Hungary, bestowed the Burgenland on the Teutonic Knights as a fief. Thereupon they persuaded the Pope to declare it the property of Saint Peter and sought to occupy it as their permanent home and possession. The king of Hungary hastened to reply to this manoeuvre by marching against those dangerous knights, and he lost no time in expelling them from his country. At this juncture an embassy from a Polish prince appeared on the scene and asked the Master-General to give him the powerful aid of the Order in his war against the heathen "pruzzi" who made their stronghold in the thick forests of the lower Weichsel. The Master-General promised his help. With his knights drawn from every part of Germany and with the hearty support of the Pope and the Emperor, he began his Christian and German crusade against the people who were later to give their name to the new State. In return for their assistance the Order demanded and received Culmer and any future conquests in Prussia as an electoral principality. Thus a German state thrust itself between Poland and the sea and predetermined all the future hostility between Poland and the constantly growing territory of the Order whose nature and tradition were conquest.

In the year 1231 the first army of crusaders crossed the Weichsel and began a systematic advance. It was sure and steady. Every district conquered was secured by castles whose long line pushed forward into the primeval forest like a mole of stone projecting into a stormy sea. Every advance was decided by a well considered plan of campaign comparable with that of the Italians in Abyssinia. At the epoch in which Dante composed his *Divina Commedia* and Francis of Assisi preached to the birds, a war of annihilation of the most cruel description raged for almost sixty years. Often on moonlight nights the Knights and their opponents clashed in mortal combat on some frozen lake until the ice broke and both sides were drowned. After the first victories the land resounded with the victors' solemn paean "Good news for all of us—the heathen have been smashed". The ancient sanctuary, the wood of Romove, was captured. The oaks hallowed with memories of pagan deities were cut down. The conquered were compelled to receive baptism. But the opposition proved stubborn and burst forth from the forests with renewed fury so that the Order decided to plant colonies on a large scale. Citizens from Lower Germany were invited to build a new town in the shadow of every castle. Settlers and peasants were brought from afar. In view of the difficulties and dangers the colonists had to face they were granted extensive liberties and privileges. They formed a militia which served under the orders of the Marshal of the Knights. It was the original nucleus of the later Prussian landwehr.

Literally with fire and sword the land was won for Christianity. Every village was burned whose inhabitants had dared to sacrifice at night to the old gods, the children were taken from their parents and educated in monastic schools. But those Prussian chiefs thus educated by force and drilled by their conquerors did not forget revenge, and the mothers bereft of their children were irreconcilable. In the darkest depths of their forests the disinherited people gathered and hatched insurrection. The bailiff of the Order on the Fischen Haff discovered what was afoot, invited a number of Prussian chiefs to his castle, and set it on fire. Thereupon the revolt burst out like a tempest. The entire conquered people suddenly flew to arms, burned the castles of the Order, slaughtered the traders and took vengeance a hundredfold. The atrocities of previous wars were as nothing to the horrors of this. A German noble who was captured was encased in triple iron and burnt alive as a sacrifice to the Thunder God, or he was fixed to a tree by a nail driven through his navel and then driven around it with whips until his entrails were torn out.

When after ten years' fighting the German rule seemed almost totally destroyed, the fortune of war was changed by the action of a marshal of exceptional skill and determination, Conrad von Thierberg. He reconquered the country by adopting a systematic plan of campaign. After ten years the revolt was crushed at last. The inhabitants of entire villages were thereupon transferred to remote districts, the conquered deprived of all means of concerted action and compelled to learn German, the chiefs reduced to a condition of serfdom.

We cannot insist too strongly that the extraordinary military, political and economic achievement of the Order whose constitution was aristocratic—it was governed by a chapter of twelve brothers—would have been impossible without its strict monastic discipline. This alone held those violent men together for more than two centuries and subjected them to a fixed tradition and a single will. Never since that time has the world beheld such a community of monastic warriors and founders of a state whose success was so enduring. Never since has it witnessed such an achievement of the human will keyed to the utmost pitch to accomplish a task of colonization in which conquest was followed by the foundation of a state, an enterprise so completely unfettered in its execution and furnished with everything that might secure the fullest output of energy, as was the case here. The forces it set in motion have continued to operate for centuries. They alone can explain the influence of characters formed in this school and their traditions upon the German people and its entire history. "The privileges, laws and customs" of the Order reveal the art of ruling and training men which inspired them.

In his book on *Prussia the Land of a German Order*, Von Treitschke wrote, "A man became a member of the

Order by taking the three vows of poverty, chastity and obedience," the foundation of every form of religious life, "and receiving in return a sword, a piece of bread and an old garment." He was forbidden to bear the arms of his family, to lodge with seculars, to frequent luxurious cities, to ride out alone, to read or write letters. Four times during the night, the brethren, who slept half-clad with their swords by their side, were summoned to choir by the sound of a bell, and four times during the day. Every Friday they took the discipline. A knight to whom an office was committed, be it at Riga or at Venice, accepted it without demur and resigned it on the following Feast of the Exaltation of the Cross at the chapter of his province. His accounts were preserved in the archives. If a brother committed a fault, a secret chapter was held which began with Mass and ended with prayer. The culprit was often condemned to eat at the table of the servitors or to receive a discipline, the "stripes being measured by the fault."

It was a successor of these Teutonic knights, General Bernhardi, who said, "It is war alone that assigns to every people its true place and the field of action which corresponds with biological justice. God reveals Himself in victory by which He makes truth defeat appearance. It is God's law that condemns the vanquished and it is, therefore, His will that the conqueror should dictate such peace terms as shall display his inner strength by his external power and greatness." (*Internationale Monatschrift.* November 1914.)

It is not without profound historical significance that this warlike Christianity is today being treated at last as a superfluous, indeed, mischievous alien element, and as such is being rejected by the most logical representatives of the political and military tradition whose misdeeds it had unreservedly approved and applauded. A repulsive mixture of the Divine law and the law of the jungle will thus meet its well-deserved doom. Nor must we forget, in

this connection, that this spiritual military state and everything to which it gave rise was the final result, returned
against Europe, of the Crusades. To point this out is not
to pronounce a moral judgment upon important historical
developments. We would simply call attention to a chain
of cause and effect and by recalling one of its most instructive and most far-reaching effects, cast light upon the
important historical era in which good and evil, spirit
and brute force, Christianity and barbarism were bewil-
deringly intermingled.

About the year 1370, the political and economic power
of the Order reached its apogee. The conquest of the
Lithuanian province of Samailenland, which had hitherto
thrust a wedge between its possessions on the coast, extended its sovereignty to Estland. There, however, on the
shore of the Baltic, a thin stratum of German conquerors
ruled a native population brooding in sullen hate. The
entire country from Lake Peipus to Lebav was tributary to
the Order. It traded on a large scale. Its commercial agents
resided in Bruges and Lwow. It sold corn and the amber
which it made a monopoly. A symbol of this seemingly
everlasting power was Marienburg, whose roots, its vast
cellars, reached in popular belief as far down into the
earth as its battlements rose skyward. At night, when the
light streamed through the refectory windows, it shone like
a beacon set high above the land, the valley of the Weichsel
which the Order had civilized. In the castle chapel a huge
mosaic of the Blessed Virgin carrying a lily showed that
here was the spiritual center of the Order. Round the
castle rested the bodies of the dead brethren. The entire
edifice, with its massive towers, turned its defiant visage to
the East. Even after a crushing defeat at Tannenberg, it
held out so long that the king of Poland withdrew his
forces, and from this invincible stronghold Heinrich von
Plauen was able to recover the lost territory.

In his book, *Der preussische Stil*, Moeller van den Bruck

praises the severe and monumental, as it were ascetic, architecture which dispensed with any decoration of sculptured foliage and displayed only a front of rough brick and windows severely rectilinear. He calls our attention to a symbolism which gave architectural expression to those ancient Christian and Roman virtues which were the source of the Order's strength. The play of individual fantasy was forbidden, the austere logic of stern resolution was supreme, everything was compelled to minister to the one sovereign aim and there was no place for lavish expenditure. What Plato said of Sparta: that there was more genuine philosophy there than elsewhere—and he had in mind the unifying power of a political principle logically applied in every sphere—is equally applicable to this religious and military state.

THE DISSOLUTION OF THE ORDER AND THE SURVIVAL OF ITS SPIRIT

All the conditions, internal and external alike, rendered inevitable the final destruction of this proud monastic edifice, though its spirit of self-assertive power and its historical curse would survive and be reincarnate in new forms. The spiritual climate changed, the period of the Crusades and the military Order to which they had given birth was long past. The Reformation knocked at the portal of the Marienburg. The peasants, the city burghers and the landed nobility, in spite of the franchises bestowed upon them, were no longer content that the destinies of a country which had grown rich should be decided by the arbitrary decrees of a rigidly exclusive caste, a caste moreover of foreign origin and bound by no family ties to the land. The Hansa towns saw in the Order's far-flung trade a threat to their own monopoly. Russia was slowly approaching the Baltic. Poland was beginning to round off her frontiers and was drawing Danzig once more into the new orbit.

In the face of all these dangers the inner strength of the Order was no longer what it had been. Moreover the vast power they wielded had rendered the heads of the Order arrogant and careless. One blow, therefore, followed another; first, the disaster of Tannenberg, then domestic treason. On the frontier revolt succeeded revolt, until finally the Order had to accept vassalage to Poland. Its end was secularization by the last Grand Master. On his death the territory now governed as a duchy became the inheritance of the house of Brandenburg. Thus the land once ruled by the Order, no longer capable of confronting alone the advance of the Slavs, withdrew into the general life of Germany. It linked itself with the second great German colonial power which, on the sandy wastes of the Mark and by centuries of conflict with the native Slavonic tribes, had achieved a similar product of stern resolution.

The immediate consequence of this fateful union was the well known policy of rounding off a colonial territory at many points divided, a policy pursued by a combination of annexation and matrimonial alliances. It was in pursuit of this policy that Frederick the Great, in the partition of Poland, seized the entire aboriginal Polish territory which cut off Brandenburg from East Prussia. Even the annexation of Silesia must be regarded rather as a continuation of the old anti-Polish policy of the Teutonic Knights than as a blow deliberately aimed at Austria. As early as the close of the fourteenth century a Piasten Duke had submitted to the Order a project for partitioning Poland. Bismarck's annexation of Hanover was a counterpart of the annexation of what is known as the Polish corridor. For Hanover was, as it were, the western and Guelf corridor which cut off Prussia from the Rhineland provinces. This step plainly revealed the fundamental policy of forcible annexation inherited from the Knights, in combination with that mystical conception of Prussia's German mission which perplexed Bishop von Ketteler but which is beyond doubt the faded tradition of the old crusade, an ideal of its nature capable of unlimited expansion. "What Prussia has been to Germany," said Gneisenau, "Germany must be to the whole of Europe. Someday, Prussia must rule the greater part of Europe."

We cannot sufficiently insist upon this lust of domination which the Prussian soul has drawn from the depth of a powerful tradition. Anyone who had understood it was aware how quickly and irresistibly the forces fed by that tradition would, after the first World War, conquer the whole of Germany. Germany's condition at the time was purely provisional. She had at her disposition neither the ideals and sources of strength, nor yet the strength, consistency and self-confidence of Prussia. She must, therefore, abdicate impotently the moment she was attacked by the representatives of the military tradition.

THE TEUTONIC KNIGHTS AND PRUSSIAN MILITARISM

The French Comte de Pange, whose family came from Lorraine, recounts in his *Soirées de Saverne* a typical impression he received in his youth of the survival of the tradition of the Teutonic Knights in the older generation of German generals. He describes General Haeseller, who long before the War commanded the troops in Lorraine: "The greyish-yellow countenance which beneath his helmet wore a surprisingly monastic expression is deeply impressed upon my memory. As is well known, he led a monk's life. He remained unmarried and his sole lodging in Metz was a small room as bare as a monastic cell. But on the ceiling he had had a map of the frontier district painted, so that as he lay in his camp bed he could think over future battles. The visage of this monk-soldier has long haunted me and I realize that he and his fellows are continuing in soldier's uniform the tradition of that great Order".

Graf von Haeseller was no barbarian. He was a chivalrous foe. In the Herren Haus he refused assent to the policy of expropriation which Prince Bülow sought to introduce against the Polish landlords. Yet in 1893 he spoke as follows in an address to his troops. "Our civilization must build its temple on mountains of corpses, an ocean of tears and the groans of innumerable dying men. It cannot be otherwise." This utterance made by such a man casts a glaring light on the entire Prussian mentality. When men like these are dealing with international politics, they take no account whatever of anything belonging to man's life as a personal spirit, nor of religion, humanity, morality or honor. International politics are simply the interplay of natural forces; and the man who stakes his strength in the game must, if he is to win, become himself but a part of merciless nature. This is the sacrifice he owes to his people, that it may not be trampled underfoot and that those may conquer who are biologically deserving of victory.

All men educated in this school display the same inner cleavage, however cultivated they may be. As soon as the conversation turns on politics their speech and thought suddenly breathe an arctic chill. It is not even political paganism. For the pagan believes in an ineluctable Divine government concerned even with political crime. But these men seem to be victims of a peculiar disease. Through generations and centuries of wars of annihilation, a virus has slowly poisoned the blood and in the associates and heirs of this barbarism has killed beyond hope of recovery the aboriginal instinct of the living human soul for the truth of the invisible world, even, or rather particularly, in the political field. Even a man of such high intellectual and artistic endowments as Frederick the Great gave proof, in the sphere of international politics, of what was little short of moral insanity. None of those statesmen who earnestly desire to maintain a moral order within the nation has ever suspected that his political methods are fatally inconsistent and that the time must come when all the blatant immorality they practice and justify in foreign relations will turn inwards and destroy all interior order and every principle of justice. On the contrary those statesmen live untroubled in this complete contradiction and in the practice of a policy of such blind materialism that for generations they have deprived the political thought of their people of every higher light and thereby of any realism that penetrates below the surface.

TWO CONSTITUENTS OF COLONIAL GERMANY

To obtain a thorough psychological and sociological understanding of the true nature of the Prussian militarism with which Europe is grappling in such a stern and well-nigh irremediable conflict we must constantly bear in mind the fact just pointed out that, ever since the union of the Dukedom of Prussia with Brandenburg, two German colonial powers of very different origin and equipment have joined forces and have supplemented each other in building up the Prussian system.

With truth it may be said that the contribution made by the land ruled by the Knights is of Christian and chivalrous inspiration and is responsible for the ultimate aim of Prussia's policy and for the spirit that has for centuries inspired the ruling class, whereas the Brandenburg contribution has been concerned rather with the subordinate aspect of this militarism. It was the great Kurfurst who gathered the last remnants of the roving *landsknechts* still surviving from the Thirty Years' War, gave them a legal status, took them into his service, and by an extremely severe discipline rescued them from the disorders of those years of war. His successors completed his work. One of the factors which had led to the downfall of the Teutonic Knights was the advent of infantry as the predominant military arm. The Potsdam Grenadiers, brought to military perfection by Frederick the Great, with the Dessau parade into the bargain, represent the Brandenburg contribution; whereas everything described hitherto, and typified by General Haeseller, was of Eastern origin and was inspired by the spirit of the Knights as it survived in the leading circles of Prussian militarism.

These two diverse strains of colonial Teutonism also differ considerably in their racial aspects. The Prussian factor in the stricter sense, is far less German, though tempered to an extraordinary hardness by its colonial and military history. As Treitschke said, it lacks a distinctive German trait, good nature. The Brandenburg and Markist element is of mixed racial composition. In many localities Wendish blood decidedly preponderates. It is distinguished by a particularly pliable, obedient, industrious, and practical character.

But we should have an inadequate notion of Prussian militarism, if we forget that it has also been fostered by the genuinely German attitude which has discovered in the rhythm of military exercises, in the strict subordination of the individual soldier to the army, and in the cast-iron discipline, something which satisfies a profound German need for ratio, for system, and for the union of factors in themselves making for disunion. Hence the militarist attitude of modern Germans must not be confused with mere bellicosity. If the army is the center of the national life, it is because it is far more than a preparation for war. As a training school of precision and accuracy, of a determination which never flinches, of reliability even in small matters, and of moral responsibility, it has gradually attracted to it the finest national virtues. William I could say without exaggeration, "our military institutions proceed from the entire moral culture of our people." In his *Frederick the Great*, Thomas Carlyle praises as the great achievement of colonial Germany the intimate union it has effected between manliness and wholehearted service in accordance with Goethe's saying in Wilhelm Meister, "Make thyself an instrument." This service moreover is complete and thorough, admitting no pretense or half-heartedness, staunch and true to the end.

THE CONSTRUCTIVE AND DESTRUCTIVE ASPECTS OF PRUSSIAN MILITARISM

German militarism, therefore, is an extremely complex phenomenon. It is a typical expression of a well-nigh inextricable mixture of good and evil, construction and destruction, barbarism and civilization, Christ and anti-christ, which, as we have seen, has characterized that phase of the great conflict between the higher and the lower worlds which is today reaching its close. Those who can pick out in this militarism strands a thousand times inter-woven, who can give each its right name and who can show how the good serves the evil and the evil serves or rather imagines it serves the good, help to prepare the advent of the new phase in which light and darkness, creation and destruction, spirit and its mortal foe shall once more be clearly divided, so that the conflict between them can be waged in full daylight.

The far-reaching confusion of thought and language which at present prevails in our judgments of the historic events of the preceding epoch is due to the fact that those who pronounce those judgments regard each only as a single aspect and will not see others which are also opera-tive and perhaps predominant. A host of critics have failed to perceive the important positive aspect of Prussian mili-tarism, indeed the presence in it of Christian asceticism and self-sacrifice; and have therefore, been unable to under-stand the historic rôle it has played and still plays in German life or the attraction it has exercised and still exercises over the German soul and the moral esteem it has won even abroad. Countless other judges have been blind to its diabolical and destructive aspect which, however, has dominated all the higher elements, employed them in its service, and by determining the aims of the system as a whole has exploited and gradually materialized everything in itself noble. I will quote a typical example of a just appreciation of the good combined with blindness to the disfiguring and corrupting forces at work. The former Hungarian Minister of Finance, Hegedus, writing in the *Pester Lloyd* (1927) expressed his gratitude to the Prussian nurse who by her unremitting care, inspired by an unflagging sense of duty, had cured him after a nervous breakdown. He said:

"Sister Margaret, this is my wish for you: may it be yours to see Prussia's former territory German once more and the Reich again strong, which produces such admirable souls, whose sense of duty is solid as bronze. The categorical imperative, the *recher de bronce*, such is the true-born Prussian lady. She belongs wholly to the state and the state to her. Sister Margaret, I wish that when a greater Germany rises from the grave it may stretch out a hand to little Hungary that we in turn may shake off the yoke of Trianon."

No, Sister Margaret, this is not our wish for you. On the contrary, we desire that from our people may be lifted the heavy curse which consists in the fatal principle that all those incomparable virtues are bound up with the idolatrous worship of an unscrupulous state, a state which bullies and plunders, and that the virtues are thus abused by it in the service of unadulterated immorality. We wish that the state you serve may at long last foster in its patriotic servants an iron sense of duty toward a value and a law higher than itself. Not until that state determines to serve sincerely the community of nations, to abandon the life of a freebooter, and to give chivalrous aid and service to the neighbors it has formerly oppressed, not until then will it be worthy of the many noble and devoted servants of both sexes with whom Providence has endowed it.

Since one of the principal objects of this book is to explain German history by studying the political materialization of the German soul as a psychological and sociological phenomenon, I will give another example which displays both the genuine Prussian virtue and its tragic diversion to the service of a principle diametrically opposed to virtue.

The grandson of Theodore von Bernhardi, writing to his father, Frederick von Bernhardi, gave the following account of his grandfather's last moments:

"When on February 12, 1887, I stood by his bed and the shadow of approaching death was rapidly descending on the old man of eighty-four, almost his last words were a grave admonition never to forget that no undertaking or achievement of the individual has any worth unless it is deliberately directed to the common good."

Here spoke that ancient and noble German attitude which has always moved from the part to the whole, from the single science to the Weltanschauung, from the particular to the universal: religious self-sacrifice, a Roman and Christian inheritance from the Teutonic administrators of the medieval *civitas humana*, the most valuable endowment of this central European people—but, as it is today, perverted into the worship of the Prussian State and military discipline. Even so, in Werther's *Leiden*, the German, craving for the eternal, became infatuated with Lotte and transferred to her a passionate love destined for a good which far surpasses her.

Is it still possible to open the eyes of the noblest Prussians to the true meaning and purpose of this devotion to the common good and to make them conscious of the fatal individualism and separatism which has perverted and narrowed their entire political thought and their craving to merge themselves in something beyond the individual? Or are they no longer capable of freeing themselves from their narrow isolation, their aversion to a universal ideal, their conspiracy against Europe; that is to say, from the arrogant anarchism of their political thought and understanding? Otherwise, even within the state their noble feeling for the common good must be irretrievably ruined by the abuse of the common good for the selfish interests of a particular community, because the state will not acknowledge a superior duty and responsibility.

Or will Prussia, which within a very narrow circle displays an iron consistency, perish from the appalling inconsistency with which it has attempted to combine lofty morality and sheer immorality, an inviolable regard for order and reckless gangsterism?

CHAPTER V

HOW DID PRUSSIA CONQUER THE GERMAN SOUL?

PRUSSIAN EDUCATION

THE answer to this question has already been suggested at the close of my last chapter. Brandenburg-Prussia, with all the forces and methods of political construction it had derived from the spirit of the Teutonic Knights, from the East and from the task of colonization, confronted the anarchy left by the Thirty Years' War. Thereby, as its consolidation proceeded, it attracted the attention of all German patriots. It was a South German, Hegel, who saw in the Prussian State the objective realization of the spirit. "That the individual will should tremble, and that we should learn the nothingness of self-seeking and the necessity of obedience is an essential part of every man's education." These words of Hegel clearly show why it was precisely the German individualist and subjectivist who sought refuge in the objective world of the Prussian State from all the dangers of the easy-going German temper. Once the order which completed it had been imposed on Germany by the Latin world, in Protestant Germany Prussia took over the function of representing objective law as against subjective mood.

The Prusso-German symbiosis, however, has still deeper psychological foundations. In a Platonic sense it may be regarded as almost an erotic phenomenon, a unique conjunction of masculine and feminine qualities—from whose wedlock what we know as modern Germany has been born—though, to be sure, with such an exaggeration of

the masculine factor that, as in Islam, the eternal feminine, Mary's contribution, has been completely lost sight
of. Could there be a greater contrast than between Hoelderlin and Bismarck? Nevertheless, after a long period of
mutual repulsion, the two types finally met and contracted
an alliance in accordance with the law of Plato's Eros that
brings opposites together and unites them for their mutual
completion. Plato called Eros "the desire of poverty for
wealth." There is also a desire of wealth for poverty, of
affluence for simplicity, as in Plato himself the exuberant
wealth of Ionic genius sought the Doric austerity and restraint. And this precisely is the psychological explanation
of the extraordinary attraction exercised on the German
soul by Prussian discipline, simplicity, authority and capacity for government; and in particular on a Germany
which had lost its roots, had been separated from Roman
discipline and Christian asceticism and strictness and had
been abandoned to its native excesses of feeling.

It has often caused surprise that a man so devoid of
exceptional gifts as Hindenburg could rise to a position
of uncontested leadership through all the upheavals and
revolutions of the War and the period which followed it.
It is in fact most intelligible. Just as there are extremely
complicated women who marry a clod because they want
the support and salvation of simplicity, so this almost
symbolic incarnation of the simplest Prussian manliness,
practicality, and reliability, promised to rescue from everything that disturbed its equilibrium a Germany, shaken
and in mortal strife with an unknown world. To be sure,
Hindenburg's face promised more than he actually possessed—but nevertheless, it radiated a security, solid as a
rock; and through it a man of undisturbed self-possession
spoke to men thrown off their balance. This was enough.

As the soft and sensitive snail builds her house out of
her own secretion, so the sentimental German has built
his hard dwelling out of an isolated Prussia. In the legend,

Siegfried clad himself with the dragon's skin. He is the German who has clad himself with the Prussian hide. But it is not difficult to see that the manliness is rather in the skin than in the inner man. That is why since Bismarck there has been such emphasis on iron and steel. The Iron Chancellor, a sense of realities hard as steel, the Stahlhelm. The man who has iron in his character needs no steel helmet. A straw hat is enough for him. Intelligent German women could tell you a great deal about the lack of iron in the character of many men who throw their weight about in jack-boots and steel helmets. That is why a real Prussian is more genuine and more tolerable than a Prussianized Saxon or a Prussianized native of Baden.

What then of Hitler? He is the complete conquest of the German soul by Prussia. Hitler continues the revolution of 1848 and by the same methods as the the victor of 1848, namely Prussian militarism. Prussia must yield to the Austrian Hitler because Prussia and the wider Germany, blended in one, are stronger than either of the two component forces acting separately. Goebbels once said, "We are Prussians even when we are Bavarians or Wuertembergers—wherever we are, there is Prussia." It is true.

National Socialism should not surprise us. It is the logical conclusion of the history of modern Germany from the moment when Leibnitz called attention to the anarchy of Germany and Europe, and the Germans—bereft of a Christianity speaking and teaching with a single voice, bereft therefore of Christian guidance in their political rebirth, and divided from their old European function by the Thirty Years' War and its devastation—gradually turned towards the nationalism of the West and imagined that in the Prussian bureaucratic state they had found the principle of order which would make them a united nation. Thus a straight line leads to Hitler from the nationalism which flaunted the black, red and gold flag. Hitler is but the logical completion of Bismarck's work, which because its ideal was the National State must exclude supernational Austria until the latter had been freed from its non-German elements.

Goering said at Potsdam, "Henceforth the step of the Potsdam Grenadiers is the step of the German people". The symbol displays clearly the meaning, and defines the last act of an historical process of three hundred years.

Nazi propaganda has brought to its conclusion this permeation of the German soul by the Prussian ideals of the state—in which achievement it was assisted by the complete breakdown in home and foreign politics alike of those groups which had once combated the spirit of Bismarck and his successors. Their representatives were no more than administrators of a bankrupt estate and lacked entirely the guiding ideal and the consistency with which they might have opened to the German people perspectives at once new and old, and thus have reestablished Germany's position in the world and recalled her from the false route she had taken.

My statement that Hitler is the complete conquest of the German soul of Prussia, requires amplification, of course. The complete acceptance of Prussia was, so to speak, but the first act. A Frenchman has said, "Hitler is the William I of the masses". They gladly accepted an ideology hitherto confined to the ruling classes. What is the explanation of this? After the German defeat should we not have expected the contrary? Was not that defeat the *reductio ad absurdum* of Prussian militarism? Certainly it was; but not in the eyes of the German people. Systematic lying had deceived them about the causes and the history of the War. For this reason the truth could not enlighten the German nation and open its eyes to the true sequence of cause and effect. On the contrary, propaganda had so completely distorted the facts of the War and the post-War epoch that the Germans were inevitably cut off from Europe and brought back to Prussia and its policy of war. Nevertheless there was a novel factor in the situation; the groups for whom Germany's only possible salvation lay in a return to the Prussian tradition put a novel gloss upon it and drew logical consequences from it.

Already in his *Preussentum und Sozialismus,* Spengler had argued that Socialism is but the consistent application of the Prussian conception of the state and its efficient defense both at home and abroad. Accordingly, National Socialism was not content with simply taking over the principles of Prussian government. In every direction it thought out its implications without flinching. Only thus could it make the army its servant and attain political supremacy. The National Socialist movement introduced a further element which was not of Prussian origin but well calculated to support the ideology of a totalitarian state, namely, the conception of the popular community derived from the Youth Movement which had originated, not from Hegelian theory but from the rediscovery of the German people by the Wandervogel and similar movements and had inspired a number of most laudable attempts to improve the condition of the working classes. The War and its aftermath put those singing and wandering young men with open collars first into Prussian, then into Nazi uniform. Their expression grew harder and grimmer. The propaganda of lies accomplished its deadly work and infected those young men with an incurable fever until at last the entire Youth Movement, which had begun as a struggle against the mechanization of German life, had become part of the state machine.

HERO WORSHIP

There is certainly an unintelligent and abstractly moralistic attitude towards the great actors in the historical drama which is unjust to the genius and the attractive qualities displayed in the persecution even of misdirected undertakings. Such an attitude has no understanding of the profound tragedy often concealed behind a brilliant façade of external success. But there is a no less dangerous attitude which uncritically worships brute force and the momentary success it achieves. This attitude is not only a fearful temptation for the man who stands alone on the dizzy summit wherefrom he must make historical decisions; it also fatally corrupts the moral judgment of wide groups and thereby finally makes them incapable of reverencing true heroism.

The great and unscrupulous founders of Prussia and the authors of its triumph have been preeminently the objects of this hero-worship which makes light of the discriminations and qualifications demanded by a truly humane morality. Carlyle's *Frederick the Great* has greatly contributed to this confused and confusing type of hero-worship. In general, this adoration of ruthless power betrays a feminine quality. Nietzsche attributed the cult of Bismarck to the desire of the member of a herd to be brutally broken in. There are indeed recent writers who will not allow to such a man as Frederick the Great a single good quality. That is a gross exaggeration.

Like his ancestor, the great Kurfurst, Frederick was beyond dispute a man who in an extremely difficult situation showed exemplary courage, determination, endurance and presence of mind. Nor can we condemn either ruler because, in an epoch when the European community of nations and the unity of the German race had been completely dissolved, he opposed the Emperor, sought help from abroad, and in return helped foreign nations. We cannot deny the good intentions of these men who, with amazing prudence and energy and a lofty sense of responsibility, established order in their own domains and employed in its service every living force at their disposal. They may well have believed that after the religious cleavage the imperial framework was no longer capable of embodying German unity and that it was the destiny of their own land to form the nucleus of a new concentration of German power.

But when this is granted we must decidedly refuse to regard their unscrupulous action as a proof of great statesmanship or as morally praiseworthy. Their vision was limited by the success of the moment. They were completely indifferent to the depth and scope of the German problem and its connection with the problem of Europe as a whole. The policy pursued by Frederick the Great was that of a thorough cynic and atheist. The saying which Schiller placed in Wallenstein's mouth, "the earth belongs to the evil, not to the good spirit," might have been said by him. He, therefore, saw no object in concerning himself with the problem of Germany. He was content to amuse his mind with arts, with intellectual fireworks, fashionable in contemporary France. He was satisfied to settle international conflict by employing the Potsdam Grenadiers, and to bequeath to his successors a well ordered state. When at Leuthen, the Grenadiers shrank from the hostile fire he shouted "What, my lads, do you expect to live forever;" an enlightening reflection for the lads.

To sum up: for all his flute playing and his intellectual interests, Frederick was possessed by the Prussian devil, in whose service he committed one of the worst crimes in history, the partition of Poland. It did not occur to him that his own state might one day perish from the final effects of that outrage. Characteristic of all those Prussian war-gods is the refusal, nowhere else so complete and so cold, to believe that international life and the destinies of states are subject to moral government. Hence they act as shamelessly and as unflinchingly as they talk. Despite their exceptional endowments where knowledge of the life-principle of states is concerned, they are low in the human scale, far below the heathen, below even the Redskins, for the latter recognize the social necessity of keeping their pledged word. They give expression to an amazingly bar-

baric attitude to human affairs and to the spiritual conditions of human life, an attitude whose causes are mysterious. Was that barbaric attitude due to the great colonial
expansion itself, an achievement accomplished with brilliant success and, seemingly without Heaven's vengeance
by incalculable plunder and murders? Was it a plague, a
black death of the soul, an infection caught from the fields
of corpses, the blood drunken by the earth and the smoke
of burned homes? Was it the dark curse of races wiped out
without atonement? We do not know. But we see with
horror that a curse broods over the land and we cannot see
how it may be lifted. For the Germans who live beneath its
ban laugh over it and add to it every hour.

MEN OF WILL AND MEN OF MIND

The problem presented by the completion and at the
same time the perversion of the German by the Prussian
character leads us to a deeper tragedy common to all mankind, the tragedy of human limitation. Bjornson once observed that it was the destiny of our race that some men
should be extremely cultured but lack will-power, while
others should possess strong will but be uncultivated. To
will anything thoroughly involves the determination *not
to will* many other things, demands asceticism, that is to
say, life-long devotion to a single ideal, clearly selected.
On the other hand, the man of rich intellectual endowments knows, sees, feels, thinks and wishes too many things
to be capable of clear-cut decision and unwavering determination. Hence the great danger that the man of culture,
lacking a powerful and concentrated will to affirm and
defend his culture, will surrender himself blindly to the
man of strong will as his saviour from instability. Will,
therefore, always conquers culture, when it is mere culture
and not Christianity, which brings concentration, determination, energy and supernatural reinforcement, and
unites in a single whole all things that in a merely natural

life diverge. The Prussian domination of Germany is the domination of the man of will over the more richly endowed man of sentiment and intelligence, and may lead to the complete spiritual impoverishment of the latter.

In spite of his grateful admiration, my father saw in Bismarck the incarnation of the modern German mentality. What repelled him most was this: expediency was made a fundamental principle of conduct, without regard to justice and truth.

"In spite of his grateful admiration." This concession to a man who was nevertheless perceived to be the bane of his country, reveals the reason and the nature of the weakness displayed by Bismarck's German opponents. Their opposition did not rest on a firm foundation. An entire tradition had been lost. A united Germany was as much the ideal of Bismarck's critics as his own, though they wanted it to be more humane and liberal. That the problem of German unity was essentially not a domestic problem but could be solved only by a genuinely European policy, of which no one was less capable than the colonial German, was seen only by a handful.

The materialization of Germany effected by the hegemony of the colonial border has, in the course of decades, materialized the expression of the German countenance. An incredibly simplified organization of the brain, a shocking brutalization of movement and thought, a rapidly increasing psychological uniformity, already expresses itself vividly in the face. Compare the faces of many S.A. men with that of "the son of the muse" at the close of last century. In his book on the human countenance, M. Picard depicts the *materialization of faces* during the past century and observes: "When man ceases to be the likeness of God and when the bestial elements in his composition are no longer restrained by that likeness, he is free to develop in accordance with his own instincts." When we compare the faces of 1860 with those of today we are horrified, not so much by the fashion in which the facial expression has altered, but that in so short a time the expression of an entire generation can have altered. The change is so sudden that it seems as though it could not have been a change from within but must somehow have been thrown on these men from without, as though the older faces had been seized and carried off and the faceless heads had been reclad in the new.

I have just described the conquest and the impoverishment of Germany by the one-sided man of strong will and we have found that an essential cause of that conquest was the uncertainty, the vagueness, the abstract character, and the uprooted state of hostile tradition, sentiments and ideas. There are two ways in which the powers of a mind, rich and sensitive, can be concentrated and made effective. The soul may be gripped by so strong a passion or so inspiring an ideal that its energies are so powerfully set in motion that even the energy of the one-sided volitional type is surpassed. Such was the case of Kriemhild who wedded Attila to make use of him for her revenge. This is the secret of Hitler, the romantic and sensitive South-German who, inflamed by the myriad lies of the Nationalist propaganda, has allied himself with Potsdam and carried Potsdam along with him to draw from its lies, like a man possessed, their full conclusions and to avenge himself on the "Scoundrels of November" and "the Dictated Peace of Versailles." When this point is reached and the German frenzy (furor teutonicus) bursts forth from the sensitive German stirred thus to madness, he displays greater determination than the Prussian—at least while the frenzy lasts.

But there is another, a higher and more permanent, way in which the sensitive spirit can be roused to action. Christianity may enter the soul, expel all shadowy idealism, overcome all obstacles, concentrate all the man's energies in the service of a supreme good, expel all fear and enable Christ to accomplish what is impossible to the natural man.

Such was the case with the first colonizers of North Germany who were Cistercian monks. Without their tenacious energy which scorned death, the conquerors could have effected nothing. This is the solution of the problem of human energy. When the mind and the will confront each other in the void, will conquers mind. For the mind cannot will without His aid Who concentrates the soul on eternity and sends her into the world to serve eternity. The Germany of a dechristianized, abstract and romantic culture which Bismarck defeated could effect and defend nothing.

ROME AND PRUSSIA

Mussolini once said, "We are Roman Prussians." With far greater truth a Prussian could say: "We are Prussian Romans." In itself the state of which Mirabeau observed that war was its national industry and whose history of wars and plunderings did in fact produce in the course of the centuries many Roman virtues, afforded, in its order and outlook, a most favorable terrain for the revival of the Roman tradition. And this was in fact accomplished when, in consequence of renewed interest in classical antiquity, ancient Roman patriotism was set up as a model in the schools of higher education, and the younger generation of lawyers was molded in the spirit of Roman law. The triumph of humanism in German schools did not therefore render Germany more humane but became an extremely effective instrument for imbuing the rising generation with the spirit of ancient statecraft and above all with Roman virtues and Roman patriotism. The German past, which transcended individual states, was treated as a matter for shame.

Anyone acquainted with German schools in the period which followed the great "success" of 1870 will remember the amazing extent to which the cultured classes were educated in an attitude towards the state which was admittedly

Roman rather than German. If only the attention of the pupils in those German schools had been drawn to the movement in the later Empire towards cosmopolitanism and humanitarianism, a movement which paved the way for Christianity and the later German internationalism, the mischief would have been less. But this was not done. For it would have broken through the barriers of a narrow nationalism and opened their eyes to the community of nations—which must be avoided at all costs. This reversion to an imposing but still primitive epoch of pagan political thought was however to be expected when for centuries Christianity had almost completely abandoned the attempt to Christianize political conceptions and institutions and had retired into a religion of the sacristy which, however, in consequence of this restriction, must lose the power to spiritualize and to permeate even private life.

The revival of the seemingly obsolete Roman method of ordering human affairs and restraining disruptive forces is a proof that the representatives of Christianity have shirked their historical responsibilities and that the other factors of social organization have proved incompetent to their task. Democracy, for example, does not command the spiritual forces requisite to satisfy the imperious needs of a humanity torn asunder by the division of labor and capital and by the divergence of interests. There, whenever Christ disappears, Caesar takes His place and will infallibly close the sacristy in grim disproof of the private Christian's belief that the political world may be safely left in his hands. Thus the intrusion on a large scale, and constantly repeated, of the ancient Roman principle of government into the tumultuous course of European history measures the estrangement between the forces of traditional religion and the modern world and emphasizes their inability to mold that new world. On the contrary, the representatives of the Christian tradition have allied themselves in terror with political conservatism, and have thus given to the sole genuinely progressive force in the world—the Christian religion—the semblance of a reactionary power.

The entire Hitler movement, which sought to bring the Germans back to nationalism and began with the Roman greeting, has been inspired in its worship of the omnipotent state by the ideals of pagan Rome. Even Italian Fascism, being closely linked with Christianity, set limits to that omnipotence. No less authoritative an organ than *Italia* warned its readers: "There is a fearful logic in this conception of the totalitarian state. It extends its omnipotence to every sphere, will control the entire life of the nation and tolerate no opposition. It is confronted by the Church, her hierarchy and her eternal truths, whose power and dominion extend beyond the state and fatherland. In Italy, the Latin spirit of the Duce has avoided clashes. Owing, however, to the lack of moderation and sense of reality, so marked in German history, Germany has set her course for a conflict between religion and the nation which is as senseless as it is tragic." We must beware of entertaining the illusion that it would be a simple matter to check and reverse this degermanizing and romanizing process. To eradicate in Germany the Renaissance of Pagan Rome would require a century of reeducation in the authentic German tradition and a revival of the world policy of Christian Rome. Until then there will be merely a disciplined German-Roman anarchy but no genuine German.

PRUSSIA'S STRENGTH AND DESTINY

In the late summer of 1918, I was in the large waiting-room of the Foreign Office in Berlin, waiting for an interview with the Secretary of State. I was still under the illusion that opportune information might rescue the government from its impending doom. As I was turning over in my thoughts the most effective way of presenting my views and information, my glance fell on a huge picture of William I in which that truly royal personage was depicted in the fullness of his power, with the mien of an Emperor whose commands must be implicitly obeyed and whose will never swerved. It seemed as though from the outset the picture would remind the beholder of the sole power of ruling within these walls. In my own case the object was fully achieved. I had a clear vision of the extraordinary, indeed, unrivaled earthly power, the calculated and sure adaptation to particular social needs, the audaciously hard and logical exclusion of God from political life and international relations, which had found embodiment here. I had a vision also of how the outcast Divine truth had been readmitted into Caesar's household with all her sublime gifts of religious self-devotion and ascetic austerity as a handmaid to serve his godless ambitions.

Prussian militarism is incontestably a marvelous creation. It embodies a logic comparable with the deductions of Roman law or the architectural logic of the Gothic construction. It presents a bewitching image of the supreme moral order which holds spellbound numerous men of moral and political sensibilities who have failed to discover the fearful moral anarchy at work behind the deceptive semblance. The illusion was first unmasked in the reign of the second William, and the spirit which animates Prussianism was exposed in its highest representatives, in their policies and treatment of men, in their provocation and conduct of war, as also in every undertaking of true Prussians after the war. For all this admirable co-ordination of forces, this severe discipline which propagated throughout the state the decisions of the central authority, was wholly inspired by the spirit of war and directed to the achievement of supremacy, not to any harmonious co-operation. The Prussian prayer may be expressed by a parody of Augustine's famous saying: "Lord, Thou hast made us for war and our heart has no rest until it has made war."

The enormous strength of this Prussian system rests on a fundamental fact of human life, which popular pacifism completely under-estimates and the full extent of which Christianity alone has grasped and taken into account. That fact is the overwhelming power of enmity in human life, fed as it is by all the instincts of competition, rivalry, envy, distrust, ambition and restless activity. Prussia, which grew up in the earthquake zone of Europe, ceaselessly fighting for living space against the advance of Asia and never free from danger, must inevitably produce, as the result of its fear and its disturbed slumber on the wide and unprotected plains of Northern Germany, the social type which Herbert Spencer denominated the warrior type and which has found its clearest and most thorough expression in the writings of Treitschke and Bernhardi. As Christianity is the *supernatural* reply to the vast power wielded by man's pugnacious instincts, Prussia is the *natural* reply. With unflinching and appalling logic it has made the whole of life serve a system of iron defense and unlimited aggrandizement. The reply is, indeed, false and short-sighted. It cannot fail to create enemies too powerful to be defeated. But it has been a mistake in the grand style and has shown the rigid consistency which is alone strong; so strong, in fact, that the moral and intellectual forces opposed to it can cope with it only if they act with equal consistency. This however has by no means been the case. Something whole-hearted has faced the half-hearted. This is the secret of Prussian success in the modern world.

If, however, we compare the spirit of Prussia with the mature spirit which created the Roman Empire we shall perceive at once the fatal weakness of the Prussian system: the desire to domineer over everyone else, which in the end must involve the entire world, moved by the elementary instinct of self-preservation, against the Prussian threat. Rome respected the traditions of foreign peoples, a respect symbolized by placing statues of their gods in their temples. Rome took part with the Gauls in celebrating their national feasts. Scipio, looking upon the ruins of Carthage, exclaimed, "It is a finer thing to dry a single human tear than to burn a great city." Such a sentiment would never enter the mind of a Prussian General. He would call it humanitarian bunkum. He knows nothing but the "ruthless military necessity". He is blind to the fact that it is precisely this hideous and inhuman disregard for the rights of foreigners to live which in the end proves fatal in the military sphere by arming against him even the unarmed. The humanitarian sentiment he condemns is not mere bunkum. It is a biological organ of human nature which protects its possessor against the peril of treating the entire world except himself as though it were non-existent or the prey, impotent and devoid of rights, of another's will. Because it has allowed this organ to perish from disuse, the Prussian empire will one day perish.

CHAPTER VI

THE QUESTION OF WAR GUILT

A NATIONAL EXAMINATION OF CONSCIENCE

TEN years after the end of the first World War a German Catholic Bishop said: "Surely the time has at last come to throw over the past a veil of pardon and oblivion? What purpose is served by all these attempts to discover one party exclusively guilty of the war or by enquiries into larger or smaller shares of guilt, since these attempts simply stir up ill-feeling between nations and are detrimental to the cause of peace?" These words express a pacifist rather than a Catholic attitude. And pacifism, when it attempts a too hasty reconciliation, is a great danger; it imperils that knowledge of the truth which is the indispensable basis of a genuine peace. There is a holy deceit which would make peace everywhere but a peace of lies which must one day produce a most terrible war. The love of truth, which is the mark of a strong character, destroys many pleasant friendships. Luther said of Erasmus, "He loves peace more than the Cross." There are very many who love peace more than truth, for the latter is always a cross and produces painful separations. The desire to ban enquiry into war-guilt in the interests of peace is a pacifist temptation to which we must not yield if we care for the salvation of souls and the establishment of true peace.

Moreover, it is impossible to shelve this question of crucial importance. The guilty themselves do not want it shelved. A dark power of self-accusation compels them to continue inventing fresh lies in order to whitewash themselves and to accuse their enemies. After all, the entire

Peace Treaty rests on the principle of a reparation to be made; it must, therefore, lose all its moral authority and binding force, if the party which has to make the reparation can convince himself and the rest of the world that the wrong was committed by others and the burden of reparation unjustly laid upon his shoulders. Has not the Nazi press been claiming lately that Germany should demand repayment of the reparations imposed, on the ground of her unproved war-guilt? How then can anyone believe that the question of war-guilt can be shelved?

Even from the most severely practical point of view a thorough investigation into the causes of the first World War was from the very first day of the Armistice a most urgent necessity if a new spirit were genuinely to inspire German policy. No new future is possible for anyone so enthralled by self-love that after a great disaster he refuses to face his faults and his mistakes as they really are and to go down to the roots of his calamity. The complete absence in Germany of such a national examination of conscience has hidden the truth from the German people beneath a deluge of lies, so that today it is dominated by the same attitude, is held captive by the same political illusion which twenty-five years ago thrust it ineluctably into the first World War.

Soon after the Armistice, Albert Thomas, later Director of the International Labor Office, wrote as follows to a German student: "For the first time in history a nation which provoked a terrible war has been confronted with the question of guilt. If the German people understands what this means, itself and the world will be saved. If it does not, itself and the world will be plunged into fresh disasters." The letter displays a profound insight into the moral conditions indispensable if there is to be true peace among the nations of Europe. If, after such a catastrophe as the first World War, the nation responsible for it shows no compunction or change of heart, does not publicly

retract professions of cynical immorality, does not desire
to make reparation, the forces of morality even in other
nations are fatally fettered, and trust cannot return.

Moreover, a catastrophe which tore asunder all human
ties and made such mockery of justice and humanity as did
the last gigantic struggle of the German world against the
remainder of Europe could be repaired only by an extraordinary spiritual revival. Anyone who fails to grasp this,
knows neither what happened nor what a genuine peace
is. Restoration of confidence is subject to ineluctable
psychological laws which should have been obeyed if the
War were to be morally liquidated. If their demands cannot be fulfilled, even if only symbolically by the representative contrition, confession and satisfaction of a minority,
civilization must inevitably founder as a result of the War.
What Germany did not comprehend after the War was
that, after appalling outrages against others, justice thus
flouted must be re-enthroned in the German soul before
any external restoration was possible. And this re-enthrone-
ment of justice required *full recognition and confession of
the injustice committed*. This should have been the task of
Germany's intellectual leaders or at least her Christian
leaders. There was no such acknowledgment. In 1922 the
Supreme Council of the German Evangelical Church issued a solemn declaration emphatically repudiating German war-guilt and stating that "unexceptionable testimony is slowly but surely revealing to the world who were
really responsible."

Under the impression made by this and similar repudia-
tions of guilt, a Norwegian pastor, who had taken part in
the great Luther celebrations at Worms, published the
following reflections in the Swedish paper *Dagbladet*. "We
hear nothing at all of repentance these days. There is no
suggestion that repentance is any concern of the German
people, that otherwise it cannot receive the great gift of
faith, by the remission of sin. I thought to myself: Would

Luther at this critical time have been content to say to his beloved countrymen: 'Do not forget your history, your soul, your Gospel', and not have insisted also: 'Do not forget your sins'?" Moreover it is false to deny that in times of profound disturbances even the masses can be conscious of guilt. No less a thinker than Max Scheler in his *Vom Ewigen im Menschen* speaks of such waves of collective repentance which renew the spiritual life of an entire people; for example, when in the twelfth century, St. Bernard's preaching stirred Western Europe.

Nothing less is at stake than this: Is a great people which has fallen under the curse of a tragic and fatal aberration inexorably doomed to tread the evil path to the bitter end of self-destruction, or can it escape the doom by confession, change of heart and atonement? Such a conversion is unheard of. So was a war like the last.

HITLER STATES THE TASK OF PROPAGANDA AGAINST THE "GUILT-LIE"

In Hitler's *Mein Kampf* we read the following passage: "It is not the function of propaganda to weigh the rights of both parties but to insist solely on the rights of the party for whom it is being conducted. Nor is it concerned to investigate the truth so far as it favors the other party and place it with scrupulous honesty before the public, but merely to present its client's case. To make Germany alone responsible for the war is pure falsehood. On the contrary, we should place the entire guilt on our opponents, even if this were not, as in fact it is, the strict truth.

"The vast mass of a nation consists of men who are disposed to doubt and uncertainty. If its propaganda admits the least shadow of right on the enemy's side, the way has been paved for doubting its own right. And this is particularly true of a nation so inclined to an unhealthy impartiality as is the German. For every German is anxious not to be unfair to the enemy."

This declaration of Hitler's has not received anything like the attention it deserves. It expresses the unqualified subordination of truth and scientific investigation to the policy of the state. It clearly shows that the consistent pursuit of "practical" politics involves the denial and suppression of plain fact whenever such denial and suppression seem expedient. Those petty practitioners of "practical" politics cannot see that the day must come when truth will avenge itself on the lie and when the deception practised must prove a doom of historical import, because it has poisoned the springs of international relations on which Germany also depends; and that this declaration of war against "the right of the opposite side" must be fatal to justice at home. But it is as well that these logical consequences have been drawn. We live in an age of "debunking". The process is the victory of truth. *Magna est veritas et praevalebit.*

THE OUTSIDE WORLD REPUDIATES THE GERMAN CONTENTION

On every occasion when a representative of Germany has asked the former Allies to withdraw the declaration of German war-guilt and whenever at Geneva or elsewhere the German view has been put forward, a significant silence has followed. Why this firm refusal even to discuss the matter? Could not the Germans appeal to the fact that in the last few years a host of books had been published by writers of the former hostile alliance, some of which divided the war-guilt impartially between the combatants, while others ascribed the chief blame to the rulers of Russia?

True enough; but the writers of these books were either young men who derived their knowledge of pre-War history only from books and collections of official documents or men whose books proved that they had not the least comprehension of German militarism; whereas the memoirs of all those who had spent years in Germany before the War proved that a bellicose attitude had been worked up by an agitation reaching every section of the community. Moreover, all those who from the other side had a close personal acquaintance with the events of July 1914, or who themselves took part in them were so unanimously convinced that the military policy of Berlin had deliberately provoked the War, that in their judgment the responsibility of the guilty parties could be denied only by sheer ignorance of the facts or by intentional misrepresentation.

But in Germany this very silence fostered fatal delusions, and enabled an agitation to spread which is mainly responsible for the attitude which has today rendered a reconciliation between Germany and the rest of Europe impossible.

JULY 1914—THE FINAL RESULT OF A LONG DEVELOPMENT

The fatal course taken by events in July 1914, though the catastrophe apparently originated in an unforeseen event, was in reality beyond question the final expression of inherent tendencies in German policy which abused that event to accomplish their aims. Conclusive proof of this statement can be found in Conrad von Hoetzendorff's *Memoirs* and particularly in his correspondence with von Moltke, the German Chief-of-Staff.

Historical causes and tendencies were operative which fully explain everything. The German-Austria represented by von Hoetzendorff had completely lost sight of Austria's supernational mission. From the new Reich it had taken over German nationalism and was nevertheless astonished to discover that this centrifugal nationalism had taken root among the other nationalities of the Danube basin and found vocal expression. The possibility later contemplated by the Emperor Karl, of satisfying these demands which could not be refused within the framework of an imperial federation, never occurred to those officials of the old bureaucratic state. Moreover, they knew that Hungary would obstinately resist any concessions which might be proposed on these lines. They were left, therefore, with no alternative to the military method of rule—the suppression in good time of all movements tending to transform the Austrian Empire into a League of Nations enjoying equal rights. They wanted to make a beginning with Serbia. What Conrad von Hoetzendorff (in his correspondence with Moltke) declared indispensable for the survival of Austria-Hungary was, in fact, a necessity of his restricted military and political perspective; and his point of view was the more comprehensible because no Austrian proposed another and more far-sighted solution of his national problem.

In the German Reich there was, as we should expect, even less understanding of the Austrian question. Of this the incredible statement of Bethmann-Hollweg that the first World War was the decisive settlement between the Germans and the Slavs is sufficient proof. The Germans were a minority in the Austrian army. The German interest, represented by von Moltke, in maintaining the German supremacy in Austria was due only to the political and commercial Pan-German program: Berlin-Bagdad. The German Bank of Herr Helfferich was backing the program and wanted the Russo-Serbian danger, which threatened the Berlin-Bagdad line—during the War it became the Antwerp-Bagdad line—removed by a decisive victory. The aim of these groups, therefore, was to consolidate the German bloc in Middle Europe and to establish, in the interest of Germany's export trade, a permanent German hegemony in South-Eastern Europe.

The German vitality displayed in such projects and undertakings differs from the equally strong British vitality, in the following respect: German vitality lacks any genuine vital instinct. Otherwise, it would be aware that the life of foreign peoples is also a fact to be taken account of and is indestructible. German vitality is academic in the German fashion. Even the German military leaders were and still are doctrinaire, which explains all their miscalculations. British vitality is far more natural than German and, therefore, is instinctively aware of the vitality of foreign peoples, reckons with its elemental force, and is able to hit upon a compromise between both vital forces which is not only practicable but is life-enhancing. None of those German generals whose inflammatory speeches prepared the War, were practical politicians but were professors of strategy who persistently underestimated the strength of foreign powers—even to within a few weeks of the debâcle. In this frame of mind the German and Austrian military chiefs plotted to destroy Serbia and to exclude Russia from the Balkans. It was their answer to the problem of maintaining in existence the Dual Monarchy and the first step towards establishing a German hegemony in South-Eastern Europe. The final result corresponded with the plotters' blindness to the realities of the situation.

WHAT IS ESSENTIAL AND WHAT ACCIDENTAL IN THE QUESTION OF GUILT

The question of war-guilt is: What were the traditions, attitudes, actions and omissions which prepared and finally produced the first World War? The literature on the subject, already written in every language, would fill an enormous library. Who can guide our steps in this labyrinth? The truth is not far to seek. For it is as clear as daylight and perfectly simple. The guilt, the responsibility for the war, is so indubitable, obvious, irrefutable, that it requires no lengthy proof. We have only to clear away the rubbish deliberately heaped above it to find the clue which will guide us through the maze of notes, despatches, telegrams and lies. Then the truth is soon grasped, seeming contradictions are resolved, and one piece of evidence fits easily with another.

Anyone obliged to study the propaganda literature against "The lie of German guilt" soon becomes aware that it rests on a deliberate confusion of what is substantial and what is merely accidental, of such a sort that the reader is rendered all but incapable of grasping the essential issue or perceiving the chain of psychological cause and effect. With such a state of mind there is no arguing. We can but endeavor to render it innocuous. What then was the essential cause of the outbreak of war? What was irrelevant? What was cause and what effect?

The *essential cause* of the War was not the actions taken and the official declarations made at the close of July, but the fixed determination of the Government of Vienna, supported and abetted by Berlin, to destroy Serbia as a sovereign power by military action, even though a World War should be the result. Austria-Hungary believed it would thus solve a problem vital to its existence. Germany hoped to secure her dominion over Central Europe.

This determination of the Central Powers inevitably came into conflict with the policy which Russia had pursued in the Balkans for two centuries. By six bloody wars against Turkey, Russia had freed the Balkan peoples, had assisted in the liberation of Greece, had liberated Moldavia and Wallachia, Bulgaria and Ostrumelia from Turkish rule, at the cost of a gigantic expenditure of money and human lives. No less a statesman than Bismarck recognized this. In 1887, he wrote: "Germany recognizes Russian historical rights in the Balkans." And, in particular, the liberation of Serbia a hundred years earlier had been admittedly effected under Russian patronage. The Russians and Serbs were kinsmen both in race and creed.

Nor must we forget that it was vital to Russia to establish a new regime in the Dardanelles; for that reason alone she could not dissociate herself from the affairs of the Danube valley and of Asia Minor. In 1897 the Czar had pointed this out to Bülow. And in June 1914 a Russian

Germanophile, the Professor of History at St. Petersburg University, Mitropenoff, published in the *Preussischen Jahrbuechen* the following warning "Russia cannot possibly remain indifferent to the fate of the South Slavs. The small Balkan States protect the Dardanelles from the rear, and too much Russian blood and treasure has for centuries been expended over them to abandon them now. To do so would be the moral and political suicide of the Russian government. At every turn in the Levant Russia's attempts to solve her most vital problems have encountered and still encounter German opposition. It is now clear to them that if the situation remains unchanged, their road to Constantinople passes through Berlin."

He concluded with the appeal:—

"It is for the Germans to choose one or the other path. On their attitude to Russia peace or war depends. I can assure you that my views are shared by hundreds of thousands of my fellow-countrymen."

How then could Russia stand by while Serbia was dismembered by Austria-Hungary? Even Bethmann-Hollweg recognized that it was impossible. On February 10, he warned Berchtold (*Grosse Politiki*, 12,818): "If we look facts in the face we must recognize that in view of her traditional relations with the Balkan States it is quite impossible for Russia, if her prestige is not to suffer a deadly blow, to look on passively while Austria-Hungary attacks Serbia."

That is to say, Bethmann-Hollweg and his fellows knew perfectly well what was at stake and that the conflict could not be localized. The German military attaché to the German Embassy at St. Petersburg, Chelius, wrote directly to William II on July 26. (*Kautsky-Akten*. 291): "War between Austria and Serbia means war with Russia. This is the view of the Czar's entourage."

In short, it was well-known in Berlin that Russia had acquired a clear right, which she could not surrender, to protect Serbia and to be consulted in all matters affecting the Balkans. Nevertheless, Austria could have dealt with Serbian encroachments and agitation without provoking a bloody World War, if Russia, on the one hand, was prepared to give satisfaction to Austria's demands; and if, on the other hand, Austria honestly desired to settle the matter without infringing Russia's historic rights and damaging her political interests.

It is, however, incontestable that Russia was, in fact, prepared to make every possible concession and, with that object, brought successful pressure to bear on Serbia, but that the Central Powers, far from adopting a corresponding attitude of conciliation, had made up their minds to humble, garotte and liquidate Serbia in a fashion incompatible with Russia's traditional policy and interests in the Balkans. "In the Balkan peninsula Austria must dominate the small States at Russia's expense. Otherwise there will be no peace." (William II). On the margin of a despatch written by the King of Greece on August 2, 1914, William wrote, "It is not a question of the balance of power in the Balkans but of the combined effort of the Balkan States permanently to shake off the Russian yoke."

That is to say, there was no question of recognizing and delimiting different spheres of influence, or of respecting established rights. It was, "Clear out." The unprecedented deceit practised on the German public comprises the following misrepresentations: (1) Russia's stern refusal to permit her rights and the rights of Serbia to be trampled upon in this way was cunningly twisted into a refusal to make the concessions necessary if Austria were to obtain satisfaction and security; and (2) the diplomatic efforts made by the Central Powers to prevent any interference with their murderous attack on Serbia were represented as an attempt to save peace, whereas in fact the War could have been prevented only if the dispute had been settled by the concerted action of the European Powers and if Austria had refrained from taking the law into her own hands.

In short, no one who sincerely seeks the truth and is open to the evidence can escape the conclusion that in the summer of 1914 the European Powers other than Germany and Austria were so far from desiring war that those most directly affected by the reckless policy of Berlin and Vienna were prepared to abate, simply to avoid the conflagration, even what their prestige and obvious interests demanded. Yet, in face of this wilful incendiarism, Germans still dare to talk of the guilt-lie. Prince Lichnowsky stated the truth in his celebrated memorial:

"I am even more firmly convinced that we desired war at all costs. Sasonow's persistent entreaties and plain declarations, followed by the Czar's almost humiliating telegram, Sir Edward Grey's repeated proposals, the Marchese San Giuliano's warnings, my own urgent advice, all were useless. Berlin was unmoved: Serbia must be crushed."

In Tirpitz's collection of documents, *Deutsche Ohnmacht in Weltkriege,* the Bank Director, A. Von Gwinner says: "The entire approach to Serbia from the outset was in such terms that the conflict was inevitable. They have played a dangerous game in the Wilhelmstrasse."

The Ambassador, Count Pourtalès, reported that no financial circles in St. Petersburg wanted a war with Germany. William II wrote on the margin, "Rubbish! Pourtalès also reported that Sasonow is clutching at every straw to save peace." Yet the German story runs, "We are attacked."

It was Berlin and Berlin alone that wanted war. The entire world knew it at the time and knows it now.

President Wilson's friend, Colonel House, wrote to the same effect in his diary (January 26, 1916). "Moltke does not know my conviction that the guilt of this appalling tragedy belongs to the Prussian military autocracy." The Russian mobilization which plays such a large part in the plea of Germany's advocates was but the unavoidable consequence of the irresponsible policy pursued by Berlin and Vienna; and when the paid propagandists for the lie of German innocence quote, as they always do, the seeming exculpation of Lloyd George's remark that at the close of July a panic broke out in which all Europe's leading statesmen lost their heads, they should add that the cause of that most natural panic and therefore of the War is to be sought exclusively in the determination of the German army, German heavy industry, and Pan-German publicists, that there should be a war and that the opportunity should be seized to effect the long-desired settlement with Europe.

For all those people the hour of destiny had struck for Germany. It was not a question of Serbia but of *the extension of German power in Europe*. All talk, therefore, of the Central Powers' sincere effort to localize the conflict is a mere fraud upon the public. Anyone who wishes to know the true intentions of those who pulled the strings need only read the correspondence between Moltke, the German, and Conrad von Hoetzendorff the Austrian Chief-of-Staff. It proves that the heads of the Prussian army regarded the entire dispute with Serbia as a welcome opportunity to challenge Russia, which had already given way twice, to an armed conflict, so that German hegemony in South-Eastern Europe could be finally established. Behind this program stood the financial forces of the Deutsche Bank and its Pan-German allies. An advance to Bagdad directed against the most vulnerable point in the British Empire had long been the Pan-German program. The construction of the Bagdad railway was but a technical preparation for achieving its aim.

On January 21, 1909, Moltke wrote to Conrad von Hoetzendorff, "In my opinion the Austrian invasion of Serbia may lead to active intervention by Russia. And this would be a *casus foederis* for Germany."

In a later letter (February 24, 1909) Moltke went further. Even a Russian government averse to war, "would
be compelled to intervene by a Pan-Slav movement of the
Russian people—if Austria invaded Serbia". That is to
say, for the policy pursued by the German army, the overthrow of Serbia was but a secondary matter whose importance lay in the fact that it would force Russia into a
conflict with Germany and thus free the Danube route
for more far-reaching German ambitions.

Russia's repeated concessions which postponed the danger of war were, therefore, a great disappointment for
Moltke. On one such occasion he wrote to Conrad von
Hoetzendorff, "In this private letter I may say that like
Your Excellency I am deeply grieved that a favorable opportunity has been allowed to pass which may not even
recur."

At last in 1914, an even more favorable opportunity
arose. On no account must it be neglected. With that
intention an ultimatum to Serbia was drawn up, couched
in such terms as to make acceptance and another retreat
impossible. Count Berchtold wrote of it to the Emperor
Francis Joseph:

"The contents settled today of the note we shall present to Serbia are such that we must reckon with the
probability of war. If, however, Serbia should after all
yield, not only would that Kingdom be humbled to dust
but a fatal blow would be dealt to Russian prestige in
the Balkans."

The impression made by this ultimatum on King
Carol I of Rumania is reported by Count Czernin, the
Ambassador at Bucharest.

"I shall never forget the impression which the reading
of the ultimatum made on the old King. That clever and
experienced statesman at once realized the incalculable
implications of the step. I had not finished reading it when,

pale as a corpse, he interrupted, 'This means a World War.' "

Had the Entente really desired war they would have advised Serbia to stand firm and not answer the shameless document. What actually did England, France and Russia do? They made one attempt at mediation after another. Between July 24 and 31, Grey put forward no fewer than eight proposals for mediation, Cambon three, and Sasonow three. It was in vain. Then they began to beg for peace. The Czar telegraphed to William: "In this anxious moment I implore you to help me . . . to avoid such a disaster as a European war. I beg you in the name of our old friendship to do everything in your power to prevent your ally going too far."

All was useless. Even William had to admit of the Serbian answer: "A brilliant achievement when only forty-eight hours were allowed for reply. It is more than we could have expected. It is a magnificent moral triumph for Vienna. But it removes all reason for war and Giesel might have remained in Belgrade. Had I expected such a reply I would never have advised mobilization."

Moreover, he wrote at once to Jagow; "After reading the Serbian reply which I received this morning I am convinced that the demands of the Dual Monarchy have been in substance granted. The reservations made on a few points of detail can in my view be cleared up by negotiation. But a most humiliating surrender has been made before the whole world and thus all ground for war removed."

But it was not enough for the warmongers of Berlin and Vienna. They wanted a military settlement on a European scale, as a preventive war. William II was a swaggerer, but he lacked the diabolic determination to go to war possessed by a large number of army leaders, high officials, industrialists, politicians and bank-directors, inspired by the Prussian and neo-German desire for military supremacy in Europe. They obeyed its inspiration and never rested till the avalanche fell.

THE PRUSSIAN DETERMINATION TO FIGHT

No document could prove more conclusively that the governing circles in Berlin were bent upon war than the letter sent by the head of the Bavarian army, General Wenninger, to his government on July 29, 1914:

"The Minister for War, with the support of the General Staff, presses for the adoption of military measures in harmony with the strained political situation and the threat of war. The Chief-of-Staff would go further. He is employing all his influence to secure that the present favorable opportunity for a decisive blow shall not be lost. He points out that France's military position is at present very difficult, that Russia's is far from strong and that she is aware of it, moreover, that the time of year is favorable; most of the harvest has been gathered and the training of the year's recruits completed." What further evidence can anyone desire? Can we still believe these people were not wilfully lying when they declared: "In the midst of peace the enemy has made a surprise attack."

Moreover, countless witnesses prove how certain the warmongers were of their superiority and that they knew perfectly well that nothing was farther from their opponents' thought than a surprise attack upon Germany. Baron von Beyens, for example, in his *Reminiscences* relates that on August 3 the Bavarian Ambassador in Berlin said to him:

"What would you? We are burdened with taxation to make the army and navy more and more strong. They tell us the moment has never been so favorable and will never be so favorable again. France and Russia are unprepared, whereas Germany possesses an overwhelming superiority. It must be used."

When William II met Conrad von Hoetzendorff at Leipzig he told him that the measure was full, approved the energetic action of the Austrian Government, and added, "I will march with you. The others are not ready. They will do nothing. In a few days you will be in Belgrade. I have read a great deal about war and know what it means. But a time comes when a great power can no longer remain passive but must draw the sword." (*Aus mein Dienstzeit,* vol. II, pp. 469-470).

As early as 1911 the Austrian Minister for War, General von Auffenberg, told the Ambassador Tschirsky, "Germany and Austria-Hungary occupy the inner line. At the decisive moment they could despatch two million soldiers to the same front. The others could not do this. If I had to plan a war I would not exchange our position for that of France or England."

It is, of course, possible to doubt that in July 1914 German policy was solely responsible for the War if we allow our attention to be distracted by a host of insignificant details from the essential fact that the opposite side evinced the utmost horror at the sudden prospect of war, put strong pressure upon Serbia to make every possible concession, and, to avert the disaster, made proposal after proposal for mediation.

Moltke, on the contrary, sent by the Austro-Hungarian military attaché at Berlin a telegram to Conrad von Hoetzendorff which reached him at 7.45 on the morning of July 31. "Refuse the new proposal for mediation made by England. If Austria-Hungary is to survive the European war must be carried through. Germany will unconditionally help." It prompted Berchtold's classic remark: "Who then is the real ruler in Berlin, Bethmann or Moltke?" History has answered. The army ruled in Berlin, as Haldane had observed after his visit in 1912. "The Prussian army is getting ready to decide the fate of the world." The other countries were governed at this time by civilians of incontestably pacific temper who would never have dreamed of a preventive war. No less than Tirpitz in his *Memoirs* has censured, as an enormous blunder, the over-hasty declaration of war on the ground of the Russian mobilization. Even the *Koelnische Zeitung* admitted in an article celebrating Prince Bülow's eightieth birthday (May 3, 1929): "it is not too much to say that Prince Bülow, had he had his way, would have avoided the War. He always regarded it as the most important, though the most diffi-cult, task of a wise policy to keep the army in check. In 1913 he would have accepted the Haldane proposal for a naval truce and in July 1914 the Serbian reply to the Austrian ultimatum and would have left to the Hague court the settlement of the two points not answered satis-factorily."

Instead the criminals set the match to the powder maga-zine and sentenced more than ten millions to death.

May it then be said that Germany embarked upon the War thoughtlessly, not realizing what it involved? No: behind the apparent thoughtlessness stood the fully con-scious determination of men in high position who, behind the backs of the German people, which, with the exception of the educated classes, desired peace, had been preparing for war for years and whose attitude is revealed in the most glaring light by these words of General von Bern-hardi's (1911): "We must not be blinded by English ap-proaches to us. We may need them to postpone the neces-sary and inevitable war until we have hope of victory". Even Prince Bülow could not defeat this determination. Certainly the War could easily have been avoided. But any statesman who had avoided it would soon have made way for a more robust successor.

Bülow himself, when he supported the annexation of Bosnia and Herzegovina, was already a servant of this program and by his consent to the annexation had so poisoned the Serbian blood that an abscess must inevitably form. Had it been suppressed in 1914 it would have broken out again in 1915 or 1916. The unteachable German will-to-dominate must inevitably clash one day or another with the will of the Western Slavs to maintain their national existence and the determination of Europe to do justice to their claim. Therefore, when Grey and many others say that if the Ambassadors' Conference had been held or if there had been a week's delay the War would not have taken place, they are radically mistaken.

The War was not the result of a blunder or of want of calm discussion. It was already implicit in Fichte's speeches. It was the result of Bismarck's exclusion of the South-Eastern Germans. It was the logical product of a German aberration which had continued for centuries: *namely, the resolve to pursue an exclusively national policy in a domain whose history had been supernational* and with this aim to ignore blindly the inheritance and responsibilities of the past. It was an attempt to renew the old German expansion to the South-East and to maintain the indispensable connection with South-Eastern Europe by a wholly impracticable method: namely, *forcible domination* instead of *federation*. But this aberrant resolve of modern Germany had such a long history behind it and was so deliberate and fed by such determined energy that it would have broken up any conference of ambassadors.

DID THE RUSSIAN MOBILIZATION CAUSE THE WAR?

I have just produced the essential documents and comments which establish beyond doubt the responsibility of Berlin and Vienna for the outbreak of the first World War and the dominant German resolve that there should be a war, and I have acquainted the reader with the extremely dramatic sequence of events which in July 1914 led up to the conflict. My presentation will now be supplemented by evidence which clears up the question of German responsibility, particularly as regards certain con-

troversial points. I will begin with the Russian mobilization, which is the stalking-horse of the German propagandists and of the foreigners deceived by their sophistry.
In face of all these attempts to maintain that the first
World War was caused by the Russian mobilization, I
affirm the following points.

Even if the Russian mobilization had pulled the trigger,
the responsibility for the War would still lie with those
who, in spite of Russia's aversion for war which they
admitted themselves and in spite of most extensive concessions, obstinately persisted in a course of action incompatible with Russia's historical rights and vital interests
and thus overstepped the boundary of Russian compliance.
But it is not in fact true that Russian mobilization pulled
the trigger, releasing the fatal explosion. Not to mention
the fact that the Central Powers were still ignorant of the
mobilization when on July 30, they took the fatal decision.

We know for certain that even if Russia had not mobilized, Berlin would have found some other pretext to
declare war. For Berlin was irrevocably determined to
utilize the Sarajevo episode for a definite settlement with
Europe. This is proved by an article—among countless
other documents—which was published in the *Pester
Lloyd*, the unofficial organ of the Budapest government,
on May 27, 1916. Replying to a speech of Grey's in which
he had insisted that the War could have been prevented
had his proposals for a diplomatic conference been accepted, the writer said, "How irrevocable our determination was to handle the dispute with Serbia in such fashion
as to eliminate once and for all the criminal threat to
peace from that quarter, Sir Edward Grey may learn from
this frank declaration: Even if the Russian government
had not undertaken, or had withdrawn, the mobilization
conducted secretly behind the cloak of hypocritical assurances, Austria-Hungary would not have participated in

any conference but would have insisted on settling her quarrel with Serbia as the needs of her future security required."

Since the correspondence between von Moltke and Conrad von Hoetzendorff has been published we know that Moltke himself was aware that the Russian mobilization did not mean that war was inevitable but could have been followed by a peaceful demobilization. He accordingly advised his Austrian colleague to wait for a Russian attack on Austria.

Russia mobilized, in the first place, because the bad communications of her gigantic Empire made preparation for war extremely slow; and, in the second place, because the government wished to warn the Central Powers that on this occasion they would not yield. The German military attaché reported in that sense to Berlin: "In regard to the mobilization, high officers at the Club have told me that in view of the enormous distances it is impracticable to check or stop it and to do so would merely cause confusion. Moreover in Russia it is a considerable step from mobilization to the commencement of war and the interval can be employed for peaceful negotiation. My impression is that the mobilization was due to fear of coming future events, that it has no aggressive intent, and that they are already frightened by what they have done."

This explanation, in conjunction with express assurances to the same effect given by the Czar, should, as indeed Bülow and Tirpitz held, have made impossible any attempt in Berlin to make the Russian mobilization a reason for war. But since the guilty parties there were well aware of this, they withheld from the Reichstag the attaché's report which I have quoted and excluded it from their White Book.

In his *Reminiscences*, Bülow describes a dinner held a few years before the War at which he sat between Moltke and Bethmann-Hollweg. "On my left sat the unfortunate General whose mechanical and therefore clumsy Schlieffen strategy was to lose the Battle of the Marne and with it, if not the entire campaign, at least the prospect of a complete victory. But on my right sat *the far more guilty minister who, by the Ultimatum to Serbia and its unskillful diplomatic handling, would commit the most fearful blunder in the history of Prussia and Germany and one of the worst mistakes in the history of the world.*"

So far as it goes, this criticism is true. But it is inadequate and misses the real point. It takes no account of the diabolism at work throughout the entire episode which had no intention of avoiding war with Europe. It was not simply a matter of diplomatic bungling but of something much deeper with which Bülow himself had collaborated, namely an ambitious design to establish German hegemony in Europe which might later become a world hegemony. Clearly this design took no account of European realities. It was based on radical miscalculations and grotesque delusions. But it cannot be denied that, once its premises are granted, its execution was consistently and steadily pursued. The ultimatum was a mistake, only if there had been a sincere desire to localize or wholly obviate the struggle. But it was the right weapon to use if the purpose was to rouse Russia at last to action. Bülow had handled the Morocco episode far more unskillfully. He did not want war but attempted to secure objects which without a European war were unattainable, a fact of which at last he became convinced himself. He suffered therefore a diplomatic reverse. But the action of the men he criticizes, though mistaken from the standpoint of world politics, was perfectly justified as a piece of diplomatic strategy. They obtained what they sought, namely the first World War, which they regarded as an indispensable means of clarifying and altering the international balance of power.

THE OTHER POWERS DID NOT WANT WAR IN 1914

To complete my exposure of the persistent attempts to shift the blame of the War on to the opposite side, I shall place the following evidence before the reader.

The reminiscences of the former French ambassador at Vienna, A. Dumaine (*Notes et Souvenirs*, Paris, 1921) contain an interesting proof that Russia, in view of her internal situation was most averse to war: "I cannot tell Count Berchtold how far I would go to secure peace," the Russian Ambassador informed his French colleague, "for he would abuse the knowledge."

On November 8, 1908, Isvolsky wrote to the Russian Ambassador at Paris. "The danger of a conflict between Austria and Serbia remains the greatest danger and we shall do all in our power to prevent it."

On July 7, 1914, Sasonow wrote to the Russian Ambassador in Belgrade: "The recent events at Sarajevo which have strengthened the antipathy felt in Vienna toward Serbia oblige us to warn the Serbian government to handle with the utmost circumspection every question which is likely to make the ill-feeling even worse and produce a dangerous situation." Are these the words of a warmonger? How different were those of William II: "now is the moment to stamp firmly on the rabble."

On August 4, the Bavarian Ambassador in Paris wrote to King Ludwig: "Up to the very last moment, that is to say, when I discussed the situation with Ambassador Martin on the evening of August 2, I received the impression that the French Government were bent on averting war at any cost."

On July 18, Jagow wrote to Lichnowsky: "The more resolute Austria shows herself and the more energetically we support her, the quieter will Russia remain. No doubt a certain amount of fuss will be made at Petersburg. But Russia is not ready for war. Nor will France and England want to go to war now. I do not advocate a preventive war. But if we are faced with war, we must not shrink from it."

The same Secretary of State wrote in his *Reminiscences* (p. 189); "Had Vienna retreated the war would probably have been postponed. But Russia had shown that she was not prepared to abandon her ambitious designs and live at peace. A few years later, as Russia's military position grew stronger,—about 1917 her armament would have been completed—war would have been far more dangerous for us and for Austria-Hungary than at present. All the more, therefore, was it our duty to stand firm and support our ally without flinching."

Russia's ambitious designs consisted simply in her refusal to be disinterested in the Balkans and to allow Serbia to be crushed. In any case the German Foreign Minister plainly states in the passage just cited that in 1914 Germany could have prevented the War and that she provoked it because Russia's armament was incomplete.

To compel Serbia to implement the promised concessions and to swallow without further delay the rest of the Ultimatum, war was declared and the Austrian army prepared to march upon Belgrade. It was only the natural result of this substitution of military for diplomatic procedure that all parties affected should take military countermeasures. Even so, Russia was still prepared to negotiate. In his *Memoirs* Sasonow writes: "On July 30, I had a conversation with the German Ambassador in course of which he enquired whether we would be satisfied with Austria's pledge to respect Serbia's territorial integrity and asked me to inform him under what conditions we would consent to suspend our military preparations. At once I wrote the following answer on a scrap of paper which I handed to him: 'If Austria will agree that the dispute between herself and Serbia has become the concern of Europe as a whole and declare herself ready to remove from her ultimatum those demands which are incompatible with Serbia's rights as a sovereign state, Russia undertakes to suspend mobilization.'

"A great Power could hardly give a more striking proof of her peaceful intentions than is contained in this offer submitted to Count Pourtalès. Russia agreed to suspend mobilization in return for nothing more than a pledge from Austria to abstain from action incompatible with the sovereignty of Serbia, without requiring her to suspend immediately her preparations for war or to demobilize her troops on the Russian frontier. The offer in fact exceeded my official competence. For I had not been authorized to go so far in treating with the Central Powers. I could assume the responsibility for making it only because I knew that the Czar was prepared to go to any length in making concessions compatible with the honor and vital interests of the Russian people, and that the Cabinet shared his peaceful intentions."

Jagow refused the offer. But that he did so with a bad conscience is proved by the fact that it was not published in the German White Book any more than the Czar's telegram asking that the dispute should be submitted to the Hague tribunal.

SOME MISSTATEMENTS

An entire literature has been published maintaining that the Germans were innocent of the first World War. Of this falsification the following is an instance. Events are divorced from their context, false conclusions drawn from true premises, and a letter written by Sir Edward Grey in 1915 about the Serbian agitation against Austria has been twisted by a cunning selection of extracts so as to throw the blame on Serbia for the War.

In March 1936, an article went the rounds of the German press with the title "Sir Edward Grey's conclusive verdict against the lie of war-guilt". What was it all about? In 1912, Sir Edward Grey had received two communications from the Serbian Ambassador informing him that it was the settled determination of his government, if the Entente powers did not give Serbia a port on the Adriatic, to begin a policy of open hostility to Austria-Hungary and to incite its Slav subjects to revolt. In a letter to the Ambassador on July 24, 1915, Grey recalls those reports and observes "Serbia carried out this resolve to the letter and the present War was the result of the tension thus created."

What does this amount to? To nothing more than the fact that before the War Grey knew that the Western Slavs were revolting against the Austro-Hungarian government. But in spite of that he regarded the German government as responsible for the War, a conviction he repeated after the War in a lecture given at Edinburgh. There he said, "If the dispute between Austria and Serbia in 1914 had been submitted to a conference, the conference would have settled it within a week. Why was it not submitted to a conference? England proposed a conference. Germany refused it and Germany's unconditional refusal was, as I was convinced at the time and am still convinced, of fatal consequence."

It was, in truth. Serbia submitted. The Central Powers preferred war. How can there be any question where the guilt lies? Yet the propaganda for German innocence drew from Grey's letter the conclusion that the man who took the lead in denouncing Germany and who had called her "the great anarchist" of Europe had nevertheless admitted that the guilt lay with Serbia. *Esprits faux* is the French name for those people who from true premises draw false conclusions. Obviously the War would have been avoided, had Serbia let herself be slowly throttled and had all the other Western Slavs renounced their claim to national sovereignty. Moreover, Grey does not blame Serbia for her agitation against the Dual Monarchy. He simply remarks that the clash between the risorgimento of the Western Slavs and the vital interests of the Austro-Hungarian Empire had produced the tensions which led to the War. But the responsibility for this result rested, not with those who rose against an intolerable policy but with those who pursued that policy and rendered fruitless every attempt to settle the conflict otherwise than by plunging the whole of Europe into war.

A sophist could also argue that there would have been no war if Russia had quietly withdrawn from the Balkans and let Serbia be wiped out, or if Bismarck's Triple Alliance had not been confronted by the Entente. Neither could there be a second World War today if Germany were allowed to take everything she claims. Anyone who resists a wrong becomes obviously the external occasion of an armed conflict. But the question of war-guilt is not concerned with these superficial occasions but with the moral responsibility; that is, with the attitude of mind and the will at work behind external events. Though the victim who defends himself is certainly the final occasion of a conflict, his oppressor is guilty of it; and doubly so, when not only is the revolt due to his false policy but his reply is not to examine his conscience and alter his methods but to try repression, and when into the bargain he challenges all those nations who cannot and will not tolerate the repression. Naturally repression always arouses evil passions; the day comes when those practitioners of blood and iron find more iron against them than they can themselves produce. But the guilt is theirs. Those so-called practical politicians always see only their own iron and other people's blood. This is the astigmatism from which those statesmen of *sacro-egoismo* suffer. It proves fatal to them all.

The German propaganda article from which I have just quoted continues: "The second question (who was responsible for making the conflict between Austria and Serbia into a European war?) has received an answer equally conclusive from Sir Edward Grey. He tells us: 'Since August 4, 1914, the three Entente powers have borne continually increasing burdens and made heavier and still heavier sacrifices in a war whose original cause was the pledge given by the Czar to the Prince Regent of Serbia on July 27 that under no circumstances would Russia abandon Serbia to her fate.' "

Had the writer of the German article read Grey's Memoirs, he would have known that Grey fully agreed that Russia could not look on with indifference while Serbia was destroyed. The talk of localizing the Austro-Serbian conflict was sheer fraud, a screen for carrying out designs wholly incompatible with Russia's honor and interests. We have only to read what Grey says in his Memoirs concerning Russia's retreat, when Bosnia and Herzegovina were annexed, to see how convinced he was that on that occasion Russia had gone to the utmost limit of concession. It is, therefore, a piece of deception to assert that Grey regarded Russia as guilty of the War because she intervened in 1914.

Since the literature of war-guilt is so vast I can but advise the reader to keep the essential points steadily in view. The Entente, far from desiring war, put pressure upon Serbia to concede everything possible. Germany, on the other hand, wanted a thorough settlement between the Germans and the Slavs, and intended to use Austria's dispute with Serbia as a means to bring it about. It was this which rendered fruitless all proposals for mediation. A particularly black chapter of German diplomacy during that fatal July is the *official lie about Germany's knowledge of the Ultimatum presented to Serbia on July 25.* For any German concerned that his country should behave honorably, nothing surely can be more humiliating than the fashion in which the incontestable fact that the German government was acquainted with the contents of the Ultimatum is still officially denied. This attempt, only too easily detected, to conceal the truth, obviously betrays the bad conscience of those who had weighty reasons for concealing the decisive part played by Berlin in the action taken by Vienna; an action, indeed, which Berlin was but employing to forward a more far-reaching design which could not be achieved in any other way.

How could a German read without deep shame the language used by the British Ambassador in Berlin in July 1914, and recorded in the German White Book: "The German government habitually lies on such a scale that I am instinctively tempted to believe everything they deny." And unfortunately, irrefutable facts bear him out.

On August 1, 1914, the Wolff Bureau sent out into the world a barefaced lie. "In reply to the assertions of *The Times*, we positively affirm that the German Government had no knowledge whatsoever of the contents of the Ultimatum before its despatch." A number of witnesses whose evidence is beyond question, for example, the report of the Councillor to the Legation, von Schoen, and Tschirsky's letter to Jagow of July 11, 1914, prove that, as we should have supposed, the contents of the Ultimatum were in all essentials known to the German Government. In particular, it was aware from Tschirsky's report to Berlin on July 8 that demands would be presented "whose acceptance seems impossible." Moreover, the documents already published prove beyond doubt that on July 5, Count Hoyos and Count Szoegyeni had a meeting at Potsdam with the Kaiser, Bethmann-Hollweg and Zimmermann at which, after the delivery of an autograph letter from the Emperor Francis Joseph, the substantial contents of the Ultimatum were determined upon. At that meeting it was also decided to take military action against Serbia, regardless of the fact that it might involve war with Russia. The celebrated memorial of Dr. W. Muehlon contains the following information communicated by Helfferich about the middle of July.

"The Austrians have been with the Kaiser today. In a week's time Vienna will despatch to Belgrade a very stern ultimatum and with a very brief space for reply, containing such demands as the punishment of a number of officers, the dissolution of political societies, criminal investigations to be conducted in Serbia by officials of the Dual Monarchy, and many other measures taken without delay to give Austria satisfaction. Otherwise Austria-Hungary would declare war against Serbia."

Dr. Helfferich added that the Kaiser had given his full support to the attitude adopted by Austria-Hungary. "He had said that in his view the dispute with Serbia was the sole concern of the parties, with which no other state should be permitted to interfere. If Russia mobilized he would do the same. But if he mobilized it would mean immediate war. This time there would be no wavering. The Austrians were delighted with the Kaiser's firm attitude."

It was officially denied that a Royal Council had been held. Dr. Muehlon, however, did not say that a formal Council had been summoned. Bülow even believed—and he knew intimately the people concerned—that the ultimatum was originally drawn up in Berlin. "The Foreign Office in 1914", he wrote, "was the nest in which the evil egg of the ultimatum to Serbia was hatched. It was there that almost all the fearful blunders were made which launched us upon the war and lost it."

Another important piece of evidence that Berlin was not taken by surprise but had, on the contrary, in concert with Vienna, devised the ultimatum which must lead to war, is the information contained in the memoirs of the American Ambassador in Paris, Morgenthau. He relates that his German colleague, von Wangenheim, was recalled to Berlin at the beginning of July. On his return to Paris he told the American that he had attended a meeting over which the Kaiser presided and in which the leaders of the Army and the Navy and representatives of industry and finance took part. The Kaiser inquired whether the country was ready for war. All present agreed that it was ready, though the financiers asked for a fort-night's delay in which to dispose of their foreign securities and recall their loans. But every precaution was taken to prevent any suspicion of their design leaking out. Morgenthau thought that Wangenheim was tempted to this indiscreet confidence by his desire to impress his colleague with the fact that he had been summoned to such an important consultation. He told the same story to the Italian Ambassador, the Marchese Garroni, who made full use of the information when his country entered the War. That Morgenthau's story is true is sufficiently demonstrated by the fact that on September 26, 1915, that is to say, after Italy had entered the War, the Italian Minister, Barzilei, in a speech at Naples, referred to Wangenheim's indiscretion to prove how methodically and deliberately Berlin had prepared the War at a time when no one believed that the Serajevo assassination could lead to a World War.

Morgenthau himself relates that Wangenheim's information was confirmed a fortnight later by extraordinary dealings on Wall Street, which he could not otherwise have understood. In addition, there are German documents whose language is quite unmistakable, which prove that Berlin was well acquainted with the contents of the Ultimatum before its delivery and had approved them.

No. 106 in the German collection of documents reproduces the note with which Tschirsky accompanied the note delivered to the German Chancellor on the evening of July 21. On July 24, Herr von Jagow sent his thanks to Berchtold and assured him that the German Government was *obviously* in agreement with the contents of the note.

It was awkward for the German Government that on July 23, Hertling informed the French Minister at Munich, Alize—it was indeed the duty of a professor of philosophy to tell the truth—that he was acquainted with the contents of the Austrian Ultimatum. After the War the letter became known in which Count Lerchenfeld advised his Minister how best to get out of the difficult position, advice carried out by one of those unblushing denials which Prince Bülow had recommended as an excellent diplomatic weapon.

Germany "completely taken by surprise" by the Ultimatum was already prepared for war before its publication. As early as July 17, the Oberquartermeister on the General Staff wrote to Jagow: "General Moltke expects to return to Berlin on the 25th. I am remaining here ready for instant action. On the General Staff we are all ready. For the present there is no further preparation to be made." No other General Staff was ready at that moment. The question arises and answers itself: whom then did the War take by surprise? Who was ready for military action?

A SUMMING UP

Anyone who studies the literature dealing with war-guilt and has practical acquaintance of political life and the conduct of nations will be amazed to find that the greater part of that literature is the work of scholars whose knowledge is confined to books and archives; such men have no eyes for the real conflicts which determine the course of history, but in the interest of some favorite thesis and without any psychological acumen, they draw from the documentary material, which consists very largely of tendentious or wilfully misleading documents, intended to deceive and conceal the truth, conclusions remote from the truth and the facts of the situation. He alone can understand the problem of war-guilt who possesses a living picture of the opposing forces that for decades had kept South-Eastern Europe in a state of tension and is acquainted with the effect of modern German nationalism and militarism upon their interplay. He will perceive that it was the evil influence of these factors which acted as a disintegrating element upon the Dual Monarchy and prevented the latter from fulfilling the federal rôle which alone could have secured the peace of Europe amid innumerable conflicting interests.

The majority of those who write against the "guilt-lie" follow a twofold plan. In the first place, they produce as authoritative witnesses to German innocence, foreign scholars who have no knowledge either of Germany or South-Eastern Europe; and who, in many cases, have clearly not read the most important documents. Secondly, they put forward documents of the pre-War period to prove that foreign powers were preparing for war, concluding alliances, giving information to their allies, even inspiring the press—while carefully concealing the fact that in these cases the object was a *defensive policy* only too intelligible in view of Germany's obvious ambitions, machinations and open threats. For a time the employment of this method succeeded even outside Germany in persuading many people that the real villain of the war was Poincaré, a thesis for which appeal could be made to certain Frenchmen who, ignorant of the facts with which Poincaré dealt as a far-seeing statesman, raised the slogan of a thoughtless pacifism, *"Poincaré la guerre"*. The charge was quickly disposed of by the weighty evidence of Poincaré's political opponent Herriot, and not less by Poincaré's memoirs of which his radical opponent, Aulard, observed, that "the accused had established his innocence."

The most important memoirs written by men most intimately and personally acquainted with the events which led up to the War are unanimous in their testimony that the Prussian army leaders and high officials and the representatives of heavy industry and the bankers dependent upon the latter who were all in close league with the army, were the men who pulled the strings; so that

Vienna may be acquitted of the principal responsibility for the outbreak of such a catastrophe as a World War.

The mere fact that Vienna despatched the Ultimatum does not entitle us to regard Austria as the villain and the tempter of Germany. I have already quoted Bülow's surmise that the Ultimatum had been elaborated in Berlin. The Belgian Ambassador, Beyens, expresses the same opinion in his memoirs: "In diplomatic circles here," he writes, "we are convinced that the ultimatum and its contents are so diabolically clever, so Bismarckian, that they must be the product rather of a German than of an Austrian diplomat." All the documents recently published prove that Austria did indeed want war with Serbia but shrank back from it when she realized that it threatened to cause a European war.

The documents which prove this, and which show in particular that Conrad von Hoetzendorff retreated, are hidden away in the pages of a monthly magazine, *Die Kriegsschuldfrage,* where the archivist Schafer had collected them (1930).

Of particular interest in this connection is the interview between the unofficial emissary of the Berlin warmongers, Dr. von Naumann, and Count Hoyos in July 1914, related by the latter in the latest Austrian official publication, No. 9966. Dr. Naumann is proved to have advised the Austrian government to make the Serajevo murders an occasion for war. Otherwise, he said, Austria was doomed. In view of Russia's increasing military strength, Germany had the best of reasons to take this opportunity of reckoning with her and would gladly support Austria.

Where we must look for the will-to-war can be seen even in documents which attempt to conceal it; for example, in the well-known report of von Schoen published by Eisner. As we know, Eisner has been accused of falsification on the ground that he published only the aggressive passages of the report in which the General Staff pressed for military action and that he omitted a passage in which it was stated that the German Chancellor was doing his utmost to localize the conflict. In a conversation with me, Eisner justified the omission on the ground that he foresaw that the passage would necessarily mislead the reader as to the motives which actually inspired German policy, since no one in Berlin could have believed it possible to localize the war. When I met the writer of the report, Herr von Schoen, in Zurich, I told him to his face that Eisner's interpretation was correct, and that the policy of Berlin, even in the Foreign Office, had been aggressive, a fully conscious and unyielding determination upon war, whereas those who negotiated and believed that the conflict could be localized were mere screens. He looked at me awkwardly and for a long time said nothing. I in turn looked at him in silence, and our silence was eloquent.

THE RESPONSIBILITY OF INDIVIDUALS

Did Bethmann-Hollweg want the War? Most certainly not. But without his will or knowledge he was driven by the logic of the official Prussian attitude at work in his ministerial conscience into such an irreconcilable conflict with the attitude of the outside world that he was obliged with an appalling consistency to refrain from taking any step that would prevent war and to do everything to bring it on. He rejected the proposal for an Ambassadors' Conference, which would have prevented war, not because he wanted war but because it was incompatible with his conception of national sovereignty. No one must interfere with Austria's right to punish Serbia. He gladly adopted Pourtalès' narrow view that such a conference would be a European Areopagus whose jurisdiction must not be admitted. It was just this obdurate Prussian refusal to accept the fact of European solidarity, a refusal pregnant with bloodshed and ruin, which plunged Germany into war and into the abyss.

Tirpitz recognized the sheer stupidity, the glaring lack of statesmanship displayed by the rulers of Germany during those fateful days and hours. He lamented "the madness that slid into war". In his view, the Conference of Ambassadors proposed by Grey should not have been refused. For its refusal strengthened the hands of the party in Russia that favored war. But this stupidity was inevitable. It was the result of a clash between Treitschke's conception of the state and the unforeseen intervention of a Europe determined no longer to tolerate that conception. The European protest, ever more urgent, against the punitive expedition against Serbia, the repeated attempts to prevent a World War by mediation, came up against the design settled long since of Berlin and Vienna to create a *fait accompli* which Europe must recognize. Those statesmen could not in a moment grasp the entirely novel though long-prepared situation. It was not so easy to cast off the student-corps mentality of mid-European statecraft. But they now saw with horror that the same European community which before the catastrophe had put forward plan after plan for mediation, now became an invincible force to suppress and punish the anarchy which was the foreign policy of the Central Powers. Under such circumstances, who would not lose his head?

The Ultimatum, with its brief delay which embodied the brutal assertion of arbitrary power represented by the Bernhardis, proved the doom of the Central Powers. It left them no time to rectify their mistake and by a change of political front to accept a European settlement of the entire issue. Every decision taken lay under the curse of the Ultimatum. Nerves replaced calm thought. The German leaders had no ears for Grey's pledge inspired by the British determination to reach, if possible, a peaceful solution. "If we are successful in saving the peace of Europe

. . . I will do everything in my power to secure a settlement acceptable to the German people, a settlement that will make them so secure that no policy aggressive or hostile can be pursued against Germany or her allies by France, Russia or ourselves, jointly or singly." Berlin took no heed.

What of the Kaiser? Did he deliberately plan the War? Most certainly not. His original notes and other expressions of opinion at this period must be interpreted by our knowledge of his character. He was not the man to plan anything deliberately. To plot a World War, a demonic strength of will and nerve is required which the weak and excitable Emperor did not possess. Certainly, the Kaiser wanted a speedy and thorough military settlement with Serbia. But he seems to have felt confident that Petersburg would once again yield to an energetic assertion of Germany's will. He lacked the serious disposition and sense of responsibility which would have made him do his utmost to save millions from hideous suffering. On the contrary, he toyed with the possibility of a world-embracing conflagration, provided the German Emperor emerged from it victorious and crushed his enemies. His heart was cold as ice, but he was a sentimentalist. He swayed up and down—the very opposite of a heroic leader of men, but the typical modern German *parvenu* uncertain of himself, unprincipled and noisy, whose unholy appetite for success and whose delight in bullying he represented so perfectly that he has never had an inkling of what "princely behavior" and "royal dignity" mean.

Tirpitz observed that the German statesmen "underestimated the European spirit which inspired the Entente." That is to say, in his opinion Disraeli's remark made about the origin of the Crimean war, is applicable to the origin of the first World War. "There is one force with which no human ingenuity can cope—the unconscious machination of stupidity." This explanation is in-

adequate. It is true only of those who permitted themselves to be made use of and who cherished all those
incredible illusions of which I have spoken enough. But
those who pulled the strings knew perfectly well what they
wanted. They were far from underestimating "the European spirit which inspired the Entente." On the contrary,
they took account of it, and were aware that war against
Serbia must lead to the general settlement *which they
desired.*

It cannot be too often repeated that the publication of
Moltke's correspondence with Conrad von Hoetzendorff
was the hardest blow which the whitewashers of German
policy had to face. There could not be a more conclusive
argument against the assertion "we were attacked" than
the letter Moltke wrote to Hoetzendorff on January 21,
1909. In this letter Moltke observes that throughout
Europe there was an extraordinarily strong desire for
peace. None at that time was in favor of war. The Russian Government would do everything possible to prevent
a new war. "The internal troubles and the financial position compel this attitude. France gives the impression that
she does not desire war." That England and France would
intervene in a continental imbroglio could not be seriously considered.

That is to say, the whole of Europe was bent on peace.
There was only *one* way in which the entire Continent
would immediately be plunged into a conflagration. Moltke
knew and said what this was: the *invasion of Serbia*,
which he recommended.

And the German Commander-in-Chief proceeded to describe with an uncanny accuracy the probable course of
events precisely as they happened five years later. An invasion of Serbia was the only step which would compel
Russia to mobilize, but it would infallibly do so. In that
event, Germany would be called upon to fulfil her obligations as Austria's ally in accordance with the Treaty of

1879. She also must mobilize. "It could not be possible for France," continued Moltke, "to tolerate a mobilized Germany on her frontier. And the two mobilized armies, the French and the German, would inevitably come to blows." Nor is this all. The clearness with which Moltke envisaged the entire result of his schemes is plain in the following well-nigh prophetic words: "Europe is today so involved in mutual treaties, ententes and alliances that it will scarcely be possible for any of the great European powers to draw the sword without obliging the entire continent to take up arms . . . Whether the war will even spread across the sea I will not now inquire."

In the spirit of the views he had expressed here, Moltke addressed to the Chancellor on July 29 a communication which is a wild cry for vengeance upon Serbia, described as a poisonous growth on the body of Europe which requires cauterization. In that communication he repudiates any attempt at mediation, designates Russian intervention as insolence, and demands unconditional cooperation with Austria. It was men with such characters and such intellectual capacity as Moltke who decided Germany's fate.

In his memoirs, Tirpitz wrote, "If the German people once gets to know the truth, there will be trouble." The guilty and their champions have worked with a zeal worthy of a better cause to prevent the German people discovering the truth. The note presented by the German delegates at Versailles presumed to affirm Germany's innocence: "Even today when Germany's military power has been finally destroyed *we declare that our war of defense was unavoidable.*"

The reader of such a statement rubs his eyes. How can a war be termed an unavoidable war of defense when for years the hostile powers had been provoked deeply and openly by the crimes, omissions and blunders of German statesmen? Or when, in a wild desire to crush an enemy, so many opportunities of making a settlement, which would have secured a happy future, were refused?

CHAPTER VII

THE CONFLICT IN SOUTH-EASTERN EUROPE

THE HOSTILITY BETWEEN THE GERMANS AND THE SLAVS

IN JUNE, 1910, Minister for Foreign Affairs Kiderlen-Waechter, said to his friend the Rumanian Minister, Take-Yonescu: "We need no war and shall have no war. Unless we provoke a war no other power will deliberately do so. The Republican Government of France is bent on peace. The English are opposed to war. They will never embark on a warlike policy, whatever the newspapers may say. And Russia knows that she has no prospect of victory."

How was it four years later? At the opening of 1914? On this Tirpitz writes in his *Reminiscences*: "Never in all her long history had Germany been so powerful, more respected by the great powers or so prosperous as then (1914). In the opinion of men well acquainted by personal experience with foreign countries, for example Prince Bülow, who records his opinions in his *Deutschen Politik*, we had in all essentials crossed the mountain and made good our claim to be regarded as a great world-power. In the Far East, in Africa, in South America, and in the Levant German culture and trade were rapidly making up for time lost in the past. Only a few years more of peaceful and wise leadership and our position as a world-power would have been too strong to be destroyed." How was it that, although the Prussian General Staff knew this, it had different views and engineered its preventive war?

Several years before the War Moltke had traced for Hoetzendorff, the future program:

"My opinion is, as it has always been, that sooner or later a European war is inevitable, which will be concerned in the first place with a settlement between the Germans and the Slavs. To prepare for it is the duty of all States that bear the banner of German culture. But the attack must come from the Slavs."

Who was right? Kiderlen-Waechter and Tirpitz or Moltke? The former were right inasmuch as no European power dreamed of attacking Germany. But Moltke was right inasmuch as the nationalist movement among the Western and Southern Slavs and their desire for national independence, a desire which grew stronger as the Austrian administration became more centralized, seemed to threaten the existence of the Dual Monarchy, and the conflict which could have been settled on federal lines would inevitably provoke German militarism to a senseless act of desperate violence. Certainly there was no necessity that the Germans and the Slavs should measure their strength in war. But in South-Eastern Europe, beneath a surface of orderly relations, a conflict of historical import threatened between the Slavs on the one side and the Germans and their Magyar allies on the other, a conflict which challenged the foundations of the Dual Monarchy and produced a clash between German ambitions in South-Eastern Europe and Russia's right in the Balkans.

The dual system of Austria-Hungary should have been replaced by a Danubian Federation in which the Czechs, Slovaks, Croats and Slovenes enjoyed home rule. The Emperor Francis Joseph had in fact been willing to be crowned King of Bohemia. But Berlin and Budapest had objected. There are parents who irretrievably lose the affection of their adult children because they are unwilling at the right moment to place the entire relationship on a new footing. "Nothing binds so closely as freedom" observed Rachel von Varnhagen. It was the tragedy of the situation that the militaristic nationalism of Bismarckian Prussia viewed the problem exclusively from the standpoint of Pan-German interests and into the bargain seduced Austrian Germans from their federal traditions so that no other solution was envisaged, save the forcible repression of Slavonic aspirations. Serbia must be dismembered and the desire of the Western Slavs for independence crushed with an iron hand. It was typical of those militarists who plumed themselves on their realism that they could not see that to attempt such a solution must prove the suicide of Austria, Germany and Europe, because the rest of Europe could not look on quietly while the Southern and Western Slavs were being crushed. The first World War was due to the mistaken attempt of the Germans to prevent by force the realization in Eastern Europe of that principle of nationality to which they had appealed in support of their own political unification.

The true solution of the Austrian question, namely, federation, was stated in a letter written by King Milan of Serbia to his Minister Georgevitsch. "If Austria", wrote the King "could conciliate the Serbs within her territory by becoming a federal, instead of a dual monarchy, Serbia could join such a federation. In that case my kingdom would be content with the position occupied today by Bavaria, Saxony and Wuertemberg in the German Empire. But in that case ten million Serbs would be united in one state and our national unity would be effected. And since the other Balkan states would soon perceive the advantages the Serbs had gained from membership of this Austrian League of States, they would also join it."

The King's letter offered a solution for the problem of nationalities in the Austrian Empire. When in July 1917 I was invited to Vienna by the Emperor Karl to discuss with him the transformation of his empire into a union of independent States, once more the prospect of such a solution opened up. The blindness of the Germans banished it. Fate took its course.

THE NATIONALIZATION OF SUPERNATIONAL AUSTRIA

Ever since the Middle Ages there have been two German attitudes towards the Slavonic world. One of these was federal, sought a symbiosis, collaborated with the Slavs, and in the Southeast took concrete shape as a supernational community. The other was warlike, the attitude of the Teutonic Knights who could only massacre and burn.

South-Eastern Europe had from the outset witnessed the peaceful collaboration of different nationalities. At the very beginning of German history, long before Charlemagne, Marbod had been inspired by the universalism of the Roman Empire. The Habsburgs continued this tradition. Since, however, Prussia grew and achieved a gigantic success while the Habsburgs increasingly suffered from the disintegrating tendencies of the modern age, after Bismarck's triumph Austrian Germany became gradually and imperceptibly Prussianized and nationalized and became correspondingly incapable of retaining under a German scepter non-German peoples moved by national passions and aspirations.

The defenders of the Central Powers therefore were right in saying that the responsibility for the War cannot be judged solely by the events and decisions of July 1914, since it was but the final symptom of a more deep-rooted disease and the final phase of a tragic development which had continued for decades.

But the question remains: whose fault was it that this profound conflict of interests ended in a military struggle? Complicated political conflicts had been settled during the past decades by peaceful agreement—for example, between England and France, and between England and Russia. Why was the conflict between the interests of the Russians and their fellow-Slavs and those of the Dual Monarchy incapable of a peaceful solution? No doubt that conflict was deep-rooted and concerned national existence. But this surely was the very reason why both parties should have recognized the vital needs of each other and found a means of reconciling them. What, after all, did the War achieve? Was not the spirit in which the Central Powers treated the final phase of the conflict typical of the hideous blunders and gross omissions which for decades had poisoned the entire dispute and rendered its settlement increasingly difficult? Did Pan-Slavism in fact threaten to destroy the old cultural community of German and Slav represented by the Habsburg Empire and make a bloody decision inevitable?

Count Berchtold and other advocates of pre-war Austria always try to make us believe that an ineluctable fate compelled the Dual Monarchy to fight for her existence and her indispensable share of influence in South-Eastern Europe by a military settlement with Pan-Slavism. To which I reply: that fate consisted solely in the Austro-German and Magyar attitude which obstinately refused, despite the warnings of experience, to permit the Dual Monarchy to be transformed while there was still time into a federation of national states. It was the national selfishness of those two ruling peoples, an attitude out of harmony with the nature and mission of the Habsburg Monarchy, which destroyed that empire.

It required an appalling degree of political blindness to bring things to this pass. As late as 1917, the Danubian Monarchy could still have been saved by federalism, not to speak of all the earlier opportunities of making the change since the century opened, if only the rulers had possessed the vision to take them. Only an Austria which consistently realized her own ideal could successfully combat Pan-Slavism. Only if a progressive and genuinely supernational State had arisen in South-Eastern Europe could the Pan-Slavonic racial principle have been subjected to a higher ideal. When instead, the German representatives of the old League of Nations proved blind alike to

the meaning of their own traditions and to the needs of
the hour and imported into their supernational state the
solvent of national selfishness, they did far more than Pan-
Slavism could have done to undermine the foundation of
their own empire. Pan-Slavism gained confidence only
when it saw that the Danubian Monarchy no longer understood its own principle and thereby signed its own death
warrant, by thrusting its nationalities back upon the lower
ideal of national sovereignty and by failure to respect their
national honor, flinging them into the arms of Pan-
Slavonic racialism.

It is far from the purpose of my argument to deny or
conceal the fact that throughout the Slavonic world, si-
multaneously and in close connection with the nationalist development of modern Germany, an extreme and
passionate nationalism had arisen which constituted a dangerous threat to the existence of the Austrian Empire.
Moreover, Europe at this period was a prey to such hostile
emotions as members of a family feel when confronted
with a disputed and complicated will. But just because
this was the case, and because a clash with the vast Slavonic
world must be the doom of a state composed of Slavs and
Germans, it was Austria's paramount interest to pursue a
domestic and foreign policy which would afford the utmost
possible satisfaction to Slavonic nationalism and give it
sufficient scope within the framework of a Habsburg
Federation, and at the same time to ally itself with all the
forces which, in Russia and among the smaller Slavonic
peoples and in Europe as a whole, constituted a barrier
against an aggressive Pan-Slavism and an anarchic nationalism.

Such forces undoubtedly existed and were powerful and
important. But as a result of Austria's mistaken policy
they were partly neglected, partly rendered impotent. The
ruling circles in Russia, since the beginning of the century,
were by no means aggressive Pan-Slavs. This is proved by

the Czar's proposal at the Hague. Those acquainted with the inner history of the Hague Conference know that it was fear of the consequences of a World War which had convinced many far-seeing Russians in government circles confronted with the constantly increasing complications of South-Eastern Europe, that they could not be solved by the bloody arbitrament of war. The Central Powers had at least an equal interest in the success of an attempt to secure that these burning problems should be handled by all the great European powers. But they hoped to gain more for themselves by the old anarchic procedure. Yet even when the first Hague Conference had failed, the after-effects of the Japanese war and the revolutionary crisis at home disposed the Russian government to peaceful methods. Austria-Hungary made use of this period of Russian weakness to annex Bosnia and Herzegovina. And again in 1912 she ventured to refuse Russian pressure that Serbia should be given a port by threatening her with German "Nibelung" loyalty.

Did Russia on these occasions behave aggressively and brutally? Far from it. Nothing could be wider of the truth than to picture the giant Russian Empire of those days as inspired by warlike ambitions, on the alert to break up the Dual Monarchy. Certainly there were demands which Russia would not abandon, necessitated by all her traditions, the needs of her export trade, and her national sentiments and affinities. Such were the control of the Dardanelles, her Protectorate of the Slavs, a share in the political settlement of the Balkans. But she did not seek to obtain them by an aggressive war. On the contrary, if only for domestic reasons, Russia would have welcomed the opportunity to conclude arrangements honorable to all parties. It was the radical mistake of Austrian policy that it did not meet these peaceful intentions half-way and did not strengthen them at the right moment by a corresponding honesty, frankness and reasonableness. Austria made the same mistake in her treatment both of the Balkan Slavs and of her own.

Nor is it true that all these people were Pan-Slav and Russophil. At the beginning of the century, Serbia was Austrophil, not Russophil. Receptive and eager to learn, young Slavs thronged to the universities of Austria and Germany, and within the Austrian Empire there was much evidence of a deep affection for the German culture still surviving among the Slavs, which found powerful expression on the outbreak of the War. In the summer of 1917, I was present at a private meeting in Vienna at which a number of Slav leaders spoke of the possibility of the Austrian Empire continuing as a federal union. They unanimously expressed their hearty desire that this solution, which best suited the history of past centuries and the cultural needs of all parties, might be realized before it was too late. They deeply deplored the hatred of the Germans which had been produced by the hectoring language of the latter, by countless blunders, and by their failure to respect Slavonic traditions. They quoted Herder and Goethe, and they praised the traditional German culture as their teacher.

Nevertheless it was too late. How many opportunities were thrown away is clear from the following utterance of the Czech leader, Smeral, in 1917: "For years I have closely studied our Czech national question in connection with the ideal of a great Danubian League of independent nations of diverse race and the way in which the mutual relations between the Czechs and the German people could best be settled. For we are indissolubly linked with the Germans and must reach an agreement with them even if it is reached only by the road of dearly bought mistakes and disappointments. The events of the War, which I had foreseen for years, have not affected my views in the least but on the contrary confirmed them."

A reasonable policy which met in a generous spirit the

aspirations of those peoples for independence would have released all the psychological effects of their centuries of attachment to the German world and would have kept the Western Slavs politically united with the Germans, as French culture has won the German population of Alsace. Instead, the obstinate despotism and the complete lack of understanding displayed by the Germans and the Magyars in their treatment of the Slavs despite every warning symptom, cast away beyond retrieving whatever survived of Slavonic loyalty and sympathy. That is to say, the hostility of the Slavs towards Austria-Hungary was not the ineluctable fatality of a racial animosity but the result of German mishandling which paralyzed the efforts of those groups among the Slavs who desired to cooperate with the Germans and brought to the boil, against the German administration, its principles, and its practices, a witch's cauldron of national passions.

The German public therefore are seriously misled when defenders of the Central Powers depict the campaign conducted before the War with increasing animosity by Czech and Serb propaganda, without a hint of the previous provocation given by the Germans. Consider, for example, the humiliation and provocation of Russia involved by the informal annexation of Bosnia and Herzegovina. These territories had been placed under the protection of Austria-Hungary by a mandate of the Powers. Accordingly their status should not have been radically changed without the Powers' consent. A conference of the Powers should have been summoned in which every aspect of the annexation would have been considered and arrangements made for any necessary compensation. In the teeth of Russia, Austria-Hungary refused such an international settlement, even rejecting Count Andrasy's urgent plea that at least the consent of England should be obtained. Thus the Dual Monarchy made its intention plain to settle at its own discretion, without regard to the rest of

Europe, the problems of South-Eastern Europe which had long been treated as an international concern. Can we be surprised that the dragons' teeth thus sown yielded their harvest of armed men? Nor was this an isolated action. It was part of a deliberate policy whose object was the gradual strangulation of Serbia.

Had the German and Austrian public the least suspicion of the incredible treatment which drove the erstwhile friendly Serbia to a frenzy of hate against Austria, the official war-lie circulated among them would have long ago been killed. Only consider the following facts published by a competent authority in the organ of the Union *Neues Vaterland*:

By a commercial treaty concluded in 1906, Austria-Hungary compelled Serbia to give up completely the importation of live stock and restrict considerably the importation of meat; at the same time the favorable tariff concessions formerly granted her were withdrawn. On this basis a provisional treaty was concluded. When it was renewed in 1908, more than 35,000 head of cattle and 70,000 pigs might be imported. In 1909 the treaty lapsed and the Serbian peasants could no longer import any animals. Only in 1911 were they allowed to import 15,000 head of cattle and 50,000 pigs. This treatment of Serbia appears in its full light when we learn that in 1906 the Austrian Government refused to negotiate a treaty of commerce, unless Serbia pledged herself to purchase material for her railways only from the Austrian cartel of iron foundries and her cannon only from the Skoda munition works, even if she could purchase these things cheaper elsewhere. Serbian attempts to conclude a tariff union with Bulgaria were forcibly prevented. The treaty actually concluded could not be submitted to the Skupschina. Austria was attempting to strangle Serbia. A trampled worm will turn, and the result of this agrarian trade-policy was the Great Serbian movement. Is it easy to indulge censure of those subversive forces when they were very largely the fault of Austria herself?

Consider also the bitterness which must have been aroused throughout the territory of the Southern Slavs by the mean refusal to grant Serbia a port on the Adriatic. What would Hungary have said had she been refused Fiume? The inspiration of all these senseless irritations was to be sought not only in Vienna but in Berlin's Bagdad policy. The rail route of the Berlin-Bagdad railway must be cleared and the "scum" made to serve the interests of the Deutsche Bank and the political ambitions allied with it. It was Vienna's task to guard the line through the Balkans. At this point the interest of Budapest coincided with that of Berlin. Hence the reckless advance to the abyss.

If we read Kleinwaechter's excellent book, *Der Untergang der Oesterreich-Ungarischen Monarchie*, we are appalled by the extent of the tragic blindness which flung away such splendid opportunities of organizing the collaboration of all the peoples of Eastern Europe. He shows how the well-nigh fabulous resurrection of Czech nationality, in spite of all the systematic attempts to destroy it made by the victors of the White Mountain, made practically no impression on the Germans. He relates how a leading Austrian in the seventies used to dismiss the Czech danger with the jest, "The Czechs have one fault, that nobody takes them seriously." In 1909, the German population of Prague which had once been a German city was only a ninth of the total. Yet to advise the Germans to learn Czech was denounced as treason to the German cause. When the author of the book once expressed his intention to visit the Czech opera, a relative told him, "If you do, you won't enter my house again." Such an attitude obviously made it impossible to establish at the right time a frontier between the German and the Czech territories.

When the Czech revival was still in its infancy, it would not have been difficult to come to an arrangement. According to the plan drawn up in 1849 by the great Czech historian, Franz Palacky, the Austrian Empire was to become a union of national states of which German-Austria would comprise Upper and Lower Austria, Salzburg and the Vorarlberg, districts of Steiermark, Carinthia, the Tyrol, Bohemia, Moravia, Silesia: that is to say, the districts which were to prove the *fata morgana* of the Austrian Republic after the war. For the Czechs, Palacky claimed only the Slavonic districts of Bohemia, Moravia and Silesia and that part of Slovakia in the possession of Hungary. The periodical in which Palacky expounded this program was banned and the author put under police supervision. Had the Germans shown the foresight to accede to the proposal at the right time, the Czechs would never have demanded the entire territory once under the Bohemian crown.

The same incapacity to respect foreign traditions and the same egoism were displayed towards the other Slavonic nationalities. Therefore, in spite of the extremely strong opposition and mutual antipathy of the Serbs and the Croats, and in spite of Serbia's well-known friendship for Austria at the beginning of the century, as the result of an entire series of political and educational blunders a united South Slav front against the Habsburgs came into existence.

The un-German nationalism which had its origin in the greater Prussia led to domestic conflicts between the nationalities composing the Dual Monarchy. Those conflicts absorbed the Austrians so completely that they lost sight of anything beyond. Austrian views on foreign policy had long been dominated by an *idée fixe*, the determination not to change the internal balance of power either by further changes in the foreign situation or by altering the national constitution of the monarchy in such a way as to endanger the German hegemony in the Empire hitherto so painfully maintained. This determination to preserve at all costs an unnatural *status quo* completely absorbed Austrian statesmen in domestic problems which had little connection with the economic and social problems of the day and to a large extent rendered them insensible to the new problems raised by a changing world. It was still in the Emperor's power to incorporate into his Dual Monarchy a bloc of South Slavs as a confederate state, to create by this trialism the necessary counterweight to the German-Magyar hegemony, and to abolish the fatal dualism which deprived the Slavs of their right to a state of their own. With the help of Italy, France and England, the change which would have secured the peace of Europe could have been carried through, even in the teeth of German opposition. Instead of pursuing this far-sighted policy, Francis Joseph and his advisers took the opposite road. They attempted to settle the question of the South Slavs by force and repressive measures. Thus they not only provoked an international crisis of the utmost gravity but also brought about the intervention of the Slavs' Russian protector. On this journey to their doom there was no halting place.

I have sought to explain the connection between this apostasy of Austria from the Austrian ideal and the catastrophe of the War. Only when the mistakes of the past are acknowledged can a people be inwardly emancipated from the curse of the past. The Dual Monarchy perished because there was no genuinely Austrian policy in harmony with all the facts of the Danubian League of Nations and representing in a noble and attractive fashion the sublime political task of constituting a federation of diverse nationalities. The future of post-war Austria, indeed the future of Europe, depended on the question whether the nation which had gambled away the old Eastern Empire

(Ost-Reich) because it sought to dominate in it, had at last learned to serve Europe and thus to acquire the intellectual and spiritual power to pave the way for a federation of the Southern-European peoples and later of Europe as a whole. We know how that question has been answered.

CHAPTER VIII

SOUTH-EASTERN EUROPE DURING THE WAR

PERSONAL IMPRESSIONS RECEIVED IN AUSTRIA

IN THE year before the outbreak of war I had an opportunity, as Professor at the University of Vienna, to study at close quarters the vital problems of the Austro-Hungarian policy. I received the impression, which was to become even stronger, of a political situation headed for disaster. I saw that the modern German infatuation, against which I had vainly struggled in my youth, was pursuing its inevitable destiny on the volcanic soil of Eastern Europe and that it seemed doomed to yield its bitter fruits. I attended a celebration held in the *aula* of the University in honor of Richard Wagner. Before an enormous audience drawn from all the nationalities of the Dual Monarchy the panegyric was pronounced by a man of the highest and most well-earned repute. It was an aggressive glorification of German culture. At the close of the proceedings the German students sang the *Wacht am Rhein*.

What an incredible want of understanding to sing this national song in the university of a supernational state which depended for its existence on relegating national sentiment to the background and remaining always conscious of the political community with foreign traditions! I felt painfully the failure to make use of this splendid opportunity to bring home the value of Wagner's art to the Slavonic and Hungarian members of the audience, so as to make it possible for them to recognize in German culture a uniting factor of universally human value. Never more acutely than at this meeting have I felt conscious of how uneducated and barbaric this national boasting is. A man of natural intelligence knows the worth of his national culture and leaves it to others to recognize and express it. He does not advertise his own people, does not sing its praises. On the contrary, he is at pains to show his recognition of other nations, to promote their development and chivalrously to defend their interests and rights, thus giving an example of ripe culture. But most German-Austrians behaved like members of nations still in their cradle and encouraged every manifestation of their immature nationalism. My conviction grew still stronger that the foundation of a powerful state inspired by narrowly German ideals has proved fatal to German culture and a curse to Europe. When the race occupying the center of Europe ceased to be a bulwark against nationalism, against power-politics, and against the tyranny of the state and when it brazenly glorified instead all these things as the last word of human wisdom, Europe must be cleft asunder and a world catastrophe ensue. And this not only because the development radically contradicts the mission of Germany, a mission indispensable to the peace of Europe, but also because it must collide with the living witnesses of a federal development which had continued for centuries. The old Germany had incorporated numerous foreign elements which it was now proposed to Germanize by force: a program which must produce irredentisms of the most perilous and explosive character.

It was on Austrian soil that I realized most fully this tragic incompatibility between the new national state and the inheritance of the German past. For the Danubian Monarchy was the surviving relic of the supernational German Empire, the former league of Central European nations. Had the Austrians preserved the old German traditions of international organization, Austria could have attracted all these young nations.

In the spring of 1914 I expressed these views in the

parting lecture I delivered in the *aula* of the University on "Political Education and Self-Education in Austria-Hungary". Referring to the celebrations in honor of Wagner at which the *Wacht am Rhein* was sung, I concluded with the following appeal: "I must speak frankly even at the risk of giving offense. As a German I say to the youth of Germany: I hope the time will come when without detriment to your loyalty towards your German blood you will no longer sing the *Wacht am Rhein* here in Austria. For it belongs to an entirely different historic and cultural setting and cannot express your loyalty to the cultural community and mission for which the gold and yellow flag stands. Choose some other song, let us say, *Brueder reicht die Hand zum Bunde,* but in any case a song which extends the hand of fellowship to the race which Providence has linked with you for the common realization of a higher form of community."

Well do I remember the effect my words produced on my audience of students. The *aula* was packed, every last seat was occupied, and facing me rows of young people stood motionless like a dark pine wood. I expected an outburst. But no one uttered a sound. They all looked at me with an air of deep thought. My words were breathlessly absorbed and stored in the mind. The attacks came from the older generation. I replied to them in a pamphlet *Das Oesterreichische Problem* in which I preached the great and new task which could not be evaded by creating a Slav and a German community. I pointed out its European significance in the following terms:

"In the dispensation of Providence the Austrian problem possesses a significance for the political order and for the religious and moral culture of the entire world. A man whose nature embraces strong contrasts but who has overcome them and achieved harmony on a higher level is a source of help to many others who suffer from inner disharmony. In the same way a political body which harmonizes races of opposite character in a single community, performs a function of value for the whole of mankind. This has indeed often been urged by thinking Austrians. But its political consequences have never been thoroughly worked out. And, strangely enough no one abroad has an inkling of Austria's providential mission. The difficulties and embarrassments which beset the internal life of the Dual Monarchy are a source of amusement abroad and of arrogant self-congratulation: 'Such a state of things would be impossible in our country.' But anyone who understands the amount of organizing ability and constructive political education required to negotiate all the arrangements great and small between the nationalities under Austrian rule will know that those other states, whose domestic problems are comparatively simple, would probably fail if confronted with Austria's task and that the political forces which are silently maturing in Austria will yet play a great part in the history of Europe."

MY INTERVIEW WITH EMPEROR KARL

My lecture and address and still more the fact that it had been received without protest by my youthful audience had so infuriated the Austrian Pan-Germans against me that they have been at my heels ever since. By persistent attacks and calumnies they sought to make Germany and Austria too hot for me. Their behavior was the same when, in 1917, I made a last attempt to bring about, while it was still possible, a solution of the problem of nationalities in the Austrian Empire. Two enlightened members of the Upper House called the Emperor Karl's attention to my pamphlet and persuaded him to invite me to discuss with him the principles of a solution on the lines there advocated. The intention was that, as the first step to the transformation of the Dual Monarchy into a confederation, my colleague, Prof. H. Lammasch, a member of the Upper House should, as Prime Minister, in collaboration with me, form a cabinet to include representatives of all nationalities. Lammasch had written me that such an internal transformation of the Austro-Hungarian state might form the moral basis of a peace treaty, and solve the problems otherwise insoluble which had given rise to the War. Under the influence of his uncle, Archduke Franz Ferdinand, the Emperor had reached views practically the same as those to which I had been led by my observation of Austrian conditions and which had been completed by my study of Frantz.

In the book which he wrote about the Emperor, Count Polzer-Hoditz relates a conversation which he had had some years before the War with the then Archduke Karl about the critical situation of the Dual Monarchy and in particular about the crisis produced by the annexation of Bosnia and Herzegovina. In the Archduke's opinion, the prospect was gloomy. He spoke of the tradition of his family which had been a firm adherence to the federal principle. In his opinion we had departed much too far from it. The mistake would be bitterly avenged. Today we were no more a genuine Empire than was Bismarck's Germany. And an Empire was needed, such as the old German Empire had been. "My uncle Franz," the Archduke concluded, "has, indeed, excellent ideas for the future about which I am not in a position to say more, and which, indeed, I know only very roughly. But in my opinion, even these ideas are practicable only up to a certain point. Beyond that there is no issue left. We are heading for a catastrophe which may perhaps be our salvation."

In similar but more concrete terms and in more passionate language, and indeed with a more detailed program, the Emperor Karl spoke to me of the inevitable transformation of his Empire, when he gave me an audience one summer evening early in July 1917 in the park of his palace at Reichenau. In a state of intense excitement the Emperor strode on by my side through the twilight.

In the course of the walk he threw his cloak on to the stump of a tree. He told me of the visit made to him by Hindenburg and Ludendorff at which both generals had assured him that the Americans would never come over to Europe and that the prospects of victory were excellent.

His own view was totally different. He feared that this blind effort to force a purely military decision would lead to an unexampled catastrophe. He maintained that the war aims of the Entente should be met by a completely new federal organization of South-Eastern Europe; that this presented the only possibility of a speedy conclusion of peace, not to speak of the fact that the domestic peace of the nationalities under his rule could be secured only on these terms. He also pointed out that his dynasty had always been international and had always fulfilled an international function. He said that its present mission was to take the initiative in ending the state of warfare between the various nationalities. He evidently had no notion of the success achieved by Prussian nationalism in Austria, in frustrating any similar projects and in making the Dual Monarchy the tool of its own designs since the day when Bismarck had prevented Francis Joseph being crowned, as he had intended, King of Bohemia. In his book, Count Polzer-Hoditz has given an account of the powerful influences and machinations which converged from every side to deter the young Emperor from the initiative he had planned and to isolate him completely. The German deputies and ministers every day put pressure upon him to desist from the experiment.

These were the Emperor's exact words to me that evening: "It has long been my firm conviction that the hopeless situation of the peoples demands a radical change of policy. The tradition of bigotry and shortsightedness is so deeply rooted that a complete change of heart alone can save us. Of that change a manifestation must be given. And who can give it if not the dynasty which has for centuries symbolized the unity of the Austrian peoples and whose moral authority over its subject nations depends entirely upon the sublimity of its supernational mission?

"I am well aware that thousands of every nationality in the Monarchy have long been eager for such a fresh start, but in the Empire no one understands the purpose for which Providence has united us in South-Eastern Europe. Austria is neither a German nor a Slavonic state. The Germans, it is true, founded the Danubian monarchy. But today they are a minority surrounded and penetrated by peoples striving to realize their nationality. They can remain leaders of these young cultures only if they set an example of very high culture and meet these aspirants with love, respect and patience. Sin has been committed on all sides. The harm done must be made good. Therefore the past must be obliterated. Unless it is applied to the realities of Austria in an academic fashion, I have no fear of 'national self-determination'. If we generously grant each national group the utmost possible scope to develop its characteristic way of living, to develop its culture and to enjoy the use of its native language, they will be united with the Empire as a whole in a novel form more intimately than before and discard any impracticable excesses.

"In Austria even less than elsewhere can a political union be forcibly imposed on its nationalites from without. It must proceed from a moral union of the peoples. This spirit is the spirit which must be instilled into the young. In place of textbooks inflaming each side against the other, textbooks must be composed which will acquaint German children with the great endowments and virtues of the Slavs and inform Slavonic children of the German contribution to the world's culture and in particular to the culture of the young Slavonic peoples of South-Eastern Europe. If we settle our domestic problems in this new spirit of responsibility toward Europe we shall certainly

regain the trust of Europe and set an example for a universal league of nations in the cause of peace."

That these words were actually spoken by the Emperor
is guaranteed by the fact that I submitted my account of
the conversation to him when I met him in Switzerland
after the War. He approved both my report and its publication. The Emperor's words left me with a very different
impression of him from that which I had expected to receive. "A likable Austrian lieutenant," a colleague had
described him to me. That indeed is what he appeared on
the surface. But he combined two distinct personalities.
The man who spoke to me was not a young officer, but an
independent thinker, a ruler deeply conscious of his responsibilities and enlightened by a tradition centuries old,
who had achieved an original reinterpretation of that
tradition in which he was rooted and which was now
confronted with its most severe trial. He was, therefore,
not understood by his entourage. Certainly he was no
"intellectual"; but he was, all the same, head and shoulders
above the highly intellectual experts and experienced advisers who thought themselves vastly superior to him. Nor
was this surprising. For a man whose ideas had been
derived from steeping himself in an age-long tradition was
by that very fact rendered far superior to all those self-
conceited intellectuals and mandarins. He was, perhaps,
the most intelligent and clear-sighted of the Habsburgs. In
him that mighty imperial tree came to a late blossoming
and revealed all the hidden possibilities of genuine imperialism. He was prepared to draw the full consequences
of its tradition, to translate it into contemporary terms,
and to surrender completely the German hegemony. But
like Francis Joseph in the Bohemian question, he was frustrated by the incomprehension of a public whose outlook
had for decades been radically distorted.

I was astonished by his complete freedom from prejudice
and from the stupid slogans of a press which had imbued

even the Austrians with the German doctrine that the
hostile powers were bent on Germany's destruction. I could
talk to him about the War and its probable end as with a
brother brought up in the same intellectual atmosphere.
But this unforgettable evening also left me with the gloomy
foreboding that his ideal was far beyond his time and his
people and had no chance of realization.

The Emperor made a beginning by decreeing an amnesty, particularly in favor of the Czechs. The army was
infuriated. But the Emperor knew what he was doing and
what he intended to do. There are symbolic gestures whose
seed-plot is eternity, which proceed from recognition of
essential truth and, therefore, yield their blessing in due
time, even if from the standpoint of practical politics they
seem foolish. But I thought that the wider significance of
the amnesty should be made clear. So I left with the
Emperor a written account of what he had said to me and
took it on myself to beg him to allow me to publish it.
I hoped to place the isolated amnesty granted to the Slavs
in the context of a far-reaching program of reconciliation
between all the nationalities of his Empire and to make
his attitude clear even to the hostile powers abroad. He
consented, with the proviso that he must first submit the
text to Count Czernin. The reservation was fatal. The
Count said: "If this is published, the Prussians will invade
Bohemia tomorrow."

Obviously, the Prussians would not have dreamed of
taking such a step. Czernin showed himself in this the
short-sighted statesman whose compromises proved Austria's doom. The publication at that juncture of the
Emperor's intentions would have made a most powerful
impression in South-Eastern Europe and abroad and would
have opened a wide road to European reconciliation. But
the ruling circles in Austria were not ripe for such a move.
The Emperor felt himself completely isolated. Even his
intention to offer the Premiership to Heinrich Lammasch,

the noble Christian champion of national rights and delegate to the Hague Conference, was so strongly opposed by the German nationalists that he abandoned it. In the teeth of German public opinion, he dared not assume the responsibility of solving the Austrian problem. He surrendered himself increasingly to Czernin's false guidance. Thereby he sealed the fate of Austria-Hungary.

Before the Imperial intentions were thus dropped Lammasch and I, with the consent of the head of the Cabinet, von Palzer, invited the leaders of all the nationalities to a conference at which they were asked to pledge their loyalty to an Austria remodeled according to the plan above described. All were prepared to do so except the German representatives. The Slovene representative, Dr. Krek, made an impassioned speech in which he quoted to the Germans the words of Schiller: "Your strife achieves great things, your alliance achieves greater." I was amazed to observe that, in spite of everything that had happened, the attachment of the South-Eastern peoples to their Austrian connection was still so deep-rooted. On the lines of my pamphlet I dwelt upon the intellectual and political necessity of finding a new foundation for the community of Austrian peoples. I pointed out that the operation of the Christian leaven in the life of nations was shown by the fact that their rulers were embracing new ideals. In the conscience of the oppressor himself his victim stood up and took from him his old conviction of his right to rule. Those who opposed the demand for the revision of antiquated claims based on force would be crushed beneath the chariot wheels of omnipotent time. I quoted the passage in which Macbeth, confronted by Banquo's ghost, exclaims:

" . . . murders have been performed
Too terrible for the ear: the times have been,
That, when the brains were out, the man would die,
And there an end: but now, they rise again,
With twenty mortal murders on their crowns,

> And push us from our stools: this is more strange
> Than such a murder is."

This evocation of Banquo's ghost was too much for the German representatives. Led by Prince Auersperg, they left the hall in protest. What could one do with such people? Only a few months before the final catastrophe these gentlemen in the Upper House howled down Heinrich Lammasch who would have brought them to reason, would have dispelled their madness and opened their eyes to the facts; at the conclusion of his plea for peace, they exclaimed, "We want war and victory." Count Dominic Hardegg went so far as to call the supporters of the imperial policy of peace "pleaders for the Entente." "Whom God will destroy He blinds." Even in Austria the typically modern German had been politically infatuated by nationalism. Brains stupefied by war-mania and war-lies were incapable of seeing that German nationalism and German bullying were incompatible with the facts of Austria's historical development.

On my return to Zurich after this fruitless effort, the Swedish Ambassador visited me. He told me that influential circles among the Entente powers were disposed, if the Emperor Karl's plan were carried through, to enlarge the new South-Eastern Confederation. In their view, Serbia and Rumania might be persuaded, on the conclusion of peace, to enter a Danubian Confederation as independent States, provided that the Croats joined with Serbia and that the Hungarian Rumanians with their territory joined with Rumania. I submitted the suggestion to the Emperor. I had no hope that anything could be done even with this prospect in view. The head of the Cabinet answered sadly, *Lasciate ogni speranza.*

STEPHEN TISZA AND HUNGARY'S OPPOSITION

It must be recognized that the failure of the Emperor's project was not due exclusively to immaturity of political thought among the German-Austrians. Another cause was the incomprehensible obstinacy of the ruling circles in Hungary. Austrian statesmen could not find the key with which to solve the problem of nationalities, because it was in the hands not of Austria but of Hungary; no Austrian government was allowed to interfere in the concerns of Hungary. Least of all could the Emperor interfere, for as King of Hungary he had taken an oath to defend in their full extent the territories subject to St. Stephen's crown. When it was proposed during the War to issue a manifesto dealing with the South-Slav question, which did not expressly maintain their integrity, the Prime Minister, Dr. Wekerle, threatened to hold up the import of provisions.

It had not always been thus. There was a time when Hungary gave hospitality to all the races within her borders. For long St. Stephen's device exercised its spell: *Unius linguae uniusque moris regnum imbecile et fragile est.* (A kingdom of one language and one way of life is weak and frail.) On the foundation of this principle, laid down by her greatest statesman, Hungary maintained her political existence. "Germans," wrote Count Polzer-Hoditz in his book on the Emperor Karl, "were the builders of Hungary. They laid the foundations of her trade and industry, taught her population of uncivilized hunters and nomads agriculture and in particular the cultivation of the vine; also the practise of handicrafts and how to reclaim her waste lands; opened up the treasures hidden in their mountains; in short, brought to them the blessings and the intellectual resources of German culture. Like the Germans, the other races inhabiting Hungary were left undisturbed in their national way of living. The Magyars remained Magyar, the Germans German, the Slavs Slav. This condition of national toleration or rather national indifference was not confined to Hungary but was universal. National emancipation in the middle of the nine-

teenth century brought about in Hungary a complete
change of attitude, which also took place in other countries
about the same period."

In 1836 Magyar replaced Latin as the language of legislation. From that time onward a policy of systematic magyar-
ization had been pursued whose incompatibility with the
racial composition of South-Eastern Europe inevitably
jeopardized not only the passionately defended integrity of
Hungarian territory but the entire Dual Monarchy. It has
been the tragedy of a highly gifted people that modern
national individualism has wrought on it, precisely because
of the exceptional political energy of the Magyar character,
ravages similar to those which it has wrought in Germany.
Far-sighted intellectual leaders of modern Europe had
foreseen from the outset the evil which a one-sided nationalism must produce in this region of Europe.

As the War proceeded, the results of this policy began
to threaten the very existence of the Dual Monarchy. Emperor Karl perceived that on the solution of the South-Slav
question depended not only the survival of the Empire
but the conclusion of peace. But Tisza refused to yield an
inch. Kossuth himself had admitted that the national independence of Hungary could be assured only if a measure
of autonomy were conceded to the Slavs. Only a few
months before the catastrophe, Tisza obstinately refused
to consider the termination of the Dual System. On January 18, 1919, the former Finance Minister, Von Spitz-
mueller, declared at a political meeting in Vienna: "On
the question of the South Slavs, whose timely solution
alone could have saved the Monarchy from destruction,
Hungary displayed a truly amazing obstinacy. So far did
she carry it that the Hungarian Premier, Dr. Wekerle,
exposed himself to this question from a quarter to whose
criticism he must have been peculiarly sensitive:—"Is
Hungary then prepared to be the solitary national an-
achronism in Europe? It was Hungary that, during the

time I was Finance Minister of both governments, prevented so long as she had the power, the solution of the Slav question."

This Hungarian opposition to the most urgent demands of the contemporary situation had also led to serious tension between the ruling classes of Hungary. The heir to the throne, Franz-Ferdinand, known to favor the change of the monarchy into a federation, was falsely charged with being an enemy of Hungary, although his quarrel was only with those Magyar groups who shut their eyes to the signs of the times. Those groups looked forward with dread to his accession. A well-aimed bullet dissipated their alarms. Prince L. Windisch-Graetz, who visited Budapest immediately after the assassination, gives the following description of the state of feeling there. "Without exception political circles in Budapest were like men who had awakened from a nightmare. Tisza's party made no attempt to conceal their delight. The entire country seemed to breathe again."

I must point out, however, that in Hungary also there were clear-sighted politicians who insisted, though in vain, that even in Hungary's interest the Czechs should receive their rights. As early as September 12, 1897, the deputy N. Barth, wrote in the *Magyar Orszag*, "Federation is the inevitable goal of our political development and the best solution. German hegemony is losing ground every day because it has long been artificial." And the *Budapest Hirlap* wrote, "Bohemia has as much right as Hungary to be an independent state. It would be a good thing if the Hungarian public would reflect what the consequences will be if it supports the German predominance." The Czech deputy, Dr. Eim, enlarged upon this warning when he said, "The Magyars should not cherish any illusion. The day the Hohenzollern flag waves in Prague and Trieste, their state and their nation will be crushed beneath the German heel." How well founded all these warnings have proved!

On July 17, 1914, a deputation of the Serbian nationalists in the Bosnian Landtag consisting of the Vice-Presidents, Dr. Dimovic, Dr. Jojkoic and Dr. Vasic, called upon Count Tisza. Dr. Dimovic, as speaker of the deputation, expressed his indignation at the crime of Sarajevo. Tisza waved his hand in deprecation and said, "God willed it so, and we must all be thankful to Him."

CHAPTER IX

FROM BISMARCK TO BÜLOW AND ON TO THE WAR

I MIGHT have enlarged the title of this chapter by adding "From Napoleon Bonaparte to Bismarck." It is indisputable that Napoleon's invasion of Germany did much to shift the focus of German life and ambition from Weimar to Potsdam. But the part he played must not be exaggerated. In the language of India, Prussia bore her Karma in herself, and even without Napoleon would have pursued her path to dominion over Germany. Had he never appeared on the scene, the German soul was ready to adopt the ideal of nationalism which had come to maturity in France and was prepared to transform it into political metaphysics and Teutonic frenzy.

Long before Bismarck the romantic writer, Edgar Quinet, divined that the Germany which Madame de Staël had visited and which found expression in the German classics differed in one important respect from French culture, which was the product of an undisturbed development of centuries. German culture, he saw, did not permeate and dominate the entire nation; it was nothing more than a thin layer on the surface, beneath which volcanic forces rumbled and were already sending out their fumes into the upper air. Quinet's first impressions had been those of too many Frenchmen up to the present day who have received a friendly welcome from a Germany intellectually alive and open to the outside world. Such men become acquainted with the simple and kindly German people and therefore feel with justice a deep affection for those Germans. That was Quinet's experience in

Heidelberg. He thought that for the first time he knew "the joy of living." He became engaged to a German girl and was eager to bring the real Germany to the knowledge of his fellow-countrymen. Of the volcanic Germany below the surface he had no inkling. But a few years later his eyes were opened. In 1831 he contributed to the *Revue des Deux Mondes* a truly prophetic article from which I have extracted the following passages.

"In Prussia the old universalism and political cosmopolitanism have given place to an irascible nationalism. This Prussian despotism is intelligent, active and enterprising. It needs nothing but a man who will clearly see his star. Between the people and the rulers of Prussia there exists a secret conspiracy to postpone political emancipation, to combine in adding to Frederick's inheritance, and to avenge upon France the disgrace, so long endured, of the Treaty of Westphalia.

"Unity is the deep-seated ideal, inevitable and constant, which moves the country and pervades every department of the national life. Religion, law, commerce, freedom, despotic rule, everything alive across the Rhine tends in the same direction. This unity is no temporary harmony of conflicting passions which the next day may dissolve. It is the inevitable development of northern civilization. Though we know so well the power of ideas we pay no heed to this movement of intelligence, indeed of genius. We actually admire it, naively thinking it will prove an exception to everything we know and will never aspire to pass from the mind to the will and from the will to action and will never covet social power and political strength. Meanwhile these ideas, which should have remained disembodied spirits haunting an unfathomable depth, are rising up before us as the genius of an entire race. And that race is placing itself under the authority of a people not more enlightened than itself but greedier, more active, more aggressive, and with greater practical experience; and is entrusting that people with its ambition and its resentments. It is Prussia, therefore, which the North is making its weapon today. Yes, and if it is permitted to do so, it will gradually push Prussia from behind to a murderous attack upon the ancient monarchy of France. What we are witnessing today in Germany is a fall of the spirit. The heavenly Jerusalem is crashing into the abyss. No hand can arrest her doom.

"Hitherto Prussian despotism has been violent and unjust, but it has not troubled to lie. Its weapons have been open: audacity, daring, defiance. It has not poisoned them with deceit. But deceit will corrupt the future. If the wedlock between force and fraud is once achieved we may say goodbye forever to all we have hitherto known of German life, intellectual honesty, penetration, magnanimity, genius. All these will perish, drowned in a blend of good and evil, justice and injustice, truth and falsehood. Who can picture a German Byzantinism? It will mingle the vices of the South with those of the North, an appalling combination: Machiavelli refuted by Frederick the Great and realized by the Tugendbund (the society for the Promotion of Virtue). For your own sakes, a thousand times more even than for ours, spare the world such a future."

Everything has fallen out as Quinet foresaw it. His prophetic vision is truly amazing. I must anticipate what I say in my apocalyptic Epilogue, concerning the hideous blend of good and evil, the spiritual and the bestial, truth and falsehood in this period of world-history, and how Germany has realized this inextricable confusion in politics and in men's souls. The insight of this French Christian, who was far from being Germany's enemy, foretold all this a hundred years ago. A single word often suffices to reveal to the man gifted with insight a spiritual state which the rest of mankind have not perceived after living with it for half a century.

Keeping Quinet's prediction of the future development of a Prussianized Germany before our minds, let us now consider the more important events of the decades which linked Bismarck with the first World War. Since it is the purpose of this book to show the philosophical, psychological and religious significance of events, I can attempt no detailed history. I must be content to pass judgment on particular events and developments which were specially pregnant with future destiny and in which tendencies operative for centuries found their clearest and most mature expression. Searchlights will be thrown on the most significant moral attitudes and the weightiest responsibilities.

St. Matthew's Gospel opens with a genealogy; "Abraham begat Isaac, Isaac begat Jacob, Jacob begat Judah and his brethren." So we may say, "Bismarck begat Bülow, Bülow begat Bethmann-Hollweg, Bethmann-Hollweg begat the first World War." Bismarck's sober estimate of the European situation would no doubt have avoided many blunders committed by his successors. We have only to read Lord Granville's reminiscences to see the prudence and self-restraint with which the Iron Chancellor avoided causing the least uneasiness to the rulers of Britain's world-wide Empire.

But this does not alter the incontestable fact that Bismarck was the source and the embodiment of the curse that has lain upon modern Germany. In his person a tradition at once far stronger and narrower than he, namely Prussianism, conquered the German people, took control of their destiny, and forced upon them an un-German policy. The skill and prudence with which his genius moved forward and the intoxicating successes which attended the hammerstrokes with which he threatened Europe gave to the cynical materialism and the reckless disregard of right which inspired his policy a powerful hold over his contemporaries and completely overcame the moral repugnance of the German people.

Certainly Bismarck would never have advised the visit to Tangiers or the despatch of the *Panther* to Algeria. But it was his war policy which erected an insurmountable barrier of hostility between France and Germany and imbued the German nation with a passionate desire to humiliate France. He inaugurated power-politics among a people temperamentally disposed to excess and to unbounded desires and whose blindness to facts plunged the nation headlong into what was regarded as practical politics.

Bismarck would have laughed at Bülow, as in turn Bülow's acuteness laughed at Bethmann and Jagow, and as Jagow would certainly have laughed at Hitler. But they are all products of the same school. Each in turn inherited all the difficulties bequeathed to him by his predecessor's policy. Each attempted by means increasingly foolish to conjure the evil which Germany's growing isolation inevitably produced. Therefore, Bülow's policy, certain to alienate England, was the result of the divorce which Bismarck's narrowly German policy had made between the people of South-Eastern Europe and the new Germany imprisoned by national barriers. Hitler's desire to break through this barrier is proof of a sound instinct. But he has remained bound by the Little German and Greater Prussian methods which Bismarck initiated and which can never rescue Germany from its isolation and its contracted sphere of action to unite once more the world of the Rhine and the Elbe with the world of the Danube and with the East. Germany's life demands the wide space which only the trust, the sympathy and the cooperation of the world can give her. She was suddenly thrust into a narrow dungeon and fed upon the illusion that she could break her way out by blood and iron and threats. The fatal incompatibility which ensued between the Prussian religion of war and Germany's vital needs belonged to the very essence of Bismarck's policy.

Bethmann-Hollweg in his memoirs defends himself against those who blame him for the U-boat campaign and other short-sighted blunders committed by the German conduct of the War. It was not his fault, he urges, that military power in Germany has been deified beyond all bounds as the solution of every difficulty.

Clemenceau observed that war is too complicated to be left to the army. Ludendorff says that politics are too difficult to be left to the politicians. We are in two different worlds. In Germany the policy favored by the army must dictate the policy of the civil government because the latter recognizes no other political instrument than war or the threat of war. Power-politics are the politics of the generals and must end in a military dictatorship in one form or another. When William II dismissed Bismarck, *Punch* published a cartoon which attracted world-wide attention entitled "Dropping the Pilot". But the pilot had guided the ship on a wrong course and into a sea thick with rocks from which her successive helmsmen could not save her. Bismarck was too intelligent not to see the true position before he died. Bülow relates in his memoirs that the Iron Chancellor on his death-bed cried in delirium, "Russia, Serbia, England."

I have quoted Quinet's prophecy of the day when Prussia in the pursuit of her anti-European policy would combine violence with deceit. If we consider from this point of view the methods employed to provoke the wars of 1866 and 1870 and compare them with the methods employed to disguise the German action in July 1914 and transfer responsibility for the War to the Allies, we shall see how faithfully the disciples have copied their master and, indeed, have improved upon him.

On June 19, 1866, Princess Victoria, afterwards the

Empress Frederick, wrote to her mother, Queen Victoria, as follows: "Not a day passes on which this evil man" (Bismarck) "does not work with the utmost skill against what is good and defeat it. He is pushing us into war by twisting and turning everything to suit his ends. No sooner have we begun to hope a little and see a way of escape from the blind alley than we learn that it has been closed. *Such is the network of lies that merely to hear of it confuses one's brain. But it is skilfully woven, and despite his disinclination the King is increasingly enmeshed in it without perceiving the fact.* No one in Berlin wants war, nor does the King. But Bismarck is bent upon it and with that object conceals from the King the despatches of warning received from foreign powers."

In exactly the same way the war of 1870-1871 was engineered and the responsibility thrown upon the ruler who had been caught in the snare and had allowed himself to be trapped into an unguarded declaration of war. As early as 1864, Bismarck had explained to the Russian, Ewert, his domestic program and its implications for his foreign policy. "I intend," he told him, "to buy some, to frighten others, to beat others and to get them all on my side for a war against France." The succession to the Spanish throne provided the opportunity for that war.

Busch, Bismarck's publicist colleague, relates how he was entrusted with the task of working up discreetly a press campaign against France. The facts were presented in such a light that it seemed as though the entire provocation came from France. The notes published in 1894 under the title *Aus dem Leben Karls von Rumaenien* prove beyond doubt that Bismarck was intriguing behind the scenes in the question of the Spanish succession, which was made the pretext for war, and that he moved his pawns, though in his Reminiscences he denies it. Exactly as it was in 1914. Busch relates: "When the Spanish question became serious Moltke looked ten years younger. But when he learned that the Hohenzollerns had relinquished any claim to the throne he became immediately old and tired."

Bismarck himself informs us in his Reminiscences that at the historic luncheon with Roon and Moltke when it was decided to arrange the famous "flourish of trumpets", he unfolded his plan as follows:

"If on behalf of the Emperor I communicate this text, which makes no alteration or addition to the telegram, by telegraph to the press and to all our embassies, it will be known in Paris before midnight and not only by its contents but by the way in which it has been published will it act as a red rag to the Gallic bull. We must strike if we do not want to be beaten without a struggle. But our success depends upon the impression that we ourselves and others receive as to the origin of the war. *It is most important that we should be the party attacked.* French arrogance and excitability will serve our purpose if we proclaim to Europe, so far as it can be done without the ear-trumpet of the Reichstag, that we are fearlessly confronting the threats of France." When the soldiers grasped their host's meaning they displayed, Bismarck tells us, a delight which astonished him. They suddenly recovered their appetite and spoke in tones of joy. Roon said, "God lives still and will not let us be put to shame." Then, as in the first World War, God was claimed as an appanage of the German army.

What do we think of such men?

Bismarck always spoke of the French with contempt. "France is a nation of ciphers, a herd of cattle. . . . They are thirty million obedient niggers, not one of them rings true. They are not to be compared with the Russians or Italians, let alone with us Germans. . . . Scratch a Frenchman and you will find a Turk." A Cardinal implored him not to inflict further humiliation upon a nation which had suffered so much. "The humiliation," Bismarck interrupted at once, "will soon be forgotten and we are not called upon to feed the French monkey with sugar." Assuredly the peace terms were not sugar. Roon relates that when Favre was informed of the terms his hair went white in a quarter of an hour. But the conclusion of peace was Bismarck's first experience of the spirit which the war and its success had aroused in the German people. He was compelled to yield to the army and to take more from France than he himself thought wise. The worst annexationists were the college professors.

In a moving letter to David Strauss, Renan uttered a warning against a peace of this kind. "Is it worthy of Germany to annex by force a province bitterly opposed to the annexation and which will never forgive the sack of Strasbourg? It is a decisive hour. There are two currents of opinion here. Some argue, 'Let us bring the loathsome business to as speedy a conclusion as possible. Let us cede everything asked of us, Alsace, Lorraine. Let us sign the peace. But then *deadly hate; uninterrupted preparation for war; an alliance with any power willing to make one; complete acquiescence in every Russian ambition; a single object in life; a single motive for living; a war of extermination against the German race.*' Others say, 'Let us save the integrity of France, develop the necessary constitutional organs, make good our mistakes, not in order to dream of a war of revenge in which we should be the aggressors but seeking the alliance of Germany and England which would lead the world further along the road of a free civilization.' Which of the two policies France will choose, it is for Germany to decide. And she will also decide the future of civilization."

Intoxicated by victory Germany decided as Renan had foretold.

THE IRON CHANCELLOR'S FIRST HEIR

Within the limits of this book it is obviously impossible to tell the complete history of the Bismarckian era. I have merely sought to make plain the diabolism of that mighty

figure. "A man will arise in Prussia," Quinet had written.
More than six centuries of colonial Germany embodied
in him its ruthless, irresistible advance and its triumphant
contest with the primeval forest, the native race and its
primitive passions, and applied it to the anarchic state of
Germany and her relations with Europe. The beneficent
inheritance of a gigantic task fulfilled by self-renunciation
and marvelous discipline, was combined in him with the
accursed inheritance of ages passed in exterminating or
oppressing human lives. German kindliness, Austrian
baroque, French civilization and "insouciance" were
thrown overboard. His unexampled success blinded his
contemporaries and in wide circles destroyed men's faith
in a moral government of the world. Thus was constructed
on the ruined foundations of the moral order an external
order permeating every sphere of life. On the foundation
of an arrogant dissolution of the last links with the community of European peoples there arose a self-confident
and seemingly indestructible sense of security.

The most fatal characteristic of this Prussian advance
against Germany and Europe was not its enormous power
and self-confidence but its betrayal of the intellect, the
Christianity, the humanism, the music, and the universalism of Germany. The Germans regarded this new cari-
cature of Geranmy as the crown of German intelligence,
humanism, music and universalism and gladly devoted
their entire being to its service. It was no doubt the design
of Providence to reveal by this apostasy how uncertain of
their own values, how faithless and devoid of character,
all those guardians of "intellectual culture" had become.
To display this truth was Bismarck's greatest achievement
in God's service. His successors completed his work.

But we are here concerned with the political results of
Bismarck's work. His genius, caution, skill and cleverness
in dealing with opponents, which he had inherited from
the tradition of the Teutonic Knights, had created an

undertaking which depended entirely on its director and founder. It tempted, however, his successors to gamble with the vast political capital he had left them and to engage in increasingly desperate attempts to enlarge the power of Germany. They could but provide another proof that power infatuates and that the instincts and passions which Bismarck's achievement had aroused in the German people must of their very nature increase the national blindness. Selfishness always begins with cunning and always ends with infatuation. Only respect for the rights of others opens men's eyes to reality and to the simple but fundamental fact that oneself is not the only person in the world.

In the largest castle that the Crusaders erected in Syria, the Kalaat-el-Hosn, there is an inscription written in the finest twelfth-century script, which the Hohenzollerns would have done well to inscribe on the coat-of-arms in all their strongholds. *"Sit tibi copia, sit sapientia, formaque detur: inquinat omnia sola superbia si comitetur."* (Wealth, wisdom, beauty; all these pride defiles, if it accompany them).

Bismarck's first heir, William II, inherited an almost inexhaustible capital of prestige, power and national wealth. All were squandered. No device can more truly express the tragedy of this brilliant life and the moral emptiness and barbarism beneath its surface than those words, *"inquinat omnia sola superbia, si comitetur."*

WILLIAM II AND BÜLOW

In his official organ, the *Post*, Bismarck published on February 24, 1887, the following reply to stories circulated in the English press that in the event of war Germany intended to march through Belgium. "That it is not the policy of Germany to begin a war because she believes it will be forced upon her, Prince Bismarck most emphatically declared on January 11. *Moreover, Germany would*

never begin a war by breaking a European treaty. It is
believed in England that the French fortifications have
made it impossible for a German invading force to cross
the Franco-German frontier and that the German General
Staff must, therefore, contemplate an invasion through
Belgium. We do not think English journalists, however
sharpsighted, can so easily discover the plans of the German
General Staff. *In any case, they are mistaken in supposing
that our policy is determined by the views of the General
Staff and not vice versa. Neither Belgian nor Swiss neutrality will ever be violated by Germany. The German
Government sets too high a value upon its reputation for
the strict observance of the Treaties which European
Powers have concluded to preserve peace."*

The most distinctive feature of the reign of William II
was the subjection of the civil government to the views
of the General Staff. This was but an apparent contradiction of Bismarck's policy. For as I have just shown, his
policy was at bottom simply a policy of war and the threat
of war, though as a result of his deeper knowledge of the
resources and traditions of foreign powers it took a wider
strategic view; was more cautious, prudent and patient.
That is to say, at bottom the General Staff was not subject
to a genuine political policy but to a more mature and
more clever militarism which kept a short-sighted gangsterism under control. But as soon as the far-sighted practi-
tioner of militarism with his sense of realities had been
removed from the scene, the war politics of the new Reich
were displayed in their naked ugliness, both on land and
at sea.

When in 1912, Haldane visited Berlin, it was Tirpitz
and not Bethmann-Hollweg who conducted negotiations
with him. The heads of the Foreign Office were in such a
subordinate political position, were so unskilled and so
lacking in a genuine knowledge of foreign countries, that
they had no authority as compared with the army. This

was shown by Moltke's action in July 1914. There were, indeed, occasions related in Tirpitz's memoirs when those civilians at the Foreign Office in their ignorance of the world were more militarist than the army. Bülow's policy was militarist through and through. He was a very dwarfish Alberich who flourished Wotan's sword. He thrust it in turn in the faces of patient neighbors and thought himself mightily successful when they yielded to childish provocations; although they, on their side, anxiously discussed the situation together and agreed that the day would soon come when they could give way no longer. One of them called Germany the *bateau ivre* (the drunken ship): a giant hulk whose movements and course were incalculable and whose movements were directed by no principles either of the ideal or the practical order but by whims, impressions and dark forces.

Those who after the first World War published the huge collection of German official papers hoped that their bulk would bury the awkward Kautsky documents out of sight. But their hope was not fulfilled. The editors desired to prove that in the decades before the War the policy of the German government was peaceful. They could not establish their thesis for the simple fact that the representatives of the German determination to go to war were not in the Foreign Office. Germany's genuine rulers, the army and its allies, the manufacturers of war material, did not want war during those decades, because Germany was not yet ready for war on two fronts and at sea. The great War in which Germany would settle accounts with Europe, and change in her favor the balance of power in Europe and throughout the world, was relegated to the date when it did in fact break out. Even so, those who desired to wait for the right moment had no little difficulty in repairing the damage done by the tactless and stupid gestures of the arrogant Emperor. William II has claimed credit for preserving the peace of the world for forty years. To this we must reply that it was due to his good luck, not to his intelligence, and that we have to thank neither him nor Bülow that on several occasions before 1914 the world did not go up in flames.

After Bismarck's retirement there were five distinct groups who sought to exploit and to increase the power which Germany had acquired in the one-sided fashion they favored and in accordance with their particular traditions and interests, for they all lacked a comprehensive vision and wide knowledge of the world. With this object they influenced the Kaiser, bending him now in one direction, now in another, and thereby making German foreign policy seem confused and changeable. The army, the navy, the mercantile marine, heavy industry, the leading banks (Helfferich and the Bagdad interests),—the Pan-Germans had adherents among all these five groups (Bernhardi), and did but carry to its issue the application of nationalism to the German world. Today Hitler has harmonized all these interests and schools of thought. He has continued Greater Prussia and Pan-Germanism, has united army and navy in a single program of rearmament on a gigantic scale, and has subjected every industrial and financial group to the policy of his Nazi state. But immediately after Bismarck's retirement the various groups were at loggerheads. One group was for expansion in the West, another for expansion in the East. And William II's foreign policy expressed this lack of a fixed and simple aim.

German policy during those decades has been reproached for the fact that it was neither definitely Eastern nor definitely Western in its orientation. But we must remember that behind this hesitation the tradition was operative that Germany is the land which mediates between East and West and that her interests and traditions attract her and bind her to both. The mistake was to make this mediating function the occasion of endless fluctuation, whereas Germany should have brought both worlds together and ren-

dered to each its due. She lacked the indispensable comprehension of her European responsibilities and the courage
to follow the path they marked out for her. Her very mistakes and embarrassments bore an involuntary and unconscious witness to Germany's true vocation in Europe and
to the responsibility such a vocation brought with it.

Bülow liked to pose as a man of cosmopolitan sympathies. At bottom he was an extremely narrow-minded
Prussian with sympathies correspondingly restricted. Bismarck also was a Prussian whose horizon did not extend
to the German people as a whole. But at least he was
aware that the wider sphere was governed by other laws
than the more limited sphere, and he deliberately chose
that Germany should set bounds to her ambitions and
remain a purely continental power. Bülow desired to make
the narrower sphere rule the wider and hoped to govern
the world from Potsdam. This was the Germany which
suddenly entered world-politics without cosmopolitan
sympathies, world-wide ideals, or understanding of the
outside world.

When Germany's interests abroad were rapidly expanding and when the substitution of federalism for militarism
was an urgent necessity, this man of limited intelligence
felt himself more than ever obliged to defend every German interest by shaking the German fist. The enormous
growth of German commerce—it doubled between 1897
and 1907—had been accomplished without a fleet to protect it. Moreover, an obvious fact which escaped Bülow's
notice, commerce can be protected only by the navy which
controls the sea. In consequence of his petty conception
of foreign politics and of economics, Bülow was inevitably
drawn more and more completely into the unbounded
ambitions of the new monarchs of industry whose ideal
was a Prussianism applied on a world-wide scale.

The memoirs of General von Bernhardi's father acquaint us with a most significant Prussian type. Bernhardi

was a nephew of the romantic writer, Tieck, and thus belonged to a highly cultivated family. He was himself an art connoisseur of the first rank. His accounts of his travels show him to have been a man of unrestricted intellectual interests. But he has only to touch on politics to become at once a narrow Prussian, with a heart cold as ice, who speaks and thinks like a savage. The spectacle thus presented of a Jekyll and Hyde, whose political outlook is devoid of anything genuinely German, is positively terrifying.

It was the same with Bülow. Though he posed as a more cultured man than he really was, in politics he was nothing but a heartless and narrow-minded gambler who moreover had deluded himself into believing that his diplomatic manoeuvres could have saved Germany from the catastrophe for which he was himself to blame. Bülow's book *Deutsche Politik* is an unintentional picture of the contrast between the gigantic problems set by the new age in the field of foreign politics and the wholly inadequate means with which the traditional Prussian statecraft attempted to solve them. It is as though Providence had compelled the Prince to compose a damning indictment of his own policy.

THE GERMAN ATTITUDE AT THE HAGUE CONFERENCES OF 1899 AND 1907

The attitude of the circles responsible for German policy and of their supporters has never been displayed more clearly than in connection with the Hague Conferences of 1899 and 1907.

When in 1898 the Russian government threw out a feeler for gradual disarmament, William II wrote on the margin of the document in which the suggestion was made, "If he makes such a proposal to me, I'll give him a smack in the face." Of the Hague Conference of 1899 he said himself that he only consented to take part in it so as not to give offense to Russia. "As I don't want to be blamed abroad for refusing, I have consented to take part in the folly. I spit on all these resolutions."

When we contrast the reception given to the proposal to call the first Hague Conference by German political groups and the German press with its reception in other countries, we are seized with a foreboding of everything that was to follow. *Throughout the world almost unanimously the Conference was warmly welcomed. In Germany there was an almost unanimous chorus of scornful disapproval.*

Professor von Kahl voiced public opinion when he wrote, "Our German forefathers would turn in their graves at the thought of complete disarmament." Other powers, which were not military states and did not share the romantic exaltation of war reconciling German taxpayers to the armaments bill, saw in the Hague Conference an opportunity to put an end to the ruinous armaments race, to devise machinery to extinguish the conflagration of war, and thus to get rid of the universal insecurity with its paralysing effect on economic life. To such considerations German public opinion was deaf. The entire attempt was regarded as a piece of bluff intended to disarm Germany, or as at best the product of an unpractical idealism. The Kaiser declared that the best guarantee of peace is the sharpened sword.

The Germans had no conception of the strong traditions and the sociological factors on which the movement abroad for world-peace was built. They did not know that British pacifism in particular was not empty theorizing but the sober and practical readiness to apply, to disputes between nations, methods of conciliation which had been elaborated to settle industrial disputes. Moreover the reaffirmation of British belief in free trade at the beginning of the century had brought the representatives of British commerce into the pacifist camp. The best articles against

militarism were published in the leading commercial organs. Every day the conviction was gaining ground in influential circles that British security, in face of vast improve-
ments in weapons of destruction, should be sought not in
the use of force but above all in an attempt to achieve an
international agreement.

In America, as also in England, traditional religious
pacifism was incomparably stronger than in German
Protestantism, which had sold itself to Caesar. And in
America also the peace movement was far more than an
ideology. It expressed the cosmopolitanism of the leaders
of business. Their slogan, *we want a consolidated world,*
expressed their desire for the orderly and reliable conditions which would give the widest scope to their capital,
their technical invention, and their pioneering energy.
These commercial groups had more to do with the Russian
disarmament proposals of 1899 than was known at the
time. In this spirit the United States had done everything
possible to preserve peace between the States of America.
In the single decade between 1899 and 1909 the United
States had concluded no less than thirty-three arbitration
treaties, whereas Germany during the same period had
concluded the same number as San Domingo, Haiti, Cuba,
Panama and Persia, namely one.

The admissions of the German Professor Zorn and the
reminiscences of other delegates to the Hague Conference
clearly show the profound impression made upon those
jurists, educated in the Prussian tradition, by collaboration
with representatives of the traditions just described. Professor Zorn, who had expected nothing but fine ideals, was
shown an entirely new world of extremely practical possibilities and hard facts. He became acquainted with men
who belonged to real life with every fibre of their being
and who had behind them the most powerful traditions of
their culture and their economic system. But Zorn, who
was himself converted by the conference to the Hague

ideal, was impotent to avert the disaster which the militarist attitude of modern Germany was inevitably preparing for Germany and the world. The spirit, which in
the third year of the War was expressed by General von
Loringhofen when in his *Lehren des Weltkrieges* (Lessons
of the War), he denounced a League of Nations and arbitration as "an intolerable tutelage", was too deeply rooted
in modern German thought to permit a change of attitude
while there was yet time. The German mind could not
respond to the appeal made by the rest of the civilized
world.

Could anything be more significant of Germany's tragic
isolation, the result of her deliberate choice, than the fact
that Prince Bülow's book *Deutsche Politik* does not so
much as mention the Hague Conference? German policy
and the Hague Policy were in fact irreconcilable. They
were irreconcilable because the policy of Modern Germany was at bottom not *German* in the old and true sense
but *Prussian*. The Germans had arrived on the scene too
late to take part in the division of the world and Germany
was now behaving like an uneducated parvenu. Instead of
trying to reach an agreement with powers which had long
been engaged in the work of colonization and colonial
administration, Germany sought to frighten the rest of
the world by threats of war and by boastful speeches.

The behavior of the German delegation to the Hague
Conference laid the foundation stone of the Entente and
the "encirclement" of Germany. The leader of the delegation was Prince Muenster. He had not the least notion of
the importance of the Conference and tried to persuade
everyone he met on the steps of the Peace Palace, were he a
willing or an unwilling auditor, that the whole thing was
humbug. The American Ambassador, White, wrote of
him: "Count Muenster, in spite of all his outstanding
qualities—he is a fine example of a dignified German no-
bleman—is unquestionably steeped in the ideas which pre-

vailed half a century ago". The observation applies to German foreign policy as a whole. The American delegate, Dr. Holls, admirably described the German attitude when he said, "The train is about to leave and if the Germans will not take their seats, they will be left behind on the platform."

This was in fact what happened after the Conference. But we put it down to envy and malice. The German delegates to the first Hague Conference had received instructions to vote *against any measure of disarmament* and against a Court of International Arbitration. Their uncompromising rejection of disarmament had already made a very bad impression. When they proceeded to oppose the Court of Arbitration the storm broke. The Italian delegate, Count Nigra, addressed Professor Zorn in words of deep emotion and spoke of the great responsibility which they would incur before posterity if the project failed. In conversations which lasted for hours, Ambassador White endeavored to make Prince Muenster understand the issue at stake and the unpopularity which the German Emperor would incur throughout the world, if the German government sabotaged the entire plan. The much vaunted German love of peace would not appear in a favorable light if on this issue Germany opposed the rest of the world. At last he was successful. Zorn returned to Berlin and obtained at least acceptance of the Court of Arbitration.

Zorn's conversion to the principles of the Conference gave hope that the second Conference held in 1907 would witness greater progress and produce further agreements. England brought up first the question of disarmament as a matter of urgent importance. The pacific Premier, Campbell-Bannerman, besought the Conference for the sake of humanity to tackle disarmament. In an article in the *Nation* he declared that the British government which, by reducing the estimates for 1906, had given a proof of her *bona fides*, was prepared to go further if she met with similar dispositions in other countries. The sole answer of the German government was a threat not to attend the Conference unless disarmament were removed from the agenda.

The second blow delivered against the rest of the civilized world was to replace Zorn by two other delegates. One was Professor von Stengel, known for a book he had written against the movement. The other was Geheimrat Kriege who exasperated the Conference by the dry tone in which he combated every proposal the other nations had at heart and which alone could have prevented war. In his book, *Die Internationale Beschraenkung der Ruestungen* (International limitation of armaments by international agreement) Wehberg observes:

"By far the most important, indeed the chief, problem before the second Hague Conference was to conclude a treaty of universal arbitration. Again Germany frustrated the project by raising far-fetched objections. All the difficulties she raised were mere pretexts to give a semblance of justification to her opposition to the entire principle. In consequence the Conference ended, as Zorn said, in general confusion. In every country, Germany's attitude caused profound disappointment".

To such complaints the defenders of Germany always retort: "The other nations are no better. They also have practised power-politics and indeed on a far larger scale and with far greater success than Germany." Such a retort evades the essential point. Germany's isolation was not due to the fact that Germany alone had pursued a policy of force, the rest of the world a policy of justice; but to the fact that, whereas at the Hague the other powers wished to cease sinning and to create an order of international justice, we Germans under the spell of Prussia's military traditions were inflexibly determined to continue in the old path. Indeed the Kaiser declared on the occasion of the Conference; "Peace is only secure when it is protected

by the German Michael's sword and shield. So long as
unredeemed sin bears sway over mankind, so long will
there be war, hatred, envy, and conflict, and one man will
attempt to over-reach his neighbor. And nations are subject
to the same law as individuals."

The reply of the *Nowoje Wremja* to this speech expressed the unanimous opinion of the rest of the world
whose insistent desire Germany was opposing with such
fatal results: "The German Michael's sword and shield are
not the only way of protecting peace. Germany is probably
in a better position than any other nation to promote
Russia's noble design. As for seeking one's own advantage
at one's neighbor's expense, it is by voluntary renunciation
of such advantages that the peace of the world can be
secured". But Germany was determined that the rule of
force should be perpetuated. Unanimous complaints of
the civilized world against the intolerable financial burdens imposed by the armaments' race evoked from the
German military representative at the Hague the following answer uttered in an exasperating tone, too well
known: "The German people is not oppressed by the burden of taxation. It is not on the brink of the abyss. On
the contrary public and private wealth are increasing. The
standard of life is rising every year."

Certainly we must not forget that other powers raised
objections to compulsory arbitration and that it was
widely doubted whether complete or gradual disarmament were practicable until public opinion on international questions had undergone a more profound change
and until more powerful guarantees of an order of international justice had been achieved. None would have objected to the German delegates raising these difficulties.
Their scoffing and triumphant dismissal of the entire attempt to place international relations on a new basis and
to prevent the imminent European war increased the
isolation of Germany and left the world under the im-

pression that peace would have to be organized not with Germany's collaboration but against Germany. The discussion of international disarmament was simply the framework within which the nations desired to explore the possibilities of international agreement. It was the first tentative step towards a new union of the European peoples.

After the defeat of Germany this was understood even in German diplomatic circles. In 1919 men dared to say what later on was once more passed over in silence or denied. In that year, Director Simons of the Foreign Office said to a representative of the Dutch paper, *Nieuwe Bureau*. "In my opinion the German attitude in 1907 towards arbitration and disarmament was one of the essential causes of the war of 1914 and of the German defeat." And the former Foreign Minister Count Brockdorff-Rantzau speaking in the Reichstag on February 14, 1919, said plainly, "We admit that Germany's attitude at the Hague Conferences towards these two fundamental questions (arbitration and disarmament) was an historic sin for which our entire nation must now do penance. It was due not merely to an exaggerated fear of the practical difficulties but to a false estimate of the respective values of might and right."

THE DISPUTE ABOUT MOROCCO AND ITS BEARING ON WORLD HISTORY

About the middle of the eighteen-eighties Bismarck said to Count Paul Hatzfeld, the foreign secretary, "Besides the Balkans, there are three wasps' nests on our planet, the Mediterranean, the Persian Gulf and the American Monroe Doctrine. God grant that Germany may never poke her fingers into any of them."

Bülow, however, lost no time in poking his finger into the most dangerous of these wasps' nests, namely Morocco. He was pushed into it by Holstein whom King Edward in a conversation with the Secretary to the Embassy, von Eckardstein, had called a "devilish mischief-maker". But the devilish mischief-making was in fact the work of powerful, wealthy and arrogant groups. Holstein was merely their tool at the Foreign Office.

In London and Paris the question has often been asked why Berlin pursued this policy of constant provocation in Morocco. The reason is simple: the Pan-German power-politicians in all circles wished to follow Bernhardi's program and to provoke in the colonial sphere a conflict with France and thus start the war they wanted. Holstein, who had long been hostile to France, welcomed this opportunity to make use of Russia's temporary weakness for a final reckoning with France.

Notice the significant coincidence of dates: "On January 13, 1905, Port Arthur surrendered. On February 12, the German Consul in Tangier informed the French Consul, Cherisey, that Germany did not recognize the Morocco agreement. On March 11, Russia was defeated at Mukden and General Kropotkin was obliged to retreat. On March 23, the German government announced the Kaiser's intention to visit Tangier and on March 31, he arrived there and made his famous speech. On May 28, the Baltic fleet was destroyed at Tsu-Shima and on June 6, Delcassé was dismissed on the demand of the German government. A few days later, as a reward for this master-stroke, Bülow was made a prince." (Paléologue, *Un grand tournant de la politique mondiale*.)

The facts of the Morocco crisis and their interconnection are buried beneath a mountain of documents and literature. But the psychological significance of the episode and its bearing on world politics must be displayed. It is with this object that I have selected it for treatment from a mass of events which filled those decades, laden so heavily with the fate of the world.

In 1880 the representatives of the European powers after

prolonged negotiations signed a convention at Madrid. It was an international regulation of Moroccan affairs and in particular of the economic interests of each power. When, at the opening of the eighties, France laid the foundation-stone of her vast colonial Empire which was finally to extend from Algiers to Timbuctoo and Dahomey, and from Senegal to Lake Chad and the Congos, she already contemplated completing it by annexing Morocco. To compensate for her expulsion from Egypt in 1881, on Bismarck's advice she established herself in Tunis. Bismarck also informed Ferry that he was prepared to recognize a French protectorate of Morocco when the right moment came for it. This protectorate was, indeed, necessary to secure the French colonial Empire in Africa.

Certainly it was a failure of tact on the part of France that she did not ask German approval of the agreement she concluded with England in 1904 to ensure British consent to a French Protectorate of Morocco as compensation for renouncing Egypt. The Germany of Bülow and Holstein made the omission the pretext for a policy calculated to set the European powers by the ears and to wound France to the quick, a policy which was senseless even from the German standpoint. The Kaiser visited Tangier. He declared the Sultan an independent ruler, though his authority over a country defenseless and in a state of anarchy could not be taken seriously. Morocco was the last refuge of French self-respect, sorely wounded from the severe blow it had received in 1871. There was every reason to be magnanimous and not to wound it further.

Ménager les amours-propres is important for the French. It counts much in the art of dealing with them. Without it, it is equally impossible to achieve lasting success in handling foreign nations. Those who knew France well agree that by 1900 the thought of *revanche* was all but dormant and that the teaching body in particular were passionately attached to pacifism. The Morocco episode

blew up once more the flames of patriotism. Behind this
attempt of German foreign policy to humiliate and thwart
France in spite of her desire to be conciliatory, the French
detected a fixed hostility to them. They reacted violently
against it. "Every time the French were beginning to
forget *revanche* they were reminded of it by a hefty kick,"
an Austrian diplomat observed to Prince Lichnowsky.
Even so convinced a pacifist as Jaurès suddenly lost patience because in the provocative manner employed by
Germany he detected a malicious intent. "What can be
done?" he wrote in *Humanité*; "our country passionately
desires peace. But this prudence is not fear. If France is
the object of a disgraceful and unjustified attack she will
rise with all her strength to defend herself against it."

The *Daily Graphic*, which throughout the affair favored
Germany, declared that if Germany wished to remain on
friendly terms with France and England she must address
herself to them and not to the Sultan. As regards the first
Morocco crisis, I am convinced that anyone who carefully
studies and compares the French Yellow Book and the
German White Book will receive from the irrefutable evidence they provide a very bad impression not only of
German policy but of the deliberately misleading way in
which the White Book was compiled. He will further
become acquainted with the part played by the Pan-
Germans and those who stood behind them. He will also
learn the fatal effect of their speeches and writings on the
world's attitude towards Germany.

Here I can only call attention to the articles in *Export*,
urging German traders to profit by the growing Moorish
hostility to France. Equally instructive are the numerous
Pan-German resolutions reported by the French Ambassador in Berlin demanding territory in Morocco for German colonists and a base for the German fleet. "The
English had seven times more interests in Morocco than
we. But it never entered their minds to adopt an attitude

in the least resembling that adopted by Germany." In view of the fact that the White Book does not contain a single complaint between April 1904 and February 1905 of any setback suffered by German trade, the sudden attacks are explicable only by Pan-German influences which goaded the German government into making the perfectly intelligible extension of French political influence in Morocco the excuse for a German aggression whose deeper motive must be sought in German designs on the country.

It is well known how in this dispute, which threatened to kindle a world-conflagration, the French government under Rouvier retreated—partly because it was aware of the neglect of military preparations due to the pacifist effects of the Dreyfus case—and, to calm the howling pack of Pan-German wolves, forced the Foreign Minister Delcassé to resign. Delcassé's dismissal is instructive, not only for the light it throws on the spirit which animated the Germans, but also because it exposes the fatal error of that false pacifism which has done more than anything else to inspire the worst elements in Germany with renewed confidence in the success of their machinations and in a policy of calculated intimidation.

Paléologue relates in his memoirs that Delcassé alone did not lose his confidence. "At this critical moment of our history he embodied in an outstanding degree the deepest instincts of the national spirit. The fact that he came of peasant stock and belonged to a family which had been settled for centuries on a flank of the Pyrenees on the border of Aquitaine made him doubly representative." Delcassé said in fact to Paléologue, "These Germans commit one folly after another. I am very far from deploring this Tangier gesture. Nothing could have such a salutary effect on the English as a Hohenzollern vessel which hoists its flag on the coast of Morocco opposite Gibraltar." He saw at once that the essential and saving counterstroke must be to hurry the Franco-British Entente and that the hour had come when England would ask for it.

In May, 1905, England proposed an alliance with France. At once an emissary of Bülow's, Count von Donnersmarck, turned up in Paris and made things hot for Rouvier and his friends. It was known, he said, that Delcassé was conducting negotiations for a military and naval alliance with England. Germany would regard it a ground for an immediate declaration of war. The Russo-French alliance was enough—an Anglo-French Entente on top of it was too much. Before the British fleet could inflict much damage on Germany, the French army would be defeated and the way to Paris would be open. Moreover, France was wealthy enough to pay for any damage done by the British fleet. At the same time Rouvier was handed a note to the effect that the German Chancellor refused to have any further dealings with M. Delcassé.

Count Donnersmarck pointed out that the bearings of the present dispute far exceeded the immediate occasion. The entire future of the relations between France and Germany was at stake. It must be one of close alliance or of war. "Yes, a close alliance or you will conclude an alliance with England." One of Rouvier's friends, to whom the Count had spoken in this strain, told Paléologue, "There is nothing for it but a rapprochement with Germany. Delcassé, our Foreign Minister, is a national danger. For God's sake demand his resignation." So easy was it to intimidate these men.

Delcassé, on the contrary, maintained: "This is all bluff. And even if it were meant seriously an immediate alliance with England would be doubly necessary." But Rouvier accused Delcassé, at a Cabinet meeting, of attempting to isolate and encircle Germany. Germany, he said, felt herself threatened and humiliated. Delcassé's fall was determined. Now, however, the French learned an instructive lesson, which they would often receive thereafter, though they would never take it to heart. The German government was not appeased by the sacrifice of Delcassé. On the contrary, Radolin's demands continually stiffened and his attitude became increasingly threatening and arrogant.

That Germany would stand solidly behind the Sultan, Mulay Abd el Aziz, was the Ambassador's last word at his departure. Rouvier, who had taken Delcassé's place, was thoroughly disillusioned. On his return home he sat crumpled up as though he had received a stunning blow, his head in his hands. Bülow, it appears, had received a grave warning from Italy, delivered in an interview between the Foreign Minister, Luzzatti and the Ambassador, Count Monts; and it was this warning combined with the British attitude that finally made him accept the decision of the International Conference for which he had himself asked. The story of the interview of May 1, 1905 has been told by the French Ambassador, Camille Barrère, in the *Figaro* (1931). Like Count Donnersmarck in Paris, Count Monts, he tells us, said that the hour had come for a definite settlement with France, a settlement for which the events in the Far East had provided a favorable atmosphere. France must choose. If she sincerely wanted peace, so much the better. If not, there would be a fearful war. England was far too selfish to come to the help of France; and even if she did, it would be too late. Germany would compensate herself in France for any losses at sea.

Luzzatti told the Ambassador how greatly he deceived himself. The entire world knew that the conflict in Morocco was nothing but an objectionable way of exploiting the battle of Mukden to humiliate France and to intrude into her colonial Empire. England would certainly not tolerate it, and in the war would destroy the position which Germany had laboriously built up in the outside world. For England knew that a German victory would be far more dangerous to her interests than the victory of Bonaparte; "public opinion throughout the world entirely approved Delcassé's policy of defense and condemned the German aggression."

Bülow also was warned by the Councillor to the Embassy, von Eckardstein, who had been asked by Rouvier to approach the German political leaders at Baden-Baden and inform them of the willingness of the French government to come to an understanding. According to Eckardstein's account in his memoirs, Rouvier complained of the wild and aggressive writings of the Pan-Germans which prevented any friendly and permanent agreement with Germany. Eckardstein reports Rouvier's words: "What is your government's object in persistently pursuing this aggressive course in Morocco? I admit that we may have made mistakes on our side and I and my colleagues are ready to make good any breaches of the Madrid Convention unwittingly committed, by open and direct exchanges of views between both governments. But your government does not appear to desire such an exchange of views."

Rouvier strongly urged a direct agreement, instead of referring the entire matter to an international conference. In his conversation with Eckardstein, Bülow insisted on the conference and refused to negotiate directly with France. Germany would enter into discussions with the Sultan alone and did not shrink from any possible consequences of her decision. Eckardstein warned Bülow that nothing would be achieved by an international conference which would only "advertise our isolation to the world." Bülow insisted that, on the contrary, France and England would be completely isolated. Finally Eckardstein said that, in the event of war, England would help France with all the resources at her command. Bülow replied with a smile, "You will never convince me of that."

By such blind mischief-makers, the German nation was driven to disaster. Everything fell out as Eckardstein had foretold. France accepted the Conference, and the Conference in all essentials upheld the French point of view. Germany recognized her isolation and refrained from direct dealings with the Sultan. A later discussion with France confirmed the *modus vivendi* in Morocco.

That the Agadir episode did not result in war was due to the fact that England suddenly intervened and took up a firm attitude, to the surprise of Germany; the Kaiser informed his Foreign Office that he wished the entire episode brought to an end as quickly as possible. Germany received by way of compensation a piece of territory in Central Africa. For a trifle, Europe had been kept for years in a state of tension and under the threat of war. Professor Haller was right when he wrote in the *Sueddeutscher Monatsheften* in January 1917, that is to say, in the middle of the War: "The political situation which produced the war was the work of the Bülow era. The war is the fruit of the encirclement policy and the encirclement policy was the answer to Prince Bülow's policy." The truth could not have been stated more clearly.

The Morocco episode is, indeed, of decisive importance for the question of war-guilt. It expressed an attitude which must inevitably produce the catastrophe at some place and time. And we must add: Whatever the responsibility of Germany's rulers, the position was not as it has always been represented since the War and as Wilson assumed it to be. A peaceful people was not dragged to the slaughterhouse by lunatic leaders. On the contrary, a people which had become bellicose demanded a bellicose policy from its rulers. Not, indeed, the simple peasantry and workers. But almost everyone of a higher social standing than they; that is to say, all the educated classes had been infected by militarism, and extensive circles demanded in loud and threatening language even far more than the diplomats, who were after all in contact with foreign countries, could approve. Those, therefore, who through the press and other forms of propaganda imbued the German people with these lunatic ambitions were far guiltier than their rulers.

DELCASSÉ WAS PERFECTLY RIGHT

Did the French statesmen in this affair apply the right treatment to the attitude displayed by Germany? I reply frankly: in handling the Morocco question Delcassé, denounced as a warmonger, was the only French statesman who met the attitude represented by Bülow as it should have been met. And if Lloyd George had not finally spoken with the right accent instead of talking like Rouvier, the Agadir episode would undoubtedly have led to war. Rouvier mistakenly believed that he could preserve peace and induce Germany to behave with moderation by letting it be known in Berlin that France desired peace at any price. When Lord Lansdowne on behalf of the British government offered an Entente so close that it practically amounted to an alliance, Rouvier feared that Germany would regard it as a *casus belli* and impressed upon Delcassé that he must be extremely reserved in his negotiations with Lord Lansdowne. "Surtout ne vous concertez pas."

The radical misunderstanding of German psychology which lay behind this timidity is traditional in certain humane and pacifist French circles and is not yet extinct. France escaped war in 1911 only because Lloyd George spoke the language which should have been used in 1914. France failed to escape war in 1914 because in 1905 Rouvier had not grasped the proffered hand and from mistaken fear of German threats left the Franco-British Entente so loose that Germany could believe that Britain would remain neutral. Rouvier did not dare to act decisively because, as a result of the wave of pacifism which swept over the country after the Dreyfus case, France did not feel prepared to face a German attack. That is to say, a false pacifism on the French side which took no account of realities fatally fostered and strengthened German bellicosity and gave rise to the misleading expectations entertained by the German warmongers that France would never make a firm stand—even in 1914. When you have to deal with an opponent who interprets generosity and a conciliatory spirit as fear and weakness and who understands no other language than armed force, you must either talk to him in that language or surrender and yield everything he asks. In such a position retreat will always produce war.

CHAPTER X

THE CONFLICT BETWEEN ENGLAND AND GERMANY

WAS BRITISH COMMERCIAL RIVALRY A CAUSE OF WAR?

THE motives which determined British policy during the twenty years preceding the war of 1914 can be understood only if we have grasped the social and moral character of the British principle of free trade as it permeated the entire British outlook and if at the same time we can justly appreciate the nature and basis of the British Empire, as was done by Moritz Arndt for example in his *Versuch einer vergleichenden Voelkergeschichte*. Only such an insight into the British outlook and its historical achievement gives us the clue with which we can make our way through the maze of detailed events and place every detail in its right setting and in its relationship to the whole.

Something must now be said of the belief widespread in Germany that British commercial rivalry inspired the so-called encirclement and brought England into the War. The belief can indeed claim the support of isolated utterances and views entertained and expressed by the representatives of particular British industries threatened by German competition. It can also appeal to the fact that during the grave slump which hit British trade in the middle nineties the nation suffered from an attack of panic. It was only natural that Britain, which until the end of the seventies had been the world's workshop, should have been faced with a crisis in consequence of the increasing competition of Germany and other manufacturing countries of the Continent, and that as a result a section of public opinion was converted to protection and imperialism. The German propaganda of anti-British lies has cleverly contrived to exploit statistics belonging to this period of crisis, while concealing the brilliant expansion of Anglo-German commerce which followed it.

A decrease of British exports at that time signified merely that British economy, whose principle was free trade and a division of labor between nations, sought to adapt itself to the economic development of Germany by withdrawing capital from businesses incapable of meeting foreign competition. England now began to develop pre-eminently her mercantile marine and became the world's carrier. The number of vessels built and the tonnage of her mercantile marine far outstripped those of Germany. Hence, in spite of the fact that German competition reduced particular British exports, British commercial prosperity increased. Indeed it could not have been otherwise. It is an inherent law of world trade that every nation is at once the customer and the purveyor of the rest and cannot therefore be damaged by the commercial prosperity of other nations. In this sense Lord Farrar argued in an article in the *Contemporary Review* "Does trade follow the flag?" that those who could not learn the truth of the Sermon on the Mount from the Gospel could learn it by studying the laws of international trade. He addressed his argument to the tariff reformers then in office. But even they were far-sighted enough to offer Germany a commercial alliance.

How was it then that in spite of all these fears the former ironmaster Joseph Chamberlain, who led the tariff reformers at the close of the century, became Germany's friend and made her an offer of collaboration whose sincerity and importance, as the German diplomat Hamann wrote in his memoirs, were unfortunately not grasped by the ruling classes of Germany until it was far too late?

This speedy accommodation to the German competition which had at first presented such a threatening aspect is easily explained by the fact that the far-seeing Englishman had soon realized that the losses to British trade due to German competition were compensated three times over by the increasing prosperity of the manufacturing countries which provided fresh markets for goods, a fact soon brought home to Englishmen by the fantastic rise in their exports. That is the reason why Chamberlain's tariff policy was so soon defeated.

A man with expert knowledge of the commercial situation, the German consul Kiliani, has pointed out (*Neue Zuercher Zeitung. 1919*) "The alleged economic defeat of England by German competition and the German threat to her trade must take their place among exploded myths. The great boom in British trade which set in with the year 1900 makes nonsense of the talk of its defeat. In reality England was never more wealthy, and never produced more goods than in the year before the War. And as regards Neptune's trident—the increase in British tonnage between 1891 and 1900 and again between 1905 and 1908 was more than double that of the German increase. The increase in the number of vessels built in British dockyards was more than three times the increase of German vessels built and twice the total number of German steamers built."

Knowledge of these facts was not confined to a handful of statisticians. For a decade before the War all Englishmen possessing any measure of education were acquainted with them and they were contested by nobody.

Had the English really desired to destroy their German competitors, they had long possessed a much simpler weapon for this purpose than arranging a World War. They had merely to restrict the hospitality hitherto freely accorded to their German rivals. Far from this, German traders, in spite of the irritation aroused in wide circles of

British industry by the practice of dumping, were on precisely the same footing as British subjects. British coaling-stations were at the free service of the German merchant service and navy. Indeed special German dumps were permitted there so that German vessels could everywhere be supplied by German firms. Until August 1914 a German trader in Nigeria, at Bombay, Calcutta, Singapore and Hongkong could carry on his business under the same conditions as a British firm. Moreover this freedom was conceded, though England did not enjoy similar rights in the colonies even of friendly powers. What freedom of the seas was then to be fought for?

It was certainly one of the most disgraceful features of the anti-British campaign during the War that no German voice uttered a word of thanks for this generous and, in view of certain German practices, extremely long-suffering hospitality accorded by the British Empire, though, in fact, *modern Germany had earned the greater part of its wealth on the back of the British Empire*. It was only in the Swiss *Neue Zeurcher Zeitung* that Herr Said-Ruete reviewing Rohrbach's *Der deutsche Gedanke in der Welt* wrote the following salutary reminder: "German trade has indeed thriven best hitherto in countries under the British flag where the British had made great sacrifices of blood and money so that the German merchant might then come along with his walking-stick in hand and find— as indeed for the most part he gratefully admitted—a profitable field for his expert knowledge and industry in which he quickly achieved a level of prosperity he could not have attained at home."

We have only to think of the splendid opening which the order and security established by Britain in Egypt provided for German industry. German labor had a large share in providing the materials and the plant required for constructing the huge dam at Assuan and the harbor at Suakim, not to speak of the German locomotives purchased for the Kenneh-Assuan railway and the network of small lines laid down in the Eastern Delta. A German sat on the committee of Governors of the Egyptian National Bank. The German Orient Bank was established with many branches. A German mortgage bank invested German capital. A German firm of cotton manufacturers had an extensive market in Alexandria. German capital was invested in Nile steamers and in coal dumps. German firms of worldwide repute made large profits in Egypt. In Melbourne twenty years earlier one German firm of wool exporters had existed alongside four British firms. Now the proportion had been reversed. Yet, as the head of one of these German firms told me, the victorious Germans had not been exposed to the least unpleasantness or underhand intrigues as a result.

In these matters the Englishman took generous and wide views. His free trade philosophy told him: "Treat the foreigner everywhere better than ourselves. Give him a free hand. We shall profit by it in the end". And he was convinced that the artificial protection of national industry must prove detrimental. He believed that if British industry was to be healthy, the Englishman should be forced by foreign competition to confine himself to those spheres of industry and commerce in which his traditions and national endowments assure him supremacy. Where such an attitude prevails it is impossible to be jealous of the success of another nation. And even if such jealousy made a temporary appearance in isolated circles specially hit by competition, it did not, as the continuation of British hospitality conclusively proved, influence the dominant spirit of British economics and British commercial policy.

We should read in this connection what the Hamburg merchant Hagenbeck in his pamphlet *My flight from Ceylon* relates of the consideration and trust with which he was treated until the outbreak of war. Although not naturalized he was actually made a British official. This is not the treatment accorded to the pioneers of a nation against which one is preparing a war of extermination. If in the years immediately before the War, in many places a feeling of animosity against the Germans was growing up, the "Honorable German merchant" was well aware of the malpractices of newly arrived or shady German firms which provoked it. And many of the Honorable German firms recognized that the new German policy of power and prestige, with its speeches and threats often positively idiotic, must gradually excite suspicion of the legitimate growth of German trade. When in 1913 in the course of a lecture at Basle the Pan-German Admiral von Breusing said, "We have not yet got to the point at which we can take colonies from England," it is not surprising that wide circles of such a great and proud people as the British were angered and disturbed by such alarming declarations and began to reconsider their hospitality. When General von Bernhardi publicly advised that Germany should pick a colonial quarrel with England or France in order to seize the supremacy she coveted, such a program, avowed so shamelessly, naturally provoked hostile comment and made the English look around for guarantees of security.

Even after the War the City, the center of British trade and finance, persisted in the same tolerant attitude. In every respect those circles have encouraged Germany's economic and commercial recovery and fostered it by credits. The *Times*, the chief organ of British commerce, adopted after the War an attitude of avowed friendship towards Germany. Such things are a clear proof that England had not gone to war from commercial jealousy of a German rival. In that case every possible obstacle would have been put in the way of German recovery.

But even if we assumed that the majority of British trader industrialists and merchants were animated by commercial jealousy of the Germans, the simple and undeniable fact would remain that after Joseph Chamberlain's fall one pacifist Cabinet succeeded another, a fact which commercial-jealousy propagandists cannot deny. Again, the *entente cordiale* with France was not concluded until Germany had refused several offers of alliance and until the German attitude at the Hague Conferences and the threats just mentioned against the British Colonial Empire together with the German naval armament, had produced their effect. But how remote this defensive entente, concluded in view of an eventual German attack, was from any purpose of injuring Germany or depriving her of any possession is most clearly proved by the fact, that, as late as the year before the War, England was ready to consent to such a large increase in Germany's Central African Empire and to treat her so liberally in the matter of the Bagdad railway that even Helfferich in his memoirs expresses his astonishment at the lengths she was prepared to go in making concessions.

THE GERMAN NAVY AND BRITISH SECURITY

Is a greater provocation of English feeling conceivable than the telegram sent by the Kaiser to the Czar: "The Admiral of the Atlantic greets the Admiral of the Pacific"? Even our hurried program of naval construction would have been tolerated, had not repeated threats given it such a sinister interpretation. This brings me to the real cause of the estrangement between England and Germany. The conflict between the two nations inevitably grew more exacerbated and finally issued in war, not because the English ruling classes were lacking in political and economic sense and failed to understand the needs of Germany's expanding industry, refusing it the necessary scope and colonial support, but because the ruling circles in Germany did not possess the understanding to reach an agreement with powers longer in the field and the tact to win their confidence. It was a period when the German merchant was piling up wealth with truly gigantic success as a guest of the British Empire. It was, then, of the first importance to build up German and British cooperation in a spirit of trust based on a mutual recognition of rights and fairplay, and on the foundation of such a tested and morally secure community of interests to improve Germany's position in the world. This was the moment when in Germany even groups by no means Pan-German began publicly to speak and write as though our foreign policy should aim at making England compliant by threatening those points of her Empire where she was most sensitive and nervous.

A typical example of this kind of political thought or rather of the complete abdication of thought in favor of the most deplorable infantilism is the following utterance of the notorious Dr. P. Rohrbach: "It is our interest to preserve in Anatolia an independent power which will enable us to put pressure upon Great Britain at the most sensitive spot in her Empire, the frontiers of India and Egypt. If we fail to find a point from which we can threaten the vital interests of Britain we shall be placed in a position of permanent disadvantage in dealing with her." The Apostles of German hegemony spoke and wrote in this strain, and then they were astonished when finally the world they threatened sought to secure itself by a mighty coalition. The German aim in foreign politics was not to reach a broad understanding with British interests. On the contrary, these interests must be threatened, when and wherever they were vulnerable. In view of such a policy it is indeed surprising that on the eve of the War England was prepared to make extensive concessions to our Bagdad scheme.

In harmony with this attitude and with these threats was the noisy propaganda for a large navy and the rate, far in excess of our genuine needs, at which the navy was in fact increased under Tirpitz. England had good cause to

fear that this fleet would one day be employed to carry
out the designs so loudly proclaimed. The situation produced by this naval program and the bullying threats and
hostile agitation which accompanied it were described
with exceptional clarity and objectivity by Lord Haldane
in *Land and Water* (October 1919).

Reviewing the memoirs of Bethmann-Hollweg and von
Tirpitz, he showed that England's hostility to Germany
has been provoked by the threat to a command of the sea
indispensable to her security as an island power. The
growth in foreign navies, he pointed out, compelled England to seek friendly relations with them, and do her best
to eliminate causes of friction. England did not seek military alliances but pursued a policy dictated by commercial
considerations—and therefore aiming at the maintenance
of peace. Though Tirpitz did not actually desire war he
wanted Germany to be sufficiently powerful to subordinate
British interests to her colonial expansion. His method
was a naval program which could not fail to arouse England's instinct for self-preservation. It was this threat which
forced the entente with France and Russia. Otherwise
these countries might have been forced later into the
German orbit and their navies united against England's.
The ententes were therefore the only way in which England could maintain a command of the sea and secure herself against the threat of invasion.

The fundamental mistake of the entire German naval
policy was the complete failure, due to the ambition of
the groups which sponsored it, to grasp the real position of
Great Britain and therefore to respect sensibilities bound
up with the very life of an island state. Germany's principal frontiers are land frontiers, England's are the sea. In
Sir John Seeley's words (*The Expansion of England*) the
British Empire is "a Venice which embraces the globe,
whose streets are the sea." Germany derives her subsistence
to a large extent from her own soil and from overland

imports. Great Britain would starve if she lost command
of the seas. Therefore, as Sir Edward Grey said in Parliament on March 29, 1909, there can be no comparison between the importance for Germany of a navy and the
importance for England. A strong navy would enhance
German prestige, and increase her diplomatic influence
and her power to protect her commerce. But it was not
vital to her, a vital necessity to secure her food as it is for
England. Already Germany possessed the strongest army
in the world. If we would judge justly the misgivings
aroused by her ambitious naval program we must ask ourselves what would have been the feelings and thoughts of
the Continental powers had Great Britain, which already
possessed the strongest navy, begun to form a huge standing army comparable to Germany's.

Haldane pertinently observed, in the article above mentioned, "Von Tirpitz's school would not be satisfied so
long as it could not dominate British sea-power. It would
have accepted a two to three standard, for it would have
sufficed to put Germany in our place, with allies, and
disrupt the Entente. But it was a matter of life and death
for us that Germany should not achieve this ambition.
Otherwise our security against invasion, and our supply
of foodstuffs and raw materials would have been endangered. Had Germany been friendly, or had a League of
Nations been in existence, such a position might not have
produced such fatal results. But the policy of the school
to which von Tirpitz and the Kaiser belonged made the
situation increasingly dangerous and the Entente indispensable."

In the second volume of his Reminiscences, Freiherr
von Eckardstein quotes the following remark of the Austrian Admiral von Spaun à propos of the Kaiser's notorious speeches and telegrams insisting upon the unlimited
expansion of German naval power. "I do not regard your
Emperor's utterances as wise. He will end by arousing

the suspicions of Great Britain and will drive her into the arms of France and Russia. If Germany seriously attempts to build a navy equal to the British, it will prove disastrous to her. A country in the geographical position of Germany cannot afford to make England her enemy." This was indeed the opinion of all those competent to judge. But the modern German megalomania seemed to lie under a curse compelling it to follow the path of suicide.

That Bülow's policy was that of a gambler out of touch with reality is sufficiently shown by the fact that in a speech on November 14, 1906, he thought he could dismiss the entire problem, grave as it was, in the following terms. "Why should not we have as much right to build men-of-war as the Italians, Russians, Japanese, Americans, or French, or even the English themselves?"

Certainly Germany had a right to build as many warships as she wished. But in that case she must be prepared to reckon with the permanent and dangerous enmity of Great Britain on top of all the other enmities she had incurred. For, as we have seen, in view of the international situation England was obliged to secure her imports by a navy superior to that of any other power. The German naval program, which could be directed only against England, forced upon her such an intolerable increase in her naval expenditure that public opinion was becoming more and more clamorous against such a state of affairs, and finally on the failure of every attempt to reach an agreement shortly after the second Hague Conference made inevitable the "encirclement" of Germany.

Despite the blind folly of German policy the desire for a friendly solution of the conflict remained strong in influential British circles, and between 1899 and 1912 one attempt after another had been made to reach an agreement. Their importance and sincerity was fatally misunderstood in Germany. This misunderstanding was inevitable, since the Prussian mind is incapable of grasping what an agreement really means. To the Prussian an agreement means surrender to foreign interests, a restraint placed upon one's ambition by a compact with the foreigner. The modern German, educated in the school of Treitschke, desired and hoped to gain his ends without such interference. This is the outlook Treitschke had instilled into him. If our empire has the courage to pursue energetically an independent colonial policy, a clash between our interests and England's is unavoidable. It is natural and logical that the appearance of a new Great Power in Middle Europe should involve a settlement with all the other Great Powers. We have already settled accords with Austria-Hungary, France and Russia. *The final settlement, the settlement with England, will prove the longest and most difficult.*

The European nations, challenged and frightened by such a program as this naturally did not allow it to develop freely. Not to have realized this was the miscalculation of this Treitschkian school. It was also the miscalculation of those who behind the scenes supported the policy of Modern Germany when they worked against a "premature" understanding with England and believed that such an agreement would unduly hamper the development of our national strength. Nobody dreamed that this policy of unrestrained ambition at the expense of the rest of Europe would provoke a worldwide coalition against Germany and thus hoist her with her own petard. Therefore, the last attempt to reach an understanding, made in 1912, was doomed to failure. When Jagow says that though in his opinion Grey sincerely desired peace he "had allowed himself to be too deeply entangled in the net of Franco-Russian policy" he quite forgets that it was Germany's consistent policy that drove England into that net—for the Entente had become her sole remaining security against the danger of starvation. Had Germany desired to prevent British intervention in a continental war, her policy should not have compelled England to seek the protection of the hostile group of powers which of course involved her in the corresponding liability to come to their assistance.

Lord Haldane, who in 1912 returned from Berlin sorrowful and full of foreboding, convinced that the Prussian army leaders were preparing to put the fate of the world to the test, has left us in his book *Before the War* (1920) a most exact description of the mentality which prevailed among those who really ruled in Berlin, namely the General Staff. Behind the scenes the General Staff not only decided German policy but decided by repercussion the policy adopted abroad to meet it. In England, for example, the government, it was felt, must shape its policy in view of Tirpitz's plans rather than in view of the declarations of prominent German statesmen; not because the latter were regarded as liars, but because it was fully realized that in the last result the Kaiser's military advisers made all the important political decisions. In everything he says Haldane makes it clear that the impotence of the German statesmen in face of the army was due to the fact that the civilians themselves at bottom thought as soldiers and at best had no clear conception of the motive and indispensable conditions of a peaceable international agreement.

We must not forget that every British cabinet, even when the German naval threats had begun, was bent on peace and even restrained the growing irritation of the British public at German naval competition. I need only call attention to the breadth of view displayed by British statesmanship. On the one hand they effected a complete understanding with France and Russia as security against Germany's triple alliance; and on the other hand at the Balkan conference they showed such readiness to meet the German and Austrian case that the British representative won the confidence of his German and Austrian colleagues. Moreover they ventured to make most important concessions to Germany, not only in Africa, but in the matter of the Bagdad railway in spite of the threatening German propaganda. In the event of war these concessions might cost England dear, since the route thus yielded was the speediest route by which to transport troops to the Suez Canal and India. Such considerations, however, were subordinate to the desire to promote appeasement by a practical example.

This pacifist policy was by no means inspired by an abstract idealism. It was an application of the federal principle which had been followed in the British treatment of the Boers. It was not simply a precept of the specific morality "of the industrial society" described in Herbert Spencer's sociology. It was also dictated by self-interest in view of the fact that British statesmen were compelled by the rapid growth of foreign navies and the incalculable development of the art of war to secure their sea-routes by more effective and more permanent methods than the British naval control of the seas. From this point of view the enormous importance attached by British policy to the success of the Hague initiatives is most intelligible. At the first Hague Conference England produced detailed proposals for a permanent Court of International Arbitration. Germany secured their rejection. At the second Conference England proposed a comprehensive discussion of the armaments question. Germany threatened that if it took place she would not be represented at the Conference. Sir Edward Grey was not daunted by these failures. He continued to attempt to preserve world peace by far-reaching agreements concluded in individual cases.

An example of this policy was his attempt to solve the problem of the Balkans. Even von Tirpitz is obliged to recognize this attitude on the part of Britain. He admits that a year before the War the so-called encirclement did not constitute a serious danger to Germany. And he is well aware of the degree to which Britain was prepared to meet

Germany. But surprisingly he ascribes it to England's fear
of the German navy. He had always said, he tells us, that
only strong action would make any impression on the
British. In itself this is true. But it is absolutely false if it
is taken to mean that the British will give way when the
foundations of their national existence are attacked. Strong
action impresses the British only when it is inspired by a
vital need which their practical good sense shows to be
well founded. But as soon as they are confronted with
lawless pride and the demand to give place to someone
else, they are the very last people in the world to be impressed by it. On the contrary, all the toughness, prudence
and firmness of a race tried in a stern school of conflict
come into play and they carry on the struggle to the
bitter end.

What did Tirpitz's armaments avail then? Was he not
proved to have made a thorough miscalculation? He now
tries to put the blame on others. But a sound estimate of
the political and military situation should have shown him
the risk of trusting solely to armed force and terror and
how much more advantageous it would have been to come
to a timely agreement with foreign powers and set bounds
to ambition. But the Prussian mind was incapable of
seeing it. And this precisely has been the tragedy of
modern Germany—that the limited outlook of Prussian
Junkerdom, which had no understanding of the outside
world and could not estimate the vital interests of other
nations or their resources and to which the conception of
peaceful agreement was incomprehensible, was now called
upon to conduct a worldwide policy and pit its Prussian
way of handling men against a superior political experience, thereby incurring the anger and scorn of the entire
world. Moreover the British foe with whom Prussianism
collided stood fundamentally for the old Teutonic freedom which had found an asylum in Great Britain.

THE TURNING-POINT IN THE RELATIONS BETWEEN GERMANY AND BRITAIN

Spender, in his *Reminiscences*, speaking of the conclusion of the entente with France, expresses the view that the turning-point of British policy was the necessity of meeting the threat of the German naval expansion by transferring the British Mediterranean fleet to the North Sea and making arrangements with France for the protection of the Mediterranean. Germany's naval expansion made it a moral obligation, if not a military necessity, for England to make arrangements to protect the North Coast of France thus left unprotected. England was compelled to assume this responsibility by the pressure of the German naval program. In 1899 an alliance with Germany was in sight. If the Germans had not drawn back at the last moment, history would have taken an entirely different course. Spender's explanation of the entente with France and Russia is of very great interest and plainly shows what fatal consequences for Germany and for the whole of Europe followed from Tirpitz's senseless and unrestricted naval program and from the threatening language of German nationalist circles.

One asks oneself in amazement how the men responsible for Germany's destiny could have misapprehended so completely on four cardinal points the immutable laws which must determine the policy of the Great Powers with whom Germany had chiefly to deal. They could not see (1) that Russia would never tolerate the localization of the Serbian conflict, (2) that under no circumstances would France admit a Germany which immediately exploited economic concessions for political ends in her African colonies, (3) that England would never permit a country that was threatening her with an unrestricted naval program to get a footing in Morocco, and (4) that England's vital interests would not allow her to remain neutral in face of a German attempt to conquer France.

The question arises: Was the first World War due simply to the incapacity of the German leaders to grasp what stared them in the face and what they had been repeatedly told by friends abroad and by their own ambassadors? It is true there is a French saying that nothing is so apt to give us a conception of the infinite as human folly. But when, as in this instance, folly seems to exceed even infinity we cannot help asking: is it likely all these things passed unperceived? Is it not more probable that those German groups responsible for the clash were well aware of all the consequences of Germany's conduct, that they did not avoid them precisely because they needed war to carry out their design, and that they deliberately provoked war—convinced like Bernhardi that war is the sole biological test of strength and that it was high time to bring the actual balance of international power, which was biologically unjustified, into harmony with the real strength of the peoples concerned.

They secured the biological decision they had invited. But they were not convinced by it and they are now repeating the test. They will have their way; but sooner or later they will be thoroughly taught the truth, obvious enough at the first test, that the strongest biological forces in humanity are in the last resort moral and spiritual forces and that these forces will shatter the entire edifice of shame constructed by this modern German and purely animal biology. The great disillusionment which befell those groups arose from their fatal overestimate of themselves and in particular of their power of external organization. It made them judge Russia to be incapable of going to war, treat France as decadent, and regard England as on the decline.

Moreover even those who saw more clearly than their diplomatic agents were deceived about England and did not foresee that she would come to the assistance of France. A conversation bearing on this point, and of the highest historical interest, took place towards the end of July, 1914. Shortly before war was declared the French Ambassador in Berlin, Jules Cambon, called on Jagow.

Cambon began, "May I speak to you as man to man?" Jagow agreed. "Then allow me to tell you that your determination (to go to war) is extremely foolish. You can win nothing and you stand to lose a great deal. France is in a position to put up a much better defense than you imagine. And you may be assured that England will not repeat the serious mistake she made in 1870 and allow us to be defeated. Believe me, I am not talking idly; and you will admit that I am one of the ten Europeans best acquainted with the international situation. I am certain that both material and moral reasons will compel England to intervene and that she will not hesitate to come to our assistance. Have you considered the appalling consequences of the action you contemplate? Alone, with no other ally than an empire rotten to the core, you will face the entire continent."

Jagow looked at Cambon with a slight smile playing on his lips and replied: "You have your sources of information. We have ours and they tell a very different story. We are perfectly certain that England will remain neutral."

There is no doubt that Jagow sincerely believed this— as did Bethmann-Hollweg who, as is well known, was dumbfounded when the British Ambassador informed him of England's decision to join in the War. When he made his notorious remark about the scrap of paper, the guarantee of Belgian neutrality, he still failed to see that the scrap of paper stood for British security on the coast of Flanders.

CHAPTER XI

ALSACE

ALSACE has played an immensely important part in the long conflict between Germany and France. In Goethe's time Alsace was intermediate between the two countries. The Alsatians scarcely knew whether they were German or French. "We are German-Frenchmen", they said. Then came the annexation by Germany, and the Alsatians suddenly made the discovery that among them alone the true Germany survived and that the new Empire was being increasingly degermanized. Their attitude did not pass unnoticed by the French, who thereupon began to hope that one day without a war of revenge Alsace would return to them. They understood that the incorporation of Alsace into Bismarck's Empire had not been the return to the mother country of a German land which had been stolen from her, but the brutal wrench of a piece of the oldest and least corrupted Germany, which has always been in close contact with the West and had linked France with the German world, from its providential union with France, with the result that Europe was more lacerated than before.

This was Gambetta's view when he wrote to a friend: "The man who falsified the Ems telegram will attempt another act of treachery. But our coolness, our self-control, will save us from repeating the mistake of 1870. Bismarck has succeeded in welding a divided and impotent Germany into a mighty, well-disciplined and powerful Empire. He was not so well-advised, either in our interest or in his own,

when he demanded the annexation of Alsace-Lorraine,
and thus planted a seed of death in his own work. In an
epoch of such advanced civilization as our own, peoples
cannot be annexed against their will. A material annexation is never followed by a moral annexation. The Germans have torn the heart out of Europe." The thought of
Europe recurs in Gambetta's letters. He rejects the temptation to disturb the peace of Europe by an abuse of the
principle of nationality. His ideal was to secure the balance of power in Europe by restoring order and justice in
Europe.

Certainly Alsace is German and always has been. When,
as a Prussian student educated in a Prussian Gymnasium,
I walked from Freiburg through this lovely country and
its hills I felt like a man who as a baby had been stolen
by gypsies and now suddenly found his mother. Medieval
Germany greeted me, its free cities and great Christian
art, its open and impartial vision for what lay beyond the
German frontiers, its role as a bridge between the nations;
there came to me the memory of the old German internationalism and its recognition of a common Europe above
national boundaries. At the same time I observed with
astonishment when I stayed with an Alsatian family at the
foot of the Ballen d'Alsace that the purely German people
who had made me conscious of my German inheritance
met with a passive resistance those who came to regermanize them. I could not understand it at the time. Later, during the War, and after it, I understood.

Precisely because Alsace had preserved the ancient German tradition and because the French monarchs had
protected in Alsace the old German liberties which elsewhere had been destroyed by reactionary rulers and militarism, the Alsatians felt a far closer bond with Western
civilization than with the spiritual and political Germany
which had arisen from the ashes of the Thirty Years
War. Their sense of this bond found expression in the

unanimous protest of the Alsatian deputies against the annexation of 1871. After the Franco-German war, when a degermanized Germany undertook to regermanize Alsace and in the shape of a noisy Prussia fell upon the country to colonize it for fifty years, only to treat it after fruitless attempts as "a people whom it is impossible to trust", the blindest must see clearly that Alsace had remained genuinely German.

Thus the devotion of the Alsatians to France was in fact the proof that they had retained stubbornly the old Germanism which had been the instrument of European union and had always sought and found in the French genius the necessary complement of its German character.

THE RELATIONS BETWEEN FRANCE AND GERMAN ALSACE

Immediately after the declaration of war, the French paper *Illustration* published a large cartoon in which an advancing French officer was shown stretching out his arms to embrace an Alsatian girl. That is to say, while the fire of hate between France and Germany was blazing most fiercely a Frenchman embraced a German. The French regarded as their first and most inspiring war-aim the reunion of Alsace, a purely German people, with France. The cartoon brought home to me, more clearly than ever before, that between France and Germany there exists an invisible political Eros which for centuries has been an active historical factor and whose theatre of operations was Alsace. In a lecture delivered in Berlin shortly before the war Boutreux said that the French and German characters were not antipathetic but complementary; he explained the psychological cause of this political Eros operative between the two peoples. It was and is an incomparable disaster that these two complementary peoples should ever and again be torn asunder by lamentable misunderstanding and tragic historical conflicts.

Even after the war of 1870, a peace like that of Nikols-

burg would have made possible a speedy reconciliation
with France. To conclude such a peace would have been
the work of a statesmanship far greater both from the
foreign and the domestic point of view than the petty
practical statecraft of the following decades. That petty
statecraft was at bottom nothing but skillful gambling
with small resources to cover up a portentous blunder and
temporarily to allay or postpone the results it had produced in all directions. The re-annexation of Alsace-
Lorraine created a Europe from which the conflagration
of a World War must inevitably burst forth.

To wrench the passionately democratic Alsatians from
an organic union into which they had grown for two
centuries and to disregard their loud and despairing protest against the separation, displayed a political outlook
to which the rest of the world could not reconcile itself
—the more so, because this policy of the mailed fist became
the regular policy of Germany and gave fresh offense on
every new occasion of conflict between Germany and the
rest of the world. It was no accident that the Zabern affair
proved the storm signal of the coming war. The brutal
and stupid behavior of the military and the retreat of
public opinion after a brief protest was a warning: "We
have learned nothing. We have no point of contact with
the views, the outlook, and the needs of the world around
us. We challenge the entire world; come on and receive
a good hiding."

We must not forget that the bond between Alsace and
France was already so close at the epoch of the Reformation that influential circles in Strasbourg maintained that
Alsace was intellectually part of France; and the leaders
of the humanist movement came to a large extent from
Paris. The Thirty Years War and the condition it left
behind did much to alienate Alsace from the Empire.
Habsburg rule was so unpopular that on more than one
occasion the Alsatian cities asked Richelieu to make them

part of France. France had contrived with brilliant success to win the German heart of Alsace—not least because the French kings most carefully preserved the old German liberties which in the Empire had been destroyed by the establishment of the territorial autocracies. Colbert advised Louis XIV to govern his newly acquired province so that the inhabitants would be better off than in any other German territory.

Every French government has followed Colbert's advice. "Il ne faut pas toucher aux affaires d'Alsace" was the motto. The old families were left in authority, and only one Intendant was appointed to act as a link between the provincial government and the entire nation. Alsace kept its individual culture. None could detect in Goethe's description of the parsonage at Sesenheim the least discontent with the existing state of affairs or the least desire to return to the Empire. In 1828 the President of the Colmar Court of Appeal said to Charles X, "Our beautiful province after centuries of devastation is indebted to your royal house for more than a century and a half of prosperity and peace."

But it was the French Revolution that completed this conquest by French culture of the Alsatian people, deep in whose veins ran the strong old German love of freedom. It combined German idealism and the old urban democracy with the new ideals of human liberty. Nothing has severed German Alsace from the Empire and turned its history into wholly different channels more deeply than the domination of the world of thought by the French Revolution.

It would therefore have hardly been possible to devise a more painful martyrdom for the Alsatians than to place them under the heel of Prussian officials and officers. They would not have been genuine Germans had they permitted the splendid organization and economic progress achieved by the German government to reconcile them to

such a violation of their sentiments and thought. Hence
the separation of the Alsatian people from France was
incomparably more painful for both parties than the
separation of Alsace from the old Empire had been. Moreover the fact that the step was taken without the consent
of the population concerned was a sore outrage to the
democratic feeling of the Alsatians.

Citizens of the German Empire who have no intimate
acquaintance with conditions in Alsace can have no notion
of the strength of the tie which bound her to France, how
extensive had been the intermarriage between the Alsatians and the French particularly in the nineteenth century, and how closely after the Revolution the epoch-
making events of the Napoleonic era, with the bond they
created between Alsace and the French army, had linked
the entire country with the destiny of France. In 1854
L. Spach called Alsace "la province je ne dirai pas la
plus gauloise, mais la plus patriotique de l'Empire française". Most important of all, France, despite all the jests
about "squareheads," never failed to realize how much
this Teutonic element meant for French culture, the reinforcement it brought of qualities necessary to counter-
balance certain one-sidednesses and dangers of the Gallic
temperament. 1871 destroyed this symbiosis which might
have constituted an irreplaceable foundation for the cultural union of the two peoples. How illuminating in this
connection are the words which Renan wrote to David
Strauss at the time of the Franco-German war and how
unconvincing and ungenerous was the latter's reply.

"Your German fire-eaters," wrote Renan, "argue that
Alsace is a German land unjustly torn from the German
Empire. Remember that nations have always settled their
boundaries in the rough. If we once begin to argue in this
way about the racial composition of every district, the door
is opened to endless wars. There are five French-speaking
regions which are no part of France. And this is beneficial

to France herself. Slavonic territories belong to Prussia. These irregularities serve civilization. For example, the union of Alsace with France has enormously assisted the spread of German culture. Alsace is the gate through which German ideas, methods, and books normally reach us. And it is beyond dispute that if they were consulted, an overwhelming majority of the Alsatians would choose to remain French."

ALSACE AFTER THE WAR

The reintegration of Alsace into the French Republic was not indeed accomplished without difficulties. *La France laique* clashed with a deep-rooted Catholic tradition. Parisian centralization came into conflict with local privileges centuries old. The Alsatians were justified in opposing legislation which endangered their dearest tradition. Unfortunately this critical moment was abused, by elements strongly imbued with the modern German outlook through their education at school and at the university, to organize a movement of propaganda for Alsatian autonomy which could only weaken the position of those Alsatians who were fighting for their native traditions. The significance of Alsatian traditionalism was perilously perverted when its defense was made a weapon of German propaganda against France. Those groups of Alsatian Catholics were doing a poor service to the Catholic cause who, in their intelligible annoyance with the over-hasty policy in respect of language and education pursued by their new rulers who had not yet made contact with the distinctive Alsatian character, more or less made this German propaganda their own and supported its one-sided attitude instead of taking up an unambiguous and independent position.

The mistakes made by those Alsatian Catholics were due to the fact that the older generation concerned knew only the France which had expelled the religious orders, and had no inkling of the serious and profound religion of Catholic France. Nor did they perceive that even secular France had preserved more of the humane Catholic tradition and more of the Latin spirit than many German Catholic circles infected by Prussianism. Like their German brethren, the Alsatian Catholics were blind to the diabolism of the Prussian spirit, could not see it as a violent force disrupting the entire civilized order, and could not comprehend that this unknown Germany, whose nature was not fully unmasked till Hitler's advent, is thrice as dangerous to the Catholic tradition as *la France laique*. Moreover we have only to wander through Alsace and talk to the people to discover that the humanity and freedom of French rule are far more congenial to the Alsatian than the modern German drill.

In my opinion nothing could better express the true, natural, and historical relationship between Alsace and France than the words addressed to Poincaré when he visited Alsace by the *doyen* of the Alsatian burgomasters, Nicholas Kieffer of Ittenweiler:

"Permit me as the doyen of the burgomasters of the Lower Rhine, an old man whose best years were passed before 1870 and who has represented his fellow-citizens for forty years, to express the joy and gratitude he feels at your presence in our midst. It is the true and loyal Alsace that speaks by my mouth, the true Alsace whose heart has never changed.

"My little village lies in the heart of the province among the vineyards on the road from Koenigsburg to St. Odile. Your name, M. le Président, is on the lips of all its inhabitants. For we know your sincere love of peace and justice and that you are working for our happiness. It is France that we honor and love in you, France that no one shall assail, France our mother. May this fact be understood everywhere. And equally dear to us are our vineyards, the woods which clothe our hills, our soil which we cultivate by the sweat of our brow, and our freedom purchased so dearly.

"Today you have once more defended it and once again served our fatherland.

"For yesterday and today, M. le Président, we thank you on behalf of hard-working Alsace. Vive la France."

What an international tragedy is contained in the short account I have given of the part played by the Alsatian question in the great conflict between France and Germany! What light is thrown upon the entire question of war-guilt when the question of Alsace has been understood! This Alsatian question, precisely because it is concerned with a country intermediate between neighboring peoples, divided by bloody war yet made to complete each other, will be solved only when Germany and France are once more reconciled. But this reconciliation is impossible until Germany has recovered her true self and France also has undergone a change of heart and healed the tragic cleavage within her own soul. Then and not till then will Renan's words come true: "When France and Germany are reconciled, the sundered halves of the human soul will be reunited".

CHAPTER XII

THE MODERN GERMAN CULT OF WAR

W E HAVE studied hitherto the conflicts which produced the first World War. "All that passes is but a
parable." And all these conflicts are parables which reveal in turn the attitude and the determination which
stood behind them and gave them birth. The publication
of official documents cannot by itself answer the question
of war-guilt, the less so because many of those documents
are deliberate blinds intended to conceal a particular attitude and tendency.

The collection of German papers covering the period
up to the Morocco crisis seems at first sight favorable to
German innocence. No warlike intentions find expression
in them. But the picture is totally changed when we study
the political literature published between 1894 and 1905
or between 1905 and 1914. For it shows how the German
people were slowly poisoned by a virus deliberately administered to them by the wide circle of soldiers, heavy
industrialists, financiers, and Pan-German publicists. These
men devised the program of a German bloc in Europe,
thought out all it involved, and exploited every conflict
with other European powers in order to work up popular
feeling and create a public opinion which again and again
forced upon German statesmen a mode of action which
their knowledge of the facts condemned as impracticable
and mischievous. I invite you to ponder carefully the
following confessions and to ask yourself whether such
programs would have been publicly put forward in other
countries.

In the May number of the *Prussischen Jahrbuecher*

for 1896, R. Martin, an official of the Foreign Office, published an article, entitled "Mehr Lohn und mehr Geschuetze," in which he wrote: "The entire situation invites the German people to war, the great father of all good. In my opinion the greatest benefit we derive from the annexation of Alsace-Lorraine is that France can never be reconciled to it and Germany therefore for years to come must be armed to the teeth. A nation of fighters is never conquered." The publication of such a reckless article in an official organ could only make us disliked and distrusted abroad. And such a confession was far from being unique.

As early as 1896 an editorial in the *Grenzboten* (48) declared that German foreign policy should be governed by the following principles:

"We maintain that when the good of our country requires the annexation, subjection, suppression or destruction of a foreign people, we must not be deterred from it by considerations of Christianity or humanity. Accordingly, we entertain no objection to the utmost use of our military power, provided it will within a reasonable time achieve the end for which it is employed."

It would be difficult to find in the political writings of other nations such a program of shameless gangsterism. No doubt many individuals abroad have held similar views. But they have never dared to express them in an editorial, for they would have met with the severest disapproval from the overwhelming majority of their fellow-countrymen. In Germany the profession of such sentiments could unfortunately count upon hearty support from the ruling classes, from the industrialists, and from all those who held militaristic and nationalist views.

From the middle of the nineties onward men infected by the modern German power-delirium were frequently to be met in the smoking compartments of express trains; with loud and raucous voices they expounded the program of Germany's future world-hegemony and blew away all qualms of conscience or considerations of civilized conduct as lightly as the smoke of the cigarettes they held between their stout fingers. All these people, who had grown up in the intoxicating atmosphere of force triumphant and unscrupulous, could conceive of Germany's position and role only as a constant threat to the interests of foreign nations and as successful attacks upon them. Overnight Germany had become a great power, but had not acquired the political civilization which entertains wide views, reckons with the outside world, understands it and wins its confidence. A Junkerdom of Prussian landlords, allied with the industrialists, supposed in their immoderate ambition that by the most primitive and crudest weapons they could solve the gigantic problem of sharing the world's resources. The growing strength of a people capable of enormous achievement was combined with the narrowest and most reactionary traditions of banditry. When a world, hitherto everywhere friendly, at last became aware of this anarchic mentality, and took up a firm stand against it, those folks could do nothing better than inform their German public that an unadulterated envy of German virtue had suddenly taken up an attitude of hostility and distrust towards our entire policy and achievement. This explanation, of course, gave a further stimulus to aggressive German nationalism. On April 25, 1913, the following appeared in the *Berlin Post*:

"The pressure of the nation's will is forcing us to relinquish the policy of renunciation we have pursued for years and to replace it by a policy which pursues positive aims, a policy which seeks to strengthen our position in Middle Europe, to settle finally with France and England, to enlarge our colonial Empire, to provide new German settlements to receive our superfluous population, to take active steps to protect Germans abroad, to secure naval bases and further to increase our armed strength in proportion to the increase in foreign armaments. These are the tasks to which we must devote our immediate future . . . obviously the danger of war is by no means remote, but on the contrary deeply rooted in the actual situation."

Nor would it be easy to find in any foreign magazine for boys anything like the following extract from the *Jungdeutschlandpost* of January 25, 1913:—

"War is the noblest and the holiest human activity. For us too the joyful and sublime hour of combat will strike . . . yes, it will be a joyful, a sublime hour for which we should be secretly longing. The uttered wish for war is often idle chatter and ludicrous sabre-rattling. But silent and deep in the German heart should live delight in war and longing for war . . . we laugh to scorn those old women in men's trousers who are afraid of war and whine about its cruelty and horrors. No, war is splendid. Its sublimity raises man's heart far above earth and the daily routine."

The *Berlin Post* for January 28, 1912 wrote:

"Who are the men that rank highest in the annals of our nation? Who inspire the warmest affection in German hearts? Such men as Goethe, Schiller, Wagner and Marx? Not those men, but Barbarossa, Frederick the Great, Bluecher, Moltke, Bismarck, the men of blood and iron. These men who sacrificed thousands of lives are the men who arouse the tenderest affection in the hearts of the people and receive from them a gratitude little short of adoration. For they did what we should do in our turn . . . yet our people fail to make the practical application. Everyone knows the entire nation is aware that only in attack lies salvation."

Those abroad who persist in saying "The German people did not want the war" should bear in mind such language as this. There was an extremely influential and powerful section of the German people which desired war with their whole heart and worked for it. By means of verbal and printed propaganda its views obtained an ever more exclusive hold of the educated classes down to the teachers in the elementary schools.

The ruling generation had been prepared by Treitschke and his collaborators to respond to such propaganda. Hermann Bahr tells us that, when he was a student in Berlin, Treitschke in his huge lecture-room was educating an entire generation in the maddest megalomania. He tells us that he left Zeller's peaceful lecture-room and mingled with Treitschke's enormous audience. In the philosopher Zeller he saw that noble type of mind "whose mere presence seemed to vouch for the reality of an invisible world." Treitschke showed him an uprooted and Prussianized Germany at peace neither with herself nor the world outside.

I too as a student had the same experience of Treitschke's lecture-room, left with a shudder, and returned to Zeller's world. And when twenty years later I gave a lecture in Berlin, and in order to refute them, quoted Moltke's words that perpetual peace is a dream and not even a beautiful dream, they were greeted with an outburst of applause even wilder than that with which Treitschke's lectures had been received. At the same time the son of a Belgian colleague of mine was in Berlin. He wrote to his father most alarming accounts of the impression made upon him by the mentality of the nationalists and their dominant influence. From his letters I will quote the following:

"You know the deep affection I have for Germany, and it is most painful to discover how completely I have been deceived about her. By her cult of force, her self-worship and her contempt for all other nations, Germany has become a danger to civilization. Her attitude is barbaric and finds expression in a barbaric art. Formerly a moonlight night could touch a German to tears. Now the Germans are moved only by the titanic, by the application of material force. The inhuman ugliness of all the Bismarck memorials and the statues of Germania can be explained only by the most groveling adoration of brute force. Germany has indeed retained her innate mysticism. But it has fallen from heaven to earth. It is with a mystical love that the contemporary German regards his cannon, his men of war, his machines and his money—everything for him is an instrument of power."

In all "patriotic" circles the young Belgian found Pan-German views. He was constantly told that Flanders must return to the German center of Europe. An older student said to him, "By their nationality and history, the shape of their skulls, and their linguistic derivation, the Flemings belong to the Reich in which the Pan-German ideal demands their inclusion. It may be necessary for us to use a little measure of force before they realize this themselves. But they will discover that a benefit has been conferred upon them. When," the Belgian continues, "my face shows indignation my interlocutor replies with incredible naiveté: 'Why excite yourself? Can't you understand that we need the Netherlands?' "

Obviously Hitler's program is but the final expression and the official sanction of a Pan-Germanism widely spread in those circles which possessed power, wealth and arms and which were the guardians of the national tradition and of what has increasingly become the political philosophy of Germany. Years ago, for example, E. M. Arndt wrote: "Every country whose language is German is German. We must therefore work for the union of all speaking a Teutonic language. For that is the way to achieve the greatness of our dreams. Let us set about it and arouse in all German lands a sense of their common Teutonic nationality. Such a program will of course provoke sooner or later powerful opposition, even produce a European war. We must hope it may not break out before we have prepared the minds of Germans for the realization of our ideal."

The historian Oncken wrote (*Germany or England*),

"The fate Belgium has brought upon herself is hard for individuals, but not too harsh for the Belgian state. For the historic destiny of the immortal great nations is so important that in case of necessity it must overrule the right-to-existence of states which cannot defend themselves." And Friedrich Naumann observed (*The Ideal of Freedom*), "History teaches us that the progress of civilization is possible only if the national independence of small nations is destroyed. History has decided that there shall be ruling nations and subject nations, and it is not easy to be more liberal than history. We must jettison something of the old petit-bourgeois ideal of history, in order to think out consistently and realize the ideal of a scientific civilization. Man has no irrefragable right to be ruled by men of his own nationality."

If a Germany actuated by this spirit is placed after another attack under the tutelage of the rest of Europe, the step could not be better defended than by quoting these last words.

As early as 1859 the *Augsburger Zeitung* declared that it was Germany's duty to conquer Austria. That the majority of Austrian provinces were inhabited by non-German populations mattered nothing. "At all costs the German nation must annex them, for they are essential to our development and greatness."

Masaryk in his *Das Neue Europa* (Berlin 1922) expressed the conviction, based on a personal observation extending over decades, that Prussian militarism and Pan-Germanism share between them the guilt of the War. Pan-Slavism, he points out, did not possess any program of armed aggression and was on the whole defensive in character. Pan-Germanism, on the other hand, was the offspring of the Prussian philosophy of war and of the aggressive export policy of modern Germany, and was inspired by the German dream of world domination and annexations to be effected in every portion of the globe. Masaryk speaks of a veritable "Mathematics of aggression." He was always astonished, he tells us, by the French and English indifference to it. He had warned his own people by articles and lectures of the danger which threatened it and was at work on a larger study of the same question when the War interrupted him. He was convinced that the War was inevitable, since the most powerful military and economic groups in Germany regarded Austria as the bridge to a German domination of the route from Berlin to Bagdad and with that end in view were determined to oust Russia from the Balkans and deliver a blow against the British Empire.

In 1912, General Bernhardi, in his *Deutschland und der naechste Krieg*, advised Germany to "pick a quarrel with England or France in the colonies and thus bring on the inevitable war". And elsewhere: "Our people must be convinced that the preservation of peace never can or ought to be a political aim."

The Vice-President of the Pan-German Union, Freiherr von Gebsattel, declared in 1915: "On three occasions we have advised war: in 1905 against France, in 1911 against France and England, and in 1912 against England, France and Russia together. In 1914 also we desired war, because we regarded it as necessary to save our people from the false path on which it was in danger of entering".

During the war, Class, the President of the Pan-German Union, in a pamphlet entitled *Zum Deutschen Kriegsziele* wrote: "The prize of victory must be determined solely by the needs of our people without regard to the wishes or feelings of the defeated. France, that moribund nation, we can defeat so thoroughly that she will never rise again, and we shall do so. And if fortune favors us, we can reduce England to the position of a harmless island state."

In 1913 war was so close that the warmakers found it advisable to make sure that as many European states as possible would remain neutral and to persuade certain neutrals to throw in their lot with Germany. In November 1913, King Albert visited the Kaiser at Potsdam. Moltke was invited to attend their meeting and heard the Kaiser inform the royal guest that war with France was inevitable, would shortly break out, and would certainly end in the defeat of France. If the small states wished to secure their national existence they would do well to join Germany in good time. King Albert ordered the Belgian Ambassador in Berlin to acquaint the French Ambassador Jules Cambon with this conversation, which so closely concerned the guarantors of Belgian neutrality. Some ten years earlier the Kaiser had made the same proposition to King Albert's father and promised him several French provinces if he would permit the German army to march through Belgium. It was perhaps this fact which made the Western Powers attach less importance to the Kaiser's subsequent démarche than it deserved. For when in the following summer the German army invaded France through Belgium it was evident that the French staff had not seriously reckoned with that possibility.

After all the proofs I have brought of the literally mad infatuation, the romantic dream of world-power, and the unscrupulous militarism that possessed the rulers of Germany, will anyone persist in speaking of the common war-guilt of all the European Powers? Surely everyone must admit that it was Germany that desired war, and the responsibility for a world catastrophe must be sought in Germany's attitude.

Whatever sins the other nations may be guilty of, Germany's sin, which has made her guilty of the murder of fourteen million men and of causing unspeakable suffering and privation, unexampled devastation and boundless economic disorganization, is *the sin of warmaking, of militarism and of the idolatrous adoration of the state and of power*. This sin is the fountain-head of all the mistakes, crimes and blunders of German policy, the supremacy of the army, the deliberate or irresponsible production of situations which must lead to war, the war aims, the prolongation of hostilities, and finally the incapacity to view the catastrophe in the right light and to make good the wrong done. Only those who have a firm grasp of this fundamental fact of contemporary German history can read the documents correctly and thread their way through the complicated maze of forces and events in Central Europe. The truth about the war-guilt may indeed be concealed for a time by the propaganda of falsehood. But it will always reappear in the light of day.

CHAPTER XIII

GERMANY DURING THE FIRST WORLD WAR

GERMAN VIRTUES

IT IS not surprising that the Germans waged the first World War in the same spirit in which they had provoked it. The German conduct of the War displayed once more on the vast theatre on which the forces of the European powers gathered in conflict, on an enormously larger scale and, as it were, lit up by the glare of the conflagration, all the contempt of right and all the anarchic worship of force which had inspired German policy for so many decades. Crimes were committed which cannot be passed over in our indictment of Germany's attitude. For they had momentous historical consequences. The entire history of the postwar period is inexplicable apart from the German behavior in Belgium and Northern France.

Just because the original sin of modern Germany broke out in this catastrophe and revealed its appalling ugliness, it is our duty not to forget the German virtue which also in this unexampled trial showed to the full its great and enduring worth. It was indeed virtue in the service of vice, but virtue none the less, with the hope it brings that hereafter it will devote itself to the service of genuine good. There was in truth a great and extensive Germany which had no responsibility for the War and was completely alien to the spirit which had produced it. Its only share in the War, a perfectly innocent share, consisted perhaps in the defenseless humility and ready obedience with which it permitted itself to be led to the slaughter house with an unshakeable trust in its leaders and their explanations. "We were attacked in the midst of peace."

There is a most expressive German word which enshrines everything that is best in the German character. It is "Schlicht"—simple. It is said of those who never think of themselves, not even of their suffering, sacrifice, loyal service. That human life consists in service, suffering and renunciation they regard as a self-evident fact to be taken for granted. God only knows what all those unimportant people suffered during and after the War from privation, hunger, overwork. They were silent and uncomplaining, with no heroic airs, loyal and true when everything was crashing about them. What infinite bravery and patience there was in their unwavering endurance, year in and year out, in a situation bereft of joy, beneath a dark sky! The sinologist Wilhelm says that the boundless patience and resignation with which the Chinese have borne all the calamities that have afflicted them guarantees a great future for their race. The same can be said of the Germans. When the day of doom overtakes all those degermanized and brutalized elements of the German nation, whose maniacal arrogance has divorced German policy from all the great noble qualities and traditions of the German, then at last this underlying Germany with all its high moral and human endowment will find expression even in the political field.

But we are not concerned here with the moral greatness shown by those simple sufferers but with the actual conduct of the War. That high moral qualities were displayed here also has been chivalrously recognized by Churchill in his memoirs. Who can measure the brave endurance, the devotion to duty, the discipline and the unquestioning surrender of life and health of the Germans who fought through those four years of war against a world in arms, hurled unremittingly from one front to the other, slowly worn down by hunger and the excessive burdens laid upon their strength, attacked by new weapons which their country could no longer provide and disheartened by the inexhaustible American reinforcement of their foes? If the War gave full rein to a centuries-old tradition of ruthless savagery, the Christian spirit of humble sacrifice which had inspired so many generations worked its miracle. There was an inexhaustible moral capital to draw upon, Prussian asceticism, the German effort to do perfectly what is to be done. All this inherited virtue was exercised beneath the heavy barrage of hostile fire, on sentry duty, as men awaited death in the trenches or went over the top. What an indescribable contrast there was between the spiritual forces of Divine origin which here spent themselves with the utmost fidelity to duty and the godless purpose they served!

Pacifists have lacked the freedom of spirit to recognize this nobility in soldiers at war. War must no longer be admitted to possess any nobility. But whatever may be said against war, we must not forget that the extreme tension it produces between life and death has always drawn from man's highest moral endowments a well-nigh superhuman achievement. This is certainly no reason for provoking war or retaining it as a permanent element in human life. No one wants a plague because doctors and nurses are often spurred by it to extraordinary heroism. But we must be just.

In 1864, before storming Duppel's lines, the Prussian General Manstein issued the following order of the day: "I count with complete confidence upon the energy of the soldiers. Grapeshot is no reason for halting or turning back. We take it for granted that our flags will fly above the Danish lines." This is a fine example of military courage. Prussian militarism owes a great deal of its attraction to the fact that it has inspired so much courage, whose brilliance has blinded men to the dark and destructive forces of evil hidden in the background. This attraction can be defeated only by an even greater heroism which goes deeper and embraces every aspect of life. Christian propaganda is to be blamed for so largely failing to see this. We can be wholehearted opponents of a bellicose policy and yet not desire, as the pacifists would like, the martial aspect of history to be omitted in teaching it. For we must not forget that in war the noblest human qualities have been admirably displayed and weak men incited to superhuman needs.

THE GERMAN CONDUCT OF THE WAR

Would it not be better to keep silence about this appalling and discreditable chapter of human history and bury inexcusable crimes in the grave of oblivion? That unfortunately is impossible. The historic fact of the Versailles Treaty is inexplicable apart from the German conduct of the war. And the entire postwar policy of the victors was to a considerable extent influenced by the memory of the crimes committed by the German High Command. Above all, for the German people, of whom the generation educated after the War has been taught only the brilliant successes of the German army, an unsparing account of German war-crimes is indispensable. Otherwise it will be impossible to purge the German soul of the poison which has infected it. We should remember that St. Augustine himself in his *City of God* pillories the historical brigandage of Roman history while recognizing Roman virtues. For it was their combination that explained the Roman Empire. During the war a German general whose conscience had suffered sorely from the crimes he had been compelled to witness observed: "There is no army in the world in which the individual soldier commits fewer excesses than the German—and there is no army in the world in which the High Command is guilty of worse outrages."

Thus the entire responsibility for the German war-crimes rests, not upon the German private, but upon the ruling class. Its members also possess most admirable private virtues. But their personal morality serves a completely immoral principle. In this lies the essence, the strength, the weakness and the curse of modern German militarism. This attitude of mind, this subordination of all other considerations to military advantages, has produced that conception of "military necessity" which is treated as the supreme law overriding every law of God and man. In the end this "necessity" is confronted with other necessities, greater and more powerful, which evoke resistance and counter-attacks, and thus reduce all the brilliant successes achieved by this ruthlessness to hideous defeat.

An article published by Captain W. Meyer describes as follows the systematic devastation of Northern France by the German Army:—

"The label 'Alberichbewegung' covers an appalling reality, nothing less than the deliberate devastation of the entire country between Arras and Soissons till it became literally unrecognizable, the systematic transformation of a lovely and fertile district into a barren and lifeless wilderness. The Alberich movement has enormously increased our unpopularity abroad. We should place ourselves in the position of the inhabitants of this devastated area and enter into their feelings. We shall understand better then many clauses of the Peace Treaty. It was the depth of a severe winter when these people were turned out of their homes. They lost everything, absolutely everything. Moreover, in the deportation many families were inevitably separated, husband from wife, mother from child. When and how were they reunited? They and their possessions were nothing but inanimate factors in the general's strategy. From the standpoint of humanity this Alberich movement was a hideous crime. From the strategical standpoint it was justified. He who wills victory at any cost must also will the necessary means. This is pure logic."

The author forgot that in our times a hideous crime can never be a road to final victory. The reason he has stated himself. The Alberich movement enormously increased our unpopularity abroad. The burning wrath it evoked became an unyielding determination to fight against us and for the first time restored mobility to the enemy, just as it was the Zeppelin raids that led to the introduction of conscription in England. Even apart from this, how can it be wise to wage war without regard to the necessity for international cooperation on the return of peace?

It cannot be too strongly emphasized that the devastations which cost us most dear were not those involved in the actual conduct of the War, though for these also the responsibility lay with those guilty of making the War, but were those deliberate acts of destruction committed partly out of the savage desire to inflict the utmost possible damage upon the enemy's country, partly from the desire of the German industrialists to cripple foreign competition.

The official account persists in affirming that St. Quentin, Cambrai, Douai and other towns were burnt only by the enemy's shell fire. That is untrue. Here as elsewhere the thorough destruction was due to German incendiary bombs and every kind of elaborate device for mining and kindling fires. American and French troops in pursuit of our armies have produced photographic evidence of this. For example, the mine holes in the pillars of St. Quentin cathedral were photographed and the photographs published in the *Revue Hebdomdaire*. It is to the impression left by such spectacles that we owe much of the fearful bitterness which lies behind the Versailles Treaty. Before the German troops left their positions in front of Rheims the entire city for no rational motive was systematically bombed in concentric circles, street by street. When the inhabitants contemplated the mass mounds of wreckage they were at a loss to understand the method employed to accomplish such diabolical destruction.

In proof of the senseless and criminal inundation of the French mines, I quote the following details from a speech of the President of the Civil Engineers of France, E. Gruener, replying to the statements of German engineers:

"About September 1915 our German colleagues systematically destroyed, one after the other, the mines of Courrières and Lievin. It was not enough for them to flood the galleries and make it impossible to restart mining quickly. They flung into the pits every conceivable object, cages, cables, even the corpses of men and animals to infect the water and make it enormously difficult to drain it off. By throwing casks of dynamite into this medley they were confident of causing explosions during the work of salvage. After Lievin they turned their attention to Lens. Every surface installation of whatever nature was methodically blown up, room by room, machine by machine. The business men beyond the Rhine would not be guilty of neglecting to destroy the offices, the plans and accounts, or demolishing completely the thousands of workmen's dwellings. Of the 12,000 houses of Lens and the thousand in the neighboring villages and towns not a stone was left standing.

"The Germans behind the front had been convinced that they could enjoy a permanent conquest. Until the beginning of October 1918 therefore they had continued to work the undamaged mines. Then came the irresistible advance of the Allied armies. Our enemies were not taken unawares. They had made the most minute and careful preparations. On October 6 all the pits owned by the mining companies of the Nord were still working. By October 12 not a single chimney was still standing in any coal mine of the Nord and Pas-de-Calais. Everything had been blown up in these districts where not a single shot had been fired, and some 220 pits were made unworkable for years. Some would require ten years before they could be worked again. The mines were filled with some 60 to 80 cubic metres of water. A production of over 20 million tons, which was increasing at a rate of more than a million tons a year and by 1920 would have exceeded 26 million, possibly even 28 million tons, had been destroyed and certainly cannot be recovered before 1930. A population of 100,000 workers is homeless. Every house has been made uninhabitable when not completely demolished. The material damage done to the coal mines alone exceeds two and a half milliards."

This was the work accomplished during the last weeks of the War without the least military necessity. One is appalled by the infatuation, which during such a debâcle made this attack upon the foundations of the enemy's economic life. It is astounding that, after such outrages, those Germans who are well aware of what they did to their enemies and of how they did it have had the impudence to denounce the peace of revenge and, most surprising of all, that the men who ordered them have never been brought before a German court but are, on the contrary, honored by wide circles as national heroes.

First-lieutenant Whitewell, who was in command of the pioneers attached to the 73rd English division stationed at Cambrai, stated on October 16, 1918 his "conviction that, with a few exceptions all the fires in Cambrai and most of the demolitions were the work of the enemy done out of pure spite. The fires are almost wholly confined to the inner part of the city. The buildings could not possibly have been destroyed for military reasons. In many cases there is actual proof that buildings were blown up by dynamite placed in the cellar. Dynamite which had failed to explode was taken out of many cellars."

The *Muenchner Post* of May 4, 1921, speaks as follows about these devastations committed during the retreat: "If idealists have hoped for more from the Entente than the latter could or would perform in the Peace Treaty, they cannot be blamed for the disgrace of Versailles. It was the fruit of the merciless devastation ordered by the High Command which, even during the retreat, wantonly destroyed mines and factories on a large scale. The ruin created by this vandalism has cost Germany the demand by the Entente for reparations on an astronomical scale under which Germany is being crushed."

From the beginning of the retreat until barely twenty days before the Armistice the High Command, under the plea of military necessity, systematically destroyed everything in the war zone which possessed any material, artistic, or even moral value. It will suffice to mention the testimony of an officer whose honorable character demands our respect. On his own behalf and on behalf of his brother officers he "felt himself obliged to declare the devastations ordered a disgrace to the High General Staff and to the German nation."

President Wilson in his second note to Germany, after a request for an armistice, wrote on October 14: "The German armies, on their enforced retreat from France and Flanders, are pursuing a policy of wanton devastation which must be regarded as a direct breach of the rules and usages of civilized warfare. The towns and villages when not destroyed are stripped of everything they contain, often even of their inhabitants. It cannot be expected that the nations allied against Germany will agree to an armistice so long as these inhuman acts of pillage and devastation continue, which they rightly regard with horror and intense loathing."

Wilson's note made a powerful impression on the retreating troops. One of them wrote shortly afterwards in the *Berliner Volkszeitung*: "We read Wilson's note with its serious charges of pillage and devastation. We also read the German comment upon it: lies, humbug. Then we looked each other in the face, flung the newspapers in the mud, stamped upon them and cried like babies. Many stood there dumb as clods of earth, gazed with eyes wide-opened in horror and unseeing, and thought of what they had done yesterday and the day before, what they had requisitioned, pillaged and destroyed."

My friends in the west of Switzerland informed me of what they had learned from Allied sources, that it would go hard with Germany if these devastations were not stopped immediately. Germany would be treated in accordance with the law of retaliation, "An eye for an eye, a tooth for a tooth." I went to Prince Max, who told me at once that the necessary steps would be taken. As I was informed later, he had a stormy interview with Ludendorff. Finally, the order required was given.

But the devastated areas presented a hopeless picture. Months after the conclusion of hostilities, French mayors were informing their fellow-citizens "that they must abandon the hope of rebuilding their villages." The French commissions which followed the armies were reduced to despair by the spectacle they witnessed and did not know where to begin the work of reconstruction. They were particularly struck by the deliberate malice which had inspired the damage done. In many places the fruit trees had been cut down in rows or, as the owner of a property at Noyon told me, the walls were left intact but the fruit trees trained against them cut down. The French peasants were beside themselves with rage.

In 1918 a Swiss spoke to a German of the folly of these devastations and asked him: "After this, what will you do if you lose the war?" "We will organize sympathy" was the answer. They did, and most successfully. Their barbarism counted on the humanity of others.

A particularly deep impression was made on the population concerned and on world opinion by the deportations carried out. These were begun in Belgium to satisfy the alleged needs of Germany industry. 120,000 Belgian workmen and with them students, business men and artisans were ruthlessly carried off in open trucks like cattle without being given time to put on warm clothes. Hundreds of women and girls followed the mournful cortège, weeping and sobbing, to the Pahot station where the unfortunates were packed into goods trucks. "No civilized state can force men to work in this way", General von Bissing had at first objected. He was soon compelled to obey.

In his book on Belgium under German domination, the American Ambassador Whitlock says that he asked himself: "How could we have lived through those horrible days . . . this return to slavery? I could have written to my government that we must despair of humanity. I felt ashamed to write in the cold style of an official report when one should rather have vented one's wrath and disgust by crying aloud, have flung diplomatic correctness to the winds, and have called things by their right names, slavery not deportation."

A German staff officer, who during the war traveled constantly up and down Belgium in charge of a hospital train, sent me the following personal observation of the way in which the Belgian workers were deported:

"I was on the station at Charleroi when a trainload of deportees was sent off. The men were very scantily clad, without overcoats, and carried under their arms small bundles containing a few possessions hastily flung together. As they passed through the station, they expressed their indignation at their cruel treatment by loud protests, on which the German stationmaster suddenly turned on the poor wretches the full force of the station fire-extinguisher so that, soaked to the skin, they traveled to Germany in icy trucks. But I could say nothing; my officer's uniform would not have saved me from being lynched by the German soldiers. For the officers and privates present burst into a shrill cheer and diabolical laughter when the stationmaster performed this fine piece of practical joking which reduced a hundred or more men to such a pitiable state.

"Behind the front thousands of Belgians were employed laying railway lines, digging trenches, loading munitions and provisions—a flagrant violation of international law— and moreover under conditions which caused numerous deaths and permanently ruined the health of many others. When anyone died as a result of these hardships a small packet of clothes was sent to his relatives. And this was all. The indignation expressed by the entire civilized world became so great that the deportations were finally discontinued, to be resumed, however, during the great offensive of 1918. Then nothing less than manhunts were organized to obtain labor for the Western front. Strong bands of military police armed to the teeth made their way in broad daylight into cafes, public houses, cinemas and circuses and dragged off any men they found there between the ages of 15 and 60. No consideration was shown. Fathers were brutally separated from their children, husbands from wives, engaged men from their fiancées, and driven at the butt end of rifles to the 'Flandria Buildings' near St. Peter's station to be incorporated into the battalions of civil workers. Very soon no male inhabitant of Ghent showed himself in the street. It was a useless precaution. At night the military police invaded private houses, seized these unfortunates in their beds, and dragged them off. Motor trucks were dispatched to the villages to return the following morning packed with new slaves, all of whom had been seized in bed". (Since my informant is at present living in Germany, I refrain in his interest from giving his name.)

These deportations were not confined to Belgium. They

took place in France also. The worst occurred in Lille and Roubaix where thousands of women and girls of all classes were suddenly deported for labor service. I had an opportunity of talking to an entire group of evacuated French mothers who were being sent from the North to the South of France through Switzerland. They were all in despair, because their daughters were labor slaves in the Ardennes under military supervision while they themselves had been driven from their homes. "Elles seront bonnes pour le ruisseau," they concluded. Later a German student who had been serving on the Western Front wrote to me: "during the war something awoke in me which every poilu, every Czech, and every Tommy knows: fear, a peculiar horror of men who are not human," a horror of the inhuman militarism devoid of moral character which the entire German conduct of the War revealed in all its hideousness.

Three years after the War I asked a French colleague who resided in the neighborhood of Lille to collect for me some detailed experiences of the period of occupation. He replied, "Nothing doing. The people say it was such a nightmare that they cannot talk about it."

Moreover the Germans further disgraced their country's name by their gross failure to fulfill the obligations incumbent upon belligerents in neutral countries. The luggage of a German diplomatic courier to Norway, when seized and officially opened, was found to contain a number of materials for sabotage, and a larger store of them was then discovered in a depot. There were infernal machines in the form of briquettes of carbon, candy-sticks with little tubes of gelatine containing bacilli, fountain pens filled with prussic acid, and pencils which burst into flames when cut. The feeling aroused by the discovery in Scandinavia was intense. Branting called the Germans "bandits".

The Zurich bomb trial during the War revealed the incredible fact that the German General Staff abused neutral hospitality to supply anarchists with explosives and bacilli. The German Consul-General in Zurich, Faber du Faure, called upon me after the War and bitterly complained that the army had compelled him to house in his consulate all those illegal and criminal weapons of war. All his warnings and entreaties had been brushed aside. Breaches of neutrality were, it is true, also committed by the other side. But not by such methods nor on such a scale, nor by a General Staff nor of such a nature as to endanger a neutral country. On this subject we should read G. Lechartier's book, *Intrigues Diplomatiques à Washington* (Paris, Plon). We are told that Count Bernstorff knew nothing of all this. But this precisely is typical of modern Germany that the theory and practice of the army have been so completely removed from the jurisdiction, norms and considerations otherwise recognized that it is sufficient by itself to raise the entire world in arms against us.

Unfortunately it is too little known in Germany that after the first English air-raid, that on Freiburg in Breisgau, a reprisal for the torpedoing of hospital ships, there was an important debate in the House of Lords in the course of which the distinguished Bishops and Peers, led by the Archbishop of Canterbury, unanimously condemned such reprisals. Then the continuation for several months of murderous German air-raids stirred the British public to such indignation that their demands for reprisals could no longer be resisted by the Government. Lord Selbourne for example said: "What is immoral when the Germans do it cannot become right when the English do it. The greatest danger of this war is that we shall sink to the German level." Lord Buckmaster said, "If we once sink to the enemy's level, we may perhaps win the war, but it will not be an honorable victory." A mother who had lost two sons in the war wrote to the *Times*: "I have given both my sons to the war, my only two sons, and they will never return to me. I gave them gladly and do not regret it. But if I must live to see Englishmen sent out to murder German women and children and innocent non-combatants, then I should certainly begin to ask: 'Did my sons die in vain?' My feelings, I believe, will be shared by all who have suffered from the war as I have."

Ought not we Germans to be ashamed that not a single voice was raised to this effect among us, either in the Reichstag or by any dignitary of the Christian churches? On the contrary, it was the Catholic Erzberger who wrote: "In war the utmost ruthlessness, if rationally applied, proves in fact the truest humanity. If we could wipe out the whole of London, it would be more humane to do so than to allow a single fellow-countryman to shed his blood on the battlefield, provided such a radical course would restore peace most quickly. Hesitation, softness and pity are unpardonable weakness. Decision and ruthless action are strength and bring victory."

In the spring of 1917 I sent Chancellor Bethmann-Hollweg a protest against the German conduct of the War, pointing out at length the enormous political and moral harm it caused. I quote here the opening passage of my protest:

"Your Excellency, as a teacher in a German secondary school, whose professional duty is to defend the traditional ideals of the German soul but whose mouth has been closed by the censorship, I do myself the honor to transmit to you this expression of my profound grief and my earnest protest against the fashion in which the war has lately been waged. Such conduct, I am convinced, not only dishonors the German name but arouses in our enemies such anger and bitterness that the prospect of an honorable peace becomes more remote, and the restoration of assured commercial relations, indispensable to our economic recovery after the war, is rendered more impossible every

day. I know that in saying this I am the mouthpiece of
many voices now silent."

These and similar warnings were in vain. The impotence of our politicians in face of the army can be gauged
by the fact that in the summer of 1917, during the agitation sponsored by our government itself for a peace by
negotiation, night after night Zeppelin raids were made
on London though Kuehlemann had actually spoken of
the moral atmosphere in which alone a peace could be
negotiated. The *Manchester Guardian* asked with justice
whether the poisonous fumes which the raids generated
and the bitter indignation of the British people at these
senseless acts of savagery could create such a moral atmosphere.

THE GERMAN ARMY IN BELGIUM

Countless discussions between Germans and foreigners
anxious for reconciliation are opened by the latter with
the question: "Do you condemn the German invasion of
Belgium and the outrages committed by the German army
on Belgium soil? Did you condemn them during the War
or only since the War?" The question is asked to discover
how far both parties accept the same moral code. Unhappily the majority of Germans fail to pass the test satisfac-
torily—not least because they are insufficiently informed
of what happened in Belgium or completely deceived about
it—whether it be the original breach of neutrality, the
massacre of almost 5,000 civilians, the burning of entire
towns or the deportation of Belgian workers to Germany.

The Belgians, who had suffered more under the German occupation and from the German conduct after the
War than any other nation, though they were perfectly
innocent and had scrupulously fulfilled their obligations
as a neutral state, vainly awaited at the end of the War
some German expression of regret or shame for what had
happened. Indeed, that no word was said about these

things, in Germany, either officially or unofficially, by the nation as a whole or by any group or individual, and that no trouble was taken to discover the truth, to brand the guilty and to offer their victims the most elementary human sympathy, seemed to the Belgians almost more inhuman than the crimes themselves.

A short time ago, an article in a French paper asked: "Why this oppressive, monstrous, appalling silence maintained by Germany about the outrages committed by the imperial army? Why have the Germans failed to condemn these crimes, to stigmatize them as the excesses of an hour of madness? Why this horrid silence of the masses, of the educated classes, in fact of the entire nation, as though the Germans were possessed by a devil of pride which will not permit them to accuse themselves? Why, we persist in asking, this fearful silence? How is it possible that no one stands up among all these monographs, documents and collections and makes the simple avowal: "We were mad, we condemn our frenzy, it was inhuman"? The wrong committed against Belgium did not consist only in the massacres of innocent people and the deportations, but above all in the invasion as such.

A Swiss colleague told me during the first year of the War, that he was in the staff room of a German University where he was teaching when the news of the invasion of Belgium was received. Everyone was horrorstricken. Two days later the official excuses, the necessity of defense, had done their work. None of his colleagues any longer questioned "Germany's sacred right to march through Belgium," as it was stated later by the theologian Krebs. Krebs found fault with the Belgians for refusing to allow his people to march through when they asked leave to do so in order to defend their Providential position in the world. This complete abdication of the German conscience in the face of the official pleas had been prepared by fifty years' worship of a national success built upon downright breaches of justice. It was also the product—as also were all the excesses committed by the Germans in their conduct of the War—of a boundless national conceit which treated the rights of others as of no account and did not scruple, as for example, in the deportations of Belgians for forced labor and similar deportations of French women and girls, to reduce entire populations to slavery and in the alleged interest of Germany to treat with a relentless logic human beings as they were treated during the barbarian invasions.

The utter lack of compunction displayed and the open or silent complicity of the intelligentsia and of Christians in such behavior is designated by an astonished world "the German mentality". The breach of Belgian neutrality, the deportation of Belgian workers, the murder of 5,000 innocent civilians might seem but a minor aspect of the entire problem of war-guilt. In reality the psychology revealed by German behavior towards Belgium is the key to the entire problem of war-guilt. It displays in a particularly glaring light the operation of a mentality for which military necessity—understood moreover in a most short-sighted fashion—is the supreme divinity which tolerates no other good beside, still less above, itself. The entire world in fact judged German war-guilt by the German treatment of Belgium, in which the ethics of the military state was displayed in all its nakedness. Not even the German-Austrian gangsterism of July had so clearly revealed its barbaric nature.

HAD BELGIUM ABANDONED HER NEUTRALITY?

When the treaty of 1839 was signed "in the name of the Holy and Undivided Trinity" by the five great powers, the German League, and Holland, Belgium's territory, independence, and neutrality were guaranteed. As Prussia's juridical successor, Germany explicitly recognized the Treaty in 1911 and 1913.

On July 31, 1914, the German Ambassador in Brussels declared that Belgian neutrality would be respected. On August 1, he repeated the declaration. On the evening of August 2, he handed the Belgian government the German ultimatum in which the treaty was not mentioned. The Belgian reply, in which Belgium appealed to her faithful performance of her international obligations, stated that she had no knowledge of the alleged French plans of invasion and was ready to defend her neutrality even against France and could not believe that she would be compelled to abandon it towards Germany in order to defend her independence. This reply was never made known publicly in Germany. The Wolff agency gave out that no reply had been made.

Even in the fourth year of the War, a German religious paper, which dared to appeal to moral theology, spoke of a right of necessity which it was a sacred duty to make use of. In fact, it was this so-called act of necessary self-defense, a false plea if ever there was one, that finally placed Germany defenseless in her enemies' hands. Even the worst sophistry about the necessities of defense had hitherto sanctioned only resistance to an aggressor. An attack upon an innocent third party had never before been justified as lawful self-defense.

The reckless charges against Belgium by which it was sought to justify the invasion were an almost greater wrong than the violation of her neutrality. They could confuse so completely the moral judgment of Germans only because those who published the documents found in Brussels tampered with the text in such a way as to mislead the public about the true significance of the conversations between the British and the Belgian staffs which they recorded. In the first place, the talks were called conversations, not agreements; and in the second place, they contemplated the eventuality not simply of a war between France and Germany *but of a German violation of Belgian neutrality,* as was explicitly stated by a sentence inserted in the text, not a mere marginal note.

The decisive words were published in the official and semi-official German publications of the French text as an unimportant detail; so that the entire German press proclaimed that Belgium had abandoned her neutrality before the War. In reality, her attitude had been irreproachable. The German plan to march through Belgium in the event of war had come to the knowledge of the Belgian government, which was therefore obliged by the treaty to apply to one of the other powers which had guaranteed Belgian neutrality. The application did not commit Belgium except in the event of a German invasion. In 1912, when a member of the British General Staff threatened that England would effect a landing on the Belgian coast even without Belgian consent, the Belgian government behaved most correctly. They obtained an assurance from England that she did not contemplate violating the Belgian neutrality.

In view of all this, how had the *Norddeutscher Allgemeine Zeitung* the face to write on October 13, 1914, "The papers discovered are documentary proof of what the German government knew long before the outbreak of war, that Belgium had an understanding with the Entente Powers. They justify the action taken by our army." On August 27, 1914 the same paper had written, "Moreover we affirm that no attempt had been made from the German side to justify the invasion of Belgium by the guilty conduct of the Belgian Government". And on August 4, the German Secretary of State said plainly that Germany had no complaint to make against Belgium whose attitude had always been perfectly correct.

In Brussels the German government justified the invasion as made necessary by the threat of French invasion. General Emmich's proclamation affirmed: "Our troops acted under *the compulsion of sheer necessity,* since Belgian neutrality had been violated by French officers who had motored into Belgium disguised, to attack Germany."

It was all lies. Not a jot of proof has ever been given for these alleged plans or acts. On the contrary, the German Staff later admitted that the entire French strategy proved that the French had no intention of marching through Belgium. Nor had England planned any violation of Belgian neutrality. The neutrality of the coast of Flanders had always been a vital British interest and Britain would never have been so stupid as to destroy this safeguard by her own action.

Our German teachers of international anarchy—the few exceptions prove the rule—were at pains to obscure these plain truths and by every conceivable perversion of the facts to establish the imaginary guilt of Belgium and the German right to invade the country. For one reason alone the English and French could never have seriously contemplated invading Belgium, namely that England did not want the theatre of war to be so near her own shores. In 1914 Germany knew this quite well. In the autumn of that year the *Kreuzzeitung* stated that Northern France had been most markedly denuded of troops, which could be explained only by the fact that Joffre had concentrated his entire strength on the Eastern frontier. The French staff had in fact reckoned too confidently "on the protection of Belgium by the international treaty."

Belgium's preparations for defense were nothing but a most comprehensible attempt, demanded indeed by her international obligations, to secure herself on the side where she was actually threatened. If the Germans had not invaded Belgium, the plans envisaged for English and Belgian cooperation would never have been carried into effect. Unfortunately the hypothetical nature of the Anglo-Belgian arrangements is persistently misrepresented in Germany; for example, when the correspondence of the English diplomat Nicholson was recently published.

Nicholson had been charged in 1912 to discover what the attitude of the Belgian government would be if France or England should ever be compelled to defend the neutrality of Belgium against Germany. The correspondence proves beyond a shadow of doubt that both parties agreed that British forces would enter Belgium only if she had first been invaded by Germany. Nevertheless the German press proclaimed jubilantly that now at last it was plain who had first contemplated the violation of Belgian neutrality.

WHAT HAPPENED IN BELGIUM

To obtain even an approximately true picture of what happened in Belgium we must personally visit Dinant and Tamines and numerous villages on the road and hear their inhabitants' story: Here thirty people were shot, here the parish priest was shot, here the entire village was burnt. Shots, we are told by the Germans, were fired from the houses upon our troops. Is it probable, one asks oneself, that these terrified people really attempted such senseless resistance? On the pretext that the German troops had been fired upon, a large part of Dinant and its suburbs was burnt and 674 of its citizens were shot at different points in the town, among them many old men, 92 women, and 22 children under ten years of age.

In many places in the town there are monuments or tablets to the memory of the groups of citizens shot "Victims de la barbarie allemande". What an honor for Germany! A few survivors whose wounds were not mortal managed to creep out of the heaps of corpses under cover of darkness and save their lives. Beneath one such heap lay a fifteen-year old boy who fainted when he awoke to see his entire family—two sisters, brothers, father, grandfather, and mother—lying around him. The soldiers clouted him and compelled him to dig their grave. Today he is a doctor in Dinant. At another place over a hundred factory hands were placed against a wall to be shot. When the manager, an elderly man well-known for his acts of charity, hurried to the scene and said to the officer in charge: "I will give you all I possess if you will spare the lives of these poor fathers of families", he answered, "We don't want money, we want blood".

At Tamines at seven o'clock in the evening of August 22, 1914, six hundred men who had been confined in the church were brought out into the square in front of it. The Germans surrounded them with machine guns and for five minutes fired into this mass of humanity. 374 were killed. The rest, wounded, crawled away during the night to the river or back to their homes. The survivors relate that the most appalling feature of the massacre was the fact that, after the firing ceased, soldiers prodded about among the corpses with their bayonets to stab any who were still moving and had not the sense to feign death. A teacher in a German gymnasium sent me the report of an innkeeper he knew who, when on service, had been compelled to take part in this bayoneting, which he regarded as the most terrible of his war memories. No German document has dared to maintain that in Tamines there were franc-tireurs. The German White Book keeps silent about the entire episode.

The fate of Dinant and Tamines was shared by Louvain and countless other places, for example, Andenne, Aerschot, Ethe and Vise. The cry was raised: "Shots have been fired." No one asked whether they had been fired by German soldiers, by retreating French, or by regular Belgian soldiers. The order was given in such cases to burn the locality and to shoot the inhabitants. In Ethe 256 houses were burnt and 277 civilians shot. The wife of the burgomaster of Aerschot tells us that she was compelled to witness her fifteen-year old son and her husband being driven to the market-place with the butt ends of rifles; they were made to kneel down and two minutes later: "What was dearest to me in the world lay lifeless on the stones." At Andenne 211 inhabitants were shot and 41 houses burnt. A total of 5,000 non-combatants of every age and both sexes were massacred in this way and some 10,000 houses destroyed. At Surice the German soldiers suddenly spread the report that a girl of sixteen had fired upon an officer. In consequence 58 persons, among them four priests, were mown down by machine-gun fire and 130 houses burnt.

"We are convinced," wrote the Court Chaplain Dryander, "that on our side war will be conducted with a self-control, conscientiousness and humanity unexampled in the history of the world."

These words are part of the picture. They are but another form of the arrogance which inspired those savage executions.

WHO FIRED THE SHOTS?

The source of the shots which killed German soldiers as they entered Belgian towns or villages is the question on which the entire controversy turns. The German White Book and still more the Meurer Reports deserve severe censure for speaking only of shooting by civilians, as though there were no Belgian and French troops in the field, contesting every inch of ground with the German invaders and as they retired from a town or village shooting to the last from the shelter of the last houses or clumps of trees. Did the German White Book hope to throw dust in the eyes of the Germans and the neutrals who did not realize this fact and thus to shield the guilty at all costs? Meurer states that concealed franc-tireurs fired from the heights above the Meuse on the German troops in Andenne. How does he know that they were franc-tireurs and not the Belgian soldiers driven from the town? From such a great distance were the men who fired the shots clearly visible?

A conscientious report should have carefully weighed such allegations, and its author should have taken the trouble to acquaint himself with the movement of troops on both sides. It is, indeed, a most remarkable fact that, wherever the French offered armed resistance to the Germans, houses were burnt and a considerable number of non-combatants mercilessly shot. The red line of burning streets and massacred civilians follows accurately the line of the French retreat. Where, however, the French troops did not encamp or put up a fight, the houses were not burnt and the inhabitants were not slaughtered.

There can be no doubt that the German troops entered Belgium obsessed with the fear of franc-tireurs and that this obsession distorted all their observations and statements. When, for example, they entered Robertville, a little German town on the frontier with a Walloon population, they imagined they were already on hostile soil. German veterans of 1870 were taken as hostages. During the night the least noise provoked an outburst of reckless firing. Grazing cows and horses were shot and a house which showed a light very late was fired upon. An officer had already given the order to burn the houses when the parish priest, Father Heinen, explained the true state of affairs and calmed the panic-stricken soldiery.

You can judge what happened in Belgium where there were no German clergy whose word was believed and who could, therefore, prevent the burnings and massacres. "At Marchienne-au-Pont", P. Lemaire relates: "The Hanoverian troops were received by an outburst of machine-gun fire. French soldiers posted in front of the bridge over the Sambre decimated them as they entered the rue Neuve. A subordinate officer, treated for a wound by Dr. D., told us that he saw his comrades falling like flies and no one knew where the shots came from. It was naturally assumed, he added, that the inhabitants had fired from their houses. The entire street therefore and others in the

Monceau district were set on fire. 251 houses were burnt and 60 non-combatants shot."

The German High Command was guilty of allowing such executions to be ordered by young officers on the mere allegations of soldiers. Lemaire writes: "Like a horde of savages or rather of wild beasts whose cruel instincts had been given free rein they fell upon the civil population, slaughtering without compunction whatever came in the way of their rifles or bayonets. What are we to think of this savagery? Is it war or the kind of war waged in the twentieth century by Germany, a so-called civilized country?"

Wherever at the last moment there were reasonable officers who had the humanity to order an enquiry into the origin of the shots as soon as the clergy entreated them with tears to do so, the innocence of the civil population was soon established. Father Nieuwland relates a typical example in his eight-volume work. At Florennes three Uhlans, one of them an officer, made their way into the place. At the corner of the church they were met by shots fired by the retreating French soldiers who had concealed themselves at the extremity of the village. The officer, who was wounded, fortunately noticed the French uniform. He was treated in Doctor Rolin's hospital. Since he was an honorable man, he lost no time in ordering the commander of the approaching German troops to be informed of the truth. Otherwise, he said, Florennes would have been burnt to the ground. But for this fortunate circumstance not a stone of the village would now be standing because the "inhabitants had fired on our troops."

The third number of the *Allgemeinen Rundschau*, devoted to Belgium, printed a large number of similar instances in which a timely investigation immediately proved that the shots had been fired either by regulars on their retreat or by German soldiers shooting at fowl or at cats.

The true account of the fearful outrages in Dinant is clear evidence of the way in which there arose hallucinations and false explanations of the real facts to which these crimes were due. The German soldiers faced death for the first time when they encountered French troops on Belgian soil. This made them exceptionally liable to lose their heads and yield to panic. Had the invasion of Belgium been preceded by several months' experience of war, probably those panics would not have arisen. At any rate the soldiers would have known that shots ricocheting from rocks or the walls of houses may wound or kill men. Ludwig Renn, relating in *Der Krieg* his memories of the investment of Dinant, was still convinced that shots had been fired by civilians from factories and private houses. But when later he visited Dinant the truth became clear to him. "My first experience of fighting was the struggle for the Belgian town of Dinant. At the time we believed it was a house-to-house fight. A year later I revisited Dinant and examined the bullet marks on the walls. The shots had not been fired from the houses but into the streets from the opposite bank, therefore, by the French soldiers. We, however, believing the inhabitants had fired upon us, shot non-combatants en masse."

The most convincing proof that this psychological explanation is correct is the fact that in other theatres of war similar crimes were committed as the result of hallucinations or shots fired by the retreating army or by German soldiers themselves. For example, at the Polish town of Kalisch, which had in fact welcomed the German troops as liberators, a stupid commander, Preussker, lost his head and suddenly ordered the town to be burned because a few shots had been fired and because some soldiers had stated that Jews wearing the kaftan had fired from garrets. The affair was hushed up, since the army leaders were themselves ashamed of what had been done. When Major von Manteuffel lost his head and burned Louvain he behaved exactly in the same way as his colleagues in Poland. Even German Alsace witnessed similar scenes. St. Martin was burnt on the pretext that the inhabitants had concealed French soldiers who shot at night. A friend of mine was an officer there. He told me that he had the greatest difficulty in preventing another village from being burnt, because from time to time little white clouds rose from the house tops. He proved that they were small clouds of dust caused by French bullets striking the houses.

I will conclude my indictment by speaking of an in-human practice which was also a gross breach of inter-national law and aroused peculiar indignation in Belgium, the employment of masses of Belgians as cover against the fire of the retreating French soldiers. It is described in P. Lemaire's book (*L'Invasion allemande au pays de Charleroi*):

"In the district of Charleroi it was the regular practice to make hostages march in front of the German troops, wherever the French put up a resistance; the natives were employed, without distinction of age or sex, to shield the Germans from the enemy's bullets. The Germans broke into houses like savage hordes, and without respect for weakness, illness, or childhood drove the miserable wretches on in front of them with abuse and blows. There was no mercy for them. They must march on. They were given no time to dress, to take food, or to put on warm clothing against the cold of night. Women could be seen in their underclothes, without stockings, in bedroom slip-pers, old men without headgear, dragging themselves along, infirm and ailing, happy if they escaped actual blows. Small schoolgirls, more dead than alive, clung to their mothers' skirts and cried unceasingly. There were fathers, anxious about the fate of their families. There were babies, carried in their mothers' arms. And there were priests, driven on with blows like obstinate cattle. I saw many of these people after their ordeal. They were ten years older, and whenever the children caught sight of a German soldier they fled in terror."

This picture concludes my account of the outrages committed by the Germans in their conduct of the War—a small selection from the entire tale of horror. I invite the reader to consider the facts here related and then to ask himself whether he still feels entitled to denounce the "disgraceful" Treaty of Versailles or whether he does not begin to understand the reaction of Europe against the mentality which inspired those outrages.

POSSIBILITIES OF PEACE IN 1917

Were genuine opportunities of making peace in 1917 wantonly neglected? Were they once more neglected the following year, when Wilson published his first offer, the Fourteen Points put forward in January?

The reply must be Yes and No. Certainly the opportunity was real. But public opinion in Germany was far from ready to take advantage of it, to understand and accept the indispensable conditions on which alone peace was possible. This is sufficiently proved by the fact that within a few weeks of the debacle Hertling did not dare to pledge himself unequivocally to the unconditional restoration of Belgium but still hoped to use Belgium as a pawn in the diplomatic game.

Chancellor Michaelis has been blamed with as much justice as severity for his rejection of the Papal offer of mediation. In fact his refusal made no difference. No one at that time could have brought the German people, the victim of lying propaganda and in a process of passing from one illusion to another, to accept the only terms on which the Allies were prepared to make peace. The German attitude was clearly reflected by the ambiguous attitude of Michaelis. Even the most peace-loving of our opponents were determined to destroy Prussian militarism either by a victory in the field or by applying the principles expounded by President Wilson. The latter course, however, was impossible until the Prussian system had been morally defeated in the hearts of the German people, and until Germany had genuinely renounced power-politics. A merely external acceptance of an unfavorable military situation and the result of the Allied blockade was not enough.

But there was no trace of such a genuine conversion. The opposite state of mind was glaringly displayed by numerous symptoms, not least by the protest of eleven hundred university professors against a negotiated peace. The lie in the soul, as Plato terms it, that is, a profound inner mendacity and self-deception, which had been widely spread by the falsification of war propaganda, led many of those who must have known better, journalists of the more progressive press, for instance, to contradict daily what they knew perfectly well. They continued to repeat such phrases as "The enemy's will to destroy us" and "hostile imperialism", when the truth was that even the pacifists in the Entente countries refused to compromise with the mentality still dominant in Germany. That is why Lord Lansdowne said at the end of August 1917, "The German people are deceived as to the reasons which compel us to continue the war."

In January and February 1918, before the great German offensive, Wilson made a final attempt to obtain a sincere and practical acceptance of the new order by Germany. The reply was Brest-Litovsk. The new order was impossible without Germany's sincere acceptance of it. At that time her acceptance would have inspired confidence and been the proof of a change of heart. After the debacle her acceptance proved nothing. For that reason the peace concluded in Paris could not be a Wilsonian peace. The essential condition of such a peace, *faith in a regenerate Germany,* was wanting. Only in accord with a new Germany could Wilson have triumphed. Since that was lacking, the world inevitably fell back into the old paths; and the ideal of justice must yield to the anger of the victorious nations and their mistrust of Prussian militarism which though outwardly overthrown had learnt nothing.

It would have been better had Wilson never budged from his official position that the Fourteen Points were intended to apply only to a situation in which there was no conqueror or conquered. In that event their acceptance would have proved a genuine abandonment of the old attitude. To a Germany which openly scoffed at his principles when it was planning the great offensive, but greedily grasped at them when it had been reduced to impotence, he should have said: "Sorry, but my Fourteen Points are no longer available. Now take the peace which you intended for others and which is the only kind of peace you can understand." Then the false German charge against the President, that he broke his solemn pledge, would have been impossible and the Peace Terms would have been adapted to the mentality of those who had broken the peace of the world.

At the very moment when Wilson issued his great appeal for a peace of justice, Germany was about to conclude in the East a peace of violence. The reaction of Western Europe at that time to the German action is of particular interest at a time when the situation is identical. Germany's designs and conduct in Eastern Europe flatly contradict the language she uses in Western Europe. This was pointed out in an article published by the *Westminster Gazette* in February 1918.

"It is our duty," said the writer, "to tell the Chancellor frankly that the desire for peace among the Western Powers which seek a peace which shall rest upon an enduring and honorable foundation is weakened every day by the disclosure of Germany's treatment of Russia. Brest-Litovsk shows us how much the renunciation of annexations claimed by the German statesmen is worth when they are in a position to rob a defenseless neighbor. Germany cannot apply two different methods. She cannot plunder in the East and expect to conclude a favorable peace in the West. She cannot play the part of a bandit in the East, of a saint in the West, and expect the latter pose to be taken seriously. If the German people approves what is being done in Eastern Europe in their name, they must be prepared for the consequences—a prolongation of the War and the impossibility of reaching an understanding with other nations. We should like to believe that the German people are sensible enough to understand this, in spite of the fact that their rulers have not the wisdom to point out to them what must be the inevitable results of the attitude they have adopted, so long as other nations retain their self-respect and power of resistance."

Equally applicable to present conditions were the arguments against simply returning the conquered colonies without solid guarantees for the establishment of a new order of international justice. The pacifist General Smuts said: "We cannot permit the establishment on both coasts of Africa of submarine bases which would endanger the communications by land from one end of the African Empire to the other. The British Empire is not like Russia, Germany, and the United States, a compact mass, but is scattered over the globe and is therefore dependent upon the maintenance of its communications by land and sea which we must protect by every lawful means. Until the attitude of Germany has been radically changed and militarism finally discarded we must pursue a policy of legitimate self-defense and treat the occupied German colonies as a pledge for the future peace of the world."

Ten days before Wilson made his second great peace-speech at Baltimore, he was compelled to read in the news-headlines the following résumé of a speech by Hindenburg: "Hindenburg in favor of a peace of power." Wilson re-

plied: "Well then, power let it be, power to the utmost."
And he kept his word.

Later Hindenburg, in a reply to a question about the
possibilities of concluding a negotiated peace, said that
Germany had to choose between "Fighting till victory had
been achieved" or "Complete surrender". It all depends
on what we are to understand by surrender and what
Germany it is that must surrender. Certainly the modern
Germany of power-politics must surrender. And that surrender would have involved the righting of many historic
wrongs. Belgium and Alsace would have to be returned
and the partition of Poland made good. All this would
have been a blessing for the German people. But there was
not the remotest possibility of the German people and
their rulers understanding this and accepting such a peace.
Peace was therefore impossible before the debacle. The
other European powers were ready to make it; Germany
was not.

Toward the end of August 1918, I visited the Imperial
Chancellor von Hertling at Berlin to put the situation
frankly before him. I pointed out to him everything I have
just said about the indispensable conditions on which
alone the Entente would make peace; and I pointed out
the disastrous effect of the arrogant speeches of our generals and enumerated all the sacrifices the German nation
must be prepared to make while there was yet time, if it
would avoid a worse fate. I watched his pale and tired
face. He gazed at me with glassy eyes as one in whom hope
is dead. Like a man who has lost his foothold and is being
swept by a torrent, crying out to someone on the bank,
he replied with obvious embarrassment: "You are right.
Unfortunately you are right. I believe you. But what can
I do? What do you expect me to do? The High Command
does not share your point of view."

With a heavy heart I walked slowly down the stairs. In
the Wilhelmstrasse I caught sight of the notice of a new

film with the expressive title "The Dead Man at the Helm." "It is true," I said to myself, "A dead man is at the helm and the ship is heading at top speed for the rocks."

THE GERMAN MILITARY DEBACLE AND ITS CAUSES

The German debacle was the inevitable result of the fact that Germany had gradually united the entire world against her aggression. The progressive entrance of the whole of Europe and later of the entire world into the conflict between Serbia and Austria may be regarded as the tacit expression of a new solidarity of mankind. Modern Germany, whose political thought had departed ever more widely from that of the rest of Europe, was incapable of recognizing, before it was too late, the political and moral factors which inspired the combination against her. Nor has she yet understood them. Therefore, she cannot see that a second aggression of a similar kind will provoke an even greater combination of hostile forces.

Those who were responsible for the miscalculations which led to the German defeat were lying when they ascribed it to the so-called stab in the back by the German malcontents. A Prussian officer, Major von Kroecker, expressed the truth most simply when he wrote in the *Berliner Tageblatt* of May 12, 1920: "The revolution was not the work of unscrupulous elements but the inevitable result of the blindness of our political and military leaders to the limits of our power of endurance."

That the common people and their leaders finally revolted against the senseless slaughter is most intelligible. But this legitimate stab in the back against infatuated leaders came too late. It could not affect in the least the debacle which America's entrance into the war had made inevitable. The material causes of the defeat were stated, as follows, in 1920 by a member of the Reichstag, Payer, replying to the *Republikanischen Reichsbund*:

"We lost the war because our enemies far outnumbered us and our allies and because they had access to the supplies and resources of the entire world from which we were debarred. Our army corps were drained of their strength, their number had diminished lamentably, and our reserves were utterly depleted, whereas the Americans alone were putting into the front line more than 250,000 fresh troops every month. The intensified U-boat campaign did not achieve the promised success. We had nothing similar to oppose to our enemy's tanks. Lack of man-power made it impossible for our troops to take the necessary periods of rest. For years both the soldiers and the civilian population had been under-nourished. Our allies were defeated one after the other. Privations, the continued loss of human life, fear of further sacrifices, and the increasing apprehension of defeat had weakened the morale of the army and the people. The nation had lost confidence in the General Staff and its bulletins. Our private soldiers felt ever more keenly the disproportion between the sacrifices demanded of them and those asked of the officers and the Staff. It was impossible to banish this despondency by commands or propaganda."

On November 5, 1918, General Groener was obliged to inform a cabinet meeting that, on the Western Front, 58 divisions worn out by fatigue were confronted by 96 Allied divisions. On November 10, Erzberger was empowered, with the consent of the General Staff, to conclude an armistice after the Staff, who were acquainted with the severe conditions demanded by the Allies, had attempted to secure their modification on eight points. Hindenburg, however, had expressly stated: "Even if the attempt be unsuccessful the armistice must be concluded." Where then were the November traitors?

To give the reader some idea of the network of lies which have obscured the plain facts and imbued the German people with the delusion that revolutionary agi-

tation robbed them of final victory, I will quote the words
spoken by General Graf von der Goltze in the stadium at
Berlin on August 24, 1921, with reference to Erzberger.
"By accepting an incredible armistice, scoundrels have
made the German people defenseless." Applause from an
audience of thousands lasted several minutes.

HITLER'S CAMPAIGN AGAINST THE NOVEMBER TRAITORS

A few weeks after the Armistice I crossed the Lake of
Constance on a Bavarian steamer plying from Lindau to
Rorschach. During the crossing I was present at a dramatic
argument. A customs officer was standing on the deck, a
man of the middle class who had obviously served as a
non-commissioned officer in the war. Suddenly from the
ventilator a stoker appeared, black with grime, to get
some air. The two men exchanged a few words and were
off upon a discussion of the War and the revolution. The
stoker shouted: "We had enough of the fraud, the coffee
and herrings, and on top of it all, being shelled and sleep-
ing in mud. And the American airmen. What for, I ask
you, what for? We half-starved wretches were to defeat a
million well-fed Americans. On coffee and herrings! The
lunacy should have been stopped a year ago."

The wind shook the vessel and clattered at every port-
hole, but the officer's voice rose above the blast: "Just
wait, now you won't even have the coffee and herrings.
Why couldn't you idiots have held out a few weeks longer?
Then we'd have had a different sort of peace. Our enemies
had had enough of it. They would have soon given in. It
was a disgusting thing to stab us in the back like this."
And he continued to pour out all the nonsense which had
been pumped into the German people to keep them stupid
and ignorant. Anger burst from every word, like the col-
umn of smoke from the funnel. The speaker was obviously
heart and soul with those who had engineered the War, a
human embodiment of the German war mind—which

combined the idealism of the poor with the greed of the bourgeoisie for success and world domination and big business, the delight of taking part in foolhardy enterprises, and a hard callousness to the fate of the oppressed—and vented it all in bitter hatred of that section of the German people which was content to live on the land like their forebears, which had kept free from the intoxication to which their fellows had succumbed, which saw through their delusion and were appalled at their rulers' arrogance, and which had long known in their bones that the War must end in a collapse.

Whenever I read a speech by Hitler I am reminded of that argument between those two Germans on the Lake of Constance. Like the non-commissioned officer Hitler embodies the sentiments of all those bourgeois combatants in the first World War, the fiery indignation of all who staked their money on the wrong horse and saw all their impossible hopes trampled in the mire.

HITLER THE VOICE OF THE NAMELESS MASSES

Read the following passage from the speech Hitler made when he was contesting the Presidency with Hindenburg. He regarded the contest between them as a summons to the German people to "Decide about the request for an armistice on November 9, 1918 and its results". It must end in the condemnation of that event and its consequences. Here are Hitler's actual words:

"I may perhaps be asked by what right I have come forward as public prosecutor? With the right, in the first place, of a man who belongs to the nameless masses, the masses whom you defeated on that November 9 and flung into misery. With the right of one of those anonymous millions who have hitherto been unable to defend their cause but have now found in me their advocate against you. I know today that behind the charges I bring against these men stand the majority of Germans. And if the

German people had not been hypnotized by a press directed by those who have an interest in November, 1918, every man of them would already have joined the ranks of your prosecutors and judges."

This is obviously the psychological complex of 1918. It is the voice of the non-commissioned officer on Lake Constance, the expression of a bitter disillusionment after a superhuman struggle of four years and of the wrath of a man ignorant of what really happened, with no knowledge of its true causes, and bemused by a complete misconception of the quarter where the responsibility lay. The astounding and almost unprecedented fact—for such a deception of an entire nation by its government has never before been known—was that it has been and still is possible to found a vast popular movement on an explanation of the causes and effects which produced the German defeat that is demonstrably false and thus successfully to divert the attention of an intelligent nation from the real criminals.

The amazing lack of foresight which followed the peace, the persistently renewed falsification of the actual result achieved by the instruments and methods of warfare employed by the deceivers, the fashion in which the lower and the higher rank of the civil and military hierarchy lied for each other about the real situation, and the way in which the entire nation was blinded by a press which lied, under compulsion at first but later freely, has exceeded anything one could have thought possible.

The formidable and only too successful campaign to deceive the Germans about the real causes of their defeat, produced the most far-reaching historical effect; it placed Hitler in power. Those who governed the country after the War are responsible for this result. They did nothing whatever to enlighten the nation as to the true reasons for their defeat. Since any thorough study of the German debacle must investigate the responsibility for making and prolonging the War, they shrank from placing before the people, perplexed, shaken and ready to fall prey to any demagogue, those facts which alone could have enlightened their minds and touched their conscience. This fear was not solely a fear of offending the Nationalists. It was also due to the fatal mistake of supposing that an acknowledgment of the truth would have given a handle to the conquerors to make the Peace Terms even more severe. The Allies obviously knew the truth without any acknowledgment of it by the Germans but an admission of the truth would have contributed enormously to give them confidence in Germany's new rulers.

This observation concludes all I have to say about this most painful chapter in our history, our responsibility for the first World War. I have now to deal with the world's answer to our guilt and its attempt to prevent a recurrence of the disaster.

The Treaty of Versailles focused the reply of Europe and the rest of the world to the German aggression. The sentiments which the world then entertained in regard to Germany and which Wilson himself shared when he had been shown the devastated areas of France, was expressed most strongly in the document known as the Covering Note. Very few Germans have read it. I will quote the most important passages:

"Only on the firm basis of justice is a settlement possible after this frightful war. The German delegates demand justice and call upon us to do justice to Germany. Germany shall have justice. But it must be justice toward all, to the dead, the wounded, the orphans, to all who today are wearing the garb of mourning, that Europe may be freed from the domination of Prussia. To save freedom the nations have piled up a war debt of thirty thousand million. Those who stagger beneath its burden must receive justice. So too must those millions whose lands, homes, vessels or goods have been ruined, wrecked or pillaged by German ruthlessness. For this reason we have insisted so strongly upon Germany's duty to make reparation to the very utmost of her ability. That is the fundamental condition of peace. For justice requires full atonement for the wrong done. Therefore, we demand that those who bear the fullest responsibility for the German aggression and for the acts of inhuman barbarity which have disgraced the German conduct of the war should be surrendered to the judicial condemnation they have hitherto escape.

"And for the same reason Germany must for several years be subjected to special restrictions and arrangements. Germany has destroyed her neighbors' factories, mines and industries, not in the course of fighting but in the execution of a deliberate plan aimed at securing the market of these nations before their industries can recover from the damage inflicted in cold blood. She has robbed her neighbors of everything she could plunder and make use of. On the high seas while their passengers and crews vainly sought to save their lives she has sunk the vessels of all nations. Justice demands compensation for all these losses, that the nations thus wronged shall for a time be protected from the competition of a nation whose industries are not only undamaged but have actually benefited by the equipment stolen from the occupied territory. This compensation will involve hardships for Germany, but hardships she has brought upon herself. Someone must suffer from the results of the war. Who is it to be? Germany or the nations on whom she has brought such suffering?

"To refuse justice to those who are entitled to it is to risk fresh disasters for the world. If the German people or any other is to be deterred from following the example of Prussia, if humanity is to be freed from the belief that a state is justified in using war to achieve its selfish ends, if antiquated ideas are to be relegated to the lumber-room of the past, if nations like individuals are to be made subject to law, if there is to be any possibility of reconciliation and appeasement in the near future, those responsible for making peace must have the courage to uphold justice in her austere purity and not sacrifice her for the advantage of an easy-going agreement."

CHAPTER XIV

THE TREATY OF VERSAILLES

WILSON AND CLEMENCEAU

A CIRCUS once announced as the brightest item on its program the offspring of a fish and a rabbit. When the public that evening flocked to the performance they read the announcement "Unhappily the little creature died today and only its sorrowing parents can be seen."

So has it been with the Treaty of Versailles. It was the offspring of parents so diverse that it could not survive. And today not even the sorrowing parents are visible. Both died from chagrin at the abortion they had produced. Jacques Bainville has remarked: "The Treaty of Versailles was too severe for its mildness, too mild for its severity—that is to say, its thoroughly justified provisions, for example, the demand for German disarmament, could have been carried out only by providing much stronger guarantees for their enforcement than those actually required."

The reparations demanded should have been completed by an effective system of financial control. Why was it not established? Because from the outset the new and the old worlds clashed. The respective leaders of these conflicting forces were Wilson and Clemenceau. The former represented the ideal of a new international order to which all other guarantees should be subordinated, as he explained on January 22, 1917: "These are the American principles, this is America's policy. We cannot stand for any other. And these are also the principles and the political ideals of all far-seeing men and women in every nation, of every enlightened community. They are the principles of humanity, they must prove victorious."

So far as the profound significance and spirit of his ideals were concerned, Wilson was certainly right. But he overlooked the fact that these ideas originated in America, that is to say, came from a world of emigrants, men who had been removed from their forefathers' graves and from all the historical frontiers, complications and resentments of their world. He took no account of the realities of Europe, nor of the passions and suspicions provoked by the War. He thought it possible to superimpose the new order on a Europe still smoldering from the conflagration, as a peasant throws a hen coop over screaming fowls. Clemenceau confronted him with a more realistic language. "The French are Germany's nearest neighbor and liable, as in the past, to be suddenly attacked by the Germans. The strongest wish of the French peasants on the border is to recover their cattle stolen by hundreds and thousands and which they can now see feeding on the German side of the frontier. These peasants keep on crying out, 'After all we have won, can't the Germans be made to give us back our cattle?' "

Clemenceau wanted to see the meaning and reality of the new order shown first by compelling the guilty to make good the damage done. Nor was he prepared to trust either reparations or security against a new attack to an order still wholly in the air. He required substantial guarantees. The reminiscences of Wickham Steed, Nicholson and Baker contain accounts of most interesting discussions at the Congress.

What finally emerged was neither Wilson nor Clemenceau but an illogical half-Wilson and an illogical half-Clemenceau. Reparations were demanded which were materially and morally justified but from the economic standpoint completely utopian and unattainable. No trouble was taken to make the transfer of the payments practicable within the international economic order. Attention was fixed too exclusively on a broken window which the man who broke it is legally and morally obliged to repair. Moreover the victors thought that, by a few clauses whose execution was left to the supervision of a small mixed commission, they could get rid of a military system which was the product of centuries and which had taken complete possession of the German soul. In a world of still active volcanoes whose eruptions had stopped only for lack of lava, the security of all against all, and in particular the security of the conquerors against the revenge of the conquered, could, it was believed, be achieved by nothing more than a written agreement in the framework of an institution still in embryo. The victors did not see that lions cannot be kept in a paper cage and that in the despiritualized and anarchic Europe of today entirely different methods must be employed to create and maintain order.

"There is peace," Maurras observed, "when the law-abiding folk are stronger than the bandits." Power-politics then? Yes, power in the service of law. Such power is more spiritual than an utopian pacifism that surrenders the world to the bandits and forgets that, in face of physical opposition, Jesus Himself had recourse to the whip of cords. That is to say, the Treaty of Versailles was not a flawless masterpiece. It was marred by grave defects. But they were not those alleged by its German or its pacifist critics.

In spite of these defects we must remember that the Treaty inaugurated an important historical advance. To perceive this we must distinguish its three main aspects. The *first* was concerned with the temporary provisions, reparations and disarmament. The *second* was the attempt to fix permanently Germany's Eastern frontier in accordance with the principle of national self-determination. The *third* was the creation of the League of Nations to whose protection all the other provisions were entrusted. The two last aspects undoubtedly turned European civilization, and indeed the civilized world, in the right direction.

Wilson was so disheartened by the failure of the Treaty to give full effect to his original ideals—a failure due as much to American as to European opposition, that he left Paris very ill and never recovered. On December 13, 1918, the *SS. George Washington* reached Brest. On the 14th, accompanied by the French President, he drove through the Champs d'Elysées amidst cheering crowds. "Vive l'Amérique, vive Wilson!" A large banner, hung across the street, bore the words "Salut à Wilson, le Juste."

The same Wilson returned to America a broken man. It was his merit, which cannot be praised too highly, that he called the world's attention to the necessity of a new international order and truly pointed out that, without it, no treaty provisions could endure and must lack any security for their observance so that it would not be long before a second catastrophe overwhelmed Europe. But, being a descendant of Scotch Puritans, who had inherited the thin and abstract pacifism which the Puritan tradition had produced in America, he failed to see that, in order to realize his ideal, Europe required far more time and far more religion than he calculated upon; and that in the meanwhile, provisional securities and solutions were necessary to provide the breathing space and the intellectual freedom indispensable for a permanent settlement. The most important of these temporary securities was the American guarantee of the French frontiers. When this was refused Clemenceau's victory over Wilson became inevitable.

WILSON AND GERMANY

All who were present at the Peace Congress of 1919 know the pains Wilson took to give effect to his Fourteen Points and how he was finally compelled to renounce

hope of complete success because the horror aroused by
the four years' War and by the German occupations was
so intense that the need of security and the disbelief in
the conversion of the defeated rendered inevitable a compromise between Wilson's peace and a peace of security.
The Germans who had laughed the Fourteen Points to
scorn and had proceeded to launch their poison-gas offensive, and up to the last moment had sought a peace dictated by victorious power, were not entitled to ask for
any peace other than such as they had themselves imposed
or sought to impose. They should rather have thanked
God that the ideals they had scorned had saved them from
a worse fate and stood as a screen between themselves and
the victors' need of security. Those who had called down
the Divine judgment of such a war should have been grateful for what Wilson was able to obtain.

The Germans also forgot that all the abuse directed
against the Allies between the Armistice and the conclusion of peace negotiations strengthened Clemenceau's
hand and weakened Wilson's. For it gave the impression
that the new Germany which now confronted the world
was a mere façade behind which the old forces were awaiting their hour. Eisner, the President of Bavaria, addressing a Socialist Congress at Berne, in order to enlighten
the German public gave a true account of the devastation
wrought in Northern France. The German press conducted such a violent campaign against him that it led to
his murder. He had in fact said to his English and French
comrades, "I have pronounced my own death sentence today. Henceforward I am a condemned man temporarily
reprieved." He knew the German people. And he also
knew that the entire German Left was a condemned and
temporarily reprieved man and would receive no thanks
for having liquidated the national bankruptcy with the
assent of those who had been responsible for it and had
temporarily fallen from power.

Our Nationalists have never suspected the harm they have done their country by their persistent complaints of the "disgraceful" peace. For this description of the peace utters the evil and unrepented war-lie in the face of the plain truth that the disgrace consisted, not in the Treaty but in the War begun in 1914; and that the peace, whatever traces it bore of the still raging War, nevertheless by the concessions it made to the principle of plebiscitary self-determination and by its inauguration of the League of Nations represented a considerable advance, and an advance which the conquered had not merited, upon all previous peace treaties. During the War Professor Otto von Gierke had cynically proclaimed the principle of German peacemaking:

"Hitherto in all the great wars of history the defeated have always accepted whatever terms the victors chose to dictate. But this they tell us has been altered by the advance of civilization and is incompatible with the modern sense of justice. Twaddle! *So long as war continues, the right of conquest will continue.* In the nature of things conquest confers the right to determine whether a conquered state shall be permitted to retain its independence; and, if so, what conditions shall be imposed upon it. And this is just."

The Germans should judge the Treaty of Versailles in the light of these words and be thankful that M. Clemenceau was very far from being a Herr von Gierke.

THE NEW EUROPE AFTER 1919

Rejoice ye mountains and exult ye hills
Wide o'er a land redeemed—once more his wings
Poland's white eagle spreads
(Polish Song of 1848).

Providence often brings to naught the plans of men and makes use of them to clear the air and pave the way to new developments. So was it with the first World War. It was intended by the Germans to bring the Western Slavs more completely than before under the German yoke. Its failure·gave birth to three new states.

The Treaty of Versailles was the logical result of the foundation at Versailles of the German Empire. Both historical events, that of 1871 and that of 1919, are so to speak mutually involved and merely represent two stages in the operation of the same principle. For both events sprang from the same fundamental principle to which at Versailles Louis XIV had formerly set the seal, the principle, namely, of a nation united and proudly conscious of its national unity. In the shape of the second German Reich Bismarck in 1871 had given solemn confirmation and constitutional expression to this principle, derived from Western Europe, of the national sovereign state. But the natural result of this solemn rebirth of the national principle was to awaken the same ideal throughout Eastern Europe, just as the influence of the German cosmopolitan humanism of which Herder was a typical representative had taken extensive hold upon the entire Western Slavonic world.

From the outset Bismarck had foreseen the result. He was fully alive to the logic of the principle of nationality which he had adopted. When in 1848 the national movement had resuscitated the Polish question, he spoke against the doctrine that the Polish districts of Prussia should be granted independence in the name of the principle of nationality. He said: "The logic of such a doctrine would make us set up on our South-Eastern frontier a new Slavonic Kingdom, restore the Italian Tyrol to the Venetians, and constitute out of Moravia and Bohemia an independent Czech state extending far into the center of Germany. A national movement by the Poles of Posen can have no other reasonable aim than the establishment of an independent Poland."

These words contain in substance the entire Treaty of Versailles. And nowhere is it more evident than in this picture painted by Bismarck's fear that the Treaty, simply drawing the consequences of the principle to which the entire history of modern Germany appealed, embodied it politically. The foundation of the Reich in 1871 and the restoration of Poland in 1919 are but two manifestations of the same historical force and ideal.

The portentous mistake of the German-Austrian policy in Eastern Europe favored by Bismarck, with its illogicality and narrowness, was its attempt to prevent forcibly the development and operation of its own principle: thus making the latter a lie or at best a half-truth instead of a fundamental first principle, and inevitably provoking sooner or later a clash with the national resurrection of the Western Slavs. Certainly this resurrection in its turn gave rise to unforeseen difficulties. But these difficulties, which had been completely overlooked when the German problem was being solved on the lines of national sovereignty and which were incapable of solution along those lines, demonstrated clearly that Bismarck's solution conflicted with the realities of Central and Eastern Europe.

The Treaty of Versailles did not impose an artificial solution of these problems. It simply drew inevitable conclusions hitherto artificially suppressed by force. The Treaty of Versailles, like the treaties of St. Germain and of the Trianon, completed the eastward advance of the principle of nationality. Even if the conflict between the Western and Southern Slavs and the German overlordship had not broken out on the occasion of the Sarajevo assassination it would have done so on some other occasion. The growth of Slavonic nationalism could no more be checked than the contemporary movement of the Far Eastern peoples to shake off European tutelage. And the German people, which had embraced with such ardor and consistency the principle of nationality on its journey from

West to East and had realized it politically, should understand that they cannot deny to others what they have
claimed for themselves—and least of all, to those who
had behind them centuries of brilliant existence as independent states. Certainly the execution of this national
principle hit Prussia very hard. A third of Poland had
been annexed by Prussia. When Poland now rose from
the dead she rose in the very midst of Prussia. It was
painful but impossible to prevent; it was the inevitable
reparation for that crime of partition which Gratuy called
Europe's mortal sin. The new frontier, it is true, cut clean
through the entire economic network of those regions,
thus conflicting with the most elementary needs of mutually dependent populations.

But human rights must take precedence of economic
considerations—and moreover, in the long run, to the economic benefit of all concerned. It was in Germany's power
to pursue a policy which would arouse confidence in her
intentions and thus complete the excessive nationalism of
Versailles by linking in a close community the peoples it
had separated. Germany decided to adopt this policy of a
revisionism, which looked forward, not backward, fifteen
years too late, when Gdynia had long outstripped Danzig
and when Poland had solved in this way her export
problem.

It is of interest to observe in this connection how the
Treaty of Versailles re-established in the Vistula basin a
rational situation overthrown by Prussian aggression.
Danzig for example, which in the Middle Ages had been
the port through which the Slavs exported their produce
and which Frederick the Great's annexation had cut off
from its economic hinterland—Frederick the Great, wrote
Schopenhauer's mother, fell upon my unfortunate native
city like a vampire—once more resumed in the main its
former function. A great future was opening up to it and
business circles were increasingly attracted by new pros-

pects. But German nationalism gave a different word of command, and economic interests must be remorselessly sacrificed to its execution. "What was German must be German again." Countless foreigners, deceived by German propaganda, have advocated the return of Danzig and the "impossible" Corridor, thereby displaying their complete ignorance of the facts. Simply to have returned Danzig and the Corridor would have condemned to starvation the populations thus handed over. For they are completely dependent upon the Polish hinterland.

A far-seeing German policy would have solved the German-Polish problem decades ago on very different lines and have extended the German economic sphere in the East. It would have liberated the Prussian and Austrian Poles; and having done so, would have brought them into close economic federation. The result of the misconceived and narrow policy actually pursued was, as might have been foretold, to restrict instead of to enlarge Germany's economic sphere in the East.

The new Germany was blind to the fact that the independent Western and Southern Slavonic states created by the Treaty of Versailles had given her a new field for her exports, whose exploitation in peaceful collaboration with the Slavs would have repaid tenfold any territorial losses. Bitter disasters still await Eastern Europe, that unhappy region already soaked in blood, before its bloody history is finally atoned for and overcome. Those frontiers were the point at which the westward movement of the Teutons turned back upon its steps and stained every inch of soil with German and Slavonic blood. No League of Nations and no treaty will abolish the effects of that curse. Only the Saviour's Precious Blood can erase the incalculable wrong and the Satanic hate which here have had free rein and still hold captive men's minds and hearts in bonds seemingly unbreakable.

The solution given to the difficult problem of Upper

Silesia throws no less light upon the general German problem than the decision to hand over to Poland the Polish inhabitants of the so-called Corridor. The Treaty of Versailles prescribed a plebiscite. To the utter amazement of the German Nationalists who had attempted to overawe the Poles of Upper Silesia by every species of terrorism, so large a proportion of the population which had been separated from Poland for eight centuries voted for union with her that the frontier had to be drawn through the heart of the manufacturing districts. How is this result to be explained? By the fact that the non-German population had been ill-treated for centuries. The desire no longer to be second-class citizens prevailed over all other considerations. "What madness to divide manu-facturing districts mutually dependent", German critics exclaimed, and their criticism misled many foreign visi-tors to the country. No doubt—but this precisely was the encouraging feature of the plebiscite—the rights of hu-man beings prevailed over the rights of coal.

What prevented the foundation of a new community of mutual trust that would gradually have rendered the political frontier invisible? The blindness of the German Nationalists prevented it, against all the interests of the people concerned. Three months before the plebiscite a committee of Protestant and Catholic clergy of Upper Silesia asked me to plead with the League of Nations to leave both portions of Upper Silesia in one state. They promised to work for reconciliation between the Germans and the Poles. After consulting those in charge of the plebiscite I replied that the League had simply to super-vise the plebiscite but had no authority to dispense with it. If the Poles of Upper Silesia could be made to feel that in future they would be placed on an equal footing with the Germans, that is to say, if they were appointed to posi-tions of trust, they might perhaps decide to remain with Germany. The head of the department of the Foreign

Office which dealt with Upper Silesia also approached me. I gave him the same advice. It was not taken. The Nationalist terror had free course. Teachers of Polish sympathies were flogged before their pupils. The result was soon evident. The government dared not take any steps to present the entire question to the German public in a truer light. They did not understand it themselves and left the *furor teutonicus* to do its work unchecked.

WAR-GUILT AGAIN

We are brought back once again to the question of war-guilt. If Germany had been innocent or even only in part guilty, Versailles was iniquitous and Europe owes Germany reparation for it. And this is in fact what is maintained by the Germans who attack the guilt-lie.

Many Frenchmen are content to reply by pointing out that clause 231 of the Treaty merely demands from Germany reparation for damage done, just as a civil court may order damages, without raising the question who was responsible for starting the War. But the question is not so simple. Devastation so malicious and so barbarous goes far beyond anything that would be considered a matter of civil damages. If German propaganda is justified in its contention that the German invasion was an act of legitimate self-defense against a hostile combination, the Allies were the real aggressors. The question of guilt cannot therefore be ruled out. So well have the Germans understood this, that they have spent fabulous sums to persuade the world of Germany's innocence. And if Germany could be proved innocent the consequences are plain and fearful. We cannot therefore insist too strongly on two authoritative declarations which make plain the indissoluble connection between the reparations demanded by the Treaty and the Central Powers' responsibility for the War:

Poincaré said, "If it had not been the Central Powers that provoked the War, why should they be condemned to pay damages? If the responsibility for the War had been divided the costs must in all justice have also been divided." And Lloyd George said, "In the view of the Allies, Germany's responsibility for the War is fundamental. It is the foundation on which the Treaty of Versailles has been built. If the admission of German guilt is rescinded or given up, the Treaty is destroyed."

Schopenhauer devoted a most important chapter to "The Primacy of the Will in Self-Consciousness". His psychology is of the greatest political importance today. Nowhere has truth been sacrificed so ruthlessly to the will as in this question of war-guilt. Germany's campaign to clear herself of responsibility for the first World War is the second great World War she has conducted. This war also will be lost by Germany. The evidence against her is too strong. And this second defeat is the psychological and moral presupposition of Germany's true restoration and the salvation of Europe.

CHAPTER XV

THE GERMAN WAR AGAINST VERSAILLES

I HAVE sufficiently proved that the peace of Versailles was not a peace of revenge or the exaction of tribute from a vanquished foe but a peace of reparation and security; which, however, linked up these two aims with the inauguration of a radical settlement, including reparation of the secular wrong done to the Poles. Those who criticize the obvious mistakes, the lacunae and the injustices of the Treaty must not lose sight of the enormous difficulties of a peace in which not only the whole of Europe but a large portion of the rest of the world was concerned and which moreover was concluded during the anarchy that followed the first World War and in face of the most uncertain prospects. Who could guarantee the future political development?

Under these circumstances, to combine the necessary provisions for security and compensation with the new ideas of international order, to harmonize a host of detailed recommendations by experts with the general principles to be embodied by the peace was so difficult a task that in the nature of things only a very defective treaty could result. The entire course of future events, all the possibilities of correction, relaxation, modification and shortening the period of occupation, depended on the attitude adopted by Germany to the European reaction against four years of crime and madness.

Conceivably Germany might have awakened after the War, as from a bad dream, and have looked back with horror on what had been done. It was at least possible that wide and influential groups should have recognized that the entire policy of modern Germany had been, for a nation engaged so extensively in international trade, a mistaken policy even from the material standpoint, and that a second attempt must be fatal.

Precisely the opposite happened, as indeed might have been foreseen after a defeat so unexpected and after a War into which the vast majority of the nation had entered without misgivings and whose crimes it had justified or denied. From the Right to the Social Democrats a storm of protest against the entire Treaty swept the land. The organ of the Social Democratic party denounced, on behalf of the children, the return of the cows, but said nothing of the French departments from which they had been stolen. All the injuries done to others during the previous four years were forgotten. Nothing existed save German suffering and German loss of territory. Reparations were "The enslavement of the German people". That foreign nations also had to suffer severely from the effects of the War, that the manufactures of France were ruined whereas German industry was in a position to resume shortly its victorious advance—all this was forgotten. To get rid of reparations became the slogan of the groups in command of wealth and arms and with a tradition behind them. Propaganda which cost hundreds of millions of marks—literally and demonstrably these sums were spent—was organized with money which should have been spent on the restoration of France, to excite the German people against France and the Peace Treaty. Millions of pamphlets, published in almost every European language, even Portuguese, distorted all the facts and misplaced the responsibilities so that the Germans, who since 1914 had been convinced that we had been attacked, were now equally convinced that their guilty foes were determined to make use of their victory to impose upon the German people the servitude of unjust and excessive reparations.

If the War was a hideous crime, this Hugenberg propaganda was perhaps even more criminal. It lied to the German people on such a vast scale, so deeply embittered them, deceived them so completely about the facts and the true culprits, and so blinded them to the real cause of their privations and isolation, that they were ripe for a Second World War.

"Are you French?" a chambermaid in Berlin asked a French Professor in 1922.

"Yes."

"Well then, remember what I say. The first war we were forced into, the second we shall make of our free choice."

Why? The propaganda, the everlasting propaganda of lies. In a true sense, Hitler is Hugenberg's legitimate son. Hugenberg had infected the German blood with his lies; Hitler is the reaction of the veins to it; that is to say, the reaction of a serious, logical, and sentimental people which has simply drawn the inevitable conclusions from this complete perversion of the facts.

Towards the end of 1919 Lord Snell, one of the leaders of the Labor Party, visited me in Berne. In our conversation he said, "All might have been so different if only during the months after the Armistice you Germans had spoken a single word of sympathy for Europe, and of regret for what had been done, and given some trustworthy assurance that you had been converted from your former ways and were prepared to repair the damages done." I replied: "Anyone who had said officially anything of the sort would have been assassinated." Our rulers were less concerned about what they would say to Europe than about what to say to their own people.

In his book *Das verlorene Afrika* (Lost Africa) Captain Paasche had the courage to point out to his compatriots the true reasons why they had lost their African colonies.

"Few Germans", he wrote, "are aware of the gulf which divided them from the rest of mankind and that it will be more impossible than ever to convert the world to their antiquated moral ideas. The German ideology is dead in the outside world. We rode the national ideal to death. Shrill and monotonous sounded our slogans: *We are it, our right to a place in the sun, we above everyone else, the first place for Germany, awake to power.* Always the delusion that Germany could prosper by violence against other nations, peoples and markets, that our interests are separate from those of others. Always the cry, Germany needs, we need, our workers need. . . . Everything we Germans prided ourselves upon has turned to our shame and will remain so. . . . Be sure of this, Germans; you will be excluded from the community of nations, unless at last you turn against the system that has made you the butcher of your neighbors and has finally crushed you. . . . The world will not receive you again till you are once more human. It has been your destiny to push the ideals of nation and fatherland to madness. Recognize now the men who have led you astray, the men who are guilty of the War, the bellicose professors and clergy. Prussian teachers have actually given the categorical imperative, the form 'Do whatever the General Staff bids'. . . . Foreigners knew that German brains and wealth were completely at the service of brute force and that one day the man to whom divine wisdom was ascribed had but to press a button and everything German would break out in an avalanche of destruction, guns, armor plate, chemical products, the bones of grenadiers, philosophy, men, printing ink and concrete. . . . There is an entire edifice of doctrine, education and foreign policy which we must abandon."

Captain Paasche was attacked on his own estate by Nationalists and murdered.

In vain Karl von Ossietsky wrote: "The revision of an intolerable treaty presupposes the revision of an intolerable attitude of mind." He is in a concentration camp, from which not even the Nobel Prize could set him free.

The watchword was issued from the very first: the Peace

Treaty must be destroyed at all costs. Erect a pacifist façade and behind it prepare the war of revenge. To that façade belonged many honorable men who genuinely desired a different Germany in future. They were powerless. Those who possessed the money, the arms, the tradition, and the press sought what is called in theological language "the restitution of all things".

REPARATIONS SABOTAGED

"France has fulfilled her obligations honorably. She has risen from her defeat and achieved her regeneration. Full of admiration for this great nation which must have laid crushing burdens upon herself to pay off her gigantic indemnity the German Reich has entered into negotiations with the French Republic and hopes they will result in the complete evacuation of her territory before the date fixed by the treaty." So spoke William I in the Reichstag on March 12, 1873.

This quotation presents a very different picture from that presented by Germany's struggle against the payment of reparations. Yet there was this important distinction between the two cases: tribute, in the strict sense, was imposed upon France, whereas the payment demanded from Germany was reparation for damage done, of which the largest part was the malicious destruction wrought during the retreat. That section of the German people which had any knowledge of the destruction wished to make honorable restitution. Even the political leaders wished it. But they had neither the courage nor the ability to do so against the will of those who possessed the real power. The latter were determined to sabotage the reparations.

The two years before the London ultimatum of 1921 were simply frittered away. France was obliged to borrow ninety thousand million, not including the interest, in order to begin her reconstruction at her own expense. This produced a corresponding deficit. On March 10, 1923, the director of the Darmstadt and National Bank, Berlin, wrote in *Menschheit*, "Actually France has not received from us a franc in ready money. The thousand million marks in gold paid since the London ultimatum have gone to Belgium in virtue of the provision giving her priority. Certainly gold is not the sole medium of payment. Germany was also bound to a number of most important payments in kind whose money value was to be included in the reparations. She was to deliver ships, coals, dyes, machinery, locomotives. But the deliveries of these things have been irregular. The entire world, not France alone, is convinced, that Germany was bound both by her Treaty obligations and on moral grounds, and was financially able, at any rate until the middle of 1922, as the exchange then stood, not only to make deliveries of material for the work of reconstruction but gold payments as well."

In the opinion of this financial expert of the first rank Germany was then perfectly capable of paying. "The War," he wrote, "had piled up wealth in the hands of the manufacturers and merchants, and agriculture also had enormously profited by it. All classes of producers were doing very well." Skillful taxation would have brought in enormous sums without substantial detriment to the national economy.

But there was no intention of paying and the government dared not impose the taxation imposed on the wealthy in other countries. Later the *Schweizerische Finanzrevue* stated most truly, "The entire world knows that the German nation has never had the intention to pay what it was her duty to pay for the reconstruction of Europe. . . ." And the American *Saturday Evening Post*, in a review of the German manoeuvres, printed the following assertions commonly made in Germany: "Germany's guilt is a lie. The Treaty of Versailles was the worst crime in modern history. Reparations are tribute. America joined the Allies in 1917 because she had lent them her money. In international intercourse the debtor is supported by the creditor. The object of the Hoover plan of 1931 for paying reparations is to protect the two billions of American money invested in Germany. For the debt obliges America to be Germany's political friend."

In the occupied territories the French sought to compensate themselves for the failure to deliver the material promised by felling trees in German forests. Thereupon the German press raised a wild outcry. To the journalist who protested the loudest I sent the following quotation from Pestalozzi: "If you burn down your neighbor's house and he cuts down your trees to rebuild it, what would he think, do you suppose, if you shouted to him, 'You have no right to those trees'?"

The groups in economic control of Germany began a campaign in the press, contrary to their own better knowledge, against Wirth's policy of fulfilling treaty obligations, and made the German people believe that they were not capable of paying when in fact they were. Thus, though they could have prevented it, they provoked the French occupation of the Ruhr and then by making the state pay the cost of this war of passive resistance, they plunged entire classes of the German people into abysmal poverty.

When the German state had shown itself unable to make those in control of German finances pay their debt, the French occupation of the Ruhr enforced payment. Those gentlemen realized that the injury France could do them by the occupation would cost them dearer than payment. The German failure to pay would have been less provocative if in Germany the state, the local authorities, and the industrialists had not lived so extravagantly. Everywhere new railroad stations were being built—whereas in France, even large towns were content with poor station buildings—also vast stadia, municipal buildings and the like. "We could not afford such luxuries," said the French. The refusal to deliver the material, which was certainly deliberate, led to the occupation of the Ruhr. Even such pacifists as the sociologist Lévy-Bruhl and Ferdinand Buisson approved of it.

On the French entrance into the Ruhr, the correspondent of the *Basler Nationalzeitung* sent the following report to his paper: "The German heavy industrialists think they are sufficiently strong to hold out. They are aware that the English and the United States are afraid that by uniting under a single control the iron ore of Lorraine and the Ruhr coke, France may secure a monopoly of the continental iron and steel manufacture. They therefore expect to receive from these countries the credit necessary to finance their defensive against France. Their objects are to mobilize public opinion everywhere against the French action and to compel the French to take increasingly severe measures, then to increase the French coal famine, and finally to reduce the exchange value of the franc and thus make the French weary of the conflict. In itself their plan of campaign is not without a prospect of success. But it takes too little account of the fact that the difficulties immediately facing France are much less than the suffering which resistance is bringing upon the German people."

This report reveals powerful and unscrupulous German intrigues and at the same time throws light on the motives of certain groups in England which, instead of giving the French the unreserved support they had a right to expect from the British guarantee, encouraged the Germans in their resistance and persuaded themselves that by doing so they were humane and generous, whereas they did nothing but harm—harm moreover to the economic life of the entire world.

Poincaré, the statesman responsible for the occupation of the Ruhr, was henceforward regarded by the Germans as the devil incarnate. Their judgment of his character was entirely false. Neither before nor after the War was Poincaré a nationalist, an enemy of Germany or a warmonger. But to the core of his being he was a lawyer; therefore, also an advocate of international law, a Latin jurist, an opponent of war. As a native of Lorraine he understood the modern Germans, was therefore convinced that a war was inevitable and did all in his power to prepare France and her allies for what must come. After the War the *leitmotiv* of his policy was to enforce the payment of reparations not merely in the interest of France but also in order to re-establish the reign of law in Europe. It was with this motive, not to destroy Germany, that he entered the Ruhr; and he spoke the truth when he said that without the occupation of the Ruhr the Dawes agreement would never have been concluded. There are people who realize that they will have to pay their debts only when the bailiffs have entered their house and put their seals on the piano. The occupation he regarded as an obvious and inevitable step.

When the question of reparation had been settled by an international agreement Poincaré regarded as equally obvious the gradual but deliberate restoration of normal relations with Germany. The supremacy of law to which his entire life had been devoted, and which was also the moral inspiration of his work for the restoration of French finance, could be achieved only by an order of international justice. The first attempts at the Hague to set up such an order he had warmly welcomed and promoted. When Germany wrecked his hopes he saw in her attitude the plainest proof of her rulers' warlike intentions.

This criticism of the German attitude does not deny the grave mistakes committed by the opposite side. The reparation figures of astronomical size disheartened the Germans. The entire problem was treated as if it were compensation for a broken window-pane. It was not thought out and treated in the framework of world economy. No one approached the Germans as man to man. The Allies left

them to welter in anarchy and were content with the role
of bailiffs. There were still men in Germany who spoke
out frankly. The Entente sat by and watched with a smile
the suppression and rejection of their criticism until by
degrees free speech was made impossible. The infamous
fabrication of war-lies continued without much attempt
at concealment, terrorist associations of every kind were
formed and were active on a large scale, the press and
public opinion—in any case both were a very dubious
factor in Germany—were at sea, anxiety and fear spread,
every coward and rascal made haste to fly the super-
patriotic flag.

The Entente saw all this happening under their noses
and did absolutely nothing. It would have been so easy,
child's play in fact, to call a halt to all these paid venal
scribblers, whether soldiers or civilians of higher or lower
rank. Those of us who at that time risked life or position
to enlighten the German people and bring home to them
their responsibilities, indeed to prove to them where their
true interest lay, could not blame too severely the fault
committed by the victors in failing to take the necessary
steps to cure the anarchic condition of Germany. When I
said this to an influential Frenchman, he replied—and his
answer was not without a measure of truth—"You are certainly right. But you have only been a few days in France."
It was 1923. "If you stayed only a few weeks you would
see how untrue it is to speak of 'victors'. God alone knows
which of our two peoples has endured the worse blows,
has been bled whiter, is the greater nervous wreck, has
been the more ruined. We have as little thought to give
to Germany as Germany to us. And I assure you we did
not enter the Ruhr because we had no mercy for the
Germans, but to show their rulers who was master, which
must benefit Germany herself. But your people always
stand solidly behind their seducers."

One thing is certain. The bad faith of those who possessed the real power in Germany was undeniable. It did incalculable harm to Germany's position in the eyes of the world and in countless ways interfered with and postponed a reasonable settlement of the problem of reparations.

A VISIT TO THE GERMAN AMBASSADOR IN PARIS

In 1925, shortly after the campaign of passive resistance had broken down, I discussed the entire question of the relations between Germany and the rest of Europe with the German Ambassador in Paris, von Hoesch. I was introduced to him by a German officer of high rank who shared my views. But it required courage on his part to receive a German who, because he had publicly condemned the passive resistance at that time, was the subject of most violent attacks in the national press.

The Ambassador alluded to my position in the matter when he remarked, "It is said that you have cut yourself off from your fellow-countrymen." I replied, not in jest but with a deliberate purpose, "So much the worse for my fellow-countrymen." He almost fell flat at such conceit. But I hastened to add in the most serious tones, "An individual may be in the right against his entire nation, if the protest he makes is based upon a great and venerable tradition and on an intimate knowledge of the facts inaccessible, under present circumstances, to the vast majority of the Germans. There are very few Germans who know as I do the extent and wilful malice of the devastation ordered without any military necessity by the German High Command. Therefore, in my opinion there is a moral obligation to make reparations. But those who wield the real power in Germany refused to pay this debt of honor. Therefore, the French were fully justified in making use of the rights accorded to them by the Treaty."

Naturally the Ambassador and I did not agree. Nor, indeed, was he in a position to say what he really thought. German ambassadors after two or three years in Paris always became very friendly to France and began to see the conflict between France and Germany in such a new light that they had to be transferred to another capital. This indeed happened to von Hoesch. At that time he was an enthusiastic admirer of Stresemann and argued against me that after such a war, debacle and peace there would naturally be a section which could not change its attitude so quickly and that it depended entirely upon the French whether these people were gradually thrust into the background. French militarism however—at this point I interrupted him. I said there was no such thing as French militarism. Behind the French determination not to let themselves be tricked stood not the French army but the small peasant who sat amid the ruins of his farm and said "never again war". And as regards our Nationalists, before very long it would be plain that they were not losing ground, but becoming constantly more powerful. Therefore, the French could not be too strongly warned against living in a fool's paradise, as indeed Heine had already warned them.

It was most instructive to observe how this entirely honorable and well-intentioned man who, as the son of a leading manufacturer, came from a group in touch with the outside world, swallowed all the clichés so cleverly devised and disseminated by the ruling class in order to prevent Germans from studying freely and frankly the causes of their national defeat and to throw the blame for everything, dishonorably and against their better knowledge, on the enemy.

After the War I spoke to a large number of German diplomats of long standing and great experience, for example, the future Ambassador Solf. In private conversations they expressed views which hardly differed from my own. Herr von Hoesch, who had been comparatively but a short time in the service, had no diplomatic experience of the period before the War. This made him an optimist. But as I was informed by one who knew him intimately, the rise of militaristic nationalism to power gave him such a shock that it hastened his death.

GERMAN DISARMAMENT AND REARMAMENT

I propose to say little on this topic. For the facts are known to everyone and we are concerned only with their bearing on the psychological, political and moral problem of which my book treats.

For the supporters of the old tradition the disarmament imposed upon Germany was the most humiliating provision of the Treaty and the provision whose effect hit them most severely. On the other hand, the reaction of a continent ravaged by the German military machine was, as we should have expected, primarily directed against this formidable danger.

Only those intimately acquainted with Germany can understand what the disappearance of the army meant to the entire nation. Other nations have a population of civilians and an army to defend it. But German society was built on the army and its regulations, its views and notions of duty. The army was as much an instrument of social education as of national defense. It was to this educational function that the officers who had served in the War appealed when after the War they gathered the undisciplined young loafers into patriotic associations, in many places accomplishing magnificent work.

Many German defenders of the institution, however, have had eyes only for its educational aspect and have completely lost sight of the purpose the army was designed to serve abroad and the disastrous moral effect on the German people produced by the object for which the army existed and by the traditional glorification of war which accompanied it. If the Germans are in fact incapable of any other national aim than the concentration of the nation's entire forces on total war or of any other inspira-

tion than the feeling which military maneuvers so naturally produce and which the Crown Prince once expressed
when he exclaimed, "Heavens! if only this were the real
thing", the rest of humanity will certainly determine
sooner or later to place such an abnormal people under
permanent supervision.

The disarmament clause of the Treaty of Versailles gave
Germany providential and final opportunity to free herself from this militarist obsession which devoured all the
national strength and to substitute for compulsion a free
choice. This would have released a nation, whose economic links are worldwide, from the prison-house of Potsdam and enabled her to pursue a genuinely European
policy. It would have been the greatest and most decisive
reparation she could make. The opportunity was not
taken. Instead, the military foundation of a German war
of revenge was systematically laid and built up. Germany,
as she persistently maintained, had completely disarmed.
She had indeed got rid entirely of her antiquated armament but only to replace it by new armament, and in the
background of the small legal army to reconstruct, like an
enormous shadow, the old army. That this was possible
was due chiefly to the unteachable British illusion about
the "new" Germany combined with the British policy of
balance of power, which entirely misconceived the German
situation.

We, the German defenders of peace who were kept fully
informed by our numerous friends in the army of the successive stages of the German rearmament whose pace increased tenfold after Locarno, did everything humanly
possible to reveal to our own people and to foreign countries the extent and the danger of this breach of the Treaty.
It was all in vain. None would see or listen. It seemed as
though every statesman preferred to leave his successors
to face the serious conflicts which any effective interference
would produce rather than to tackle so explosive a prob-

lem. Among the few who faced the truth was Herriot. But like Tardieu he was prevented by British influences from placing all the damning facts before the League. Nevertheless we did not abandon our efforts. We regarded it as a debt of honor to the country that there should be at least a few Germans who, at a moment when the Entente were preparing to make concessions and conclude agreements with a Germany in whose honor they trusted, would expose the trickery of German rearmament.

In 1926 when the League Assembly held an important meeting we published and distributed a pamphlet based on intimate knowledge of the facts. The pamphlet described the extent, the speed and the object of German rearmament, with proofs and comment. Many thoughtful people were alarmed. But the governments refused to be shaken from their apathy. Stresemann however lost his self-control and called us *"Lumpen"*—rogues—for which he later apologized to a relative of mine.

The most fatal and depressing aspect of the situation was the fact that in the struggle against this gigantic fraud which finally proved fatal to it, the German Left completely let us down. They concealed everything, kept silence about everything, indeed actually attacked those Germans who had the courage to say what they should have said themselves. Instead of honorably informing the Entente of the truth, they did not scruple to talk of a disarmed Germany, though they knew perfectly well that Germany had already prepared her industries and finances for war and had rearmed on a large scale. There existed moreover, an abstract German variety of pacifism which persistently agitated for the disarmament of other nations and persuaded itself that the responsibility for German rearmament lay with a France "armed to the teeth". Yet, as they must have known, the resurrection of German militarism was deep-rooted in a tradition and a mentality well-nigh ineradicable, whose representatives allied themselves with international pacifism in order to disarm their opponents by appealing to their own principles. In Geneva, German nationalism and international pacifism collaborated in the interest of the former: truly one of the greatest comedies in the history of mankind.

This collaboration was made possible by the abstract nature of this international pacifism which misled the idealists of world-peace into inviting the Prussian wolf, cleverly disguised in sheep's clothing, to work with them and into giving it in the name of equal rights the freedom it sought—namely the freedom to produce, by employing the high German military potential, a thorough inequality of armaments. The trick would have succeeded if Hitler's program had not awakened in time a world drugged by pacifism to the grim reality of German rearmament and its aims and given it the opportunity to make up for lost time. The spectacle silenced at last the persistent repetition of the argument that a completely disarmed Germany had been promised universal disarmament and that the breach of this promise by the Allies justified the Germans in secretly rearming. For the amazing extent and rapidity of Nazi rearmament proved that the foundations must have been laid long before, and that, under cover of Locarno, rearmament had been enormously speeded up—cleverly disguised under all sorts of innocent-looking provisions in the budgets—and that the handful of Germans who had denounced the talk of a disarmed Germany as an impudent fraud had been right after all.

Our attempt to enlighten the world was assisted by soldiers who could not hold their tongue. Colonel Hierl, for example, an intimate friend of Hitler's, in 1929, gave away the entire program: a preparation for war behind the screen of pacifism:—

"There are two sorts of pacifism. There is genuine pacifism. This is due to a weak and sickly constitution or mental blindness, but it is sincere. And there is a hypo-

critical pacifism. The latter is a weapon of political conflict and in fact assists the preparation for war. Lulling the
enemy to sleep with pacific phrases it hopes to persuade
him to neglect his armament. The narcotic vapor with
which we surround him conceals our own preparations
for war. It is from this point of view that we should regard
the Kellogg pact to renounce war and the disarmament
conferences of the League."

What a tragedy it was! All these well-meaning men in
Germany and abroad, whom our Colonel called weak and
sickly, fell into the trap laid for them and did everything
expected of them. The fox preached to the geese and the
geese believed everything he said. When at last he took off
his mask and the trick was discovered, they stared at each
other dumbfounded. Why did they not give earlier heed
to our warnings, definite and supported by solid evidence?
There is a German flight from reality. But it met an
English and French flight from reality which also had its
distinctive causes in the national character.

The real attitude of the German militarists was expressed in the following passage from a leading article in
the *Militaerwochenblatt* which appeared in September,
1932. "No one who possesses military superiority cares a
straw for pacifist phrasemaking. Only one consideration
can prevent a nation from going to war: the risk involved,
the fear of defeat."

CHAPTER XVI

FALSE AND TRUE PACIFISM

PEACEMAKING IN THE AIR

WHAT could be more natural than that after the incalculable suffering of the War, the cry "Never again" should have resounded throughout the world and that the desire to secure permanent peace should have become the dominant sentiment of mankind. Under the actual conditions that desire found expression by adherence to Wilson's League of Nations, a purely institutional pacifism. Men forgot that, if war were to be abolished, atonement must be made for a crime which had darkened the face of heaven. They forgot that the law, a thousand times flouted, must recover its supremacy in the law-breakers' souls, before it could be effective in this novel institution and they were quite oblivious of the fact there must be trustworthy proof that the guilty had genuinely abandoned their unscrupulous program and ambitions and also proof that the new peacemaking machinery was working well and not being abused to assist a preparation for a war of revenge.

The danger was that a superficial pacifism might prevail and that in the interest of international trade and a rapid reconciliation between the nations such a pacifism might demand that everything which had happened should be speedily consigned to oblivion and a radical treatment of the evil denounced, as troubling the waters unnecessarily. There was every inducement to close wounds before they had been washed and disinfected. To be a pacifist was to be pro-German in the worst fashion, to echo the unre-

pentant protests of the war-makers, and to seek reconciliation *at any price* though the intellectual, moral, and religious conditions under which alone the nations could
once more collaborate had not been realized.

Men were everywhere talking of the "Abolition of War"
and seriously persuading themselves that it could be abolished by international cartels of manufacturers placing
reparations on a commercial basis, and by intellectual
cooperation: and even that a United States of Europe could
be botched up over the plague pit, so that the entire catastrophe should finally prove a blessing to the continent.

More than twelve millions were killed in the War, eight
millions were crippled, millions more suffered from its
effects, incalculable suffering was the lot of millions of
wives and mothers. Is it credible that all this could be even
gradually forgotten and put away as though it had been
an inundation of the Yellow River, that atonement and
purification could—and in the unfavorable atmosphere
should—be dispensed with?

Certainly we need an organization for maintaining peace
throughout the world. But the first step, which should have
been taken towards this end after the War, was to make the
cause of the disaster plain to the entire world and to fix
the responsibility for it on those who had represented war,
which is a plague and a catastrophe, indeed the bankruptcy
of civilization, as a blessing and as an indispensable instrument for forming human character, the touchstone of every
value and the tribunal to decide which nations were
worthy to survive, a tribunal whose verdict God Himself
must accept. Those enemies of peace should have been
deprived of every chance to resume their deadly game. But
the attempt should not have been made to obliterate all
distinctions of national character by an abstract and cosmopolitan pacifism.

Nothing is more likely to lead to war than a pacifism
which is out of touch with reality and so fails to perceive

the diabolical element in human life and to exorcize it by
the only appropriate means. This is true of the past as
well as of the present. After the warmongers of Berlin,
the English and French pacifists were most responsible for
the first World War. They denied the obvious danger, and
when they could deny it no longer, they prevented the
adoption of the only measures which could have averted it.
"France is unprepared for war—" this was what Germany's
military leaders informed Vienna at the end of July 1914
as the decisive reason why the risk of a World War could
be taken. Who was to blame for this? The same doctrinaire
pacifists who in the past had prevented Napoleon III from
paying attention to the urgent warnings sent him from
Berlin by the French Colonel Stoffel.

Who was to blame for the fact that in 1914 Berlin
counted upon England's neutrality? Not Sir Edward Grey,
who could not speak or act in advance of English public
opinion. The fault lay with the purblind pacifism of the
City and of the radical idealists which, as is proved by the
reminiscences of Wickham Steed and of Spender, put such
pressure upon the Foreign Office to hold its hand, that
nothing was done to enlighten and frighten the warmongers.

The humanist Masaryk, who was well acquainted with
the Prussian neutrality, observed when speaking of the
Allies' decision to save 100,000 lives by not marching to
Berlin: "The omission will cost you far more than 100,000
lives."

Many Frenchmen blame the makers of the Treaty of
Versailles for not having put an end to Prussian hegemony
by dividing Germany into a federation of independent
states. This indeed was Paul Cambon's view. These critics
certainly show greater knowledge of the evil from which
Germany suffers than do the majority of Englishmen,
whom it is hard to wean from their love of Prussia. Nevertheless they are mistaken. For they take no account of the

strength of Nationalist propaganda. The War did nothing to cure the German nation of its Nationalist ideal. An enforced division would have done no good. Germany would have resounded from one end to the other with the clamant agitation for reunion, and a weary world would have given way to it in the end. Only an experience that will shake its confidence, no regime imposed from outside, can convert the Germans from the ideal they have cherished for the last 130 years. If after the next catastrophe it is desired to separate Prussia from the remainder of Germany and at the same time to organize an efficient control of Germany, this will be possible only if the whole of Europe is correspondingly reorganized. In any case all such measures are merely technical and must ultimately prove impotent in face of the spiritual problem in the background. This spiritual problem is the core of the German problem. Its solution waits for a miracle—the spiritual rebirth of the European nations. I shall return to this matter later in the book.

BRITISH PACIFISM AND THE GERMAN QUESTION

British pacifism is something totally different from doctrinal pacifism in other countries and from the natural pacifism of the French. In England also there exists a doctrinal pacifism deeply convinced and with a long tradition behind it. But the political power wielded by the British love of peace is not derived from it but from *the logic of Britain's economic position as the center of world trade,* her Empire scattered throughout the world, her experience of confederation, embodied by this British Commonwealth of Nations, and not least from her employment of arbitration to settle trade disputes.

From her Empire Britain has acquired a vast knowledge of different peoples and great wisdom in handling men, the art of waiting, of conciliating conflicting interests, and discreetly guiding without parade of domination. Since

Britain in her colonial administration has had such constant practice in reconciling the most divergent interests, she has acquired an extraordinary capacity to make terms with any new powers that may arise in the world. This is the secret of her Empire—and also the explanation of her conciliatory attitude towards Germany, indeed of the offers of alliance she made to her.

Another reason for this attitude to Germany was the collaboration of both peoples in the commercial field, in which the English learned to appreciate highly the complementary qualities of the Germans. The blunders of British policy after the War were in large part due to the sincere wish for a good understanding with Germany and to sympathy with the open-hearted type of German seaman.

But there was a third reason for it. A most intelligible result of the ecclesiastical separation which tore England apart from the Continent was the policy of the balance of power. This policy sought to secure England by never permitting the continental nations to unite or one continental power to achieve hegemony. Unfortunately England's spiritual separation from the Continent fatally prevented the English from understanding the psychology of continental Europeans. It is positively astounding how for many decades British statesmen have so completely misunderstood the mentality and political development of the Germans.

In his study of England's relations with France and Germany, *Idealism and Foreign Policy* (1925), A. Ramsay shows that the English conception of Germany dates from the Napoleonic wars and has not been corrected since. In 1850 Palmerston said that a German confederation with Prussia at its head would be an excellent arrangement for Germany. No one troubled about Prussian militarism. On December 10, 1870 a leading article in the *Times* maintained that of all the continental nations Germany was the least dangerous. And this point of view has never been radically altered.

British political thought, which has been molded by international commerce, is so diametrically opposed to the political thought of Germans steeped in the military tradition of Potsdam that the British have never yet fully grasped the tendencies of the latter. The Englishman saw the extent to which Germany had become an industrial and commercial nation. He therefore believed that Germany's interest in world trade would gradually find expression in German politics. He did not know that the Nationalist ideal was omnipotent and compelled the industrialists to think in the political sphere in terms not of international commerce but of power-politics. Potsdam ruled Essen. Hence no opposition was aroused by the Kaiser's remark in a speech at Bremen—that it was the task of the German merchant throughout the world "To drive in the nail from which we can hang our armor." No Englishman has yet recognized what was clear to the Frenchman Edgar Quinet as long ago as 1833. Certainly the reality of the military threat is at long last perceived. But up to the last moment it was still thought possible to divert by "arrangements" the German determination to regain her power.

I once saw in a newsreel a most impressive picture. English engineers at Scapa Flow had filled one of the sunken German warships with compressed air, and it slowly rose to the surface with all its funnels and masts from the foam of the defeated waters. The picture was a symbol. With British help the unconverted Germany of 1914 has gradually emerged from its submersion. And the hour has come when England realizes her miscalculation in assisting that resurrection and sees what a totally different policy she should have pursued towards Germany if she was to aid the birth of a new Germany instead of resuscitating the old, closing her eyes to all its plotting at a time when she and France should have been resisting in concert the rebirth of German militarism.

Today the vessel so marvelously refloated is showing her gratitude by training her guns on the coast of Britain. Edward VII knew Germany and understood how her rulers should be treated. He nodded approvingly when Clemenceau said to him at Marienbad: "Sir, don't forget. It was not by your naval victory at Trafalgar, brilliant as it was, but by the battle of Waterloo, a very small affair, that you cut Napoleon's throat". He had the territorial army in mind: and it is opportune today to remind the British of Clemenceau's hint.

In his reminiscences, Wickham Steed relates that when he returned to London after twenty-two years' absence in South-Eastern Europe, in a lecture delivered at the Royal Institute for International Affairs he expressed his amazement at the insular isolation of England whose public was completely ignorant of continental developments which might produce a conflagration overnight. How could British diplomacy, dependent as it was on a public opinion so blind, pursue a far-sighted policy. He lamented the fatal influence on foreign policy of the financiers who lent money abroad. He said that the supreme danger for England was the so-called pacifism which built upon the mirage of other nations' good intentions. Statesmen were needed who could not only provide for the material defense of the country but also educate the public to use the strength thus acquired as honor and duty demanded.

CHAPTER XVII

FRANCE AND GERMANY

THE so-called rapprochement between France and Germany, so far as it did not deliberately confine itself to mutual acquaintance and look away from all the tragic and irreconcilable conflicts which have determined the immediate history of both nations and of Europe as a whole, had of late years become more and more a farce. The actors on both sides pretended possibilities of mutual understanding which in fact did not exist. Smiles and gestures of friendship concealed the dark background in which, as they well know, a new struggle for life and death was awaiting its inevitable hour.

The following utterances of Hitler's prove how deceived they were who believed reconciliation possible. In *Mein Kampf* he says: "We recognize the reasons which render an agreement with France necessary. But such an agreement would effect nothing if it were regarded as the final objective of our foreign policy. It can and will be nothing more than a screen covering the extension of our national *lebensraum* in Europe." Germany, he says, must not accept the present position in the West. She must on the contrary strike France down in war without quarter. "Only when this is fully understood in Germany so that the vital will of the German people is no longer wasted in mere passive defense but concentrated upon an active and final settlement with France, a decisive conflict in which the Germans will fight for great objectives, will it be at last possible to end the everlasting and fruitless conflict between France and ourselves; provided, that is to say, Germany really regards the annihilation of France as a means to the future expansion of our people in other directions".

These and similar statements have never been retracted. The book has been and is now employed as a Bible in the political education of the coming generation. Moreover, as I have shown, it represents the consistent development of Pan-German ideals a century old, the ideals whose danger to Europe and to France in particular Quinet pointed out. These quotations from *Mein Kampf* may be completed by Rosenberg's statements in his *Das Wesensgefüge des Nationalsozialismus.* "France is now not only the Rothschild republic but the outpost of Africa in Europe. She is therefore a danger to civilization which threatens all the white races. . . . The notion that the pacification of Europe required above all else a reconciliation between Germany and France was a mischievous illusion from the outset . . . It is impossible to pronounce the word Locarno without laughter".

Certain peace-loving French ex-servicemen told us some years back: "We must have a talk with Hitler". What good would it have done? You don't parley with demons. Hitler is a man possessed by an historic mania, he is the lava-flow from the German volcano which is gradually advancing upon the villages it will swallow. Would anyone reason with lava, to persuade it that it would be better to stop and turn back? The problem of a Franco-German rapprochement cannot be treated as an isolated political question. It cannot be solved unless Germany is converted from her mania and returns to her better self, and this can be brought about only by an historical judgment, not by conversations. Moreover the two nations can come together only if France recovers her true self and shakes herself free from a century and a half of revolutionary abstractions, which in turn is possible only if the other France emancipates itself from the bondage of mere reaction, and recognizes and deepens the Christian truth which, though superficialized and cut off from the whole, is contained in the revolutionary ideals and has given them their explosive force.

It is not easy to do justice to such a man as Briand. A member of the Chamber once said to me: "Briand lacked the distinctively French ability to rid ideas and feelings of vagueness and to express them clearly and precisely". This is true. But the Celt, the Gaul, in the Frenchman is wont on occasion to break away from Latin discipline, to lose his critical and sceptical caution, and to welter in ideals of world emancipation. The French Revolution was such a Gallic outburst which continued to rage until the Latin Bonaparte once more chained up the Celt. Briand was a pacifist Jacobin, a spokesman of French revolutionary abstractions, who applied the gospel of world-emancipating reason to the problem of universal peace which after the horrors of the War was on everyone's lips. No one had felt the War so deeply as this Frenchman. It was Briand who expressed with a passionate eloquence and in the language of world revolution the burning desire for peace, a desire elemental, simple, eternally human, of all who had fought in the War, of all mothers and wives, fathers and grandfathers, after the slaughter. For a time he seemed the spokesman of the entire nation. No one opposed him. Without hindrance he was free to proclaim to the world his country's devotion to peace. And the entire world replied with a giant echo as from mountain crags.

How did it come about that opposition gradually made itself heard and constantly increased until it finally became loud even among the Left? Briand's closest friends voted against his election to the Presidency. In spite of the enthusiastic support of a group of like-minded Radicals he became more and more isolated.

For one thing the lyrical epoch of pacifism could only

be an overture to the practical work of peacemaking. But Briand remained the bard of a United Europe. When it came to practical measures he failed. He was ignorant of the Europe he wished to unite and had no conception of the immovable aims of the Germany he hoped to save by concessions from the grip of Nationalist propaganda. So he was seduced by a fatal optimism into the Locarno policy which lulled Europe and France to sleep with unreal guarantees and encouraged the Germans to demand equal treatment too soon, since its psychological conditions had not been realized. The inevitable refusal provoked such indignation in Germany that these illusions and their disappointment produced worse embitterment and made the fulfillment of the new dream of peace still more remote.

At the time of the Thoiry breakfast, I wrote in *Menschheit* that if the French evacuated the Rhineland, for every French soldier who left, three Stahlhelmers would march in. I was mistaken. There were not three Stahlhelmers, but ten. When a meeting of the Stahlhelm at Coblenz sent Briand a message of thanks for liberating the Rhineland the Frenchman's political influence was at an end.

When Christ appears, Caesar's power fades. When Christ departs, Caesar rises again and organizes anarchy. The abstract ideals of the revolution and of humanism cannot create a new Europe. We are on the threshold not of a golden era but of an iron age. Only when we have passed through it will new spiritual forces come to birth and displace the unsatisfying powers that bear sway in the period of militarism. That Briand literally fell asleep in the Chamber was symbolic. This pacifism which is ignorant of human nature is blind to the work of the devils, thinks to conquer hell by playing the flute, and is totally incapable of dealing with the gigantic international problem of our time. It must gradually display its impotence, become silent and sleep. Already in the distance the chariot wheels of

Mars were thundering along the road. But Mars too is
impotent, is but a thundering impotence. Mankind however is still unaware of this. Therefore it must experience
once again the impotence of human power. A more evident judgment must smite the guilty. The reckoning must
be more obvious to all. Then and not till then will the
dawn break.

MAGINOT THE REALIST

The *Echo de Paris* published a merciless but apposite
cartoon. Briand was depicted asleep on the ministerial
bench in the Chamber; in front of him the gigantic figure
of Maginot, towering more than a head above all the
ministers and wearing a steel helmet and awakening Briand
with a blast of his trumpet.

While Briand indulged the pleasant illusion that he
had sufficiently protected France's eastern frontier with
the garlands of Locarno, Maginot was erecting along that
frontier a rampart of concrete which extended from the
frontier of Belgium to Basle. In doing so he was not a
militarist, but a defender of the humane civilization of
France, though he defended it with steel and iron. Maginot's idea was right. War is not prevented by garlands,
illusions and abstract phrases but only by moral and
religious guarantees given by the depths of the human
soul, guarantees that unite nations by a spiritual bond
and by their common subjection to a supreme Good—or
failing these, by iron strength.

Maginot, an Under-Secretary of State, went to the front
as a sergeant in 1915 and was twice seriously wounded at
Verdun. The effects of his wound were visible when, lean-
ing on a stick and with the expression of a man who has
bravely borne severe pain and crippling wounds, he reviewed troops or took part in a public function. He was
a man, moreover, from whom anxiety for his country's
future had banished all light-heartedness. He was never

wearied of warning his countrymen to look facts in the face. In every word he spoke, in every fibre of his being, he was Briand's opposite. He was a sturdy Frank from Poincaré's Lorraine where he now lies buried, the wounded sergeant of Verdun, the neighbor of the Germany, the thought of which overclouded his soul, a man with no prospect or hope of a future in which the historical tension between the two nations would be relaxed, a hard soldier fighting his part in the Franco-German tragedy.

THE MAID OF ORLEANS DEFENDS FRANCE

St. Joan could not be represented better than by her statue in rue de Rivoli. It depicts not a heroine of romance, but a daughter of the people simple and unaffected, whose strength is derived from her parents' farm. She looks straight in front of her, irresistible, believing, clad in plate armor, *"La finesse cuirassée,"* but nevertheless a woman in every vein with no trace of bellicosity in her countenance— a symbol of the French people which is not militarist and does not desire war but which in the hour of supreme danger works miracles of self-defense.

Many years ago General Rampont, then commanding the troops at Orleans, invited me to Orleans for St. Joan's feast. I stood on his balcony facing the huge front of the Cathedral around which a flock of pigeons was flying. At last the central door opened and the Catholic procession came out and made its way slowly to the center of the city. At the same moment the door of the neighboring Mairie, a radical-socialist center, opened and another procession emerged and joined the Catholic. This was another symbol. In the Maid of Orleans both Frances unite, otherwise such bitter foes. There is no French militarism in conflict with a French pacifism. The army is nothing but an instrument of the civilians' peace-policy.

The tomb of Napoleon at whose feet Europe once lay

is not a shrine of French patriotism. No rousing speeches are delivered there. No lamp burns night and day. The Saint has put the conqueror of Europe into the shade. If we think over the significance of this, we shall understand the difference between France and Germany.

CHAPTER XVIII

FROM EBERT TO HITLER

THE SOCIAL-DEMOCRATIC PERIOD

THE historical epoch demarcated by the three names Ebert, Stresemann, Hitler was pregnant with the destiny of Germany and the world. It will find its historian. Here I can deal only with its essential psychological characteristics. Once again Europe and Germany have clashed. The entire chapter might well be entitled "Illusions and Awakening".

Three things determined the part played by the Social Democratic leaders after the debacle. In the first place, the majority of them belonged to labor groups which before the War had concluded wage agreements with the employers. These agreements remained in force throughout the War. And after the War they played their part in conflicts with foreign powers. In the second place, it was deemed advisable to make use of the popular leaders to calm the masses exasperated by the defeat. And in the third place, it was also desirable to present the Allies with a democratic façade and at the same time to discredit the revolutionaries in the eyes of the nation by leaving to them the liquidation of the national bankruptcy. After the inglorious fall of the German Left, the liquidations were severely criticized from every quarter. No doubt by their complete subservience to the nationalists they merited their fate. But there is much to be said in their excuse.

The Left represented a Germany without a tradition. Their optimistic trust in Prussia as the bulwark of the Republic showed that they were wholly unaware how impotent was the position of a party without roots. They did not see that the dead were mightier than the living and that the Prussian Right had behind it a massive tradition centuries old, a tradition of domination and terrorism which went back to Byzantium. They did not perceive that democratic Germany would inevitably be thrown aside without the least trouble the moment it had done its work of giving militarist Germany the opportunity it required. Abroad the German Left harped on its vast numerical majority. It was blind to the fact that this majority was confronted by an energetic minority trained in the art of exploiting the cowardice and indecision of majorities. In brief, the parties of the Left in Prussia were piles of wind-swept sand; those of the Right thick hard clay, or rather granite.

The French Left was equally blind to this. They believed that as after the French defeat the Republic had passed through several critical years, it would be the same in Germany and that trust and patience should therefore be shown to her. They forgot that the modern French state was the property of the Left, built upon its ideas and principles and that the Right were merely allowed a lease-hold. In Prussia, on the contrary, the Right owned the edifice. The state was the product of their ideas and traditions. The Left was the leaseholder here and the Social Democrats sublessees. The building still kept its former owners' furniture. The gallery was hung from end to end with their ancestors' portraits, nothing new had been introduced, with the solitary exception of a secondhand gramophone and when it was turned on it played the old marches and patriotic airs. This was the situation from which everything else followed.

I never tired of warning the German Left that their speedy doom was certain unless, before it was too late, they stood up to the Right. They dared not do it, not on any single point. In 1922 I said to the Minister Koester:

"You really must do something to put a stop to the propaganda of lies about war-guilt". "Impossible", he replied, "impossible; on the contrary, we must yield to the Nationalists on this point. We cannot afford any dissensions just now".

So it went on until Hitler organized his stormtroopers. The worst insincerity of the German Left was that, when they were constantly receiving further proof of the powerful assault threatening them from the Right, they declared the suspicions of foreign nations unjustified and appealed to the "peace-loving majority of the German people". Yes, this majority loved peace so much that step by step it yielded without a struggle to the warlike minority. And it was this which made the French increasingly anxious. The legend of "the Two Germanies" has had far too long a life and has deceived Germany's neighbors. Certainly the two Germanies existed as wolves and sheep exist. The mistake was to believe that the sheep could restrain the wolves.

GERMANS' DOUBLE GAME AT GENEVA

"Foreign policy," we read in *Der Tag* for May 26, 1928, "is the art of playing with an impenetrable disguise to conceal our powerful patriotic determination, and with hidden cards".

Stresemann took office when the Right, encouraged by the success of the patriotic associations, thought the time had come to adopt an aggressive policy. Stresemann shared their aims but had a juster appreciation of the respective strengths of Germany and the Allies. Moreover the industrialists and financiers wanted to regain the world markets and were therefore in favor of postponing the conflict and securing further concessions by a parade of pacifism. In Geneva Stresemann was the popular representative of Germany's double game. All the enthusiasts for the League were pro-German. Germany was playing pacifism in grand

style against the "Conquerors". No one noticed that
Geneva was working for Berlin, not Berlin for Geneva,
that Locarno would simply make a breach for Potsdam to
march through.

Was Stresemann a "good European"?

When someone spoke to Bismarck of Europe's protest
he replied "What then is Europe?" Stresemann knew very
well what Europe meant for postwar Germany: a charm
with which to close Europe's eyes. No, he was not in the
least a good European. He was and remained to the end a
German Nationalist, completely indifferent to Europe.
Throughout his life he thought wholly in terms of power-
politics and was perfectly well aware of the fact—which
was indeed frankly admitted by a pamphlet issued by the
German People's Party on the occasion of a party meeting
held in Hanover—that the Revisionist program could not
be realized without a war of liberation. By a policy of
understanding he meant simply that the neighboring states
should be persuaded for some time to come to give freely
what could not yet be taken by force. He persuaded the
German Nationalists to remain in the background and to
keep silence for a time so as not to alarm those who were
living in their fool's paradise abroad. When he had successfully played his last card and his work was done, at
once the war cry of the unconverted and unteachable
Nationalists rose anew. Stresemann was simply the most
gifted player of the German confidence trick which professed the pacifist principles of Western Europe as a
screen for their opposite, the restoration of German power.
"He has tricked us", Clemenceau observed.

His policy was indeed a vast piece of deception though
he was probably unaware of it himself, since he had
received his political education in the school of fox-and-
wolf and took their methods for granted. But deception it
was, notwithstanding; it consisted in extorting concessions
in the name of pacification for which no solid return was

given and which were granted on complete misrepresentation of the facts. His death therefore was a benefit for Germany and no loss to the cause of European peace. On the contrary it cleared up the situation. He was followed by men who did not say "Locarno" when they meant "Potsdam", or "Gingerbread" when they meant "Steelhelmet". It was at least a gain in frankness that the true German attitude and the real strength of the Nationalists should be revealed, that it should be realized that Locarno had been but an opiate, and that a genuine rapprochement was possible only under very different circumstances and conditions than the statesmen in Locarno's orange-grove had made themselves and others believe. "In reality", the Comte de Saint-Aulaire wrote in the *Figaro*, in an article on Stresemann, "Stresemann, the good European, was Europe's great enemy. That is to say, he was simply the obedient servant of the modern German ideal. He therefore sought to restore order at home in order to create disorder abroad, to reconstruct Germany in order to destroy Europe". Though this may be unjust to Stresemann's motives it is an accurate statement of what his policy amounted to in fact.

BRUENING THE CATHOLIC PRUSSIAN

In Berlin the riddle used to be asked "What is the difference between Bruening and a violin?" and the answer ran "Both are held in the Left hand and played with the Right". Bruening was the last nominee of the screen policy. He was put forward by heavy industry and the Higher Command as Michaelis had been during the War, and was as well intentioned as he was insignificant. He was the typical Prussianized Catholic who had swallowed with astounding credulity all the misrepresentations served up by the Nationalist press; he reproduced them sincerely and with an air of authority, and his mind was hermetically sealed against all evidence to the contrary. He had the excuse that he had been placed in a most impossible situation. He had to champion the German claim to equality of treatment at a time when foreign distrust of Germany was being rapidly increased by the Nationalist Movement, a distrust to which the German behavior in the matter of reparations had considerably contributed.

Vladimir d'Ormesson contributed to the *Figaro* an account of the Disarmament Conference held at Geneva while Bruening was Chancellor. That article is a most trenchant criticism of the false pacifism that refuses to face facts: "It was not long before it became evident that all the proceedings at this Disarmament Conference ignore completely the existence of the real Germany. No account is taken of the essential facts which make the present situation what it is. What are they? That the unarmed Reich is a fiction, that the determination to rekindle a world conflagration as soon as Germany once more possesses the necessary armament is proclaimed more brazenly every day, that these armaments are being feverishly prepared whereas the defensive strength of France is gradually diminishing so that there is danger that the respective strengths of the two countries will be reversed, and finally that the slogan of equal armaments is preposterous so long as national sentiment differs so widely. On the one side is France passionately devoted to peace; on the other Germany intoxicated with the craving for revenge. The deliberate refusal to face these untoward facts empties the Genevan battle of words of all significance, places the discussion on a false basis and makes the Disarmament Conference a sheer abuse of trust and a screen for Prussian militarism."

The lot of the statesmen who held office in Germany during those years of transition was not enviable. The entire policy pursued by Geneva towards Germany was vitiated from the outset by a fundamental mistake. The attempt was made to mollify Nationalist Germany and to strengthen the German Left by inviting Germany to international cooperation. It was with this view that she was admitted to the League. The admission was too hasty and involved contradictions which embittered instead of ameliorating the situation. Germany was a member of the Council while the loyal performance of her treaty obligation was still under the supervision of the League. This was an impossible position; it incited Germany to make claims for equal treatment which, though logical, were obviously incompatible with the exceptional position in which she was still placed as a result of the War.

It should have been one thing or the other. Germany should not have been admitted to the League until she had discharged all her obligations. The effect of her premature admission was inevitably to make the continuance of her exceptional treatment intolerable to the Germans and seriously to confuse the international outlook of the nation. If a criminal under police supervision were given a place among the officials of Scotland Yard he would lose his mental and moral balance. Such a policy was international quackery.

Moreover, this ambiguous and obscure position encouraged Stresemann to ask Briand for one concession after another in order to mollify the violent Nationalists at home. The plea was false, as subsequent events proved. Every concession was greeted with stormier outbursts and treated as a concession made by the culprits' bad conscience to those they had shamefully deceived and wronged. The Nationalists said: "It is we who are to be thanked for all these successes. Without our agitation Stresemann would have gained nothing." In fact, the agitation should have been a reason for refusing any concessions until certain definite and clear conditions had been completely fulfilled. Instead, Germany received real concessions in return for mere scraps of paper, of value only to collectors of autographs.

Bruening failed to see that foreign nations were beginning to have enough of this policy. Like Stresemann he was a henchman of German industry which was seeking to regain its foreign trade. In its service he harped in his speeches upon the restoration of confidence. But he did not venture to offer any political guarantees, so that a French paper asked, "May we not then ask for security, that our milliards shall not be returned to us in the shape of bombs?"

The general situation was completely lost sight of, as was the fact that the world's security depended entirely on Germany's sincere renunciation of violent methods. Acknowledgments of German obligations would mean very little when the political outlook for German trade was brighter. Bruening refused to face these facts nor indeed was he in a position to give any guarantee.

Theodore Wolff wrote, "Germany does not understand the world and the world does not understand Germany".

The hour came when Germany decided to withdraw into herself and seek compensation in the East. It was Hitler's hour.

PART II

CHAPTER XIX

THE PRUSSIAN TRADITION OF THE TEUTONIC
KNIGHTS REVIVED

WHAT Hitler represents I have sought to make clear in several chapters of this book. He links contemporary Germany with the fountainhead of the Prussian tradition described in my account of the Teutonic Knights. Indeed this German order of knights has been deliberately revived by National Socialism, in the form of a picked body of leaders, who with the devotion and disciplined life of a religious order will thoroughly think out and consistently apply the National Socialist conception of the State, the Prussian outlook, and the Pan-German program. Their children are to be educated in the stronghold of the Order. At Marienburg the Baltic German, Rosenberg, delivered a speech in which he defended this return to the tradition of the Knights. Hitler also seeks to revive their tradition in as much as he has adopted for the whole of Germany their policy of expansion to the East. As the Knights made their Eastern conquests for their Order, he intends to employ the concentrated forces of Germany to conquer territory in the East.

The Nazis forget that times have considerably changed since the Teutonic Knights flourished and indeed that the Order broke down because its policy of conquest finally provoked a combination of hostile forces. Nor was the bloody work of the Knights representative of the policy pursued by Germany in the East for two thousand years. In Silesia and on the whole of the South-Eastern border German policy was very different. Otherwise the Pole

Sobieski would not have sacrificed himself to raise the Turkish siege of Vienna.

Hitler is the point at which the oldest Prussian tradition has blended completely with the Pan-Germanism which made such a profound impression on the Austrians excluded from the Second Reich and which took possession of Hitler as a schoolboy. The reader will remember Quinet's prophecy: "A man will arise in Prussia". To the second act of the drama he might have attached the title "A man will arise in Austria". The second man was to continue the work of the first and carry it to its logical conclusion. Hitlerism is the final result of abandoning the original German ideal, operative for a thousand years, an ideal not confined by nationality but aiming at a synthesis of the national distinctions in Europe which would give Germany access to Eastern Europe in the sole practicable fashion by federal union.

Cardinal Otto von Rauscher uttered a prophetic warning. "At Sadowa Prussia gave a mortal blow to the old Empire and with it the international German ideal. Murdered Austria will one day be fearfully avenged." His prophecy is in course of fulfillment and will be fulfilled more completely. Austria's revenge for the destruction of the international Empire is the fact that an Austrian, possessed by the *furor teutonicus*, has conquered Germany, taken Prussia along with him, made the Prussian tradition his servant; and that, in consequence, Germany in a frenzy of irreconcilable hate against the foreigner has gathered all her Germans for a mortal conflict with the rest of Europe. Thus Sadowa is avenged.

HITLER AND PRUSSIAN MILITARISM

It is worth looking a little more closely at the relation between Hitler and Prussianism.

When America entered the first World War the American Ambassador Walter W. Page wrote to Wilson: "I see

no other hope of defending the ideals which we hold dear
than to eradicate Prussian militarism as thoroughly as a
surgeon removes a cancer." The operation proved a complete failure. The surgeon did not cut deep enough. The
operation merely increased the energy of the disease deep-
seated in the victim's body.

Prussian militarism after the War took hold of the
vast middle class in Germany impoverished by the War
and by inflation. With diabolical cunning it turned their
anger and disappointment at the defeat and its result
against the peace treaties and those who had signed them.
In turn, the revived middle class took possession of Prussian militarism to use it as their weapon against the treaties.
Two evil passions perceived their mutual need. Hitler
was the point at which they met.

Goebbels was therefore justified in saying: "We are
Prussians even if we are Bavarians or Wuertembergers;
wherever we are, there is Prussia." *Furor teutonicus* and
Prussian organization, Pan-Germanism and Prussian lust
of conquest joined hands and concluded their alliance for
life or death. The revolution that failed in 1848 was now
successfully accomplished by the methods of its erstwhile
opponent, Prussian militarism. Remember how Kant
erected the Prussian imperative of duty into the categorical imperative of his ethics, thereby more deeply Prus-
sianizing the Germans than any Prussian military successes
could have done. Hitler has completed this union of will
and feeling between Prussia and the German mind and
has made it the psychological foundation of that "union of
all Germans" of which Bismarck laid merely the first
stone.

How was an Austrian able to make himself master of a
Prussian Germany? The answer is simple. The region in
which Hitler was born is the most emotional region of
Germany and, as a border land, has been in a state of
chronic excitement produced by the ceaseless friction be-

tween Czech and German. Into such an emotional powder-
magazine Prussian propaganda fell like a match. Nowhere
was Pan-Germanism so orgiastic as in this district. It was
the frontier disease. Accordingly, Hitler, a man of the
Austrian frontier, became the greatest missionary of Prussianism and overcame the enmity of more than a century
between Prussia and Southern Germany.

Hitler, it is true, has simply employed Prussian weapons
without understanding the Prussian ethos, as he has taken
from Germanism its natural Teutonic elements only and
rejected whatever centuries of Christianity had brought to
birth in the German soul. This superficiality will render
his work shortlived. Hitlerism, as a whole, is merely the
abuse by a very mediocre intelligence of powerful historic
forces and traditions in favor of the wild antics of a political power-circus. One day the manager of the show, in
spite of his whip, will be devoured by the tamed lions or
trampled by the elephants as they run amok.

It should now be clear why Prussian militarism was
not destroyed by its crushing defeat in the War. It was far
more deeply rooted in the German people than has been
believed. Even during the War Professor von Sombart
wrote: "Our militarism is the closest union conceivable
between Potsdam and Weimar. It is Beethoven in the
trenches". The position could not have been expressed
more truly. The musical and poetic Germany, the Germany aflame with intelligence, far from opposing the
militarist Germany, has placed all its mental and spiritual
gifts at the disposal of the latter. The more richly endowed
the human soul becomes, the greater becomes her need
to concentrate all her powers in the service of a supreme
good. If she fails to find this center of unity in religion,
she seeks it in some form or other of totalitarian super-
stition. Hence Germany's great classical period was bound
to end in Pan-Germanism.

After the War, misrepresenting its causes and the causes

of the German defeat, military nationalism attracted within its orbit ever wider circles of the German people. Hitler has completed the work. He has made Prussian militarism, its pagan statecraft, and its dream of unbounded annexation, universally popular. Yet there are those who imagine an opposition between Hitlerism and the German people. On the contrary, from the democratic standpoint, Hitler is the most legitimate ruler Germany has ever had, a Kaiser who owes his crown to the most genuine popular vote. He is the spokesman of all the ideas held by the leading groups in Germany ever since 1850, indeed, since Goethe's death in 1832. He is the logical expression of a century's illusion to whose utmost consequence he has given shape, and which in National Socialism has donned the garb of primitive savagery and become the program of Germany's renewal. Were a plebiscite held today, ninety per cent of the voters would vote for Hitler. And the remaining ten per cent are scattered throughout the country and are politically impotent. There is certainly considerable opposition in Germany, but about the ultimate goal of German foreign policy there is no disagreement whatever between the people and the Fuehrer.

Hitler expresses most perfectly this primitive mentality which for many years the worship of material success had induced in the German people, an attitude of mind which rendered it impossible for them to make their defeat the starting-point of a moral conversion. A Germany that had turned her back on herself, on Christianity and on the spirit of her history must be ruled by precisely such men as Hitler, Goering and Goebbels. The fact that many Germans dislike much that the party does and that they think it goes too far does not annul or atone for the fact that the political thought and feeling in Germany since 1866 has been inspired by Pan-German megalomania, by the moral insanity of Prussian policy. In fact, the butcher, the baker, the candlestick-maker, the chemist, the post-

master, the clerk, the elementary and secondary school-
teacher, have combined to push the government further
than it desired to go. Worship of the army and of war by
the man in the street has, for several decades, amounted to
a veritable diabolism. I grew up in such an atmosphere in
Berlin and when I hoped to recover from it in South
Germany found things even worse. In the North it was
simply Prussia. In the South the entire German soul, with
its Schubert, Schiller and Beethoven, had been captured
by the Nationalist frenzy and turned in fury against even
the most cautious opposition. It had infected the University of Vienna and the Austrian tobacco monopolists.
Therefore the entire nation must surely be punished by
Divine Providence, must suffer to the full the consequences of all it has done and approved. How otherwise
can its soul be purged?

THE DESCENT OF THE UNHOLY GHOST

I have just said that Hitler is a man of mediocre intelligence. How then could he play such an important historical
rôle? We might as well ask how it was possible for the
simple fishermen and artisans who were Jesus' disciples
to inaugurate a movement the like of which had not been
known. There is an outpouring of the Holy Spirit and an
outpouring of the Unholy Spirit. The apostles spoke with
tongues on that Pentecost Day in Jerusalem. The servant
of the national demon spoke with tongues in the Sport-
palast in Berlin. Precisely because Hitler is so thoroughly
mediocre, a man who has surrendered himself unreservedly
to the national spirit without personal ambition or desire
for individual aggrandizement—"I am one of the nameless German masses"—he was chosen by the unholy spirit
of Pan-German frenzy to be the vessel of which it would
take possession. This is the psychological explanation of
Hitler. He is a chapter in the history of this epoch of
collective madness which is just opening.

In London, Sir Austen Chamberlain asked me if I thought there was any possibility of dissuading Hitler from his absurd ambitions. I replied by quoting the Indian Proverb: "The man who rides a tiger cannot dismount." Who can reach an understanding with a mountain torrent, conclude a treaty with a volcano? These obsessed men do not themselves know what design will take possession of their heated brains tomorrow or what patriotic program may capture even against their will the inflamed imagination of the people.

René Benjamin showed profound knowledge of the German mentality when he wrote in his *Les Augures de Geneve*: "The German's loyalty, his will, his reason, his capacity for hard work, everything about him, is devoured by a flame which suddenly bursts forth from the depth of his soul, the secret of his temperament, his heritage, his alarmingly mysterious national destiny. Treaties, pacts, discussions, precautionary measures, concessions, all these count for nothing in comparison with this doom, pronounced by his own nature. Even if the whole of Germany, united in a vast national choir, were to swear with the utmost sincerity that henceforward they would behave as lambs, their sincere intention would be a guarantee of straw. Against their will they would suddenly be transformed into wolves."

For our comfort Tolstoy observed "God always sends from Heaven fresh troops of children". Among them he sends fresh troops of German children, and the day will come when their German souls can once more be fertilized by the genuine German ideal and with the aid of the living Christ be emancipated from the curse of the past. Then Germany will at last be able to make restitution to the world for the evil she has done it. But before that day comes, omnipotent Destiny must once more speak to the German people and raze to the ground their castle of dreams.

CHAPTER XX

A CENTURY OF ABERRATION

HENRI MASSIS once said "Hitler has not made Germany but Germany has made Hitler". The preceding chapters have justified his words by showing the connection between National Socialism and the last century of German history and by manifesting thereby that this Nationalist demagogue has merely drawn the logical consequences of a hundred years' aberration of the German people. The geographical position, the endowment, and the economic needs of the Germans combined to impose upon them the performance of an international function. But the so-called Nationalist movement alienated Germany from herself, from the spirit which had achieved her history, from her fundamental character, and from all the essential laws governing her economic life and functions, and thus brought her into mortal conflict with her true nature and the entire world around her. Systematically deceived by her seducers about the real cause of this conflict and fatally deluding herself about it, she fell a victim to a frenzied hatred of her true self and of the entire world. She believed herself encircled, fought a conspiracy which existed only in her imagination, entrenched herself with an impossible autarchy, and by striving to dominate the world sought in vain to obtain what she could have easily obtained long ago by peaceful cooperation with the outside world.

Bismarck, William II, Hitler—these are the leaders of the movement which has divorced Germany from her true nature and her providential task. There is a French policy that expresses the French character, the spirit of French history, and the conditions of national existence. And there is a British policy of which the same can be said. But there is no German policy which is in the same way a faithful expression of Germany, of her more than millennial history, and of the laws determining her life. What has passed for such for almost a century is Europe's nightmare and Germany's tragedy. It was imposed on the Germans by their most un-German and barbaric elements, blindly welcomed and assimilated by them as a providential means of promoting their national greatness and prestige. The spiritual disease spread from above downwards. Could Frederick the Great have dreamed that the son of an Austrian customs officer would lead the entire German people to worship at the shrine of Potsdam? Could Maria Theresa have contemplated the possibility of this final victory of Prussia over Austria?

Fichte's panegyric of Machiavelli and Ludendorff's political campaign against the Christian heritage are two manifestations of the same spirit. But we must never forget that this political barbarism which threatens our civilization today is but the final result of that great historical experiment known as the "secularization" of politics which attempted to divorce political thought and conduct from the religious and moral tradition of Western man. This secularization was promoted by the technical necessity of a division of labor between the ecclesiastical and the secular authority; this division was justifiable. The error consisted in completely divorcing political practice from the illumination of principles derived from the invisible world, which principles alone are genuinely practical and realist.

"Place me somewhere East of Suez, where there ain't no Ten Commandments," sang Tommy Atkins in Kipling's well-known ballad. The whole of modern politics has been practised "East of Suez where there ain't no Ten Commandments." But in Germany, the laboratory in which the ideas of the rest of the world have been thought and lived out and their consequences ordered to their ultimate implications, this doctrine also was taken with the utmost seriousness and relentlessly put into execution. This meant that the most important human relationships, international intercourse and the life of states, were wholly abandoned to every description of crime and immorality. And no one asked whether such conduct must not by degrees influence private relationships and undermine the moral foundations of the state itself. A man of such fine sensibility and so intellectually gifted as Frederick the Great scoffed at such scruples. All these power-politicians regarded the political sphere as a vast Indian reservation where the most extravagant crimes were permitted and were indeed a positive duty in the interests of the state. The unique shamelessness of German political knavery was due to the fact that the intellectuals and even the Christians heartily applauded it and, when some piece of trickery had been successfully pulled off, the court chaplains, before the entire people, gave thanks for a "miracle of Divine Providence."

Ludendorff was convinced,—as he said on many occasions—that Germany would have won the first World War if a regard for Christian morality had not prevented the military and naval authorities from waging it unhampered by scruples. In this respect, National Socialism has carried out without reserve the ideal of the German general. But Hitler did not confine himself to executing his testament. We should miss the significance of contemporary history if we failed to perceive in National Socialism the fulfillment of something of vaster scope— namely those one-sided ideals which modern man has everywhere blindly accepted, and whose nature and effects are thus revealed. Christians have abandoned politics to the lower powers without the least inkling of the terrible consequences. Therefore logical Germany had to give birth to the power which has carried a purely biological policy to its logical conclusions. Such destruction can have a positive effect when it is a case of demolishing buildings which have decayed, blowing up bridges whose arches are unsafe, exploding guarantees which exist only on paper and no longer answer to any reality, overthrowing an order which is no longer assured of its own right. For all this serves to destroy dangerous illusions and to make the true position clear.

Nietzsche performed this service. Hitler also performed it. A façade of merely apparent securities has suddenly been demolished. One screen after another has fallen. History itself seems to have speeded up. Ideas have fallen behind the pace of events. Foundations and guarantees, corroded by the work of centuries, have finally crashed to the ground amid a succession of explosions. "What goal will the car of destiny finally reach? Where will it halt, where stay its course?" asks a chorus in the *Choephorae*. That is the question we are all asking today. Only now in the light of the latest events do we perceive what the divorce between religion and politics really involves, where politics, left to itself and to man's natural instinct, must infallibly lead, and why in the end it must either attempt to eradicate Christianity or deny its own logic.

Here Hitler has executed not merely a political and a military but a spiritual testament, the testament of the moral and religious disintegration which was at the back of the political relapse into barbarism. Hitler is the political executor of Nietzsche. Those who reject Christian theology must put biology in its place and accept all the consequences of the substitution, including the struggle for existence, the right of the stronger, and perpetual war to establish it. Christianity sacrifices strength to weakness. Nature sacrifices weakness to strength. Is it not obvious that Hitler has simply realized in the political sphere with a relentless consistency this demolition of hollow façades, and a recognition of the consequences of a new intellectual and spiritual outlook?

When, in the latter half of the last century, Lord Acton visited Germany he observed that nowhere else had the destruction of Christianity made such progress. Heine saw it long before; and what is more important, he saw that the day was not remote when this work of destruction would once more release the German savagery which had been tamed with such difficulty and demolish the work of over a millennium of Christian civilization. A hundred years ago he wrote:

"Christianity has, to a certain extent, moderated this brutal German delight in war. But it could not eradicate it and when once the charm that tames it, the Cross, is broken, the savagery of those old warriors, the wild berserkers of whom the Northern bards sang and relate so much, will burst forth anew. Yes, the day will come when the old stone gods will rise from the debris beneath which they lie forgotten and rub from their eyes the sleep of a thousand years. Then Thor will spring up with his gigantic hammer and smash the Gothic cathedrals. And when you hear a crash such as the world has never heard before you will know 'The German thunder has at last found its mark.' "

It has happened exactly as Heine foretold. Half a century ago the German biologist August Weissmann, a disciple of Darwin's, published a monograph on *Rueckschritt in der Natur* (Retrogression in Nature) in which he showed that in nature a return to the primitive was often real progress, that is to say, it signified an adaptation to a change of environment. A Nationalist orator, Dr. Haupt, addressing, in September 1933, an audience of 4,000, applied that doctrine to the return of the German to the primitive. "We are," he said, "charged with wishing to return to the primeval forest. The charge is true. The primeval forest is a symbol of our people, which is a child of nature and the forest. It has returned to its origin. Our primeval people will follow nothing but the forces of its own nature. This is our reply to the Treaty of Versailles. Germany has left the path of Western civilization."

This return to the primitive as a necessary consequence of a changed environment has also been preached by another Nazi, A. Junger. He said that the striving for perfection has other goals today than it has had hitherto. Today it may be best expressed as the art of handling dynamite. In any case it has nothing to do with the spiritual or intellectual values.

Ludendorff found fault with Christianity for decrying war which alone was in harmony with the true conditions of man's life on earth. He said: "Christianity is a foreign religion which conflicts with our entire heritage, is fatal to our racial qualities, deprives our people of unity, and delivers us into our enemies' hands."

And a Nazi poet. H. Burte, declares:

> "Know thou, son of the north
> In the endless slaughter of earth.
> There is but war and war again."

Is it surprising that this German relapse into a profession of faith in the primeval forest, animality and endless slaughter has found its philosophical justification? Spengler's latest book *Der Mensch und Technik* glorifies the man of prey who alone is strong enough to fulfil the cosmic mission of the natural master. "There are peoples whose strong racial stock has preserved the qualities of the beast of prey, master races who plunder and conquer, lovers of war against their fellow-men, peoples who leave to others the economic struggle against nature in order to pillage them and make them subject. They know the feeling of triumph which possesses the wild beast when its prey is quivering in its claws."

How perfectly this theory fits the Nazi practise in Poland

and Czecho-Slovakia! Spengler however is not a Nazi. He preached his gospel long before Hitler's accession to power. This bears out my contention that the defeat of National Socialism would not change in the least the mentality which has long been deeply rooted in the most influential German circles. Such a mentality can produce only the policy of the jackal. To invite their political representatives to participate in a European Federal Council is to invite a tiger to discuss the reorganization of the jungle.

I will conclude this survey by quoting from a document which casts a grim light on the shamelessness of even Christian theologians in Germany. In 1914 the Berlin theologian, Professor Reinhold Seeberg wrote in the *Internationalen Monatschrift*:

"War assigns every people its proper place, its sphere of action, in accordance with its real strength. It brings the truth to light. It is the great assize of the nations. Its verdict is just. In war, God Himself is made manifest by victory. Then truth conquers appearance. God wills that a clear road should be opened to *effective* power. God's law condemns the vanquished and it is also His will that the conqueror should dictate such terms of peace as shall reveal by outer greatness his inner strength."

This is the evident triumph of what Nietzsche had already preached as a new law in opposition to the Christian. Life no longer accepts its law from above but erects its own blind power as a sovereign right above all laws, human and divine. Our theologians did not see that this doctrine is completely false even from the standpoint of biology, and that biology culminates in theology. Life is doomed as soon as it ceases to obey the law of the spiritual world in which the unseen principles of vitality are at work. But the Germans will not understand this till they have suffered greatly. As Germany is today, we can be certain that the last shepherd left in her fields who dares raise his eyes to the star of Bethlehem will be slain. The inner corruption of the German people, illustrated above, is already plain in every department of the national life.

I would call attention to the most instructive chapter in Hermann Rauschning's *Die Revolution des Nihilismus* which is concerned with the development of the typical member of the Reichswehr. He shows how this inner corruption of the German and of his state has produced a wholly novel type of soldier who is ready to embark on adventures but is no longer competent to face a severe test. The last war was waged with the help of the Christian spirit of sacrifice. But no one can say from what source soldiers, trained in the school of National Socialism, are to derive the spiritual strength to stand firm when the trial comes. The effects of the inner emptiness will be astonishingly visible as soon as difficult times have to be endured. An article published by Rauschning in the Zurich review, *Mass und Wert,* for December 1938, contains the following passage:

"The German people, united by force, is looking forward with alarm to another catastrophe. This fact may perhaps be concealed for the time by the lethargy which has come upon them. But the forces of opposition, forcibly suppressed, will for a certainty break out violently one day. And they will do so just when the German nation needs to stand together in solid union, and they will drive our people to a doom beyond conception.

"The knowledge of this, the fearful foreboding of it enters into the Fuehrer's dark speeches and screams at the back of the anti-Semitic outbursts. It is the mortal weakness of the German people so strong on the surface. Can a nation which is a prey to such corruption resist attack? Can it hold out even a few days against a severe strain?

"Incalculable values have been destroyed in the past six years. Everything that has been built up, all this material equipment and armament, is weak, because the most essential source of strength has been lost. In truth it is a judgment of the Absolute. Germany's power is a power to which we may apply the language of the old hymn: 'One little word can lay it low.' "

Even if this were not the judgment of a man intimately acquainted with German conditions, we could be certain that the destruction wrought by National Socialism in Germany's inner life must inevitably have the result he describes. In his book Rauschning speaks of "an exterior discipline and order behind which the destruction of all the factors of national order is plainly visible."

This is the truth. Germany is a disciplined anarchy and it may well be the case that the great strategic problems of the present World War will be replaced finally by a problem of a wholly different kind, namely what action Europe should take in face of an unparalleled interior collapse of Germany, a collapse from whose debris no new life will be able to spring up for a long time to come. Before Germany crashes down in complete self-destruction, she threatens the entire world with ruin. This is not the action of those who really possess the power to carry out such a threat. Knowledge of the intellectual and spiritual situation described in this chapter is essential, if we are to understand Hitler's advent. It is not a case of a defenseless people being overpowered by a horde of criminals but of the spiritual fall of a nation. National Socialism must not be regarded as a mere political phenomenon. It must be understood in the light of a process of spiritual disintegration which has been long in progress, of which it is the final expression, and which is closely bound up with the same process at work throughout Europe.

Those who grasp these profound causes will understand that, in our struggle against this new barbarism, military mobilization though an unfortunate necessity is only the first line of defense, and that we must mobilize forces of a very different order to combat the moral corruption at the back of the political savagery.

CHAPTER XXI

THE SOLIDARITY OF THE TWO GERMANIES

A FEW years ago a German paper published a picture
of Seldte, the Stahlhelm leader. He was depicted
shouting to his Stahlhelmers, inciting them against France
—which had at last been roused from her sleep by the
extravagances of German militarism and was fortifying
her frontier—by the lie that she harbored aggressive designs against Germany, and demanding the return of
everything that had once been German. As I gazed at his
bloated countenance devoid of any genuine German feature and read of the perpetual orgy of flag-waving and
parading in which those adult schoolboys and their on-
lookers indulged, I said to myself: "The growth and blossoming of the German soul when it was touched and filled
by the passion of Christ was a thing of rare beauty. It
flowered in the art of Dürer, with its profound devotion,
and in Bach's cantatas in which all human emotions are
so wonderfully disciplined and the soul blissful and secure
is lost in the Divine Infinity of Christ. How repulsive and
lamentable an object it has become now that it has withered
and lost itself!"

When the world read with horror the manifesto of the
93 German intellectual leaders it was perplexed by the
enigma of this neo-paganism. How are we to explain the
incomprehensible solidarity which by degrees has identified the German intelligentsia more and more closely with
the attitude of an unspiritual Prussia, with the revival of
the old Teutonic barbarism? At the close of his Hyperion,
Hoelderlin depicts Teutons of this kind as "barbarians
made still more barbarous by their industry, science, and

even religion, utterly insensible to the charm of the graces". Who knows whether in 1914 Hoelderlin would not have signed the manifesto of the 93?

Who built the bridge between spirit and animality, between German culture and the barbarism of modern Germany? German philosophers—Kant, Fichte, Hegel, deep and serious Germans, drowning in subjectivism, and craving to escape to the terra firma of objective principles of universal validity. I have had plenty of opportunity to observe in the élite of university students this extraordinary and unique development. I have often attempted to explain it to foreigners who have no faintest understanding of the tragedy and complexity of the German betrayal of the spirit. Nationalist Germany is comprehensible only when we have grasped the psychological explanation of the alliance between German idealism and the Prussian state and its policy, and the conquest of the German soul by Nationalist materialism. Other nations too have fallen victims to this form of materialism. But in Germany it has assumed the proportions of a mania and a disease, not because Germans are more materialistic than other nations but because at a particular juncture in their history they devoted their intense spiritual and intellectual energy to a materialist and national ideal—it is symbolized by Wagner's Wotan—and thereby produced a materialism and a worship of the state inspired by idealism.

In Germany the state captivated the German soul by a peculiar kind of spiritual education. The state was invested with a garb of German metaphysics and benefited by the German desire to unite every aspect of life and thought in a compact whole. Thus like Jahveh in the Old Testament it became a consuming fire. The state and the national community annexed the whole of German poetry and music. The German passion for the Infinite entered the public service and inflated what should have been something simple and obvious, the necessary administra-

tive system—indeed something of subordinate value, for
it was nothing more than the organization of the nation's
life and instrument for the improvement of human society
—into the supreme value with an unlimited claim on
man's allegiance; until a clash became inevitable between
the state thus treated as the spiritual Absolute and the facts
of the outside world.

The world, aroused from its slumber by this terrific
conflict, asked in amazement: "Where then can we still
find the Germany of Goethe, Bach and Beethoven?" To
which I can only reply, "The old orchestra has by no
means been broken up. But it has a different conductor
and plays the Hohenfriedberg march".

One of my students was a Bavarian Catholic who had
passed through the War immune from the infection. In
the trenches of Douaumont he had read a French life of
St. Theresa of Lisieux and was with me heart and soul.
His example shows that the spiritual aberration I have
just described is possible only when the mind and conscience are no longer possessed by a deep and Catholic
Christianity. Many of my best pupils fell before Verdun
and in the Vosges. During their short periods of leave
they visited me and poured out their hearts to me. Their
confidences gave me a deep insight into the unique process
by which during the last hundred years the German
idealists have sold themselves unreservedly to Prussia, and
by which spirit and animality have wedded for life and
death. One of them wrote "The important matter is to be
ready to sacrifice oneself, not the *object* for which the
sacrifice is made . . . and so we all sang in a wholly new
spirit the old patriotic songs."

That is to say, Kant's abstract conception of duty bridged
the gulf between their spiritual aspiration and their task
of slaughter. The old spirit of religious sacrifice derived
from Christianity, which had taken a strong hold upon
the German conscience, for lack of substantial nutriment

weakened to an abstract idealism and the vague desire to surrender oneself for something of higher worth. The old German tendency to the whole, away from the particular to the universal, had been confined to the narrow field of the national state. Walter von der Vogelweide's old enthusiasm for the international Empire was now given to the greater Prussia and its High Command. Philosophy was practised by dying for Falkenhayn and Ludendorff. At Verdun the French were fighting Kant. Kant almost captured Verdun. But the Maid of Orleans suddenly intervened and proved the stronger.

The wife of a German officer, Margarete Susmann von Bendemann, reviewed in the *Neuen Zuercher Zeitung* the *Kriegsbriefe deutscher Studenten* (Letters written by German Students from the front). Her review tallied completely with my own experience and explanation. "For centuries," she wrote, "German history has been marked by the persistent cleavage first opened by Luther's gigantic personality when he attempted to dam the revolutionary forces which his doctrine of salvation had released, by demanding unconditional submission to the ruler, no matter what his character and the spirit that inspires him. For centuries, right down to the present day, Germany has been suffering from the consequences of his teaching that man's free intellect and will must play no part in determining his outer life, in which he has only to submit in silence to his superior's command. Henceforward the German was no longer responsible for the external conduct of his life. Blind obedience replaced responsibility."

The writer then proceeds to show how in German idealist philosophy, which embodied the abstract subjectivism of the German intelligentsia, the German mind gradually lost touch with reality and spread its pinions ever more ambitiously in the void while Germany, in the concrete, lay helpless in the mire and was plunged in ever thickening darkness. The cleavage grew wider. "The outer and the inner life became more and more remote from each other. No foreign nation can conceive how remote from reality was the inner world of the intellectual German at the outbreak of war."

That all these dreamers of noble dreams could surrender themselves so completely to an unjust war, the writer explains by the fact that Kant's identification of duty and freedom suddenly became a living conviction in their souls—"they were all Knights of the Grail who had gone astray, who set out in search of the Holy Cup and because they could not find the road which led to it, were lost in its quest."

This uprooted idealist Germany was as inevitably Hitler's victim as it had been the victim of the General Staff in 1914. These young people approved in good faith the murders of June 30, 1934. Where the policy of Germany's rulers was in question there was no conscience, no moral law, no personal responsibility, not even a secret revolt of the heart. A dangerous state of mind indeed with which the world has once more to reckon.

German nineteenth-century philosophy, which in its arrogance considered its barren abstractions superior to the Christian faith, has been chiefly responsible for the despiritualization of the modern German. The entire nineteenth century offers the spectacle of souls increasingly alienated from God and Christ, idolizing earthly goods as substitutes for the Supreme Good they have lost. Almost all Schubert's songs are inspired by a profoundly religious devotion perverted to earthly love. A few years later this devotion was given to the nation and the state.

The nation's intellectual leaders took the initiative in this subversion of values and aims, thus surrendering the entire nation defenseless to the Nationalist intoxication. The apostasy was made easier by the fact that the object of this unlimited worship, the Prussian state, had displayed, from the outset as we have seen, many high moral qualities in its government, order and discipline which concealed from vast numbers the abysmal immorality of its foreign policy. The solidarity, so incomprehensible to a foreigner, of the moral and the immoral elements of the German people, of the intelligent and the insane, was intensified after the War by the German propaganda.

Yet another reason can be given for this uncritical support of his rulers by the modern German. After the fearful devastation of the Thirty Years War it was the ruling princes and their officials who with the utmost skill and devotion saved the country from anarchy. The people were glad to obey them, realizing Hegel's definition of them. "The people is that part of the nation which does not know what it wants." Hence the German worship of the expert. Everything combined to deliver the nation blindly into their rulers' hands. The softness, kindliness and credulity of the people sealed their surrender. When we are discussing the responsibility for the War, it is indeed important to distinguish between the hard Germany and the soft, between the ruling and the obedient. But we must not forget that those who from blind obedience take part in grievous crimes and feel no remorse for them later, cannot be held guiltless in the sight of God or man.

CHAPTER XXII

THE ACHIEVEMENT OF GERMAN PROPAGANDA

TODAY every German has clearly before his eyes the acts of political robbery committed by Hitler, but the sight does not penetrate to his brain. For his brain has been molded by the doctrine that every German act of violence is the reply to intolerable provocations and acts of terrorism committed by the opposite side.

This vast system of organized lying has completely perverted the historical meaning of every event so that as long as its literature remains in German houses, libraries and bookshops, the entire German outlook on foreign affairs must be hopelessly perverse and stupid. But this is not the worst. The propaganda makes any national self-criticism impossible for a very long time to come and prepares the German public to misinterpret completely all future events and to see them as confirmations of the supposed determination to destroy them, as manifestations of the world's envy of German efficiency, and as the conspiracy of the haves against the have-nots. Twenty years' disinfection would hardly suffice to get rid of the mania.

Yet, if foreign nations were really bent on destroying Germany, their desire would be perfectly intelligible in view of all the evil Germany has committed against foreign nations since Bismarck. But the supposed desire was in fact a complete myth. On the contrary, the former enemies of Germany were eager to preserve Germany's great virtues and endowments and to employ them for the benefit of mankind. So strong indeed was this desire that it was the source of all the unintelligent and muddled benevolence toward Germany and of all their attempts at reconciliation with her, attempts which Hitler and his forerunners craftily abused in order to assist their conspiracy against Europe. How characteristic that reply of a German diplomat during the War to a neutral who, in view of outrages committed in the German conduct of the War, asked whether the Germans did not consider the possibility of defeat: "In that case we shall organize sympathy." So well aware were these barbarians that their adversaries were not barbarians. And they did organize sympathy with brilliant success.

Long before the first World War Le Bon's *La Psychologie des Foules* had called our attention to phenomena of mass psychology hitherto unnoticed. But this psychology of the masses is only the first chapter in the psychology of the herd. The second is the psychology of the leader, the man who takes full advantage of all these new methods of influencing the herd and by his scientific propaganda enslaves the minds of the millions to his will and design. Hitler and his collaborators have made this propaganda a political weapon of the first importance. For the first time they have systematically employed Gutenberg's invention as a political instrument and have realized all the possibilities of a democratic era. The Nazi leaders know only too well that ideas and emotions are more potent than self-interest and that, if you excite a man's emotions and captivate his intelligence by cheap clichés, you can lead him to act against his own interest as easily as you can propel a boat against the stream by hoisting a sail.

To this propaganda Hitler owes all his successes. This idolator of material power is the only contemporary statesman who fully believes in the power of ideas. After the failure of his putsch at Munich he radically changed his methods and won his victory by mental weapons. When he was fighting his way to power the German Republic and the Reichswehr still possessed a defense strong enough to defeat any attempt at a violent revolution. By the hypnotic spell of his propaganda he disarmed, crippled, and even won over his opponents. The Prussian rulers could not give their tradition a popular dress and translate it into the language Germany demanded under her actual conditions. Prussia could not speak High German. It needed an Austrian to champion a Pan-German Prussianism. The Prussians did not see that the time had come to abdicate. Only three weeks before Hitler seized power General Schleicher said: "The danger from Hitler must now be regarded as removed. There is nothing more to fear from that quarter." This has been confirmed by Rauschning in his latest book. How was it that three weeks later Hitler became Chancellor?

Certainly one most powerful cause of Hitler's triumph was the effect produced on the German people by Prussian propaganda after the War. The Nazi fury was the crop which sprang from the sowing of these dragon's teeth of hatred and lies. The sowers did not foresee the explosion their seed could produce. Too late they began to discuss counter-measures. Rauschning in *Das Wahre Deutschland* (December 1938) has told the story of their deliberations. He asks the decisive question:

"What was it that drove us young conservative and nationalist politicians of the respectable middle class, together with the representatives of big business and the military leaders, into the ranks of a movement which even before it assumed the government of the country was evidently an outburst of anti-social elements?"

He then recalls the enormous task which confronted the nation, problems calling urgently for solution, if Germany were to survive—the economic crisis, the country's weakness abroad, the social unrest, an executive almost nominal, the incapacity of finance and industry to function, with a system which seemed clearly antiquated, Parliamentary government destroyed by intrigue, and the general disintegration of the community into groups maintaining their particular interests. And he replies to his question:

"How were these elements to be welded into a new order? Did we not need a new leader of the entire nation, and in particular a whip to compel and control the masses, and blend all these refractory classes and parties into a nameless mass which could be disciplined? Could anyone perform this task except a man who himself belonged to the masses, who could wield their new and disruptive forces which under no circumstances the revolutionaries of the Left must be permitted to annex."

Rauschning truly points out that all those who believed that this blind outbreak of destructive energies could be made to subserve a new order of German life have been bitterly disappointed. But this was not the first time in the history of modern Germany that such a miscalculation had been made. Rauschning reminds us that those classes who had in the past ruled Germany were united with this unscrupulous band of agitators from an anti-social stratum by their common profession of a false political realism which was totally blind to the moral conditions of national regeneration. National Socialism is the punishment of Prussianism, as Prussianism in turn is the punishment of four centuries of European Machiavellianism.

We read in Rauschning's book what Hitler said to him: "Hitler spoke contemptuously of the conservative old guard, Hugenberg and his group, because they entertained scruples about breaches of the Treaty, whereas he, Hitler, was completely free from them." In this, Hitler is the consistent representative of pure Machiavellianism and of the political realism of modern Germany. He told Rausch-ning he had read *The Prince* several times. It was indispensable for a politician. He added, "In politics I admit no moral law. We are paladins of the will-to-power. My advantage over the democracies is my entire freedom from moral or sentimental considerations." (*Hitler Me Dit* pp. 303, 305).

In this respect also Hitler is the heir of Bismarck's epoch. In 1858, the political writer, F. Bollman, in a treatise entitled *Defense of Machiavellianism* wrote, "Germany cannot be saved unless a warlike ruler arises in Prussia who, in his relations with foreign nations, takes no account of mercy or cruelty, honor or dishonor, but thinks only of his country's unity, power and independence."

I have explained how the Nazis were able to conquer the German Republic without bloodshed by the weapon of propaganda. Hugenberg's press campaign paved the way for them. By the same method, Austria was annexed without firing a shot.

This propaganda was not countered by a serious and systematic opposition employing the same methods of influencing the masses in order to defend Austria's tradition and to refute effectively the lies spread by Berlin. We must, however, remember that Hitler reaped the fruit of the decades during which Pan-Germanism exercised a powerful influence in Austria. As early as 1866 the great historian, Onno Klopp, could write in a letter to Princess Eleanor Schwarzenberg:

"Prussia has set herself systematically to win intellectual Germany to her service. Unfortunately she has been only too successful, particularly as regards the historians whose work influences political sympathies and antipathies so strongly. Nine-tenths of German historical writing is steeped in the Prussian spirit. And that spirit is the same here as in the domain of practical politics, a spirit of inveracity and falsification; but also, indeed, for that very reason, a spirit of aggression in every shape and form and above all against Austria. Long before Austria was defeated on the battlefield of Koeniggratz, Prussia's silent emissaries, books and pamphlets pregnant with her spirit of falsehood, had made their way into Austrian palaces and

cottages, had confused and deceived men's minds, and
had fettered their consciences. Falsehood is labeled truth
and truth falsehood. A power that has arisen and grown
only by injustice and violence at the cost of Germany and
the genuine spirit of her people is depicted in these
writings as the protector of Germany."

The passage gives a picture of Prussia's deliberate work.
Such a Prussia earned her success richly. From the historical standpoint, the fate which befell her victims was
not so unjust. For it was the recompense of a blind heed-
lessness almost as criminal as the far-sighted villainy of the
Prussian agitators. No doubt the successful propaganda
was assisted by the universal tendency of the age toward
racial nationalism. But, after all, Switzerland has remained
proudly loyal to her international idea, confident that to
that ideal the future will belong because it alone is capable
of solving the extremely complicated international problems of Europe? No, Austria's surrender of her tradition
reveals a deplorable weakness of character, a dullness of
soul, which more than deserved the punishment it has
received. To betray a great tradition hallowed by religion
and by a glorious history is surely a sin against the Holy
Ghost and therefore unpardonable.

I have described the part played by propaganda in preparing the domestic victory of National Socialism. The
Foreign Office and the War Office had for years been superseded by the Ministry of Propaganda without the outside
world realizing what was happening or the objective of
what Hitler has called "Psychological War" and Mussolini
"White War."

In Austria the psychological annexation preceded the
political and military annexation. The case of Czecho-
Slovakia was more complicated. It was obviously impossible to win the Czechs by propaganda. But by threats, by
fostering internal dissensions and by influencing the public
opinion of the Allies, the determination to resist German

aggression by force could be weakened; and by a twisting of all the facts those among the Western nations who cared most for political morality could be completely confused and persuaded that the Czechs had no moral right to refuse the German demand.

In the review *L'Année Politique française et étrangère* (1939; p. 303), Professor B. Lavorgne published a devastating criticism of the way in which certain English groups allowed themselves to be fooled by German propaganda.

"To read this document", he wrote concerning Lord Runciman's report, "one would suppose it was the composition, not of the British peer, but of Hitler himself. With such a docility does Lord Runciman champion the German demands, even the most extreme, that he is not only for giving Germany all the districts with a Sudeten population, but is prepared to see the whole of Bohemia enslaved politically and economically to the Reich. In short, he would yield everything not actually surrendered by the Munich agreement. We look in vain for a grain of equity in this scandalous arbitration."

Thus the Germans, by crippling the will to resist them, succeeded in rendering armaments and defensive work of the highest quality completely ineffective.

It was in the field of foreign policy that this psychological warfare first displayed its full devilry. Biologically it may be compared with the way in which certain wild beasts render their prey defenseless by squirting them with a paralyzing fluid. Its method is based on the new possibilities provided by a democratic era and which the totalitarian leaders have been far quicker than the representatives of democracy to see and to employ. It is the art of capturing public opinion and exploiting the conflicts of interests, ideas and traditions in an epoch of profound intellectual and psychological upheaval in order to spread confusion, treason and revolution in the enemy's camp. Nothing in fact has given rise to such divergencies of opinion in the Western nations, as the problem of Germany. If that problem is ever to be solved, nothing is more necessary than to create among the Allies a complete agreement about its essential conditions. Otherwise, the German art of sowing dissension will have another amazing success in crippling and dividing the conquerors in their treatment of it. Those who desire documentary evidence of the grave mistakes committed by the Allies in their postwar policy, mistakes responsible for this second World War, should read André Tribourg's excellent book *La Victoire des Vaincus* (Denoel, Paris). Its very title is a service to truth and a summons to a political examination of conscience.

Certainly the former Allies were deceived again and again by German propaganda for the right of national self-determination. This has been and still is Hitler's technique and until he attacked Poland he was amazingly successful in concealing from the Allies the general plan behind each step he took. In *Mein Kampf* he spoke frankly of the strategy he intended to pursue. "When you have to deal with spineless nations who readily submit, you must always bear in mind that they do not regard a single act of violence as sufficient reason to go to war. You must therefore take one little piece after another."

Unfortunately German propaganda for foreign consumption has been and still is more skillful, and the language of the controlled press with which they support it far more efficient, than the Allies' counter-propaganda. This was the case throughout the conflict between Germany and Poland. The German grievance and threat, at first cleverly confined to Danzig, made a powerful impression on public opinion in the Allied countries and in some cases misled it completely—*The Times* for example, *L'Oeuvre* and other organs. This was sufficient to make Berlin believe that, whatever official statements the Allied governments might make and whatever measures of mobilization they might adopt, they would behave in the case of Poland as they had in the case of Czecho-Slovakia. This fatal belief was due to the fact that the democratic statesmen took no systematic measures to inform public opinion, which both in domestic and foreign policy counts for far more than under the dictatorships, about the real bearings of the Danzig question.

Certainly the public were told that Danzig was a matter of European importance, because violent aggression must be stopped. But the man in the street asked himself whether violence could not be prevented by returning to Germany a city unquestionably German. For example, a deputy named Deat asked in the columns of *L'Oeuvre* the dangerous question "Are we to die for Danzig?" If millions are to risk death or mutilation on the battlefield, if women and children are to accept the bombardment of their homes, they must be told plainly and convincingly that the struggle is not for something slight and local, but for a great, decisive and unavoidable issue. They must be informed in language they cannot ignore or misunderstand that, though Danzig is certainly a German city and no one disputed the fact, yet, until the partition of Poland and its annexation by Frederick the Great, it was a free city outside Prussia and as such, precisely because of its free status, performed for centuries an international function as the port through which Poland traded with the outside world. For a revived Poland the assured performance of this function by Danzig is a matter of life and death. For that reason Danzig must remain a free city outside the Reich.

As regards the Corridor, when Hitler says: "I am seeking to put right an historic wrong, France to perpetuate it", the reply is that the Polish Corridor is itself a reparation. It is the reparation for one of the worst crimes in history, the partition of Poland. That partition produced a racial mixture which admitted of no other treatment than that given by the Treaty of Versailles. On that account this reparation for the partition is one of the strongest foundations of European peace. To abolish it would be a further defeat of the justice on which alone the community of nations can be built.

German propaganda, as it has become more completely the servant of the powers of destruction, has pursued four distinct aims. The first of these is to conceal the attitude behind it and to disguise its mischievous activities as a policy of peace, justice and order. In the second place, it wins over the moral, honorable and peace-loving elements in foreign countries by insincere appeals to their ideals and traditions. In the third place, it also addresses itself to the worst and most unprincipled elements, and by bribery, incitement to violence, and every species of underhand alliance and profit-sharing, attempts to make them conscious or unconscious accomplices of Germany's designs. And in the fourth place, by threats of the alarming consequences of opposing Germany, it spreads the belief that it will be the wisest course to yield to her demands.

The employment of these methods achieved such great successes in the past, and particularly since the Armistice and still more since Hitler's advent, because the world has been blind to the effectiveness of mental weapons and has treated them as something remote from the world of political realities, as though only visible objects counted for anything. Moreover this propaganda had built up a stupendous fabric of lies and falsifications embracing all relevant matters great or small, so that cause and effect, fact and falsehood, exchanged places. That so many highly educated and gifted minds have lent themselves to this work of patriotic lying is one of the most appalling episodes in the entire history of the human mind.

The character of the propaganda destined to undermine the Western Powers was determined ever since Hitler's accession by his contemptuous estimate of the Western bourgeoisie. He simply applied to the West his experience in dealing with the spineless German middle class, and believed that employment of the same weapons would bring him the same easy victory. He once said to Rausch-ning, "Time is working for us. I shall have only to deliver a slight thrust and the defenses of a doomed epoch will fall immediately. Whatever appearances of solidity these institutions and nations may still present, they are in-wardly rotten and will crumble to pieces".

His experiences of the yielding attitude of the Western Powers in face of a Germany rising from her defeat con-vinced Hitler that the dominant characteristics of this middle-class democracy—desire for peace and comfort and increased wealth, fear of social revolution, and pacifist illusions—would bring about the gradual surrender of every position occupied. In this he was thoroughly de-ceived. A great nation may give world trade the first place in its interests, and large sections of its population may succumb to the spiritual dangers this attitude involves; yet when confronted by a criminal assault upon the moral foundations of the international system and when eyes have once been opened to the assault, it may prove that it is incomparably more than the world's workshop and em-porium. This is true also of the United States, where we shall one day witness a far more rapid and active national rising against the German peril than ever was shown even in the first World War. I do not however mean to assert that those disintegrating tendencies on which Hitler counts have already been completely overcome or that they do not constitute a very real danger. Nothing is therefore more urgent than to unmask the spirit which inspires German propaganda, to make known the full scope of its aims and the subtlety of its methods, and to begin a sys-tematic counter-offensive.

The latter must consist, in the first place, of acquainting the public in all the threatened countries with its spirit and tactics. Nothing is more characteristic of these than some remarks which Hitler has made about the possibility, or rather the certainty, of enthroning National Socialism in the United States. It is to be effected, it seems, not by bombardment but by a propaganda aimed at the weaker side of American plutocracy and by exploiting the exceptionally favorable opportunities for influencing the masses which American public life presents. He said that only the German element in the American population could thoroughly transform its racial conglomerate and for the first time introduce order into an anarchy which the impotent slaves of democracy could never master, but not until they had first become National Socialists. Hitherto the American people had been simply the raw material exploited by Yankees who thought of nothing but the dollar. It was the mission of the German Americans regenerated by National Socialism to take control of the United States, in which task they would be assisted by a sound element of small landowners who still retained the energy and spirit of the colonist. It was due to false notions of freedom and equality that in America, the scum of the Balkans, Bohemia, Hungary and Eastern Jewry had been placed on the same level as scions of an old Spanish noble family, Swedish farmers, and others of pure stock. "Nothing could be easier" was Goebbels' comment on this, "than to provoke a bloody revolution in America. Nowhere else is there so much inflammable material, social and racial."

We should read the chapter in Rauschning's book entitled *The Storm Troops of World Propaganda*. He gives most interesting examples of Hitler's instructions to youths sent to foreign countries to plant this German dynamite: "I expect blind obedience from you. It is success that counts with me. I don't care what means are used. We are not aiming at equal rights but at domination. You will be entrusted with the guardianship of the countries conquered for the German people. You have to disguise our preparations for attack." Rauschning relates that he was present once at a discussion held by the German Academy at

Munich. "Henceforward I could not doubt the crime that was being committed. The Germans living abroad were being used to effect a German revolution on the ruins of the entire world."

In this connection also psychology has its surprises for us. Hitler is convinced that there is no country today which could not be disintegrated and revolutionized by the systematic employment of such methods.

Unfortunately it cannot be denied that since the end of the first World War, and particularly in the years immediately preceding the present World War, very influential commercial groups in Great Britain and France have persistently worked for a understanding with Germany without grasping the moral conditions required. Quite sincerely they have assumed that business must produce not only money but peace. They have had no conception of the mentality prevalent in Germany which seeks not business but power and business only as a means to power.

In France, indeed, there were groups completely indifferent to considerations of morality who would swallow any German affront and who were repelled by no exposure of German designs if they saw a possibility of doing business. Such utterly unprincipled men are also to be met with in certain English circles. Even now they would be prepared to make peace with the enemy of peace and effect a reconciliation at any cost with a man who, as soon as he could, would enslave, expropriate and sterilize them.

Hitler's great mistake has been to take these groups too seriously and also those who would willingly sell their country and honor to secure their property against Communism. Certainly such people existed, but when the decisive moment came they counted for nothing. It has always been a blunder of German psychology to misunderstand the fact that in the Western countries many are allowed to talk and write and unburden themselves who in other countries would have long been in confinement.

For more than a year England and France have witnessed revivals of national life and political orientations which no foreigner could have foreseen. It was not merely that men who had taken the wrong road retraced their steps. From the depths of a glorious history entirely new elements rose up and forced upon the new government a new language and a new policy.

Hitler had seen in England nothing but a nation of shopkeepers. His confidants kept him well informed of the defeatist tendencies in the British mentality, particularly among business men and in British foreign policy. But he was blind to the instinct of the race, hidden deep below the surface and never vocal, which precisely because it was conscious of its strength and the extent of its resources could permit itself considerable indulgence in "wait and see" but which when the hour struck would rise in its might and mobilize in inexhaustible strength.

Even if the English had been but a nation of shopkeepers, those shopkeepers had created a world empire. Lord Clive, the conqueror of India, was a product of the City. The Great English merchants yielded to no conquistador for warlike energy. And the moment Germany's anarchic foreign policy was completely unmasked their dynamic tradition came to the surface.

DEFENSE AGAINST GERMAN PROPAGANDA

But all this does not remove the danger that German propaganda may exercise in future a dangerous influence upon particular sections of public opinion in the belligerent and the neutral countries. It is therefore a matter of urgent necessity to organize an effective counter-offensive against the "White War", that is to say, an offensive of ideas, to correct the lies and misrepresentations and to explain the profound significance of the present struggle. A further extensive campaign is required to defend the fundamental principles of Western civilization against the totalitarian agitation. In face of the totalitarian states, it is not enough to insist in general terms upon the value of political liberty and the rights of man. We must show in the concrete what Western civilization stands for and what in it is true and good for all time and for every nation. And we must avoid all vagueness.

We must, for example, develop the meaning of order as Western civilization understands it, in contrast with the totalitarian conception of order. Order must be created in the souls of individuals before it can take root in the state. Here a hierarchy of functions must be established, and the material must be made subservient to the spiritual. Order must be educated to obey conscience and to show a strong sense of personal responsibility. Unless this inner order exists, the external is not understood and accepted by the soul. Unsupported by the conscience of individuals the state is at the mercy of every wave of collective passion; therefore to suppress the individual is to destroy the state. No momentary success obtained by forces united by external pressure can alter this fact. That is why all totalitarian states are distinguished by their utter lack of principle. Only his individual conscience binds man to the eternal Power that sanctions treaties and enables him unflinchingly to defend obligations to his fellows, which may not be violated for any price, against the tyranny of national profit and the unfettered passions of the herd. When the entire life of a state is based on a solid core of personal responsibility, as soon as the need arises the collective achievement will exceed that obtained by a system of state compulsion.

The full significance of the daring faith in freedom shown by Western Europe must be explained and illustrated by its colonial experience. "Nothing binds so firmly as freedom" wrote Rachel von Varnhagen. The history of the British Empire is a proof of this. The British experiment in free confederation has a most important lesson for the world and in particular for Eastern Europe. The need to defend Western ideals against the totalitarian states should assist considerably to clarify the former. The customary contrast between democracies and dictatorships is untenable. Portugal is a dictatorship on a democratic basis. Democrats have made the will of the masses effective but have neglected to give its proper place to leadership even in industry. If this mistake is duly corrected, democracy will be more successful than hitherto in making respect for the rights and value of the individual the cornerstone of all fruitful cooperation and all effective mass achievement.

At a moment when the Western democracies are struggling with the totalitarian states for supremacy in the Balkans, we cannot be too much on our guard against propaganda which champions a false conception of democracy, which comes into collision there with the desire to secure the political predominance of those elements most firmly attached to the soil, to national traditions and to strong government. When the Englishman speaks of democracy he always means aristocracy tempered by a chivalrous and observant regard for public opinion. The genuine and all important political inheritance of the West is the secure freedom of public opinion, the Magna Carta of personal rights, and a horror of anything that savors of the Gestapo and the Cheka. If these achievements are to be extended throughout the world, nothing is more essential than to erect a powerful bulwark against the unleashed passions of the mob, the dictatorship of particular interests, the worship of efficiency and the unprincipled intrigue of parties. This bulwark must consist in strengthening the authority of the political leader and of his executive competence. If the self-styled democracies leave to the totalitarian states this urgently needed reform they will bar the door against those who would otherwise be attracted by the genuine advantages they possess.

A favorite topic of German propaganda is the necessary opposition between owners of property and the proletariat. This is one of the most deceptive clichés employed by the champions of National Socialism. In an extremely clever editorial entitled "Reaction" the *Frankfuerter Zeitung* misrepresented the position in the following way. The hostile nations bent on encirclement were depicted as rigid reactionaries who treated particular systems and arrangements as inviolable although they had long ceased to be in harmony with changed conditions and a different distribution of power. France is always accused of opposing a static principle to the irresistible dynamism of the historic process. These controversialists and the Italians speak in exactly the same strain—they forget that in the intercourse of nations much is possible in the way of revision, concessions, transference of territory, condominium and even colonial collaboration (by chartered companies of mixed nationality) when we are dealing with gentlemen and not with gangsters disguised as gentlemen.

It is not true that French political thought is always static. On the contrary it is extraordinarily fluid and dynamic. But for that very reason the Frenchman clings to a firm order. In this he is in harmony with life itself, which requires a permanent order as much as adaptation to changing needs. Even man's economic life, which must be mobile and elastic, cannot undertake any enterprises or commitments on a large scale unless there is security on which reliance can be placed, prospects with which one can reckon, trustworthy guarantees. The Active Man, Goethe tells us, needs "Woman, the woman's hallowed repose". The static factor in human life provides the dynamic with secure lines of development along which it can advance in harmony with the laws of the invisible order. The champions of the Axis think statically when the rights of other people are concerned, dynamically only when it is a question of their own vital needs. And they refuse to see that it is impossible to combine two incompatible things. You cannot reject with scorn an order of international justice and proclaim the rule of war supreme throughout the globe, and then ask your threatened victims for presents which are wanted only to build up a position so strong that one day thrice as much can be taken by force.

The article just quoted from the *Frankfuerter Zeitung* appeared on August 20, 1939 and contained the words "Germany is striving for a new order in which the just interests of other nations will be respected as those of Germany herself". On September 1st Poland was invaded and ravaged, and thus deprived of her rights in a fashion unknown since the ages of barbarism. This is the new order which the rest of the world is invited to welcome.

FALSE PRESTIGE AND ITS PART IN INTERNATIONAL POLITICS

Anyone who lived in Germany before the Russo-Japanese war will remember how great was the fear of the Russian colossus and its overwhelming military power. Nicholas II knew better. When in 1899 he proposed universal disarmament, it was because he was aware of the inner weakness of his gigantic empire and of its military effects. Russia's defeat in the war with Japan took the military experts in Europe completely by surprise. Her failure in the first World War was a second heavy blow to Russian prestige. But Bolshevik Russia regained it in part by the millions she counts in her army. It was the tiny population of Finland that destroyed this revived prestige of huge numerical superiority, which had led men to believe the Red Army strong enough to undertake a Napoleonic attack upon Europe. Those who have learned the lesson will not wait quietly until Russia has been subjected to German organization and technique, and made subservient to Germany's ambitious design to create an Empire stretching from Flanders to the Amur.

The Finnish campaign reminds us of that page in the
Book of Daniel which speaks of the stone that broke away
from the high mountain and fell upon the feet of the
colossus which forthwith crumbled to dust. No one can
know whether the moment has already come and if the
spiritual forces required to produce it are yet ripe. But
the day will surely come when the hollow prestige of a
power built only on a material foundation will crash in
ruins, leaving nothing behind save a cloud of dust. Since
Frederick the Great and still more since Sedan, the prestige, certainly well earned, of the Prussian army has been
at least an equally powerful historical force. The marvel
achieved on the Marne might have been far greater than
it was; but the German armies were saved from an utterly
crushing defeat by their extraordinary prestige. They
could have been completely routed had their opponents
been able to credit the full extent of the confusion which
prevailed at German headquarters. The French miscon-
strued the evidence of it as a trap to be cautiously avoided.
It was not thought possible that communications between
the German army corps had been completely broken and
the General Staff dazed by the shock. The same thing
occurred in 1918. Had the full extent of the demoraliza-
tion and disorganization been grasped, a defeat of unexampled magnitude could have been inflicted upon them
without great loss to the Allies. But the prestige attached
to German generalship once more erected a powerful
barrier between the German army and its pursuers.

In the destruction of Czecho-Slovakia the traditional
prestige of the German army once more played a decisive
part. The exaggerated accounts of the military readiness
of the army circulated for years by German propaganda
in the foreign press attained their object. In reality the
German army was first and foremost a weapon of bluff.
It was far from being prepared. Its units lacked their full
complement of men, and its reserves were insufficiently

provided with arms. The latter defect was first made good by the huge store of material belonging to Czecho-Slovakia. The General Staff had categorically pronounced against a war on two fronts. General von Brauchitsch's declaration to the Fuehrer—which I quote from M. Fuchs' book *Das Oesterreichische Drama von 1936-1938*—has been confirmed by the evidence published in *Le Droit de Vivre* of October 15, 1938: "If it is proposed", the General said "to use the army to bluff by a threat of war I have no objection to raise. But for actual warfare we are not yet ready and as things are at present our army could not undertake a European war".

Even now the German military system and the spirit behind it enjoy a reputation which no longer corresponds with the facts. No doubt, enough of the old tradition survives to be reckoned with very seriously. And the technical achievement of the great era of German applied science survives. Many German virtues and to a considerable extent the Prussian sense of duty have escaped the moral corruption of National Socialism. And last but not least, the diabolical energy which has erupted from the volcano of German history survives. For all that, we can be certain that the Nazis are as incapable as the Russians of meeting successfully a severe test and would succumb to the shock of an unexpected attack on a large scale. When we are faced with the assault of a destructive mechanism controlled by powers of evil we must remember that there is no department of human activity in which the devil can in the long run replace the soul. That is why he tries to win as many souls as possible for his service. He has been more successful in Germany than anywhere else. But his work there, since it has been severed from its root, will be exhausted sooner than it might appear and his impotence will be exposed just when victory seems assured. The invisible world is stronger than the visible and does not let itself be mocked.

CHAPTER XXIII

SOUTH-EASTERN EUROPE AFTER THE WAR

PAN-GERMANISM AND THE AUSTRIAN TRADITION

IT IS a doctrine of Indian philosophy that an idea is not vanquished until its Karma, its deepest content, its life-principle, has found complete expression and its utmost consequences have worked themselves out. This is true of the idea of nationality. And it would seem to be Germany's contribution to history to realize with relentless consistency its entire logic and thereby become its *reductio ad absurdum*. I have quoted already the observations which on December 30, 1918, shortly before the arrival of the American delegation to the Peace Conference, Lansing wrote about the fatal formula so dear to his chief: that the word self-determination was packed to the brim with dynamite and must arouse hopes incapable of fulfillment. For unless the meaning of the principle is defined with the utmost caution and precision its application is a danger to peace and stability. Lansing foresaw only too truly the disintegrating effects which would follow the proclamation of self-determination as an unqualified right.

We must, however, remember that behind the principle stands a vast historical force, which moreover can appeal to Christian truth in its support. The American sociologist Hyslop in his *Democracy* truly points out that no other spiritual truth has produced such potent effects in the political sphere as the doctrine of the immortality of the soul and the infinite value of the individual soul in the sight of God. It has given birth to the entire movement to secure political freedom and with it the principle of national self-determination. But by a tragic fatality this principle of individual right developed one-sidedly on the ruins of the great Christian league of nations which existed in the Middle Ages, and its realization was not balanced by a corresponding insistence upon unity and mutual responsibility. In consequence its progressive application in Europe must prove a solvent and finally break up the national organisms into their component parts. For every Christian truth torn from its context in the entire body of Christian truth disintegrates both the soul and society.

The process of European disintegration produced by a one-sided individualism has been at work for four centuries at the roots of the national life of the European peoples. It has created the great national powers. Today, with the irresistible course of an historical process, its logic has worked itself out to the uttermost. The dynamite of self-determination blew up the last remains of the old unity of the West. The Austro-Hungarian monarchy was the first to finish. It was followed by Czecho-Slovakia. And all nations that possess foreign minorities are equally threatened. The various racial components of the disintegrated supernational states everywhere feel the attraction of their respective fatherlands. A Europe reduced to atoms must be the final result of this nationalist movement.

Eastern and South-Eastern Europe resisted this development because the application of the principle of nationality could not solve, but only confuse and entangle, their complicated racial problems. A vast Teutonic tide swept over Europe. It was followed by a Slavonic tide. Then the Teutonic tide turned again eastward, and both floods meeting in stormy clash mingled their waters so thoroughly that in those regions no clear racial frontiers can be drawn; even where Germans and Slavs to a certain extent confront one another as distinct groups, they are Slavized Germans and Germanized Slavs. These conditions gave rise in South-Eastern Europe to a German-Slavonic federal system which is so deeply rooted in the facts of the situation that there can be no doubt that it must be restored in the near future and that any solutions now forcibly imposed upon this world of inextricable racial mixtures must prove merely provisional.

But the work of nationalistic disintegration to which the Danubian monarchy was sacrificed was bound up with instincts so extremely powerful and encountered such feeble resistance from the ghost of the federal tradition, that changes recently effected could not possibly have been prevented. The defenders of unity were unequal to their task. They did not themselves understand the historical strength or the present meaning of the threatened political order, and made fatal compromise both in theory and in practice with nationalism. Their defeat therefore was a foregone conclusion. Europe, it seems, must endure to the bitter end the tragedy of this disintegration, if it is to comprehend anew the full and true significance of the principles it has abandoned and betrayed.

Equally fatal was the failure to defend the old order as it should have been defended. The representatives of the old supranational form of political association in Eastern and South-Eastern Europe could not bring themselves, before it was too late, to make the necessary concessions to the principle of self-determination and home rule, which is undoubtedly a partial truth that must not be denied if diverse nationalities are to share a common life. Yet these concessions are in fact demanded by the federal principle itself which makes provision both for particular rights and for the need of the community, a provision made by the political order of medieval Europe. The heirs of those venerable federal arrangements mishandled so badly their relations with the foreign nationalities politically united with them, that they fostered the growth of their national and even imperialist claim in the modern sense. Everything that has successively happened since 1918 is but the final result of this misgovernment. If the Danubian monarchy had treated the diverse nationalities under its rule as Britain treated her colonies, it would not only have survived to this day but would probably have become the nucleus of a wider federation.

THE CONCEPTION OF THE EMPIRE AND NATIONALISM

Constantine Frantz never tired of insisting upon the following points: Germany never was a state but simply an Empire, a league of nations, a political community comprising the most diverse forms of political associations. The conception of the Empire has been lost since Leibnitz. Prussia, departing from the traditional line of German political growth and developing on purely étatiste lines, has imposed upon Germany a form of external unity as ill-suited to her nature and vocation as a Steel-helmet to a nest of nightingales. Only in our time has the idea of the Empire been slowly rediscovered.

Frantz's thesis is equally applicable to the remaining part of the old Empire, namely Austria. In the nineteenth century, even in Austria, the idea of Empire was almost forgotten and no one grasped the true significance of the supernational community of nations which existed in the valley of the Danube. In 1841 Freiherr von Andrian published a book entitled *Oesterreich und Seine Zukunft* (Austria and its Future) in which he points out that the Austrian Empire lacked an ideal binding all its subjects together. There were a Hungarian, an Italian and a German patriotism, but no patriotism was inspired by the Austrian Empire. In this work home rule was demanded for the first time for the subject lands, and the centralized bureaucracy was attacked as the reason why there was no patriotic attachment to the Empire.

The events of 1848 brought the old imperial conception back into practical politics; and above all, at the meeting of the national parliament at Frankfort the demand that Austrian Germans should join a national German empire made the members of the Danubian monarchy aware of the meaning of their supernational community. And it was the Slavs who showed the clearest understanding of the true nature of that economic and political complex to which the inhabitants of the Danube valley belonged and which was termed Austria. The Czech historian Palacky addressed a protest to the Frankfort Parliament in which he adjured the deputies not to touch the cultural community of Slav and Teuton, whose existence was, and would continue to be, of irreplaceable value for Germany herself and for the solution of the entire Eastern problem, provided Austria understood the moral foundations on which it rested and within her state of nations would make the necessary concessions to the principle of nationality. "In truth if the Austrian Empire were not already in existence, in the interest of Europe, indeed of humanity as a whole, it would be necessary to create it. But at present Austria is drifting helplessly because for long past she has blindly ignored and denied the juridical and moral foundations of her existence, namely equal rights and equal treatment of the nationalities included in her Empire."

At the Frankfort Furstentag (Assembly of Rulers) of 1863 the Emperor Francis Joseph made a final and fruitless attempt to win the German people for the policy of imperial federation. Bismarck took care that his sovereign did not attend. He had other plans. Clausewitz had foreseen and anticipated them when he wrote: "There is but one way by which Germany can achieve political power, the sword. One of its states must bring all the rest beneath its sway." The foundation of the smaller German national state was itself a mortal blow to Austria. It created

in Austria a German *irredenta* which inflamed all the
other nationalities. Then his defeat in the war of 1866
compelled the Emperor to base his empire one-sidedly on
the power of Hungary which has consistently opposed a
just solution of the Slav problem. As early as 1865 Palacky
had foretold the result: "The day on which a dual system
is established will inevitably be the birthday of Pan-
Slavism in its undesirable form. We Slavs shall witness
it with a well-justified sorrow but without fear. We existed
before Austria, and we shall survive her."

When the Franco-German war broke out the Emperor
realized once more the need to grant the Slavs their
rights and thus to create a counterpoise to the pressure of
German nationalism which was a threat to the integrity
of the Danubian monarchy. In 1870 he let it be known
that he was willing to be crowned King of Bohemia and
he told his minister Schaeffle: "I can no longer cheat my
peoples." The selfish power-policy of the Germans and
the Magyars frustrated this last attempt at federalism. In
1875 Crown Prince Rudolf said "The future belongs to
the Slavs. Nevertheless Austria will be able to maintain
herself in existence, if she understands her mission aright,
places herself at the head of the South Slavs, and becomes
a powerful Danubian Empire."

In earlier chapters we have already spoken of the similar program entertained by Franz Ferdinand and the last
attempt made by Emperor Karl. My present intention is
solely to sketch in its general lines the tragedy of the
final conflict between the ancient imperial ideal and the
irresistible advance of a violent nationalism. Nevertheless,
nationalism is but the temporary victor. It is digging its
own grave. It is displaying to the entire world its complete
incapacity to solve the problem of nationalities in Europe.
Entirely different solutions are preparing in the womb of
Providence.

HISTORY IN A NUTSHELL

Immediately after the Turkish threat to Vienna, re-
pulsed only by the intervention of John Sobieski, the
Polish King, the Emperor Leopold invited the Serbian
Patriarch of Pecz in old Serbia with 35,000 picked Serbian
families to settle in the Austrian territory to the north of
the Danube and to garrison it. When the settlement had
been effected in the year 1690, the spiritual, economic, and
political autonomy of these Serbs was guaranteed by a
special rescript, the so-called Privilege. The districts
handed over to them were their free domain. In return
they undertook to defend the southern frontier of the
Empire against the Turks. Later these Serbs fought for
Maria Theresa against Frederick the Great, for the Emperor Francis against Napoleon, for Francis Joseph against
the Hungarian rebellion of 1848, and against Italy in
1866. Loyalty to the Emperor was their tradition, almost
their religion.

One of these Serbs, Michael Pupin, has described in
his reminiscences *(Vom Hurten zum Erfinder.* F. Meiner,
Leipzig) the effort produced upon this entire body of
Serbs by the violation of the Privilege. "When in 1896"
he wrote "the Emperor removed the military frontier and
abandoned them to the Hungarians they felt that they had
been deceived by the Emperor who had broken the oath
embodied in the Privilege. I remember my father saying
to me one day 'You must never serve in the Imperial
Army. The Emperor has broken his word. In the eyes
of our frontier people he is a traitor. We despise a man
who is false to his plighted word.' That is why after 1896
the Emperor's portrait had no longer a place in my father's
house. When I look back on those days I feel, as I have
always felt, that this act of treason committed in 1869 by
the Emperor of Austria was the beginning of the end of
the Austrian Empire. It marked the birth of Serbian

nationalism, and the love once felt by the people for the state in which they lived decreased and finally became extinct. But when the people's love for a state dies, that state must die. This is the teaching I received from the unlettered peasants of Idvor."

The tragic alienation depicted above of a particularly loyal group is typical of many similar things, particularly of the alienation of the Southern Slavs. After the first World War, an Austrian admiral, whose name I cannot mention today, told me of the shortsighted treatment accorded to the Croats in the army and navy. They were treated as men and citizens of an inferior class who could not be trusted. How differently the French monarchy treated the Alsatians, thereby making them France's most loyal children! The Habsburgs certainly rendered very great services to South-Eastern Europe. If they have not received the recognition due, the reason is that at the height of their power and in the pursuit of a power-policy the rulers of Austria fatally despised the strength of spiritual forces and forgot the right of the weak to the gratitude and honor of the mighty.

THE DISSOLUTION OF THE DANUBIAN MONARCHY AND THE ANNEXATION OF AUSTRIA

Anyone who has read the chapter of this book which deals with the problem of South-Eastern Europe and its tragic denouement and in particular with the reasons which defeated the Emperor Karl's attempt to place the monarchy on a sounder foundation before it was too late, will perceive that the failure of a mutilated Austria to maintain its independence was the obvious and inevitable consequence of the invasion of the supranational Danubian Empire by the National Socialist movement. Even if Dollfuss had not been murdered he would have been vanquished by these triumphant forces of contemporary history. He would have put up a more heroic struggle than

Schuschnigg. But his defeat would have been certain. For great as Schuschnigg's mistakes and omissions were, not even Dollfuss could have swum against the current of history. This is not, however, to say that the victorious power is in alliance with the profounder historical forces or that the future belongs to it, or that defeated Austria defended an obsolete tradition—which misconceived the political foundations of South-Eastern Europe. The contrary is true. Certainly the Nationalism triumphant today is the overwhelming outburst of a natural force: a force of elemental vitality and torrential pressure. Moreover, it is the offspring of the democratic epoch and its individualism; and precisely in South-Eastern Europe it had just realized claims which could not be disregarded and had long been forcibly held in check.

But the supernational ideal, embodied in the old Danubian monarchy, possessed still higher and more realistic claims to prevail in this confused medley of races into which it alone can bring order. The tragedy of the situation was that this ideal had grown too dim. Even bloodier experiences and collapses were and still are necessary before its profound harmony with the facts of the European situation is once more perceived. Austria herself had abandoned it too long. What was called the Austrian ideal had become no more than a timid and uncertain memory incapable of holding the allegiance either of the educated classes or of the masses. Moreover the supporters of legitimism could not learn to speak a modern language. Therefore attempts to revive the ideal were doomed to disaster, to inevitable defeat, by the might of Pan-German propaganda, supported as it was by the fashionable idol, Nationalism.

With blind infatuation Pan-Germanism forged forward on its violent course with no presentiment of a huge and living reality in its path, with which it must sooner or later come into conflict and by which it must someday be smashed. Schuschnigg was blind to the fact that he was surrounded on all sides by treason, by active or passive infidelity to the Austrian ideal. In fact, he himself radically betrayed that ideal by his so-called Pan-German attitude, which he persistently emphasized, whereas he should have understood that in the existing situation and confronted as he was with the actual Pan-German mentality, he could be true to Germany's inheritance only by the most thorough repudiation of Pan-German aims and by separating himself decisively from their adherents. Any other attitude could but confuse and mislead his own people and European observers. For the moment the true German imperialism lies under a curse which, as God wills, shall at some future date be removed and atoned for. Until that day arrives the language of Pan-Germanism must be scrupulously avoided by all serious men who refuse to compromise with open or veneered barbarism. From of old we have been commanded to pray indeed for those subject to such a curse but to hold no fellowship with them, and neither intellectually nor politically to be involved in their destiny.

In the nature of things Austria needs an intimate bond with the entire German world, and northern Germany needs Austria. But this bond must be postponed until Germany has once more recovered her true self, a recovery to which Austria could contribute by recovering her own true self, thereby assisting the revival of genuine Teutonism, until at last the hour dawns when the entire German nation can be regenerated and reorganized by this profound force of Teutonism newly born.

One of the noblest Austrian Germans who has attained an understanding of what Austria was, is and will be, so clear and firm that it cannot be obscured, K. Tscuppik, wrote in 1936 that we must not forget that the old Danubian world survived and should survive in the new Austria. Austria was not a "German" state, it comprised more than the German element in it. "We belong to the German-speaking world and belong also to an intellectual world with which contemporary Germany has nothing in common. This complete divorce of Germany from what was once the common possession of all Germans is the decisive factor. *An Austrian today cannot enter the civilized world as a German*. The claim made by certain enthusiasts that in the Third Reich there exists a secret Teutonism endowed with qualities which the world prized when they were displayed by a few Germans in the past is difficult to believe. But even if there were a grain of truth in it, *you cannot make Europe believe that a nation of sixty-five million has been barbarized against its will*. The world judges Germans *by what Germany is*. The Austrian therefore has every reason to emphasize his distinction from the Germans, his unlikeness and contrast to them. 'Austrian' is a term too clear to need explaining. 'I am an Austrian' conveys far more to the foreigner than the longwinded paraphrase 'I am of course a German but . . .' It is no fault of ours that the term 'German' has acquired this sinister connotation throughout the civilized world".

After the first World War, and above all since Germany became possessed by this revival of Nationalist mania, Germans outside the frontier of the Reich had no more important task than to keep the periphery of the German world absolutely separate from the Prussian center and to link it once more with the surrounding world in a super-national community. This was the vocation of Austria above all. By fulfilling it she could have saved Germany. But the Austrians had ceased to understand the deep significance of their bond with Eastern Europe and, remembering the historical greatness of their country, strove to escape confinement within the boundaries of the small state to which peace had reduced Austria. They were therefore tempted to attach themselves to the Prussian Reich, as Pan-Germanism understood the union.

The strength of these tendencies was evident from the way in which after the War the German Left revived the Pan-German Program of 1848 and, regardless of the fact that the situation had completely changed, conducted a campaign in favor of an anschluss between Austria and the German Reich. They cherished the illusion that Austria would be a counterpoise to Prussian militarism. They closed their eyes to the fact that Bavaria, which Bismarck had designated the transition from Germany to Austria, had fallen victim to the Prussian invasion and had actually improved upon the militarism of Prussia. At all costs, therefore, if Austria were to preserve a better Germany, it must be rendered, to the utmost possible, proof against the infection. Had not the Peace Treaty, to the benefit of Austria herself and the true good of Germany, forbidden the anschluss, the Danubian Germans would have been sacrificed far sooner than they were to a senseless agitation. But instead of recognizing this fact Austria, where the advocates of an anschluss lost all feeling for the self-preservation of their people, demanded "self-determination" to swamp Austria in a magnified Prussia. The Austrians moreover were blind to the further consideration that, all the world over and at every epoch, anyone who has abused his self-determination to attack the self-determination of another is justly deprived of it for a time. But at any cost public opinion must be excited against the peace treaties. What had happened before counted for nothing.

Austria's worst calamity was its uprooted intelligentzia which had been bemused by over fifty years of the Hohenzollern Empire, by its successful employment of force, and by its technical and scientific achievement; and which had no longer the least inkling of Germany's true mission in Europe or the meaning of its bond with the Slavs. Instead of considering how this mission might be accomplished, the intelligentzia was aware of nothing save the intoxication of Pan-Germanism and hatred of the Slavs—an attitude which was an appalling defeat for scholarship and culture. That in his struggle for Austrian independence he was opposed by the Universities sealed the downfall of Dollfuss.

The reproach had been made against Schuschnigg that he failed to open to his once imperial countrymen a new and wider prospect by working with all his might for a new Danubian Federation which would have included all the succession states. But not even a statesman of supreme genius could have realized such a project. No state was willing to surrender the least tittle of what it had swallowed when the Empire was divided or to renounce its claim to any territory it had then lost. Until the fever of shortsighted self-assertion which at present holds the nations in its thrall—and the younger nations even more than the older—has been cured by bitter experience and until the religious and moral regeneration of political thought takes place, no new federation is possible.

A HABSBURG RESTORATION PREVENTED

There can be no doubt that a restoration of the Habsburg monarchy would have reconsolidated Austria and saved her from Hitler's attack—if only because it would have reunited Austria and Hungary. Since it was desired to maintain Austria in being and since native force must obviously be mobilized for that purpose, such a restoration would have been only logical. But once again it was proved that the great dooms of history have profound causes and cannot be so lightly reversed. What the Greeks called "Mneme", the sphere of memory, is an enormous power in animal life and in the destiny of men, and is probably strongest of all in the life of nations, especially when it is a memory of suffering, repression and humiliation continued for centuries.

Hence the tragic chapter of history entitled "The Habsburgs and the Succession States". Legitimism could not save Austria because to those states it represented the restoration of the past. Therefore they passionately opposed a Habsburg restoration, an opposition which found utterance in the slogan "Better an Anschluss than the Habsburgs". But the Legitimists on their part were guilty of a very serious mistake in failing to recognize the strength and invincibility of this opposition to the Habsburgs. Their propaganda for the re-erection of the "Holy Empire" aroused the protest of those who had suffered too long from unholy repression and servitude. What guarantee was there that the claimant to the imperial throne—whose personal intentions were certainly most honorable—might not himself fall under the tutelage of groups which had learnt nothing from disaster? The ruling classes in Hungary had no qualms of conscience, no thought of abandoning the fatal obstinacy with which they had persistently prevented a reasonable solution of the problem of nationalities in the Danubian monarchy. Their sole thought was to revise the Treaty of Trianon. They saw in that treaty no instructive lesson of history, no intelligible retribution for centuries of delay. They had eyes for nothing but the rights of the holy crown of St. Stephen. The Bohemian crown of course had no rights.

Unfortunately, both in the lives of individuals and of peoples what has been squandered by an accumulation of mistakes cannot in many cases be restored. The Habsburgs and the Hussites had measured forces. The first time the Habsburgs won, and triumphantly annihilated their foe. The second time the Hussites, reawakened from the grave and enlarged into the Czecho-Slovak nation, won with the aid of the Western democracies. Their victory closed the Habsburg chapter of history *in this context*. The Emperor Karl could not atone for three centuries of German domination and was himself rendered impotent by traditions and by the attitude of an environment which were stronger than himself or his uncle Franz Ferdinand, and which would infallibly have returned had the young and inexperienced heir of the Habsburg dynasty revived the memories already submerged.

The Austrian claim that the restoration of the Habsburgs was her domestic concern was intelligible. But it was equally intelligible that her neighbors should reply "Certainly it is *your* domestic concern. But it is also *our* domestic concern, most intimately domestic, indeed a matter of life and death for us, for nothing less is at stake than whether we are to keep or to lose all we have gained. A restoration of the Habsburgs is a declaration of war against us, even if you do not intend it to be so and are unaware of the results which must follow sooner or later. It does not simply mean Otto. As we see it, it means the re-establishment of a mighty dominion which of old trampled upon us and which will make this youth of noble ideals the plaything of passions and revived ambitions and must ruin the entire work of the peace in whose spirit we are resolved to hold fast the independence of the Danubian states".

It was not without good reason that I have devoted so much of this book to the question of war-guilt. Anyone who has weighed the relevant documents and my comments upon them will understand that Austria's collaboration with the Prussian aggressors explains the historical judgment which brought the great and splendid epoch of the Habsburg Empire to a relentless and inevitable close, as it also closed the epoch of Hohenzollern rule—a conclusion rich in lessons for all ages and all peoples.

Whether in the future under wholly new conditions and after terrifying lessons and searchings of heart the Habsburg dynasty will once more be in a position to play a leading part on the historical stage cannot be foreseen. Alike in the countries governed by dictators and in the countries under democratic rule, though as a result of widely different experiences, the need will once more be felt for monarchy and for the imperial dignity. We are not entering upon an epoch of "Leaders". Demagogic dictatorship and dictatorial demagogy will lose every scrap of credit. Undoubtedly the future of the civilized world will lie with monarchy, in a new context and under new conditions.

MUSSOLINI AND THE ANNEXATION OF AUSTRIA

Mussolini's acquiescence has also been blamed as partly responsible for Austria's doom and stigmatized as a retreat before Germany. The question is fully answered by the following protocol which is the printed record of the advice given verbally by Mussolini at the beginning of April 1936 to the Austrian military attaché in Rome. According to the protocol, written down immediately after the interview, Mussolini made the following observations:—

"In 1938 at latest, Europe will pass through a crisis of the first magnitude. For the Germans have rearmed. They will begin by fortifying the Rhine so that they can remain on the defensive there. A propaganda campaign will very soon show the direction in which their next move is to be expected. There is no doubt that it will be the Southeast.

"Unless Austria takes steps immediately to provide herself with an army ready to take the field and to prepare her defenses, she will be lost. None of her friends, however quickly he comes to her assistance, will arrive in time. It will be too late. There can be no question of a gradual program to be carried out over a long period.

"Austria, therefore, must create an army ready to strike and mobile if small. Only if the Germans know (they are well aware that it is an easy matter to produce *faits accomplis*) that Austria is determined and able to defend herself quickly, even if at short notice, so that no *fait accompli* is possible and that an attack would on the contrary involve Germany in grave difficulties, will she shrink from attempting it.

"The Austrian army is confronted with an extremely hard task. We are no longer in 1866. It must be the mainstay of patriotic resistance. Therefore it must be inspired with a new morale and equipped with every weapon possible.

"This can be achieved only by universal military service which is the foundation of everything else. No one will object. Europe will understand. Austria's financial position (in the currency market) is better than that of most countries. Her economic position is no worse than that of many others, indeed better. She is therefore in a position to afford the necessary rearmament *if only she wills it*.

"Italy is able to give Austria very considerable material help if Austria wants it.

"There is already a large supply of military material in East Africa at our disposal.

"To strengthen the army would be an inestimable inspiration for the officers, the Austrian people, and in particular the youth, and would instill a salutary fear in her foreign and domestic enemies.

"There is still time, though it is running short. If Austria lets it slip, no one can help her.

"The German mechanized units, if they are not driven back from the frontier, and if there are no prepared and mobile troops to oppose them, will be in Vienna within a few hours.

"He (Mussolini) was aware that much hard work was being done in the Austrian army. But an army faced with so hard a task must be helped in every possible way. Inactivity would prove fatal".

This urgent advice clearly proves that as late as 1936 Mussolini sincerely wished Austria to resist the German threat and was moreover convinced that the certainty of such resistance would have had a decisive effect on the German plans. But since his advice was completely neglected, he could only draw the conclusion that Austria had given herself up and that there was no longer any object in defending her independence from outside.

The spiritless and disheartening attitude adopted by those responsible for Austria's destinies is also revealed by correspondence between Archduke Otto and Schuschnigg published in the *Oesterreichischen Post*. On February 18 1938, Otto asked Schuschnigg, for the sake of saving Austria and in the true interest of the German peoples, to make him Chancellor so that without restoration of the monarchy he might rally all the forces of the country for a final resistance. Schuschnigg replied that he could not be responsible for such a forlorn hope. Austria's mission was to preserve the peace to which a senseless and hopeless resistance could in no way contribute. There was no chance of success. Only if the country were confident of herself could she count upon foreign aid. Any attempt at a restoration either in the immediate or in any calculable future would inevitably involve Austria's downfall. The only task that a responsible statesman could at present undertake was to keep the road open for future developments. . . .

Both correspondents were justified. Otto could not have saved Austria. But Austria would have gone down in an honorable struggle, loyal to the last to her true self. And her resistance would have made a vast impression throughout the world and rendered impossible all the lies with which the conqueror misrepresented the true position. But Austrian Austria was not at the helm. An Austria half-paralyzed and undermined by Pan-Germanism had taken her place and could but sign her own death warrant as she passed to her doom. Since the government had not ventured to reorganize the army, and for years the civil service had not been purged of untrustworthy elements, and since German propaganda had been permitted to do its work, Austria was beyond saving. Schuschnigg was well aware of it. Indeed he was himself the surrender of Austria incarnate. True he had declared "Red, white, and red till we are dead" but he did not mean it seriously. He had taken no steps to organize this resistance to the death. He lived in a world of illusions. At Berchtesgaden he was suddenly confronted with the genuine picture of Pan-Germanism and fell crashing from the clouds. On his return to Vienna, instead of mobilizing the army, he spent two hours listening to Bach's cantatas to recover from the shock. No wonder the Potsdam cantatas were victorious.

After the annexation, an Austrian refugee, a lady of the class which cherishes the old traditions, wrote me the following words of despair: . . . "And this is the most painful circumstance of our tragedy that no one lifts a hand or raises a voice of protest, that even the Holy See keeps silence and leaves this land which has always been Catholic the prey of her enemy, I should rather say, of the enemy of all Europe. The German propaganda of lies and deceit has already got a hold upon Europe. European statesmen twist and turn so as to avoid by any possible means the necessity of taking action. And the guiding principle adopted by the press of Europe is the same: whitewash and approve every injustice rather than provoke the wrath of this seemingly all-mighty power.

"At last the Neumann project of the route to the East has been realized. From the Baltic to the Brenner and far into the Balkans, Prussian violence and lust of possession bear sway. The dam which Austria has been up to the present, has been broken down. Who cares? This is the agonizing question, which, sooner perhaps than we expect, will be answered in the same way as the Austrian question: Is there at present any power on earth or in heaven that will resist these diabolical powers?"

A German patriot who was living in Vienna on the very eve of the catastrophe and who escaped by the skin of his teeth wrote me the following account:

"In the afternoon the streets were still thronged by a happy and excited crowd. The public expected the country would be saved by the plebiscite order by Schuschnigg. Then the first bad news reached the crowd: the plebiscite had been postponed, a new government would take office, the entrance of the German troops was expected. An hour later the aspect of the streets had completely changed. As though in Paris the rats had suddenly emerged from the sewers and were swarming over the boulevards from all quarters, repulsive countenances made their appearance, bands of ruffianly youths and girls, viragos, groups of people bawling out their triumph, the vanguard of barbarism. Then for the first time in my life, cold and hard, I felt hatred for my own countrymen rise in my soul".

Hate is a diseased state of mind. But even so it is preferable to the vague Pan-Germanism which prevailed in Austria, obliterated all clear distinctions, and made it impossible to rally in defense of truth and honor and put up a determined resistance. Even many Legitimists lived in a fog, in as much as they were content to talk about the "Holy Empire" without asking themselves whether Austria were still worthy to be invested with the title. If she is to be thoroughly cured of her attitude of blind collaboration with evil and if she is to atone for her betrayal of herself, Austria must pass through her Purgatory by experiencing in body and soul the nature of that power which from a distance she has cursed, yet never ceased to adore.

CHAPTER XXIV

THE CZECH STATE

NO DOUBT the principle of nationality is an explosive which must blow up human civilization unless it is completed by the supernational and universally human principle of confederation, with all the consideration for other nations, the limitations and coordinations it involves. But in any case it stands for the one all-important and fundamental condition of world peace: namely, that the right of the individual, man or nation, must be secured, protected against the tendency to level and to reduce to a cast-iron uniformity, and the riches preserved which arise from a variety of marked contrasts whose mutual and organic supplementation can alone produce what is genuinely universal. No other result of the first World War so clearly embodied the triumph in European history of this principle of nationality as the foundation of Czecho-Slovakia. When Napoleon III, at the conclusion of the peace of Villa Franca, spoke to Emperor Francis Joseph of the triumph of this principle of nationality, the latter replied "You can call it the principle of nationality. I call it revolution." It was the clash between reaction and freedom in Europe.

The conservative elements in the British Empire understood in good time the conservative value of freedom and thereby saved their Empire and averted revolution. It was the failure to perceive that no Empire could survive unless it satisfied the demands of liberty which brought the Empire of the Habsburgs to its downfall.

The movement for Czech emancipation owed its birth

in a very true sense to the personality of Masaryk who, with the support of his most faithful disciples and friends and in face of the utmost conceivable obstacles, had achieved the triumph of his cause and now embodied, a figure of indescribable dignity, the deep-rooted national tradition of humanity and freedom. He was at once a nationalist, in the profoundest sense of the term, and a cosmopolitan. He interpreted the mission of his people as that of mediator between East and West; and it was in Asia that he had assembled the regiments whose task it would be to link up the new state with the Allied powers. After his election as President he proved a political leader of the type of Lorenzo dei Medici, a living protest against all other national leaders in Europe. Precisely because he had no desire to be a dictator he tolerated many survivals from the world of more primitive national instincts and traditions which should have been eliminated. He was convinced that his people, as they slowly matured, could progressively realize their better nature and noblest vocation, and that they would outgrow the feeling of resentment which must prevent them from consistently setting the example which they alone could set. Unfortunately they matured too slowly.

It was undoubtedly a dispensation of Providence which, on the verge of the East, confronting the unnatural and exaggerated discipline of Prussianized Germany and the baroque imperialism of the Habsburgs, had embodied the unique principle of social cohesion and coordination; for it was a visible criticism of all discipline imposed for its own sake and artificially exaggerated. This principle found complete expression in the Sokols. It was a cooperation achieved simply and without effort or strain, charming therefore, and, so to speak, born of the spirit of harmony, producing exactitude and order, free from any trace of what Dostoievsky termed "bureaumania".

THE SUDETEN GERMANS AND PAN-GERMANISM

Before the first World War Masaryk in 1896 had opposed the project of an independent Bohemian state. "We are not so simple" he had written, "as to believe that we could defend such an independent Bohemia against Germany, if the German minority were hostile to us." It required a long series of disillusionments before Masaryk despaired of the possibility of a genuine Austrian confederation and regarded the dissolution of the Danubian Monarchy and the creation of an independent Czecho-Slovakia as the only possible way to secure the national development of the Western Slavonic peoples. That is to say, he ventured upon an experiment of whose dangers he was fully aware.

He believed that the danger from Germany of which he had spoken could be removed by the victory of the Allies in the first World War. From the moment when Germany, without any interference from the conquerors, recommenced its Pan-German program and accordingly welcomed the dissolution of the Danubian Monarchy, as having removed an obstacle to the fulfillment of its aim,— the annexation of the entire German population of South-Eastern Europe—the hour of doom for the newly-created Bohemian state was in sight. Had the new Germany genuinely abandoned those Pan-German aims and returned to its millennial tradition of confederacy, it might have become, in a very different sense to its present intention, the center of a European Federation. In that case, the German minorities in the states of Eastern Europe would have become links in a common task instead of advance-guards of German conquest.

The existence of those German minorities in foreign states is an inheritance from that former international system of which Germany was the foundation. The nationalism of modern Germany was incapable of administering rightly this inheritance. It could give those minorities no sound guidance, but must necessarily drive them into increasingly violent conflicts with the nationalities among whom they lived, as it was itself in turn excited by those conflicts to a feverish bellicosity. It has as little understanding of Germany's past as of her proper tasks in the world today. Ever since the foundation of the German Empire, Europe has been sick of this fever. The first World War was its catastrophic crisis. That war arose from the conflict produced by the misunderstood legacy of the old supernational Empire in South-Eastern Europe.

When, therefore, after the War the foundation of the new Slav states compelled their German minorities to submit to a foreign government and when Germany began to work for the accomplishment of her century-old dream of the union in one state of all European Germans, sentence of death was pronounced on the new states—unless the Western Powers should honor the pledge they had clearly given to maintain the independence of those new states. But pacifist tendencies made it extremely difficult for the Powers to do this. Even before the War, those pacifist ideals had seriously weakened their resistance to Germany's power-politics, and after the War they took possession of large groups in England and in France and thus led to a fatal neglect of national armaments. (The MacDonald period.) The ideal of self-determination, of Western origin, on which the dismemberment of the Austrian Empire had been based, disclosed its intrinsic logic, with which Germany successfully allied herself to carry the process further still. Nor must we forget that it was especially difficult for England, which had granted her own Dominions self-determination and by that means retained them in her commonwealth of nations, to mobilize her Empire in order to prevent by its intervention the self-determination of the German minorities. Once on a visit to London I was complaining of the indifference shown by the English to the question of Czecho-Slovakia. A member of Parliament called my attention to this aspect of the matter "You can hardly expect us, who in every part of the globe have stood for national self-determination, even for Ireland where it was particularly difficult for us and seemed so dangerous, to oppose self-determination for the Sudeten Germans". To which I replied "But if the Irish lived on the East Coast of Great Britain and if on the continent a vast Irish Empire had armed to the teeth and if its leader had proclaimed himself the leader of all Irishmen throughout the world, would you then have granted independence?" An awkward silence followed.

But we must be just. It was impossible for the rulers of the British Empire to enlighten their public as to the peculiar nature of the situation in Eastern Europe. Events developed too rapidly. Only a handful who possessed special knowledge could foresee future events. This is the explanation of Lord Runciman's mission, which was an attempt to apply without modification to South-Eastern Europe the method by which the Irish question had been solved. But the tragedy of South-Eastern Europe in our time has consisted precisely in this attempt to solve Eastern problems on Western lines. Nor did England perceive the complete insincerity of German policy, which was not in the least concerned with the self-determination of the Sudeten Germans or of Austrians but merely sought to abuse the Western ideal in order to extend German power in Eastern Europe, that is to say, in order to destroy deliberately the self-determination of the countries she could annex, including their German populations. When in March the remainder of Czecho-Slovakia was reduced to a German protectorate England's eyes were opened at last.

Obviously then, the dismemberment of Czecho-Slovakia, like the previous dismemberment of the Danubian Empire, was an inevitable product of the forces of that one-sided nationalism which still retained its omnipotence. And the ideals which oppose it are taking shape very slowly. A striking light is thrown upon this irresistible development of modern history by the fact that as early as 1899 a German member of the Austrian Parliament, the Bohemian deputy Turk, declared amidst the enthusiastic applause of his friends: "The hereditary German territories outside Germany must in one way or another be united with Germany, as they were before 1866. A customs union with Germany would be the first step in this direction. We Germans are prepared for anything. Only let a civil war break out between the Czechs and the Germans in Bohemia, Moravia and Silesia, and the Prussian army will march in and deal with you".

This was exactly what happened forty years later.

It has been said "If the Czechs had not made the same mistakes in their treatment of the Germans as the Austrians had made in their treatment of the Czechs, Germany would have found it extremely difficult to destroy the stability of Czecho-Slovakia." This is more than doubtful. The attraction of Pan-Germanism would have prevailed in the end, the more so since Germany's attitude made it impossible for the Czechs to concede to the German population of their frontier districts the home rule which could have been granted without excessive risk, if their neighbor could have been trusted. The more unreservedly the Sudeten Germans professed the ideology of National Socialism, the more extreme became their claim to unlimited autonomy.

The Germans would not have hesitated to subject such a foreign minority in their own empire to the most severe control. This appears clearly from the principles laid down magisterially by Professor R. Huber of Kiel in his textbook of constitutional law (published by the Hanseatische Verlagsanstalt, Hamburg, page 81). Professor Huber is an official jurisconsult under the German government. "This

secure protection enjoyed by foreign minorities is condi-
tional on their acknowledging themselves politically a portion of the third Reich and behaving accordingly; any
open or secret attempt to secede from the Reich, that is
to say, any form of irredentism, destroys the conditions on
which a foreign nationality can expect protection. Recognition of a foreign way of living cannot be carried so far
as to be detrimental to a German people and Reich. If a
foreign group offends against its duty to be loyal to the
German Reich, it forfeits the rights of a protected minority. The Reich is then justified in taking the measures
necessary to defend itself against the threat to its unity as
a state. This is the obvious condition under which the
German Reich protects its foreign minorities."

This casts a grim light upon the contemptible duplicity
of German policy. The principles applied to foreign
minorities in Germany are set aside without scruple when
it is a case of German minorities in a foreign state. Such
German minorities are to have no restriction placed upon
their freedom. They have even the right to claim their
allegiance to Germany. Was it regard for the interests
of the German minority that made Henlein demand that
Czecho-Slovakia should reverse her foreign policy? What
other European state has ever before been confronted
with such a demand? But the European situation being
what it was, it was to be expected. The conflict was mortal
and admitted no solution. The development of an armed
Pan-Germanism compelled the republic of Czecho-
Slovakia to ally herself with the enemies of Germany, and
this could but alienate the German minority from a state
which could defend its existence only by preparing for
the eventuality of war with their mother-country. It was
a knot impossible to unravel even after the division of the
country at the end of September, 1938. The German
islands in the Czech rump state continued to play the

same game until the naked right of superior strength put an end to the situation.

Given the historical situation, events took their inevitable course. But it is equally inevitable that all these monstrous wrongs shall be righted and the game of political gangsterism called power-politics brought to an end. Everything that has happened hitherto is but provisional. What has been destroyed and suppressed will be revived under new forms and in the framework of more comprehensive European settlements and unions. The course of events up to the present is but the *reductio ad absurdum* of a principle whose unthinking and one-sided application will but entangle still further the problems confronting us and whose nucleus of truth, the need to secure individual rights, can be permanently realized only in the context of a new world-order.

CZECHO-SLOVAKIA AND THE WESTERN POWERS

Chamberlain's flights to Munich and to Godesburg, the retreat of the Western powers in face of Hitler's threats, the abandonment of Czecho-Slovakia, the outbreak in London of a veritable orgy of pacifism,—all this composed one of the most dramatic episodes enacted on the historical stage. It was the tragedy of that false pacifism whose blindness and weakness were no less dangerous to Western civilization than Pan-German expansion and barbarism. It was almost too late when the situation was at last seen in its true light, soon enough it is true to bar the way to wider projects, but too late to prevent the total annihilation of Czecho-Slovakia.

I have explained the reasons which made it extremely difficult for England to intervene in favor of Czecho-Slovakia and to commit her Empire to its cause. But if the English had understood that the loss of the districts inhabited by Germans meant the unavoidable ruin of the Czecho-Slovak state and could have foreseen what consequences would follow from its destruction and that it would produce a catastrophic disturbance of the balance of power in Europe, England would long since have taken up the position she has now adopted and would have won her Dominions to the same point of view.

The annihilation of Czecho-Slovakia, which made England completely change the continental policy she had pursued hitherto, was no sudden inspiration of Hitler's but the inevitable consequence of its dismemberment. In his speech of April 28, 1939 Hitler himself admitted that the mutilated Czecho-Slovakia was incapable of survival. By this admission, without realizing it, he testified to the truth that in this case the self-determination of the German minority was impracticable, because it ran counter to all the political, economic and military conditions on which alone the Czech state could preserve its independence. The entire tragedy, which irretrievably weakened the timely organization of a concerted defense against the threat of German hegemony, was the result of political amateurishness. The Western governments failed to perceive Hitler's true program, its strict consistency, and the significance of Czecho-Slovakia for what had been for centuries the supreme consideration of Britain's European policy, the balance of power.

"We cannot fight for Czecho-Slovakia" was the cry of extremely influential French circles, as though Czecho-Slovakia alone were at stake, whereas the Western powers were in fact called upon to take up a decisive attitude in prospect of a future German attack in the West. It was believed that nothing more was asked of them than to permit the German Reich to round off its frontiers. Statesmen and public alike closed their eyes to the fact that the Sudeten question had been raised simply as a strategical weapon to destroy completely the Czecho-Slovak barrier in the path of Germany's Eastern expansion, and that the German goal was nothing less than the domination of the near East and the reopening of the Berlin-Bagdad route, thereby to secure essential supplies and prepare for a settlement with the Western powers.

Is it not a striking fact today that no one in the West says "We will not fight for the Polish Corridor"? It has been realized at long last that the issue is not a strip of land but a principle, and that in the light of the essential aims of Hitler's foreign policy every position taken up in Eastern Europe is at the same time a position taken up in Western Europe. It will no doubt be argued that in 1938 the Western powers were not yet ready for war and were therefore compelled to retreat. Unfortunately they were ignorant that Germany was far less ready. Germany was in a position to make war only in the Southeast; and even if Czecho-Slovakia had dared to resist unaided, it is certain that an attack would have not been made but postponed until Germany was better prepared for it. Nor is it true that the choice was between surrender and European war. On the contrary, had the Western powers stood firm and delivered the ultimatum "Home rule for the Sudetens but no separation from Czecho-Slovakia", Hitler with Mussolini's assistance would have found some face-saving retreat. Anyone even moderately acquainted with the position behind the scenes knows that this would have happened.

Lord Runciman's report contains this remark: "The problem of Czecho-Slovakia is to eliminate from Central Europe a focus of acute political friction." The only way to do this could have been to make Germany understand once for all that she would not succeed in eliminating Czecho-Slovakia. Instead, Czecho-Slovakia was eliminated and the political tension in Central Europe rendered three times as dangerous. A most instructive example of the muddles of a false pacifism.

After the abandonment of the Czecho-Slovak Republic an article appeared in the Prague paper *Lidove Novine* entitled "Farewell to France". It is an historical document. The writer said: "We have been abandoned. The world is governed by might, not by right. Therefore our place must be on the side of might. There is nothing left for us but to go along with Germany."

This article became known in Western Europe and probably did more than a little to prepare for the change in the attitude of the Western powers. Nations that can repent of a shortsighted and unprincipled policy give good earnest for the renewal of their moral and political strength. For the Czechs, the leave-taking from the West was bitter and bloody. For they had resisted for centuries the German thrust to the Southeast and have always been pioneers of Western ideas in the Slavonic world. Hence the German wrath mounted through the centuries against the Czech doorkeepers.

Nothing is more certain than that the Czech nation will hereafter rise again, to resume once more on a larger scale its task as mediator between the East and Western civilization.

IS THE THIRD REICH THE LAWFUL HEIR OF THE FIRST?

In his reply to Roosevelt's question, Hitler spoke on April 28, 1939 of "The return of Bohemia and Moravia to the Reich". And a considerable number of recent Nazi utterances show that National Socialism has dared to put forward seriously the fraudulent claim that the medieval Empire was a national German Empire on whose entire inheritance the Third Reich has therefore a just claim. Against this it can be proved to the hilt that the two Empires have in common only the name, not a juridical title. The Empire of which Bohemia was a part was never called the *German Empire*. Until its dissolution in 1806 it was styled the *Holy Roman Empire* whose later addition *of the German nation* was never officially sanctioned. The phrase simply meant that part of the Holy Roman Empire

whose population is German. But from 1804 the possessions of the Bohemian crown belonged to the Austrian
Empire, which in 1867 became the Austro-Hungarian
monarchy.

History proves that Bohemia, including the Sudeten
districts, has always been a *compact whole* and never
formed part of a German empire or German national
state. The medieval Empire and the Empire of the Habsburgs were "a league of nations", not a national state; and
in so far as "nations" were members of this league they
were not states constituted by a racial nationality but
historical products; Bohemia, moreover, being an over-
whelmingly Czech state. The Empire to which Bohemia
belonged was a Christian Empire, and the authority of
the Emperor to which the states of Europe surrendered a
portion of their sovereignty was not a juridical but a
spiritual authority. The Emperor was looked upon as the
guardian of peace and justice, and therefore peoples and
monarchies voluntarily submitted to his rule. That is to
say, the Emperor was the political expression of the Christian ideas of justice and law which were recognized by the
peoples of Europe as powers superior to nationality.

It is therefore a gross perversion of historical truth to
represent this medieval empire as the property of the
German nation—a possession to which the present German Empire can lay claim. Bohemia, a country protected by
a powerful mountain rampart, was from the first the home
of Slavonic people. The Germans entered it as guests and
welcome colonists. For well-nigh a thousand years Czechs
and Germans lived in it side by side. To break up a community thus created by Providence in the name of self-
determination was such an outrage against this product of
the entire history of Europe that it could only have been
engineered from abroad in the interest of a foreign power.
Not a single man in those regions can affirm with certainty "I am a German, you are a Slav". For the man

who is German today may have acquired in the course of the centuries more Slav blood than is possessed by the Slavs. The Slav may be a German who became Slavonic only a few generations ago.

The intermingling of the two peoples found expression in the legal code. Bohemia, even after the battle of the White Mountains, remained a single administrative unit which no centralization dared to touch. What Mussolini said a few weeks before the dismemberment of Czecho-Slovakia, that it had been artificially inflated by the forcible incorporation of the Sudeten Germans, is false. On the contrary, the Czechs after the War had simply to take over the existing unity, historical and juridical, of Bohemia and give it a Czech name. That this christening took account only of the Czechs and Slovaks and passed over the Germans was indeed a fundamental mistake, followed by several other stupid slights inflicted upon the Germans. But in making this admission we must not forget how difficult the Germans both outside and inside the country had made it for the Czechs to trust German loyalty. Nevertheless German loyalty was of vital importance to the Czech state, since the protection of the Western frontier was at stake. In such situations an abstract right of self-determination cannot be upheld. On historical, geo-political and strategic grounds, the Czechs were justified in claiming the whole of Bohemia for their national territory. The German Empire has no historical claim to Bohemia. The Sudetens have never belonged either to Germany or Austria but to Bohemia; and the last-named had always, as a unit of mixed population, been a member of a League of Nations, not part of a national German state.

A government organ of the S.S. published on March 21, 1939 an article entitled *Space or Empire* (Raum oder Reich) which was illustrated by a large map intended to show that in occupying Bohemia and Moravia, Germany had simply taken back what had belonged to her for a millennium. It contained the following statements:

"If a wrong has now been righted and after centuries of weakness the German people once more remembers its strength and restores the ancient historic boundaries of her national empire, this concerns nobody save perhaps the robber of one or another of her territories.

"And he is the last who has any right to express moral indignation. For he has in the past exploited the weakness of a great people in the most unconscionable fashion to enrich himself unjustly.

"What has been sanctioned by the history of a millennium cannot be invalidated by peevish contemporaries.

"For we think in millennia, whereas the Western democracies, owing to the short life of their rapidly changing systems of government, can scarcely look more than a year ahead.

"We are aware of our debt to our past and have never forgotten the shameless abuse of our weakness in the hour of our national breakdown.

"We know how to defend our sacred right to the soil of our Empire and do not intend to allow ourselves a second time to be robbed with impunity of our border provinces".

The facts I have set out above show what a barefaced falsification of history it is to claim that the frontiers of the former medieval league of nations are those of a former German national empire. What consequences may be drawn from this claim when applied to Western Europe is shown by the following German utterances:

The *Reichszeitung für deutsche Erzieher*, the official organ of the union of National Socialist teachers with a circulation of 310,000, published, after the return of the Saar, a typical article by H. Dicht, entitled "The Question of the Saar and some Reflections on the Advance towards the West". The author argues that Germany must now take in hand the question of her Western frontier since German hegemony is dependent on the Western extension of the Reich. About the year 1500 her westerly advance was held up. "Under the rule of the Hohenstaufen the frontier of Germany ran from the mouth of the Scheldt to Marseilles. The peace of Westphalia reduced the extent of the Reich. Germany has her eyes on the valleys of the Rhine, the Rhone, and the Weichsel. But they can be reached only by war."

Do not object that this is but an isolated voice. The Pan-Germans before the War of 1914 also seemed isolated individuals. But it was the program they advocated which was finally adopted. For they expressed the insane logic of an aberration of the German people centuries old, a blind misconception of the meaning of the fact that the Germans were scattered throughout Central and Eastern Europe and of their historical bonds with foreign nationalities. And unhappily the entire educated classes had for decades been misled by untrustworthy leaders who fostered a collective conceit and an overweening pride of power which made them see in such shameless utterances the true expression of their own lack of moral balance. Let us not persist in distinguishing between Hitler and the German people as it really is. Unfortunately the German nation as a whole is far more responsible for Hitlerism than is often thought. Among the opponents of National Socialism there are very few genuine supporters of their country's old and honorable traditions. The rest would gladly accept all the guns Hitler offers, were they not presented with the alternative "Guns or butter". They prefer the butter. But that is not a regenerate Germany.

CHAPTER XXV

GERMANY AND RUSSIA

A PROFOUND cause of the entire German tragedy was the fact that Asia and Europe met in Germany; and the German world, indeed the German soul itself, was torn two ways by two fundamentally different forces. No doubt Germany's position was providential. It gave her the mission to mediate between the two continents. But if she was to accomplish that mission and not be merely the theatre in which the two worlds clashed, she had to achieve a synthesis of the conflicting forces. This, Germany has so far failed to accomplish. She has simply tacked from one side to the other.

During the Middle Ages and again in the eighteenth century the Southern and Western influence was predominant. But as Prussian will-to-power progressively conquered the German people, the influence of Asia on the German soul and on German history came to the fore. In this connection Asia does not mean Buddha or Confucius but Genghis-Kahn. It means the world of the wide plains and of unlimited despotisms. It means the extinction of the individual, the power of vast masses, the reduction of millions to an equality of servitude, the negation of the spiritual world and of individual conscience. Hitler represents Asia against Europe. He said once to a friend, "Napoleon was an ass. Genghis Khan for me." By that he meant: "No world empire can be built on the rights of man championed by the French Revolution. Only a barbarian can organize the world."

At this point the two worlds divide, and their quarrel

can be settled only by a new victory of the Catalaunian Fields—that is if the Russian soul is really with its tyrant. But in its depths the Russian soul does not belong to the Asiatic despotisms but is on the contrary their strongest foe and one day will be reunited with a regenerate Western Christendom. Again and again Mongol and German organizations have taken possession of the Russian soul and have ruled Russia in opposition to its deepest nature. That is why the Slavophils said "The state kills human brotherhood." All the Russian despots have allied themselves with Prussia in order to slay human brotherhood by the state, by organization and by machinery.

The period just opening of renewed collaboration between Germany and Russia is intended to serve the same purpose. It has been prepared so long by the developments on both sides that it was but a matter of time. Czarism, germanized by Peter the Great and based upon a bureaucracy of German origin, never abandoned its secret bond with Russia, and the apparent opposition between revolutionary Russia and authoritarian Prussia must disappear in the measure in which the Prussian principle is consistently applied in the economic sphere. In his *Preussentum und Sozialismus* Spengler truly pointed out that Socialism is simply Prussianism in the economic field. A totalitarian state must be socialist. Therefore Prussian state-socialism and Russian Communism were bound to meet the moment Russia abandoned Leninist orthodoxy. Both systems represent the complete triumph of society over the individual.

Rauschning informs us in his book that Hitler told him plainly: "To the Christian doctrine of the supremacy of the individual conscience and personal responsibility, I oppose the emancipating doctrine that the individual is nothing and survives in the immortality of the nation. I reject the dogma of man's redemption by the suffering and

death of a Divine Saviour and I put in its place a new
dogma of the communication of merit, namely that individuals are redeemed by the life and action of the new
lawgiver and leader who delivers the masses from the
burden of liberty".

But the triumph of society over the individual is the
triumph of Asia over Europe, whereas the West has too
often allowed the individual to triumph over society. The
truth is represented by the Christian community which
bases social life on the regeneration of the individual who
is always disposed to abuse society for his private ends.
This abuse has largely contributed to contemporary Socialist reactions, which are distinguished from each other
only by the particular class which in each case has made
the collectivist experiment its program.

Renan's book *La Réforme* contains a remarkable passage, which I here quote, about the part the German
element in Europe would play in defending private property against the growing power of socialism.

"It is probably the German race, because it is feudal
and military, that will vanquish socialism and egalitarian
democracy which are not likely to meet with a check from
us Celts. Such an issue would be in harmony with historical precedent. For it has always been a German characteristic to combine conquest with the protection of
property, in other words to put the material and brutal
fact of property acquired by conquest before any consideration of the rights of man or abstract theories of a social
contract. Therefore every advance of socialism is likely to
evoke a corresponding Teutonic advance, and I can en-
visage the day when all the countries, wherein socialism
has made headway, will be governed by Germans. The
invasions of the fourth and fifth centuries were due to
similar reasons. The provinces of the Roman Empire were

no longer capable of producing good gendarmes, efficient defenders of property."

What would Renan say were he living today and could witness the spectacle of National Socialism with its totalitarian grip of individuals and their property, and its corresponding alliance with Russian Bolshevism? Here is another proof how little security mere force can provide.

Communism is the Fascism of the proletariat. Fascism is the Communism of the bourgeoisie. The day came when they were reconciled to make a joint attack on the social order of the West. The hour of the Russo-German cooperation had struck. For National Socialism the greatest advantage expected from this alliance is not military cooperation but the disruptive effect which it is hoped the slogan "Socialism against Capital" will produce among the middle and lower classes of the Western peoples. In this way the Nazis hope to transfer the international struggle to another plane, to make it a class struggle, and to cause the Western workingman to ask himself whether his interests would not be better secured by the German-Russian bloc than by the Allies.

Everything will depend on the question whether the proletariat of the Western nations is sufficiently intelligent to grasp the fact that the struggle of the West against the German and Russian dictatorships is not the struggle of a class to retain its position but the struggle of civilization against barbarism, and that the workers' struggle for a position in accordance with human dignity can be won only where freedom and the rights of man are recognized. The forcible aggression against Finland has made a deep impression on the workers in Western countries. To what extent Bolshevik propaganda will be successful in effacing it remains to be seen.

In Western Europe the delusion is still widely entertained that any close collaboration between Germany and the Soviet Union will increase the prospects of a conservative revolution led by the Reichswehr. The hope is proved false by the simple fact that on this question the Reichswehr is itself divided. In fact two tendencies observable in the Reichswehr favor a rapprochement with Russia. One is that represented by General von Seeckt and expounded in his pamphlet *Deutschland zwischen West und Ost*. The author is opposed to Bolshevism but thinks it impracticable to isolate Russia from the political life of Europe by placing her in a species of quarantine. The attempt would only make the Russian disease take a firmer hold and perpetuate it. Only a policy which assists Russia to recover her economic health can slowly bring her back to a political and social system like those obtaining in the rest of Europe. "Russia" he says "is not a land and state such as we find elsewhere in Europe. Russia is a vast landbridge, connecting Asia's inexhaustible reserve of men and forms of power with that western division of the continent which we are accustomed to call Europe and in which the center of world power and of history is located. There is no natural frontier between Europe and Asia. Attempts to draw a boundary are the artificial constructions of geographers or politicians."

The Prussian General's attitude is the natural attitude of a man from Eastern Germany who knows the Asiatic world, knows too that Russia, as Europe's bulwark against Asia, cannot be definitely cut off from Europe and thrust into the Asiatic chaos. And it has long been shared by a considerable section of the German corps of officers.

But there is also a new and very strong current of opinion. The state of mind which it expresses is best described by the chapter in Rauschning's *Die Revolution des Nihilismus* devoted to the new type of German officer, the officer who has cast off all old religious ties and thus has abandoned completely the traditional outlook of the German officer and has become the unknown soldier of an unknown destiny. Such men are prepared for great ventures. It was they, not Hitler, who made the war on Poland. Far from objecting to the alliance with Russia they are quite ready to see Germany itself bolshevized, provided the Bolshevism is of an aggressive and military type in which the officer corps would take its place in the forefront.

Even the section of the Reichswehr still professedly hostile to Bolshevism no longer opposes a firm front to these two tendencies. On the contrary, its adherents are ready to accept the new departure in the unavowed conviction that a military alliance between Russia and Germany, which would of course involve a military and economic reorganization of the former by German experts, must lead to a gradual German penetration of Russia and the eventual overthrow of the present government which would be replaced by puppets of Germany.

In view of all this, a military alliance between Russia and Germany would be inevitable if Stalin were not Stalin, a man at least Hitler's match for cunning. Is he prepared to surrender himself and his country to a German occupation of this kind? But the further question arises, is he strong enough to refuse? Will not the exposure of Russia's weakness in the Finnish war encourage the Germans to occupy Russia uninvited?

None can foretell what will happen in that quarter. But in any case the Western powers should take steps to forestall any such developments. The Prussian occupation of Germany has already cost the world dear in blood, devastation and anxiety. The occupation of Russia by Prussian militarism in the pursuance of the Nazi strategy of aggression would increase the misery threefold.

Hitler said to Rauschning, "If ever I should decide upon an alliance with Russia nothing will prevent me from making another volte-face and attacking Russia as soon as I have secured my objective in the West".

More than a century ago Donozo Cortes wrote "A gigantic anti-christian empire will arise governed by the methods of the demagogue. Its ruler will be a man of the people, of Satanic magnitude." Did he foresee the present Reich of eighty million or a German-Russian Empire of one hundred and eighty million? It is for the Western powers to decide.

CHAPTER XXVI

POLAND BETWEEN GERMANY AND RUSSIA

DISCUSSIONS of the future peace and its terms are still dominated by a disposition to think in terms of November 1918; and to imagine the Allies, having achieved an overwhelming victory over an exhausted Germany, dictating terms that will make a third German aggression impossible. Czecho-Slovakia and Poland will be restored and the Corridor eliminated by annexing East Prussia to Poland.

But, even if the Allies defeat Germany, what if Russia protests and by her mere existence annuls all the guarantees which it will be the Allies' duty to exact from the incorrigible disturber of the peace? The difficulty cannot be overcome by pointing to the present military weakness of the Soviet Union. For who could prevent the Germans, when a second defeat had made it impossible to rearm in Germany itself, transferring their preparations for the third war of revenge to the interior of Russia by employing their most expert soldiers and technicians to build up Russia's military strength and to reorganize her economic life? In that case the Russians would have no reason to fear that a Germany held down by the Western powers would still be strong enough to abuse the assistance they gave to prepare an armed attack upon Russia. The object of such a military-economic reorganization of Russia would be a fourth partition of Poland and the re-establishment of a Germany able to support Russia in her Asiatic ambitions and able to hold the Western powers in check.

This rough sketch of the possibilities of the situation is sufficient to prove that the German problem cannot be

solved unless the Russian problem is solved at the same
time. Let us imagine an attempt to restore Poland at the
end of the present war. The Russians cannot be expelled
without fighting from the Polish districts they have occupied. If the Allies left them in undisturbed possession the
new Poland would be shorn of vast genuinely Polish
territories, and to avoid further expulsions of entire
populations Poland would probably not even recover the
lands now occupied by the German immigrants from the
Baltic. If however, the victorious armies forcibly restored
the former frontiers, the new Poland would find herself
between two great countries whose one thought would be
to destroy by joint action the situation thus created.

These considerations suffice to show how closely a genuine solution of the German problem depends upon a
reorganization of Russia in accordance with the essentially
Christian principles and conditions of Western civilization. This does not mean that Western institutions must
be forcibly imposed upon the East but on the contrary
that Russia must be liberated from the violence which her
native traditions are at present suffering from a system of
government based on revolutionary abstractions. Could
this liberation be effected, Poland should undoubtedly
join a great Russian and Polish federation. Such a federation would make it easier for Poland to solve her domestic
racial problems, secure her once for all against danger
from Germany, and at the same time put a final end to all
German imperialist ambitions in Eastern Europe. And
such a union between Russia and Poland would bring
Russia once more into vital contact with Western culture,
of which Poland had always been the Eastern representative.

In this connection it is most important not to lose sight
of the enduring Russia by fixing our gaze exclusively on
Czarist or on Bolshevik Russia. Obviously the Poles could
not be committed to the goodwill of Russia as she is at

present. But in Russia, at any time, a world at once new and very old may unexpectedly rise to the surface—and as a result of the present crisis. The Finns tell us that many dying or captured Russians made the Sign of the Cross. The peasant population of Jugo-Slavia is convinced that "Holy Orthodox Russia" is not really dead and will soon rise from her apparent grave. Members of the Communist Youth, the Comsomol, in increasing numbers attend the services of the Church and even sing in the choir. The Russians are a far more religious people than the Germans; and this will once more make itself evident in the course of world history.

In any case, Russia's return to Europe is one of the most important events of our time. It must not be regarded as merely a source of spiritual infection. Everything depends on who takes the infection. It may well be Russia that is infected—another point of view from which to consider an eventual return of Poland to a new Russian world.

CHAPTER XXVII

GERMANY AND WORLD ECONOMICS

CERTAINLY Hitler is right when he insists that Germany lacks the extensive territories producing raw material which the great sea-powers possess. What conclusions should we draw from this fact? Is Germany's lack of a colonial empire due to the jealousy and greed of those who came first into the field? Was it not natural that a nation situated in the center of the Continent and constantly occupied by her relations with Asia, which time and again pushed into Germany the peoples to the east of her frontier, could not become a first-class sea-power? Germany's contact with the sea sufficed only for the export of her products. She was, therefore, obliged to leave the development of trade overseas and the organization of colonial empires to nations with extensive coasts, nations dependent on assured commercial relations with other continents. Their empires represent the investment of incalculable sums and centuries of hard work. Is it just or feasible to expel them from these possessions and to divide the world anew? Such a course would be an immoral violation of hard-won rights. No doubt the rise of the colored peoples to self-government will involve a peaceful and gradual disappropriation of the colonial powers. But the Western peoples will resist with as much determination as justification any attempt to transfer the place they occupy to nations who are attempting to solve by the barbaric method of force a problem so extremely complicated as the colonial question has now become.

There are today, as there always have been, other ways by which Germany can secure what she cannot obtain within her own frontiers. Those nations who, as a result of their geographical position and the course of their history, have arrived too late to take part in the distribution of colonies must secure their *lebensraum* by the right not of possession but of commercial treaty, and must accept all the results of the situation in which they find themselves. The time is indeed not remote when those nations which today still possess colonies will exchange their possessions for the guarantee of commercial treaties. But the epoch of international treaties must come first.

Further, has Germany the right to complain that her vast industrial development has in fact been hampered by a lack of raw materials? German manufacturers could purchase them in the British Empire on the same terms as English manufacturers. German trade in Hong-Kong enjoyed the same treatment as British. Supported by the British Empire and enjoying the protection of the order it had established, the German merchant piled up riches and won a high position in the commercial world. Was this a refusal to let Germany have her share in the world's wealth? No doubt it was different in wartime. But who compelled Germany to make war in a world whose peoples were already bound together by a network of mutual relations?

Bismarck was well aware of this. He had no desire to substitute a German Empire for the British Empire. Lord Granville points this out in his Memoirs. The founder of the Prussian Empire was in favor of a division of labor between the sea-powers and the land-powers. He realized that the older commercial nations brought to the problems of colonial administration the centuries of experience necessary, if the moral and educational difficulties in working with the natives were to be overcome successfully and the world spared the evils arising from the employment of the wrong methods.

If Germany desired to secure for her people their

lebensraum, that is, the importation of whatever cannot be obtained at home, her policy should have been directed to winning the confidence of the older commercial nations by the peaceful labor of her citizens and by her political attitude. So far as the work of Germans was concerned, Germany was successful in this. But her policy lost her the fruit of years of industry. She could take for its device "Politics versus Economics." She succeeded in cutting off the German people, who for almost a century had been living on foreign trade, from this source of its prosperity, indeed of its subsistence. Similarly Italian nationalism— which, unlike French nationalism, is practising a species of Roman Prussianism instead of defending the inheritance of a humane civilization—cannot by any artificial autarchy compensate for the damage Italy has received, and is still receiving, from her action in severing herself from world commerce. "Steam and electricity" said Admiral Reveillière at the beginning of the century "have revolutionized the entire world. But the routine of politicians has not altered."

In fact, modern nationalism stands in such glaring conflict with the realities of the modern age and its world-economy that such a realist as Machiavelli, were he living today, would most certainly have defended against a reactionary nationalism the laws which govern it. Nor does this world-economy imply a leveling cosmopolitanism. An inevitable consequence of the diversity of national territories is an international division of labor whereby each land produces what its climate, soil, geographical position, social structure and the character of its population dictate. Hence the necessity for a mutual supplementation of resources by international cooperation. It is impossible to give every nation all it requires by putting it in possession of the territory from which those goods are derived. Such claims must produce a savage mutual war so that in the end there will be neither possession nor treaty rights but only smoking ruins.

Certainly Hitler is right when he says that Germany must obtain from the East the raw materials she requires. But does this give him the right to reduce to a state of semi-slavery the nations who possess them? Did not Germany become a great commercial power long before her navy challenged Britain and long before she threatened with political bondage those who supplied her with agricultural produce? Was it not precisely because Germany is poor in raw materials but rich in intellectual endowments and in technical genius that she became a great workshop for the manufacture of raw materials obtained from abroad and that she became renowned for the high quality of the goods she produced? Did she not obtain in this way a position in the very center of world trade? And did not her universally recognized skill secure for her, long before the first World War, a foremost place in the markets of the world? "Pride is enough to ruin everything." Germany preferred the right of possession to treaty rights; and to obtain it she plunged blindly into a War which cost her customers and purveyors.

Thus was Germany's suicide begun in 1914 and completed by Hitler's autarchy. By the first World War Germany threw away the fruits of a century of German work abroad and became the victim of an economic crisis. In consequence the greatest exporting country in Europe was brought to the verge of ruin and the economic systems of other countries thrown out of gear—particularly since the experience of the War, by cutting off foreign supplies, had obliged all the nations who had taken part in it to aim at industrial and agricultural self-sufficiency.

On this crisis Hitler supervened. Instead of bringing it to an end by returning definitively to a policy of economic internationalism, he flung himself into a campaign to recover former possessions and to acquire new ones.

By the consequent threat to the peace of the world he aggravated the critical position of German commerce. The correspondent of a Prague newspaper, after visiting the idle port of Hamburg, wrote an account of it entitled "The cemetery of ships". This loss of trade would have found expression in increased unemployment if Hitler had not invested the nation's entire capital in rearmament; which, of course, rapidly reduced the number of unemployed but hastened the decay of international commerce and thus of the German export trade.

The cause, therefore, of the gradual but inevitable breakdown of international commerce has been the solvent power of military nationalism setting one nation against another, an evil which made its appearance roughly at the same time as the international movement diametrically opposed to it, namely, the growth of world-trade. While the technical progress and the growth of commerce were linking the nations more and more closely and making them increasingly dependent upon each other, they were being driven apart by a principle of disintegration. The enormous advance in the external organization of the world was confronted with its moral disorganization. The spiritual foundations of international commerce were completely lost sight of. The years of fear which preceded the first World War, the War itself, and the fear of the second World War, have necessarily been fatal to world-trade which must develop peaceably with assured prospects. "Capital," the American financier, Vanderlip, says in his book *What Happened to Europe* "is like a rat which scurries back to its hole as soon as it sees that it can't nibble the cheese."

Behind this paralysis of international cooperation stood the spirit of Potsdam. And its logical culmination, Hitler's deliberate work of destruction, has completed it. Yet Hitler is surprised that the colonial powers drew their economic bonds with their territories overseas more tightly in order to rescue something of their commerce from the growing insecurity. He is blind to the fact that those economic bonds were but a logical result of the gradual supersession of mere dominion by federation. England has been able to retain her Empire only because she has had the foresight to exchange possession for treaty rights. Therefore England will win. Germany will go down in disaster. For all the living forces in the world are on the side of the rights of man.

Hitler wants to base politics on biology. Very well. Biology is not confined to the doctrine of Germany's vital urge, her unlimited claims, her intellectual aberrations and her miscalculations. It has also something to say of the human vitality of non-German peoples, of their elemental energies, their achievement and reserves of strength. The war in which Hitler refused to believe has come.

Given Hitler's policy of self-sufficiency, his ambition to rule the world is strictly logical. The economy of the entire globe has long since become part of the *lebensraum* of every nation; and a nation which refuses to be satisfied with treaty rights guaranteed by an order of international law and which believes that the only way to secure necessary imports is by conquering them, must necessarily aim at a military domination of the world. That is why iron and oil dictate German policy and why the invasion of Scandinavia and the invasion of the Danubian states that will follow it are inevitable stages in the process of securing *lebensraum*.

We are witnessing the final phase of the entire experiment in self-sufficiency and the delusion which inspires it. The entire world it threatens is rising up against it. The right of the strong will be stultified by the strength of right. That is to say, the military strength of all those who have a vital interest in reestablishing and strengthening the outraged international law will prove greater than that supporting the lawless frenzy of a solitary deluded nation.

The first victorious attack on a system of a morally rotten brute-force will be followed by a breakdown so catastrophic that it would not have seemed possible beforehand. We shall be confronted by an anarchy unable to provide even an authorized liquidator. We shall then find that the difficulty of overthrowing the colossus with feet of clay is as nothing to the difficulty of concluding any sort of peace with this anarchy and obtaining from it even the most elementary conditions of a new order and restored confidence.

CHAPTER XXVIII

ILLUSIONS AND FACTS

READERS of this book, which has placed Hitlerism in its full context of German history and of the spiritual destiny of modern man, will eventually ask "What are the future prospects of this German Revolution?" It is a question to which I cannot venture a definite answer. The unknown factors which may come into operation are far too many to permit any confident forecast of the issue. A modest attempt to place the relevant facts in a clear light and to banish any lingering illusions is preferable to speculating in the void.

One of the most dangerous illusions finds utterance in the wish, repeated persistently by representatives of Western civilization, that Germany may finally throw off her tyrants' yoke. As we have seen, ninety per cent of her population regards those tyrants as the defenders of German interests in the world and as the chosen champions of Germany's will and her view of the European conflict. Of the ten per cent in opposition, only five are completely reliable and convinced supporters of the common heritage of the West. The remaining five per cent may be mortal enemies of Hitler, but they have retained their allegiance to that Germany which in the political sphere has long suffered from the moral insanity which inevitably produced National Socialism.

Another illusion is to overestimate the effect of the Allied blockade on the German determination to carry on the War. Certainly the blockade is sound strategy, and will be felt. But those who count upon it underestimate the determination of the Germans not to allow themselves to be defeated, underrate too their technical resources. Rather than yield the Germans will let Hitler marshal them at public tables like the Spartans of old and feed them on black broth. And as regards money—a government which has the power to requisition all the country's resources, taking his property from A to give it to B, can hold out far longer than our political economists have foretold. Certainly the day must come when even this expedient fails. But till then the Germans will not sit still. And this precisely is the time of greatest danger. Desperate attacks will be made to enslave and pillage one neutral after another. The German occupation will be extended in South-Eastern Europe. And sooner or later Germany will assume the control of Russia, with or without Stalin's consent.

When the Allies discover that a strategy of defense and exhaustion is insufficient they too will take the offensive in one quarter or another, possibly deciding to attempt to seize Russia's oil wells. The greatest danger is that the Allies will remain inactive until the neutral countries are occupied in turn by the two totalitarian powers which would thus re-consolidate their strength so that the War would be disastrously prolonged. There is only one way in which those neutrals can escape this danger and thus prevent perilous blows to themselves as well as to the Allied cause. It is that all the neutrals should join forces and declare that an attack on one will be taken as an attack on all and bring them all into the War. The principle of neutrality must be defended as a whole if each neutral country is to secure its own neutrality. When law and justice are no longer recognized, the insolence of the strong must be resisted by the united strength of the weak.

It is very difficult for foreigners to reach an objective estimate of the positive and the negative factors of Germany's present military power. Judgments about the material factors and of how long it will be possible to hold

out, differ widely—and moreover must vary with changes
in the political situation. I shall therefore speak only of
the psychological element. We must beware of applying
to Germany our experience of Russia, even though the
German army today is very far from being as strong as
in 1914. I have already pointed out that we must know
a nation's dead before we can judge how its living will
behave. The morale of an army is always decided by the
nation's tradition. It is more important to estimate this
psychological factor correctly than to calculate the amounts
of raw material or study the decline in the German
standard of living.

Nor should we forget the diabolical energies which
inspire the men in charge of the War. It is common to
jeer at Hitler as the corporal posing as a Napoleon and
to imagine his Generals, when they are alone together,
laughing at his ideas and plans. But Hitler possesses the
strategic genius of a tiger; straining his vital energies to
the utmost pitch he watches his opportunity to make a
spring. This tension of elemental intuitions can undoubtedly effect what military experts could not, namely, coordinate all the nation's forces and capacities and, instead
of merely calculating on technical grounds the time and
place at which to strike, discover it by a psychological
clairvoyance. Clemenceau remarked that war is too complicated an affair to be left to the army leaders. The Allies
must not forget for a single moment that they are now
up against the totalitarian Wotan, not just General von
Brauchitsch or von Keitel.

At this moment Hitler embodies the German vital force
at its highest degree. He possesses, if not the strategical
genius of a Bonaparte, an elemental biological intelligence. And it is undoubtedly a source of great strength.
Since, however, it is combined with an amazing blindness
to facts of the moral order, the temporary success it
achieves will finally end in disaster.

The Germans today are still far from suspecting that all the wrongs committed against foreign nations, all the cruel and malicious passions they have fostered against their so-called enemies, all their heartless contempt for foreigners' life and happiness—that all this will turn one day into vengeful wrath against their own countrymen.

Having observed many signs long and carefully, I think it probable that after the first serious check suffered by the ambitious German plan of campaign, after the first undeniable defeat of the German army, the War will be brought to a conclusion not by a disaster in the field, nor by a revolution, but by a civil war of all against all, inaugurated by serious and incurable dissension within the ruling German groups. Heine foresaw this issue a century ago; he foretold that the other nations would watch as from the seats of an amphitheatre a tragedy compared with which the French Revolution was but an idyll. A German can but cover his face at the prospect of what such an issue of his country's tragic history must involve. Foreigners will see it as the fearful doom pronounced at the bar of history by its imminent justice.

Until a few months ago even enlightened statesmen in the Western countries regarded it as an exaggeration so gross that it compromised the reputation of anyone who seriously maintained it, to affirm that the goal of German policy to which everything else was subordinated is nothing less than domination of the entire world. Even those personally acquainted with Hitler have been reluctant to credit it. Rauschning relates a conversation in which Hitler spoke of America and said that to conquer America was one of the main objects of his policy. "In a short time we shall have an S.A. organization in the United States. We are already training picked young men for it, to whom the rotten Yankees will have nothing to oppose. Our youth will accomplish the task Washington is incapable of performing and which a corrupt democracy has completely neglected."

When the objection was made that such an undertaking would make the accomplishment of the Nazi designs in Europe more difficult, Hitler answered irritably: "When will you grasp that my struggle against Versailles and my struggle to establish a new world-order are one and the same, and it is not in our power to halt at any point? If we did, we should lose even the struggle against the Treaty of Versailles, which in fact never existed since it mistook the victors for the vanquished" (sic).

Hitler concluded by saying, "I assure you that when the right moment comes I shall organize America as I please; and when Germany advances from Europe and crosses the ocean, our strongest support will be there. We possess all the means of arousing the people. No second Wilson will arise to bring America into the field against Germany". This is true enough. To do this a Hitler is required. And he looks like the man to bring it off.

I have displayed here the farthest horizon of Germany's present policy because it reveals most plainly how boundless is her ambition. As regards Europe the opinion has long prevailed that Hitler threatens neutral countries only insofar as the occupation of their territory would be effective strategy in a war against a third party. But Rauschning's report of what Hitler said to him about the neutrals shows the fate intended for them in his project of German domination (Rauschning p. 146). They are to be gathered around the central power of Germany as vassal states, with subordinate rights and in economic bondage to Germany's needs. "The age of small states is past. I do not intend for a moment to make any concessions to those countries on humanitarian grounds. There will no longer be any neutrals. Their fate is to become satellites of the great powers. They will be absorbed. I shall advance with an iron consistency."

To understand how Hitler's policy is the inevitable result of the nationalism artificially fostered in an area whose geographical situation is such that an international federation is the only solution of the German problem, we should read the following utterance of Hitler's which throws much light on his entire attitude:—

"Don't you see the tragic mutilation we have had to endure, we the second largest people in Europe, from an unfertile soil and from insufficiency of living space? A nation cannot be a world empire unless it can live on its resources and provide for its armed defense. Only such nations are sovereign in the full sense of the term. Russia is a sovereign state, and the United States. England is a sovereign state, though an artificial one; for her sovereignty does not rest on the nature of her territory. France is still sovereign up to a point. Why are we in a worse position? Is it the result of some divine decree, which has determined that in spite of our love of work, our capacities, our industries, our military endowments, we must always remain a second-rate power, always below England and France, though we are greater than those two nations combined? You believe that no more than I do" (Rauschning, pp. 143-144). Later in the conversation Hitler added "Either we shall rule Europe or our nation will break up and crumble into a dust of small states. Don't you see why I cannot halt either in the East or in the West?"

What conclusion are we to draw from all this? Simply that a German military nationalism founded on force and on the violation of law is bound to regard the Pan-German program as nothing more than a preparatory stage on the road to more far-reaching goals. A nation whose program is a constant state of war with the rest of the world is obliged to seize sufficient territory to be self-sufficing. Hitler pushes everything to its logical conclusion. The slogan of living-space is in itself unexceptionable in the case of any country which is unable to supply its needs. But must the additional supplies which are indispensable be obtained by violence and by enslaving neighboring countries? Will the rest of the world ever tolerate this?

The medieval empire was also based on a recognition of Germany's *lebensraum*. But it effected the necessary contact between Germany and Eastern Europe, not by forcible annexation but by a federation of states enjoying equal rights. Rauschning recommended this solution to Hitler and appealed to the example of Great Britain. Hitler replied in angry contemptuous tones:

"Certainly not. That empire shows every sign of breaking up and falling irretrievably. For the will-to-power is completely lacking. When you have no longer the courage to use the mailed fist and have become too humane to command, it is time to retire from the stage. England will regret her humanitarian weakness. It will cost her her Empire. Such an ancient power, even though she has no real government, may perhaps continue to drag out her existence for a decade or so. But a new Empire is born only of blood and iron beneath the compulsion of the strongest will and the most brutal force" (Rauschning, p. 145).

Nothing could reveal more clearly than these words the spirit which inspires German policy. Hitler answered as a beast of prey would answer, could we speak to it of confederation. The savage can think only in terms of violence.

CHAPTER XXIX

TOTALITARIAN WAR AND THE DEMOCRACIES

A NATURAL result of the War, but a great and indeed a fatal mistake notwithstanding, has been to speak as though the truth lay entirely with the democracies as against the totalitarian states and as though the latter had nothing to learn from their opponents and no need to revive their principles in any respect. Nevertheless, even before the War the need to push rearmament forward compelled the Western Powers to place their entire industry progressively on a war-footing and in doing so to adopt a large number of totalitarian methods. An organized coordination of all the national forces in a unified control, readiness to strike without delay, initiative and resolution, in short a complete and determined effort and a powerful sense of responsibility ready to meet efficiently the demands of any situation that may arise—all this is now regarded in a new light and many dearly cherished habits of the old freedom are being abandoned.

No doubt the change is first and foremost an adaptation to temporary conditions and dangers. But it is more than this. We have passed from an industrial age to an age of iron. The nations are in the throes of a vast upheaval. Every right of power or of property is being challenged. Moral and religious barriers centuries old are being overthrown. Diabolical forces have risen up from the depths of history and threaten to destroy everything that opposes their fury. The champions of law and order are, therefore, faced with a grim choice. Either they must let their foes outstrip them in the consistent practise of total war and submit to unconditional surrender and slavery; or they must accept all the implications of an iron age and defend the inheritance of two thousand years of Christian civilization against anarchy and barbarism with an even greater armament and an even sterner determination than the unfettered powers of destruction can draw from the abyss of their infernal resolve. It must be shown that the Christian knight, the warrior fighting in the defense of right and of all that is most precious in Western civilization, if he will put into the field the entire moral resources of Christian discipline and Christian sacrifice, is superior even from the military point of view to powers which, though they wield an imposing military machine, have destroyed the moral and religious foundations even of military success.

It cannot be made too plain that the consistent militarism of a Prussianized Germany is served by vast energies of human will and by an organization which is not only indispensable if mechanized warfare is to be waged in three elements; it also provides a model for the solution of the gigantic problems of organization which will confront the coming age in the economic, social and political spheres. It is most understandable that the nations which have fulfilled the noble mission of defending liberty, self-determination and human rights should be deficient in the art and science of coordinating social forces. In my opinion this second World War is destined to bring home to the free peoples the full extent of the danger to which this deficiency has exposed them and to prove to them that its remedy is not simply a matter of redressing a want of balance but a stark issue of life and death.

The question confronts us: Will Germany be ruined by her relentless sacrifice of the rights and dignity of man and personal culture to the collective beast, or will the champions of freedom be destroyed by the one-sided fashion with which their free culture has neglected to train into organized collaboration the individuals it has emancipated and to imbue them with a sense of responsibility to society, unselfish devotion to duty, careful attention to detail, and reliable performance of a social function?

In spite of the vast revolution effected in Germany during the last few years something still survives of the virtue inherited from the past. It is to be found among the simple people and in the military tradition. To the demoralizing effects of war that tradition opposes its discipline, its training in the wholehearted performance of duty, the soldier's unquestioning sacrifice, his devotion to the task set him and his readiness at any time to give to its accomplishment every ounce of energy at his command, the banishment of irresolution in face of a decision for life or death. We have not faced up to the problem of Europe and Germany if we do not take these things into account and draw the conclusions from them. The complete union between Prussia and the entire German people concluded in the person of Hitler has pushed the logic of militarism to its utmost consequences so that it can be fought only by a consistency as strict as its own.

We must always bear in mind that for the contemporary German trained in the Prussian school, war is not a necessary evil but, as Mirabeau said long ago, the national industry, the supreme and most important science, the great educator and test of character, the sole means of effecting and consolidating German supremacy in the world. Therefore, all the profound seriousness of the German character, all its passions, indeed its romanticism, have been thrown into the service of war and preparation for war.

Those who are earnestly striving to defend their lives against this organized instrument of destruction which makes use of all the traditional German virtues, must be prepared to go to school with this wholehearted and consistent fashion of warfare, this keying of the will to the utmost pitch, this coordination of all energies. But this education obviously cannot be completed overnight. This precisely is Europe's peril. In Berlin, next door to the military academy which educates its pupils exclusively for the army, there is an academy of defense whose chief purpose is to train competent higher officers in every branch of the services, to coordinate their employment of the weapons of aerial, land and naval warfare. During the first World War, this coordination was still very incomplete. Today it is perfect. England, the home of decentralization, is still behindhand in this respect. It is easy to understand that nations which do not regard total war as the supreme object of human life and see themselves faced with the necessity of sacrificing their liberty to save it should shrink from the prospect. Yet there is no alternative.

Hitler unites in his hands political, military, and economic action, together with propaganda. He adapts every particular activity to the whole plan on which everything depends. Everything is prepared down to the smallest detail. Even the unforeseeable is foreseen; that is to say, instructions are given for every conceivable contingency save that of defeat on a large scale, which German pride refuses to contemplate. For that reason the Germans, so magnificently prepared for a lightning offensive, are wholly unprepared for a reverse which would confront the individual with wholly new tasks, tasks of which these men intoxicated with success do not dream, and would undoubtedly throw them into utter confusion. But for the moment the magnitude of the present danger obliges the Allies to imitate the German example of efficient operation. We cannot doubt that such a combination of free tradition with a highly developed coordination will finally show itself superior to the one-sided totalitarian system of Germany and moreover prove most instructive for the future tasks of civilization.

CHAPTER XXX

WHAT OF THE PEACE?

CHRISTIANS AND PEACE

ONLY one who for decades has had his hand on the pulse of the German people knows how serious is its intellectual and moral disease, and how completely impossible it must prove to collaborate with it in constructing a new world-order. The sole practicable course, provided that Germany is defeated—this chapter will have no relevance to the post-war settlement if she wins—will be to conclude a peace which leaves ambitious schemes for building a new international community to the future and is content for the present to make it completely impossible for the millions who now hold the tenets of National Socialism and have been poisoned by it once again to involve the German nation in a repetition of its crime against mankind.

What do those who are talking today of a true and just peace mean by it? Is the past to be simply forgotten and packed away in the subconscious, so that peace terms may be offered so generous that even an unrepentant Germany will accept them? Are all nations to consult on an equal footing about the new order to be established and is Germany to be thus permitted in the name of equal rights to exploit every opportunity which presents itself to recover her domination and for the third time to destroy equality of rights?

At the end of the first World War, General Smuts said that the final peace terms must depend on Germany's fulfillment of the moral conditions of international confidence; if she did not fulfill them the peace must aim at security and its terms must be such as to make another German aggression impossible. After the second World War only the latter alternative need be considered. Only a peace of security could be just. For it alone would give the victims of an incorrigible breaker of the peace the safety so dearly bought. Those who see the future peace as the conclusion of a life-and-death struggle with a great nation led by bandits, a nation whom the attitude of the vast majority has implicated in their guilty conduct, will understand that such a peace must unfortunately be primarily a question of the right treatment of law-breakers and not genuine pacification.

The peace will be lasting and just, only if the European reaction to the criminal enterprise and the measures adopted to secure it from a third repetition are so strong and so consistent that the weakening of moral fibre throughout the world is cured by an unbending determination to secure its victims definitely against the political brigandage of modern Germany. Only then can the question be raised of a European Federation and all the institutions bound up with it. Domestic security is assured by the penal risks involved in committing crime. Similarly in our epoch of international anarchy the peace of the world cannot be secured by institutional machinery for organizing peace but only by the certainty that the transgressor will be placed under restraint, so that the abuse of freedom will involve its loss and foreign compulsion will subject the guilty nation to the law it has refused to obey freely.

The German problem must be settled after the War, not by a pacifist England but by the England which banished Napoleon to Saint Helena.

No doubt this looks like the Old Testament, not the New. But to treat guilt seriously and to insist upon reparation and on all necessary precautionary measures is a better preparatory discipline for Christianity than the idealistic construction of another League of Nations in which equal rights are conceded to those who only yesterday planted dynamite in every European cellar and are still unable to provide any solid guarantee of a change of heart. After such a period of crime, lying and broken pledges, conversion is impossible until the offender has been sternly and with no half measures deprived of the rights to which he would otherwise have been entitled and placed under a strict supervision which will suppress the first attempt to return to the path of aggression.

This can be effected without the least brutality towards those whose intentions are upright. But the guilty, whether principals or accessories, must be handled with an iron severity. A Christian policy of peace which neglects these measures, which must precede and prepare a new incorporation of Germany into the civilization of Europe, and yields to the delusion that nothing is required but to receive the criminals and their millions of supporters straight away into a new organization for securing the peace of Europe, will soon discover that its illusions have paved the way for yet another outbreak of Teutonic anarchy.

The crimes committed by Nazi Germany are so enormous, the vast majority of the educated classes so undeniably guilty of complicity in them, and the national megalomania in which they have indulged for decades has made these crimes so inevitable, that it would be no just peace but an outrage against the millions whom the Nazis have plundered, tortured and murdered, indeed an outrage against the eternal majesty of the moral law itself and a license for further crimes, if all this guilt were simply obliterated and forgotten in a new Europe and if due atonement and reparation are not exacted.

At this point I shall be reminded of the text "Vengeance is mine, saith the Lord". But this is not the case of revenge nor even of punishment. The national guilt involved exceeds the competence of any court, and no penal code prescribes a penalty for it. It is the unavoidable necessity to secure ourselves against an intolerable national attitude and its frightful consequences, a mentality which has already cost the lives of fourteen million and plunged the entire world in disorder; and this security cannot be achieved by a so-called just peace which admits the representatives of such an attitude without further demur, on the strength of paper guarantees, as members of a new system of international trust.

We are faced with a collective beast of prey that brazenly proclaims itself and has cut itself off from human society. It is a novel form of biological degeneration, still further complicated by the fact that into this monster's composition there enters a highly gifted but uncritical and unresisting people, the German, and it is thus able to prepare for its attacks by propaganda which bears the stamp of a high intelligence. "Render to Caesar the things that are Caesar's and to God the things that are God's." These words have often been misunderstood to mean that human society is exclusively Caesar's province while the spiritual life of the individual belongs to God and must be governed by Him. On the contrary, Caesar is himself responsible to God for the maintenance of the moral foundations of human society, which may never be sacrificed to purely political considerations. In accordance with this principle Charlemagne in the year 802 made the entire population of his Empire swear to stand fast in God's service with all their thoughts and deeds. This was very different from the totalitarian state which has deified the Fuehrer and which must inevitably be destroyed by its totalitarian character, which severs it from the supreme spiritual source of its life. On the other hand, at a time like our own when anarchic forces and unfettered natural instincts have broken forth anew and are making a mock of every appeal to the spirit, many tasks must be left to Caesar which in a better future can be reserved to the competence of the spiritual authority.

Those who would have Caesar abdicate in favor of the Gospel, when it is a question of meeting the violent aggression of diabolism, do but increase the power of unprincipled anarchy. This has been proved by the experience of the last twenty years, during which extensive Christian groups attempted by generous concessions to influence men who misinterpreted their efforts as weakness and grossly abused the concessions made to them. For twenty years numerous influential Englishmen, inspired by a pacifism which was the result partly of a sectarian Christianity (which therefore lacked a wide knowledge of human nature), partly of a humanitarian optimism, have sought to restore Germany to the comity of European nations. It is one of the most important contemporary events that today England has understood that this is a task which must be accomplished by Caesar's weapons and that it is Britain's vocation to renew the work of Augustus and reestablish order throughout the world *et debellare superbos*. The *pax britannica*, of which we have heard so much but which has been flying far above the world amid rosy clouds, has at last descended upon our chaotic earth to restrain, by the forcible language alone current here below, the grossest and most brazen insurrection of human lawlessness and thereby like Rome two thousand years ago to prepare the way for the Gospel.

THE LIMITS OF AN EVANGELICAL POLICY

The London *Tablet* recently published a magnanimous article on the influence of Christianity in Germany. The writer points out the difference between the second World War and the first. We feel ourselves closer to Charles Martel than to Sir John French. National socialism is a new Islam seeking to conquer the world. When it has been defeated in the field the most important task, that of spiritual conversion, will remain to be done. We could not accept the pessimist view of certain circles in France that Hitlerism is simply the clearest manifestation of a Germany always the same. The great centuries of German Christianity prove the contrary. Everything depends on our success in combating the false religion and preaching the true by our example. British statesmen could not insist too strongly that our aim is nothing less than a radical transformation of international life. The intimate alliance between England and France is only a beginning. Other nations are welcome to join. By which I do not mean a second Versailles!

Certainly Germany's Christian past proves the existence of another Germany than that which has culminated in Hitler. No Nazi voice is heard in Bach's cantatas. Handel's *Messiah* utters a worship of God who tolerates no idols. But it is equally true that the Hitlerian frenzy is not just the inexplicable aberration of a few years, but as I have shown, the logical result of a century's development, and therefore far harder to cure than foreign Christians usually suppose.

What treatment are we to apply to this German political disease? Where in this connection are we to draw the boundaries between Caesar and Christ? The question raises a most important problem of universal application, a problem of national therapeutics, which stirs the Christian conscience to its depths and tortures the brains of politicians.

Lord Baldwin, while still in office, compared Europe to a madhouse. His comparison was lacking in accuracy. At that time no peace-loving statesman was willing to state frankly the real conditions of this European asylum. Europe was a madhouse in which their revolvers had been restored to the lunatics who had been released without a medical certificate of sanity and whose representatives had been put upon the board of governors. All this proves that those responsible for managing the asylum were just as mad as the patients. This is the real reason why the European asylum is so largely in the hands of dangerous lunatics.

Does Christianity forbid us to protect sufferers from an infectious disease from themselves, and the rest of the community from them, by placing them in an isolation hospital? If the beloved father of a Christian family suddenly loses his reason it may even be necessary to send attendants to take him to a padded cell. Is this forbidden by the Sermon on the Mount? Christianity indeed demands that such men should be treated humanely and everything possible done to cure them. But it does not ask us to treat the diseased as though they were healthy, or incorrigible criminals as though they were honest men.

It is high time to put away the misleading compunction and shame for the Treaty of Versailles which Christians have been called upon to exhibit. Certainly the Treaty is justly chargeable with making pecuniary demands impossible of fulfillment. But it is much more deserving of blame for its lack of realism and consistency in provisions unquestionably just and necessary. And it is also time to abandon the magnanimous hopes entertained of a Germany that for a long while to come will not rid herself of her spiritual and political anarchy. Certainly the spiritual appeal should not be neglected and it will be heard by those who are ready for it. But the millions whose ingrained political corruption, even if they suffer the most crushing defeat, will be on the watch how best to exploit the evangelical mercy of foreign Christians must at last be placed under such control that they can do no further harm. No one will understand such a policy better than the Christians in Germany. A few more months of Germany's biological policy and foreign Christians also will understand it.

PAX ITALIANA

Martin Luther said of Erasmus: "Erasmus loves peace more than the Cross." It is a disease of our time to love peace more than the Cross; that is to say, to seek peace at the expense of truth, at the expense of a clear and thorough-going settlement with the forces of evil. In this way we obtain a peace which lacks every guarantee of permanence, is morally unsound, an unclean peace which is at bottom a compromise with the peacebreakers and therefore contains and keeps alive the seeds of a new war.

Particularly dangerous in this connection is the pax Italiana because, in striking contrast with the clear atmosphere of its country, it envelops in the thickest mist all the fundamental moral conditions on which alone the War can rightly be ended. Up to the present day the entire theory and practise of Fascism in the sphere of international policy and the speeches and writings of its representatives have been a frank profession of Machiavellianism; that is, of *sacro egoismo*, without any recognition of duties to other nations or of a moral code. This amounts to the proclamation of a perpetual state of war and renders it impossible for any of Italy's neighbors to consider making concessions which involve trust in her intentions. Under such circumstances any concession is simply the surrender of a bridgehead to the enemy of tomorrow.

Mussolini the Roman has hitherto halted at the first phase of Roman history in the period of Punic Wars. He has not yet risen to the world-embracing universalism of the later imperial Rome which, as is depicted in Mommsen's arresting account of it, united with Hellenic intellectualism and humanity to breathe a soul into power and to transcend a merely Roman nationalism. When we contemplate the existing European anarchy we can understand the Fascist slogan "Anti-Europe". The question however arises whether by this "Anti" is meant remaining in a primitive barbarism or whether the truth has been grasped that if Italy is to remain a great power in one way or another, she must make her contribution to the construction of an international community; and that only by doing so can she overcome her domestic difficulties. In the present economic condition of the world there is no civilized people whose most elementary conditions of subsistence are not threatened by the antagonisms of the European nations. In his foreign policy Mussolini has taken the wrong road, and it would require great optimism to believe that he can find his way back from Hegelianism to a Christian conception of the state and the foreign policy it demands. He could have played a great part in Europe. He has failed to shake off the war mentality. His countenance is stamped by a strong, joyless, and convulsive tension which has communicated itself to the entire nation. He knows nothing of the repose and humanity of the great Scipio who turned an Italian Rome into a cosmopolitan Rome.

THE DOOM OF A FALSE PACIFISM

The mistakes of a false pacifism have been shown up in a most glaring light by the events in Scandinavia. During the last twenty years it was plain to those who attended international gatherings, and not least the sessions of the League of Nations, that a pacifism completely divorced from reality, whose representatives had neither eyes to see nor ears to hear, nowhere possessed so many sincere adherents as in the Scandinavian countries—doubtless because the Scandinavian peoples were disposed to judge the entire world by their own apparently secure position, and because their comprehensible distaste for conscription as practised throughout most of the European continent had neglected even a minimum of armed defense. But even if these errors were once excusable they became inexcusable and incomprehensible. It is impossible to excuse or even to understand the failure of those nations after the fall of Prague to make up in every sphere for past neglect and at last to make use of their rich resources in order to place themselves in a state of defense. Sweden could have created a navy superior to the German. Norway could have brought her coastal defenses up to the standard required by the technique of modern war. Had these states only done half as much for their army and made only half the sacrifices for their army that Belgium made for her defense, Germany could not have carried off the invasion which is now costing so much English and French as well as native blood.

It could have been foreseen that the possession by Scandinavia of raw materials of decisive importance for Germany's conduct of war must involve the Scandinavian states in hostilities. But they foresaw nothing. They had enjoyed peace and prosperity too long. They had sought to conjure the growing peril to Europe from German nationalism and militarism by no more effective method than exporting an abstract pacifism which took no account of the real forces at work in Germany to achieve insane ambitions by crime on a vast scale. In this the Germans had no better allies than those pacifists whose sole concern was to disarm not the criminals and the lunatics but the police; and who repeated without criticism all the catchwords of German propaganda about disarmed Germany and the imperialism of the victorious states.

How came it that the governments responsible for this lamentable neglect to provide for the defense of their countries were socialist governments? The reason is that their attitude was the same as that which made the German socialists blind and helpless in face of the National Socialist conspiracy. All those socialists were caught in the toils of an abstract ideology which made them look for the explanation of the European crisis in an imaginary capitalist imperialism and blinded them to the real foe of

European peace. The socialists were sworn to a program which had no chance of realization under existing circumstances. They had no practical and consistent program to meet the pressing need of humanity and of their own nation, no program which took account of historical realities and put first things first. Even in England a vague but powerful antipathy to capitalism made it impossible for Labor to judge correctly the real causes of the world crisis and to provide in good time for the nation's undeniable needs. If unprejudiced realists had not taken action before it was too late, the muddleheaded pacifism which was a legacy from the Labor government would have undoubtedly brought about England's downfall. Labor in every country urgently requires new leaders completely free from antipathies and ideologies which are inherited from the industrial revolution and which can only blind Labor to the demands of a truly progressive labor policy. For Labor, whose economic security depends on the stability of world economy, cannot be content with a purely domestic policy but has a vital interest in establishing the reign of international law. But this constructive purpose must be based, both in the political and in the economic sphere, on a thorough knowledge of human nature.

After the first World War the way in which international pacifism played into the hands of Prussian militarism was a spectacle for the gods. The orgies of academic pacifism were celebrated at Geneva, a pacifism which was intent on bringing the gangsters and their prospective victims together in one vast peace-palace, and which by paper guarantees completely lulled to sleep those who should have kept watch. Thus Geneva became an outpost of Potsdam. How many serious and well-intentioned men acted in that tragic comedy!

THE PAN-EUROPEAN MOVEMENT

Something must be said of the Pan-European movement sponsored by Count Coudenhove-Kalergi. No doubt it is

an excellent and consoling thing in the very midst of the
present European anarchy, to lift our gaze towards a
better future. But this may be very dangerous if it fosters
the delusion that as soon as the War has ended it will be
possible to erect Pan-Europe above the chaos. It will require at least ten years before the states steeped in the
conviction that war will and ought to be a permanent
feature of international life have at last realized that they
have no longer any chance of successful aggression. This
however they would certainly not understand, if they were
to be admitted as members of a league which they would
only abuse to plant their explosives and to annul all the
special guarantees which the Allies would have the right
to exact.

We must therefore renounce the prospect of a United
States of Europe, when a large part of Europe will for a
long time be morally unreliable, with an unreliability
which can be overcome only by the utmost watchfulness
of superior power and not by a premature offer of friendship. Our Pan-Europeans hope to combat Russia and Bolshevism by their United Europe which is to include Germany and be assisted by Japan. They do not understand
that German National Bolshevism is far more dangerous
than the Russian variety, more barbarous and far more
deeply rooted in the people; or that Russian Bolshevism
is a danger only when allied with Germany.

Coudenhove's proposal to entrust an anti-Bolshevik mission to such a militarist power as Japan, could produce no
good result until Western Europe—far from making Germany the champion of Pan-Europe in the East—has established order in Eastern Europe including Russia, and by
force of arms put an end to gangster rule.

The literature of the Pan-European movement, a movement to which we are greatly indebted for its internation-
ist propaganda, has until the present completely failed to
grasp the diabolism at work in the present crisis through
which human civilization is passing or the spiritual medi-

cines which alone can cure such a fearful disease. But without a thoroughgoing diagnosis of the malady which afflicts Europe no effective cure is possible, nothing in fact save a dangerously superficial treatment of problems on whose solution the fate of mankind depends. Only a profound comprehension of the true nature of the present struggle can give the Western powers the necessary authority to put an end in Asia also to a bandit empire and to free the highly gifted Japanese people from the aberration from which it would seem their own strength and intelligence cannot find an escape.

THE CONDITIONS OF A FUTURE PEACE

Surely we should proclaim today: "Let the criminals be sure that they will not escape punishment. As for the German people which has approved and abetted all their crimes and allowed such men to rule them, it will not indeed be tormented or starved; but since it has proved incapable of governing itself, it will be subjected to the most rigorous international control. The education of its children will be for a long time taken out of its hands and will be restored only when there is sufficient evidence that the noblest German forces and traditions have regained their sway over German hearts." I do not know if the Allies, in the event of their victory, will speak thus or act thus. It will be a catastrophe if they do not.

An entire library of books must also be written, particularly for the use of teachers, to obliterate the baneful effects of more than a century of official lying. If not, everything will be built in the air—like the peace of 1919. For the Germans will not be thoroughly enlightened as to the decisive facts of the process which has produced world wars and all the horrors of the recent years and which involves a genuine responsibility for them.

The proposal has been made to prevent the recurrent Prussian danger by dividing Germany again into a number of federated states and decentralizing her government. Such a measure would certainly assist considerably the revival of Germany's sound national traditions. But unless it is supplemented by the control of which I have just spoken, a violent campaign would begin immediately for the restoration of Prussia's central authority and all who served the local administrations would be threatened with murder. Even this control will be too heavy a burden upon the victors unless it in turn is supplemented by a far more effective and far-reaching defense against any attempt of militaristic nationalism to rise from its grave. This defense must consist in such an efficient organization of Germany's neighbors that both the present and future generations of Germans would be compelled to abandon any hope of reviving the old ambitions. Only in this way can we bring the Germans back to their best traditions.

That is why, in my short chapter on Russia, I pointed out that the German problem cannot be solved until the Russian problem has been solved. It was the spectacle of a vast but unorganized Russia which more than anything else tempted Hitler to make an even more ambitious version of Ludendorff's Eastern policy. It is improbable that a new Russia would consent to assist a rebirth of German militarism. It is obvious that even Stalin is dominated by fear of the secret designs German imperialism may cherish in Eastern Europe. The motive of his attack on Finland was undoubtedly to forestall Germany.

After the solution of the Russian problem the most important step which must be taken to create a stable Europe will be to organize a South-Eastern Federation. Whether a Habsburg can be placed at the head of such a federation will depend on whether the former succession states regard the general situation as so radically altered and have been sufficiently impressed by their experience of autonomy to accept such a Habsburg president under completely new conditions.

The firm solidarity of those who have shed their blood to save Europe must continue. But it needs to be supported by unambiguous pledges from the United States that any further assault upon the peace of Europe will bring them at once into the field on the side of its victims. Such a pledge would be the best of all possible guarantees. History today is no longer divided into separate continents. What happens in one continent affects every other. Indeed events in Finland or the Balkans affect the United States more seriously than events in Mexico or Bolivia.

After this War, though there will be small countries fulfilling an important mission, there will no longer be neutrals, as we understood neutrality today. Their present experience will convince the neutrals that, in a world struggle between law and barbarism, neutrality is impossible and that the only way in which the small countries can protect themselves is to get rid of an unreal outlook and, before they are devoured, to join the league of those who are defending law and international order. Such a combination of the defenders of European order, supported by an American guarantee, would suffice to ensure peace and would therefore convince those powers which at first hold aloof that they cannot achieve their legitimate aims observing honorably the principle *Do ut des*. Such a gradual conversion and practice can in time produce the United States of Europe.

The first step to its creation will be to provide a center where the common concerns of European states can be dealt with. Any further progress towards our United States of Europe will for many a long day have to contend with the mutual hostility, deep-rooted in their past history, of the peoples who side by side inhabit the Asiatic peninsula called Europe. The common possession of European civilization must first have made possible a spiritual and intellectual community between those nations, stamped as they are so strongly with distinctive characteristics.

Above all, a revival of Christianity in Europe must have released those national groups from the bonds of collective selfishness and thus have destroyed the barrier that divides them and have prepared them by its teaching to sacrifice themselves in the sacred cause of peace. Until all this has been accomplished, any organization must lack solid foundation. And you cannot build without a foundation.

I will conclude by repeating with the utmost possible emphasis what I said at the close of my chapter on the Christian attitude to peace: Europe's present calamity must be treated by two different methods which supplement each other and render each other effective. One belongs to Caesar's province; the other to Christ's. As of old the Roman Empire united the nation in its iron bonds and created the international order and a framework within which evangelists could be sent forth in every direction to win souls, so today, when the forces of an unleashed barbarism have plunged Europe into chaos, the reestablishment of order by military action in the service of elementary right is indispensable and will remain necessary after the War. But whatever external order may now be imposed upon those forces of anarchy, the eternal and spiritual power of the Christian religion must interiorize, complete and firmly anchor it in the supernatural order. Only the City of God can uphold and foster the earthly city.

This lesson the ancient world learned by most bitter experience. Today that experience is being renewed and more deeply impressed by the blood and tears of a humanity which had thought it possible to leave to lower powers the sacred art and science of political government and international organization. The sight of catastrophes as yet incalculable will produce a far-reaching and profound conversion, the spiritual foundations of human life will be plainly revealed, and mankind will awake as from a nightmare, unable to understand how it could all have happened. The distinction will become visible between true leadership and the art of swaying the mob, and men will know the quarter to which they must look for the supreme Leader of our race. *Stat crux, volvitur orbis.*

CHAPTER XXXI

THE SPIRITUAL CAUSES OF HITLERISM

A S I bring this book to a close I once again state with the utmost emphasis that the entire tragedy of Germany is in its essence a spiritual tragedy and can therefore be correctly understood only from the spiritual side.

Hitler regards nationalism as merely the first and temporary form assumed by a revolution which springs from sources far deeper than patriotism and which is, in Nietzsche's sense, biological. That is to say, in it a new type of humanity finds expression. This type is that which Nietzsche termed the blonde beast, the incarnate rejection of every spiritual and moral restraint which at present prevents man from living in a purely biological fashion in accordance with the right of the stronger and unscrupulously enslaving the masses to his aims. Hitler told Rauschning in unvarnished terms that the entire education he was giving the rising generation was directed to the creation of such a type to which the world ought to belong and would belong.

"I want fearless, vigorous, commanding, and cruel young men with the strength and beauty of young beasts of prey," (Rauschning, p. 78).

From this point of view the Hitler movement may be regarded as the greatest and most unrestrained revolt of the vital force in man's nature known to history. The first modern revolt against Christianity was intellectual. The intellectual disintegration it produced unleashed the revolt of vital energy. The program of this revolt is not new. It was the program of the Sophists against whom Socrates fought and to whose glorification of the vital forces he opposed the mysterious saying of Euripides "Who knows whether our life is not death and our death life"? That is to say, "who knows whether what you call life is not doomed irretrievably to death inasmuch as it has revolted against the spiritual secret and law of life?" All those rootless persons who play with words and concepts without ever getting down to realities are blind to the fact that this primitive materialism embodies a serious biological error which can easily be refuted by modern biology. It is not true that man's natural vitality is autonomous. The natural *élan vital* leads him to death by self-destruction or by collision with the outer world, unless it is enlightened, controlled and guided by his spiritual life.

Religion subjects man to conditions and laws of life which exceed his understanding. Those laws and conditions can be seen only by the light of religion and confine within their due bounds the instincts which hamper and restrict his intelligence.

Certainly a vast expansion of vital and bodily energy is required to defend life against the death which assails it from every direction. It is for this reason that the life-force entices man to propagate his species and blindly to sacrifice marriage, duty, wealth and health to the gratification of his sexual passion. But just because the energy of his physiological life is so gigantic and operates so blindly, the Creator has opposed to it another force of greater strength, the Cross of Christ, the supreme spiritual order, without which life must be defeated by death. The Cross is as necessary to life as is physical energy. It provides the framework within which life must develop if it is not to devour and destroy itself. But modern political biology, in its frenzy and carried away by a tempest of unrestrained vital instincts, has no conception of this truth, though it seeks to organize the entire world. It does not see that the spiritual and moral order, which even in international relations resists the blind energy of the *élan vital*, ap-proaches far more closely the profoundest secret of life, or its maintenance, health and propagation, than all the nonsense of materialist charlatans.

Watch a community of ants. See how everything serves the state, how every function is exactly determined for its good, how there are no parasites, no revolts, no strikes. How is it with mankind? Man possesses indeed social instincts but not the ants' instinct for building a state. But in its place he possesses a substitute for this constructive instinct, namely the Christian religion. Do not say, "Surely he possesses reason". Today we know that reason divorced from religion is a solvent of all human society. Christianity alone produces the type of man with which states can be constructed and maintained. The reasons of this have been stated by Augustine's profound psychology in *The City of God*. The natural man is anti-social and abuses society for his personal ends. His spiritual nature must be renewed from above. This regeneration alone enables man to be a member of society without losing himself. No jerrybuilt community put up in haste by evil passions can permanently compete with this construction of the Christian faith. It is a weakness of modern Christian apologetics that it has failed to adapt its great message to the needs of modern life but confronts this violent manifestation of a will bent on radical destruction amazed and helpless, uttering ineffective protests. Christians must speak to those deluded souls, and to those who tomorrow will fall into the trap, in terms of the language, not of theology alone but of a true biology which has grasped the fundamental biological importance of religion and morality.

An entirely new apologetic will accordingly take shape which is not content to speak from the heights but will with Tertullian invoke the witness of the human soul and turn to the facts of human life, to biology, economics, pathology, neurology and politics, and receive their testimony to the living truth. But if we are to speak in these terms we must try to understand to its utmost depths the mentality with which we have been concerned. I have spoken of a deliberate return to the savage which has often become a deliberate return to the wild beast. What difference is there between those zoological programs and the policy of wolves and jaguars?

This description however explains the mentality of Hitler and his convinced supporters as insufficiently as Prussianism explains the baffling mixture of brutality and sentimentality, of the goose-step and the Ninth Symphony, in the political behavior of contemporary Germans. Rauschning aptly describes Hitlerism when he says of it that "National Socialism is the invasion of Western Europe by the savage" and that "National Socialism is the St. Vitus' dance of the twentieth century". These descriptions taken from different parts of his book, together state the two psychological components of this social phenomenon. There is a savage in the Nazi but a savage with a crazy and disintegrated soul. From the savage he derives his shameless brutality, from the lunatic his hysteria, the rages which make him foam at the mouth, his frenzied and convulsive energy. In earlier centuries also, St. Vitus' dance was produced by the religious impulses, severed from the complete Christian truth, which took hold of barbarous masses.

Nobody who recalls the frightful and criminal nonsense poured into the German soul for a century past by a literature cut off from its roots could expect any other result than that which we now witness. The common people have kept their health, but the educated classes are in an unbalanced mental condition in which reason and conscience have ceased to resist the powerful mania. It was only to be expected that the constantly intensified propaganda of hatred and bullying, conducted verbally and in writing, should have produced the phenomena of possession we find in Hitler. We must come to understand that these enormously potent influences must be counteracted by methods which the imperiled world has not hitherto employed. In short, we are only beginning to grasp the most fearful phenomenon of our time and have not even begun to defend ourselves against it in the right way. Hitler is a key to our age. To understand him is to understand the age in which we live, and to know what must be done to build a dam against the flood.

Deeply significant is the Christian doctrine of Lucifer and his fall from heaven. Man's worst corruption comes not from below but from above, from the treason of the angel in him, from spiritual forces which have gone astray, from the spirit that has cut itself off from its Source. In such a psychosis as Hitler's there is active not only a savage released from restraint but a spiritual power, a force which has lost sight of its Goal, which has turned to the lower world, and which has excited its impulses to fever pitch. The Prussian soldier is too simple to be hysterical. Ludendorff was not hysterical. Hysteria presupposes disturbance of the higher centers. Trustworthy witnesses, above all Rauschning, tell us of Hitler's serious attacks of hysteria in which he foams at the mouth. Hysteria may be due to a pathological state called into activity by particular experiences of a deranging character. But it may also be the reflection, in the soul of an individual, of the great spiritual crisis which first overtook the European mind in the nineteenth century. That crisis consisted in the fact that the spiritual powers, robbed of their religious goal by the so-called enlightenment, have attached themselves in turn to different earthly objects and put into their worship a devotion out of all proportion to their worth.

Nietzsche's life-story sums up the entire tragedy of modern man. He knew what he meant when he said that God was dead. No one had as yet suspected what that implied and what results it would have for the soul and the world. His romantic portrait of the blonde beast, in reality the spirit's relapse into barbarism, has become a potent psychological spell and has led countless numbers to combine the brutality of the savage with a romantic idealism. We are now confronting for the first time the final result of its influence.

In fact, in the political sphere it is only today that modern man is beginning to be aware of the social, moral, political and psychological effects of this destructive secularism. The psychological result is particularly evident in such men as Nietzsche and Hitler; that is, among spiritual men who have been uprooted and have become sentimental savages. It consists in the fact that intellectual and psychical powers which for two thousand years have been developed under the influence of the Christian spiritual discipline are ignorant of the goal on which they should concentrate, of the meaning of life, and of the vocation of the soul. It is unemployment not on the street, but in the soul of man. "The Germans", Goethe said, "have lost their senses". Nothing is left save a blind determination stimulated by evil passions, an insane biology, the delusion of power and the race of masters, lust for world domination, the wild beast making his spring to Wagner's music, and the whole put forward as a new religion of redemption. If man's higher life is illusion and lies, he must surrender himself to his lower passions, not instinctively like an animal but with all his powers of mind and soul, deliberately and unscrupulously. He will live wholeheartedly as a beast of prey, will seek to annex the entire earth and to enslave all the weak, and will wage war against the Cross of Christ and all the barriers which religion places in his way.

How illuminating are the following utterances of Hitler's (reported by Rauschning): "Conscience is a Jewish invention. Like circumcision it mutilates man". "Those who look upon National Socialism as a political movement misconceive its nature. It is more than a religion. It is the creation of the supermen. I will free the German race from a thousand years' domestication."

We should indeed be glad that today this perversion has burst forth with its evil principles carried to their utmost consequences, like a volcano in eruption. It is such a warning that cannot be ignored, a warning to Christians who still imagine they are confronted with a purely political movement and not with the most thoroughgoing and direct attack yet delivered against their religion and their cultural inheritance.

Many people are saying: "How terrible that one man had the power to bring this calamity upon Europe." Such language is as false as it is irreligious. We should thank God that this unhappy man, like an abscess which reveals a disease that has eaten into the organism but has hitherto remained invisible, by his diabolical professions and acts has revealed in its full extent the spiritual disease of a great people, indeed of the entire world—a disease of which its victims are unconscious. The most sinister feature about Hitler is his uncanny conviction that in every country his propaganda can secure growing numbers, a body of secret supporters. And his supporters are not confined to political traitors. Among them we must also count the widespread decay of spiritual and moral convictions, the growing revolt against religion, the kind of psychoanalysis which makes the abdomen our "Fuehrer", and every other variety of materialist outlook. Who can tell how deep the rot has already gone, what is still standing, and what must and will fall in that day of reckoning when bills given to the devil must be paid in full?

To the whole of civilized mankind today the question is addressed which St. Ignatius asks his exercitants: "To whom do you belong? Where are you going? Choose between heaven and hell". The German eruption makes the choice easier. It compels humanity to face without possibility of evasion a logic of which it had not dreamed.

EPILOGUE

UNIVERSAL history can be understood only in the light of St. John's Apocalypse. Its subject is the fundamental theme of the development of human civilization, everything that gives significance and background to the course of events—in fact, as we see depicted on a famous altar at Pergamos, the conflict between the Gods and the Titans, the forces of heaven and hell, a struggle waged and decided in the human soul.

The story of this conflict is the aspect of history most deserving of our attention. Merely moral reflections upon historical events are clearly unable to do justice to this hidden and underlying reality of human history, for this reason alone that for centuries it has been involved in an inextricable tangle of constructive and destructive forces. Only today are we in a position to distinguish clearly between them and to recognize, as we look back upon the past, the activity of the infernal powers through the centuries.

The great advance and counter-attack of the forces of destruction against Christianity, which began at the period of the Italian Renaissance with the rediscovery of antiquity, required centuries in which to undermine all the foundations of our culture under the deceptive pretext of emancipation and the struggle for truth. Truth, science and freedom are indeed goods of very high value. But nothing has been so abused for their ends by these destructive powers as man's effort to attain them. Long ago the Platonic Socrates had proposed spiritual exercises to the contemporary youth, with the object of preventing this abuse and making them distinguish between what comes from above and the inspirations of that infernal power which is always ready to exploit a muddled idealism for lower aims.

Nevertheless, the process of so-called secularization was not in itself the product of an invasion by the lower powers. It was the inevitable result of an increasing differentiation of a human life which believed in its autonomy and could discover only by the experience of centuries that this very autonomy is subordinate to the supreme and universal truth with reference to which alone man can understand himself and do justice to the interconnection of all things. But the actual effect of this secularization has been to make room gradually for those lower powers which were on the watch to make their escape. The mere semblance that there are wide spheres—politics, for example, business or education—within which humanity can be independent and rest upon its own foundation and no longer needs the guidance of religion, sufficed to throw open to the underworld the possibility of intruding itself gradually, an intrusion assisted by the progressive liberation of entire departments of human life from ecclesiastical control, henceforward to be regulated by independent decisions of the emancipated conscience. An example of this is the way in which sciences which boasted of being impartial and unprejudiced have been enslaved all too quickly by national passions.

The effect of the process of secularization was widely reinforced by the direct attack upon the Christian Faith conducted by a misconceived scientific attitude, an abstract rationalism, a criticism of the biblical text which exceeded its competence—all this, with no understanding of the theological and metaphysical problems involved.

The first result of this work of disintegration was a farreaching loss of religious beliefs, whereas Christian ideals of conduct and humane sentiments inherited from centuries of religious influence, which moreover had saturated the entire mass of literature, persisted for some time.

Astronomers inform us that today we are receiving light
from stars which may have long ago been reduced to dust.
Similarly, many are living by the light of truths rejected
long ago by their reason. The eighteenth century, with
its spiritual atmosphere rarefied by rationalism and its
humanitarianism, is typical of this first phase of dissolution when the diabolical revolt against everything divine
had not yet dared to show itself openly.

This phase continued far into the nineteenth century
until at last Nietzsche compelled his contemporaries to be
logical by proclaiming the indecency of living on moral
capital borrowed from ideas long since inwardly rejected.
In his *David Strauss the Confessor*, Nietzsche reproached
Strauss for accepting without criticism Christian *morality*,
though he had destroyed Christian *theology*, whereas in
fact the former is bound up with the latter and must share
its fate. The scientific position, he argued, from which
Strauss had conducted his theological criticism led inevitably to an ethical system diametrically opposed to
Christian ethics and purely biological in its norms, in
which the right of the strongest must prevail and become
for man also the decisive factor of natural selection.

Nietzsche speaks of the "bridge of lies to obsolete ideas",
and proposes "to rehabilitate the ancient German ideal of
honor." No one has seen more clearly than he that for
a century past the accepted morality had been the survival
of a moral code determined by religion. "The best in us,"
he said, "is derived from the sentiments of former times.
The sun of our life has set. But the sky still glows and
shines with its light though we no longer see it." Nietzsche
was simply the logical and the most advanced pioneer of
a movement which has manifested itself throughout the
modern civilized world and taken possession first of circles
in touch with modern science, industry and technique.
From them, as its paralyzing course proceeded, it has spread

far and wide and infected classes still under the sway of tradition.

It is no exaggeration to credit Nietzsche's daring logic with a powerful influence upon the development of political thought in northern Germany. Intellectually and psychologically he strengthened and fostered the continuous growth of a political philosophy of a purely biological type and indeed inspired by a materialist biology. His influence is a chapter in "the mind's betrayal of mind"; that is to say, the apostasy of man's higher spiritual powers and their enslavement in the service of his lower nature. Without this apostasy the latter could not triumph. Lucifer is not a myth. The apostasy of the spirit from the supreme spiritual God is the tragedy of human history and in particular of modern history. The diabolical is always an apostasy of spiritual powers. The sub-human order is not in itself diabolical, it is rendered diabolical only when spirit betrays Spirit.

Though Nietzsche was a German, the French intelligentzia is at least as responsible as the German for the general demolition of religious beliefs. Paris in the Middle Ages was the intellectual capital of Europe. Such concentrations of power, however, always produce a proud independence whose fruits will ripen sooner or later. Suddenly the presumptuous intellect leads a revolution against religious tradition and authority, and the mind which yesterday served the Gospel of Christ, today takes service with Antichrist. It cannot do otherwise. For every faculty of the soul which severs itself from the life of the whole is rendered *ipso facto* the thrall of the powers of destruction and an accomplice in their work.

Nevertheless in the intellectual world of France the humane tradition of the old Mediterranean culture survived so that the revolution was not carried to its logical conclusion.

Germany, on the other hand, was closer to the steppes

of Asia than to the Mediterranean, and the Thirty Years' War was yet in its blood so that Goethe could truly say, "We are of yesterday". There were, therefore, far fewer obstacles to its relapse into barbarism, the more so since for over a century the most recently civilized elements of the German people had assumed the political leadership.

The defenders of the rights of man and other so-called achievements of Liberalism are dismayed today by the momentum and speed with which all their claims are being trampled underfoot by the Collective—the Beast of St. John's Revelation. They do not perceive that it was Christianity that deprived Caesar—and the masses which claim to wield his scepter—of unrestricted power over the individual, and by the martyr's blood secured the right of the individual conscience. The representatives of science are dismayed today by the ruthlessness with which the Collective is enslaving science to the State and making mock of its claim to serve truth. They do not perceive that the scientific conscience and its devotion to a truth sovereign above all worldly interests is purely religious in its origin and can be kept alive by religion alone.

In language of unsurpassed sublimity the Apocalypse depicts the advent of this Collective Beast, that prints its mark on every forehead and hand, to establish a uniformity of thought and action, and opens its mouth wide to blaspheme God and to vomit lies. The beast signifies a condition of human society in which the personal center constituted by the individual conscience attached to the invisible world is replaced by a collectivity, lacking any kind of intellectual and moral center, any notion of an eternal Good and Value, and whose life, as it develops, is degenerating to the condition of the slimy polyp from which, according to the scientists, individual life has slowly evolved.

The student of human history, since the entrance of Christianity into the life of nations, will perceive that the historical action of Antichrist is not simply an onslaught upon truth by the powers of falsehood but, above all, the gradual and imperceptible exploitation of spiritual forces in the service of the lower world, a process which often begins with an offer by the inferior powers to place themselves at the service of the upper world to build Valhalla on earth. The fatal confusion of both worlds has begun. In his Ring of the Nibelungs, Wagner has depicted the tragedy of this seduction. And this fall of the spirit is the peculiar tragedy of the German people, though it is also the tragedy of the whole world and the true explanation of a temporary triumph of the infernal order. Jesus foretold of Antichrist: "He shall deceive the very elect".

What is meant by this? Surely, that in the coming centuries, Antichrist would succeed in exploiting the new spiritual forces called into being by Christianity, and moreover, by this very alliance with powers of a higher order, would successfully blind even sincere Christians to the destructive nature of his apparently constructive achievements. Consider, for example, the way in which the struggle which Christianity inaugurated for the due recognition of the infinite value of the individual soul, has been abused to confine souls within the narrow prison of self-interest. A proud and selfish isolation has often invoked the right of self-determination and assumed its aureole.

The abuse is made possible only by the divorce of one Christian truth, the rights of man, from another and equally important complementary truth, God's rights over man. But every Christian truth separated from the entire organism of Christian truth acts as an explosive and breaks up the soul and society. The modern principle of nationality contains, no doubt, a partial truth of Christian origin, namely, the truth that individual distinctions and the peculiar talent entrusted to the individual should be protected. But this principle, divorced from responsibility for the world of supernational values and abused to minister to the hallucinations of collective selfishness, has contributed, more than any other force, to destroy human civilization. In this instance also forces and ideas from a higher sphere perverted and abused have given man's dark instincts a strength and historical effectiveness which without their aid they could never have possessed.

The last century represents the phase in which the confusing "Admixture of Good and Evil" reaches its height. In earlier periods vice served vice, and only too often vice was even taken into the service of virtue—"The end sanctifies the means." Today virtue serves in the armies of vice; that is to say, the higher powers of man's mind and character, severed from their source, suffer themselves without misgiving to be employed in undertakings whose ultimate object is the service of the lower powers but which present a seductive semblance of positively constructive work.

This is particularly true of the German tragedy. Like the Jews, the Germans are a people with a spiritual mission which has fallen away from its missionary ideal; in consequence, its lofty mental endowments have been easily perverted to the service of purely material and finally even criminal political aims. This, however, was possible only because the state, whose attraction was felt most powerfully by natures susceptible to moral issues, had originally been founded with the assistance of sublime Christian virtues. The Prussian state was founded by a religious order of knights who observed strictly their monastic vows and whose government and administration at the most flourishing period of the Order were widely renowned as exemplary.

We are constantly hearing of "heathen" Prussia, which was converted to Christianity only in the thirteenth century. This is a complete misrepresentation of the facts. The aboriginal pagan population which was almost wiped out played no part worth consideration in the formation of Prussia. Certainly the rulers of the Prussian state have consistently pursued a heathen policy. But that policy was carried out by Christian asceticism and Christian self-sacrifice. It was this which made it possible for Hegel to describe the State as the embodiment of morality.

A powerful current of Christian virtues poured into the body of Prussian rule when the Alsatian mystic Spener became pastor of the garrison church in Berlin. In that environment his other-worldly mysticism gradually developed into the Pietism which abandoned politics to the devil and the King of Prussia, and fostered a spirit of devout self-denial which the Prussian spirit proceeded to exploit, to make its subjects fulfil more obediently their duties to the State. The categorical imperative of the Prussian official is of Christian origin. One thing is beyond doubt: in her foreign policy Prussia has always been a gangster state devoid of scruples. "Prussianism" in the widest sense can be most accurately defined as *a highly developed morality in the service of pure immorality: an admirable order in the service of the most appalling disorder, namely the disintegration of Europe; organization in the service of disorganization; Christianity in the service of Antichrist.*

We cannot therefore draw an unqualified contrast between Nationalist Germany as the diabolical power and the other European powers and their civilization. The situation is not so simple as all that. Germany could commit such crimes and on such a large scale and with such astounding impunity, only because she had had at her disposition in these criminal enterprises the moral capital of a religious devotion accumulated for centuries. Read the letters of the fine young men sacrificed in hecatombs at Verdun and Langemark, unwittingly for a hideous crime— *"infandum scelus morte expiandum,"* said the prophecy of the Lehnin monastery—, and you will grasp this terrifying alliance between Christian and Antichrist which has shaped the destiny of modern Germany and consequently the confusion of our entire epoch and the fate of modern man.

Pagan antiquity no doubt survives to a far greater degree in modern Italy than in modern Germany. For that very reason Mussolini could tolerate the existence of Christianity side by side with his Fascist State. Hitler cannot do this. For the modern German State founded by Christian ascetics and steeped in the Christian self-sacrifice of its subjects has, for that very reason, gradually become a religion and declares, "I will have none other Gods but me." Undoubtedly when these Christian sources have dried up, the State will perish with them. But the secularism of its present rulers has no inkling of this. It is at last beginning to dawn upon the members of the Church Universal that when the contemporary Prussian state attempts to destroy Christianity, it is avenging the fatal compromise on which the leaders of the Church ventured in the Middle Ages when they sanctified the bloody and cruel war of Christian Europe against the East and rekindled it from time to time. The sword was direfully blessed in those days. And the Teutonic Knights in Jerusalem were the hardest and most seasoned stormtroopers in this war of extermination waged in the name of Christ.

That is to say, history displays four successive stages. The first of these was war in the service of Christianity, the Crusades. It was followed by the employment of the Christian virtues in the service of war. Then the State which, with the sanction and assistance of Christians, had become an end-in-itself declared war on Christianity. And finally Christians are beginning to recognize with terror, but far too late, who it is they have served and whom they have defended, and to revoke their shameful compliance with the era of power-politics.

I have described above the phase of Christian civilization in which the spiritual forces which Christianity had awakened to life have been abused in the service of the Beast. To this abuse the entire power of modern social organization owes its origin. A vast treasure of unselfish devotion was required to create it in face of the forces of social anarchy. The Cross of Christ alone could unlock the sources of such power.

The reader of Saint Paul's Epistles watches the real foundation of human society. It was refounded by the crucifixion of selfishness and the charity of Christ. Beelzebub, however, has slowly but surely made himself master of this social organization and with it has erected the empire of the Collective Beast and intoxicated its herd. And Christians to whom St. Paul cried "Ye have been dearly purchased. Become not slaves of man", have in many places become the most active servants of this Collective Beast. They have congratulated themselves on the spirit of Christian self-sacrifice which serves the Beast's designs and have not been troubled by the fact that its aim is sheer robbery and self-aggrandizement.

Beyond doubt we are confronted today with the triumph of the Beast, and Christians will in consequence have to endure the utmost trial and testing. The apocalyptic beast is not any individual tyrant but a *collective* disease, namely the barbarization and despiritualization of man by deifying the state and its social organization. Humanity will experience to the utmost—as we are now beginning to realize—that the growing centralization of human life must inevitably involve the progressive destruction of the individual conscience, of man's personal rights and of the spiritual order by the state machine. Man divorced from God is brutalized by the organization of the masses, and the collectivity degenerates into a technique on a colossal scale for satisfying man's animal needs.

Personality is henceforth regarded as a disturbing factor, indeed as treason against the mass spirit. This Collective Beast will be defeated and the totalitarian state in its first form will be broken. But, as the Apocalypse foretells, this "mortal wound shall be healed". A second and even more thoroughly organized system will join forces with the former. That is to say, the older and more modern forms of centralization, that which comes from above and that which comes from below, the military and the democratic, will unite to make the great experiment of a naked and soulless "organization" of human life— until finally the empty illusion fails and the "spiritual" foundations of all human society are made plain.

The writer of the Apocalypse does not doubt that the dominion of the Beast lies under a curse, that it can function only for a time and is doomed to be overtaken by a fearful judgment of God.

The dehumanization of man by organization is the portentous doom of the political development of the modern world—a development fostered equally by the forces of the old traditional state and the mass mind of modern democracy. That is why we are told that a second beast will arise to aid the first, whose mortal wound has been healed, and work out all the implications of its principle. What for the early Christians was the worship of the Emperor has assumed today a novel form. It has become the Caesar-worship of organization, of the mass mind, which, assisted by a servile press, increasingly beleaguers the individual conscience and threatens to overpower any attempt, by a soul devoted to God, to oppose the omnipotence of public opinion and its slogans. Genuine service of Christ can consist only in maintaining an invincible resistance to this collective bestiality. This alternative concerns not only the individual soul, which by acquiescence in the passions of the masses incurs the most fearful danger, but society as a whole, which must inevitably erect dishonesty into a principle of government and become the sport of shifting currents—if in the human soul the entire spiritual power of the Redeemer does not counteract the potent magnetism of society.

The writer of the Apocalypse is aware that only in the slow course of millennia can the leaven of Christianity penetrate mankind; and that the advent of the Beast will produce the supreme crisis in Christian history when innumerable Christians will apostatize to Caesar-worship and drink the wine of Gods' wrath. For our consolation, however, the same vision displays from time to time the small band of faithful souls who maintain the bond between earth and Heaven and cooperate with Divine grace. In truth, the Beast must finally be overcome. For those gigantic collective organizations cannot permanently live upon the disintegrating forces of the Beast. And when their higher sources of power fall, their entire organization must dissolve into atoms.

This precisely is the significance of the terrifying experience through which mankind is at present passing. Men will be compelled to recognize to what an unsuspected degree their earthly security reposes on supernatural foundations and the extent to which even the successful assertion of evil power derives from apostate powers of a higher order the force with which it triumphs. This dearly bought experience and recognition will produce in a chosen few entirely novel insights and decisions. There will be one day a Christian counter-attack of unprecedented strength. This counter-offensive will profit by the impression made on the world by the far-reaching collapse of the diabolical edifice and for a time—for everything earthly is temporary —will achieve a genuine victory of the higher world.

Already there are signs which announce the end of the phase in which both worlds are inextricably mingled. From the apocalyptic standpoint we have entered upon the new phase in which the powers of hell unmask themselves so clearly and disclose their ultimate aims and designs so plainly, completely discarding caution and rejecting compromise, that an increasing number of those whom they have hitherto deceived see at last with open eyes and are once more returning to the Sovereign Truth.

ANALYTICAL CONTENTS

PART I

FOERSTER, F. W.

INDEX